DEVELOPMENTAL PERSPECTIVES

Edited by Ruth L. Ault

GOODYEAR PUBLISHING COMPANY, INC.
Santa Monica, California

Library of Congress Cataloging in Publication Data
Main entry under title:

Developmental perspectives.

1. Child psychology. I. Ault, Ruth L.
BF721.d43   155.4   79-22762
ISBN 0-8302-2166-2

To Mom and Dad in the special spring of 1979.

A volume in the
Goodyear Experimental Psychology Series
Thomas Trabasso, series advisor

Current printing (last digit):
10 9 8 7 6 5 4 3 2 1

ISBN: 0-8302-2166-2
Y-2166-0

Printed in the United States of America

CONTENTS

INTRODUCTION

When people attend a party, introductions are generally performed. The introducer provides a few pieces of information so that the guests have some common ground for starting a conversation. Although a true dialogue between this book and its readers would be difficult, introductory remarks can be helpful as you "meet" the following chapters. The purpose and general organization of the book are described first, followed by some information about the authors.

GOALS

The main audience that the authors and I intend to reach is advanced undergraduate and beginning graduate students in developmental psychology. We expect that the readers will have taken a beginning course in child development which surveyed a large number of topics without much detail and are now taking a second course. Under the constraints of a single quarter or semester, only a handful of topics can be selected for thorough examination.

Whenever such a selection is made, the idiosyncrasies of the authors, and especially of the editor, are inevitably reflected. The topics I selected are decidedly cognitive in flavor but are spiced for other tastes as well: three chapters are explicitly cognitive in nature (intellectual, language, and memory development), one chapter treats cognitive issues from a biological perspective, and two chapters focus on socialization issues but include a cognitive perspective (among others). It goes without saying that the book takes a developmental perspective as well, by highlighting age-related changes and age-independent continuities throughout childhood.

ORGANIZATION

Chapter One leads off with a look at Piaget's theory of intellectual development. No other single individual has had an equivalent impact on the field of cognitive development. His theory serves as the impetus for literally hundreds of studies each year. This chapter presents an overview of the theory, describing briefly the four stages he proposed, and then examines the theory more critically on three issues: the role of stages, the universality of the stages across populations, and the role of training studies.

Language development is considered in Chapter Two. Parents are probably more fascinated by the development of language than by any other single skill, for language simultaneously makes the child seem more human and allows the parent new avenues for control and teaching. Since language becomes a primary mode of instruction, it is important to both cognitive and social development. This chapter presents a considerable amount of descriptive data on language acquisition in four areas: phonemics (the sound system), syntax (the grammar system), semantics (concerning word meanings), and pragmatics (the functions language serves). The cognitive-interactionist theoretical perspective, adapted from Slobin's work, provides the major theoretical framework for the chapter. This perspective proposed various "strategies" which are biasing or organizing tendencies used for processing language.

Chapter Three looks at the development of children's memory in the context of adult information-processing models. In the first major section of the chapter, three discrete stages of memory (sensory information store, short-term store, and long-term store) are discussed and the research evidence supporting the existence of each store is reviewed. Some selected topics are treated in detail, including research on rehearsal, memory scanning, the serial position effect, episodic and semantic memory, semantic accessing, and reconstructive memory. The next three sections review the evidence for memory in infants, short-term memory in preschool and school-aged children, and long-term memory strategies in preschool and school-aged children. The final section examines the adequacy of the information-processing model from several perspectives.

The fourth chapter reexamines memory and language development by considering the physiological bases of these two achievements. The authors start with the fundamentals of neuroanatomy. Then they consider the central nervous system's anatomical features which are correlated with language development (the association cortex) and with memory development (the hippocampus and the cerebral cortex). For the readers who wonder how language and memory are impaired by physical damage to the brain, the syndromes of aphasia and amnesia are described. The extent of plasticity (flexibility) in the central nervous system is the final major issue considered in the chapter.

Chapter Five, concerning the development of prosocial behaviors and moral judgments, contrasts three theoretical positions: (a) cognitive-developmental or structural theories (of Piaget & Kohlberg); (b) operant theory (of Skinner); and (c) cognitive social-learning theories (of Bandura & Mischel). The strengths and weaknesses of each position are explored and examples of research stemming from each position are provided. The links between cognitive and prosocial development are made clear in several places. For example, Piaget's theory of cognitive development underlies his theory of moral development. Children's attributions about why they and others engage in prosocial actions also reflect the impact of cognitions on socialization. As a third example, memory is an important component of Bandura's modeling theory.

Finally, the development of antisocial behavior is examined in Chapter Six. Four factors are successively applied to account for this development. The authors propose that operant principles, particularly negative reinforcement, are most important during infancy. The second factor, physical maturation and physiological dysfunctions such as hyperactivity and hypoglycemia, becomes apparent as children enter school. As children develop greater conceptual and verbal facility, observational learning plays an increasingly important role. Cognitive social-learning theory, with its emphasis on memory and information processing, is thus the third factor in the model of antisocial behavioral development. To explain adolescent and adult antisocial behaviors, a fourth component is considered. This component draws on population cycles, obtained through demographic data, to predict which age segments of the population are likely to engage in which antisocial actions.

The arrangement of the chapters was dictated in part by their interrelationships. Piaget's theory is placed first because it is referenced in the chapters on language and prosocial development. The neurological bases of memory and language naturally follow the individual treatments of language and memory. And because memory development is encountered in both socialization chapters, prosocial and antisocial development are considered last. Despite these interrelationships, each chapter is self-contained and they could be read in any order. The relative positions of language and memory and cognitive development are essentially arbitrary, as are the positions of prosocial and antisocial development.

ABOUT THE AUTHORS

At the time of the first draft of this book, all of the authors were affiliated with the psychology department at the University of Utah. Current affiliations and research and teaching interests are accurate as of 1979.

Ruth L. Ault, editor and coauthor of the chapter on Piaget's theory, was an assistant professor in developmental psychology at Utah. She is now at Davidson College. Her primary research interest is cognitive development, especially incidental and intentional memory development. She maintains secondary interests in parent-child interactions and applications of cognitive development to instructional situations. Her teaching interests include child and adolescent development, cognitive development, and experimental design.

Anne Vinsel, coauthor of Chapter One, is a graduate student in social psychology at Utah. She describes her research interests as privacy regulation, nonverbal communication, cross-cultural interaction, and the philosophy of science.

David H. Dodd (not to be confused with David K. Dodd) is the author of the chapter on language development and is an associate professor in experimental psychology at Utah. His research in children's language development focuses on pragmatic factors in the comprehension and recall of texts and observed events, and language interactions between parents and young children. He teaches courses in the psychology of language, language development, cognitive psychology, and developmental psychology.

The author of the third chapter, on memory development, is Marigold Linton. She is a professor of experimental psychology at Utah. Her research interests include long-term memory for real-world events and the application of information-processing principles to issues of minority education. She teaches courses in information processing, experimental methods, and practical aspects of memory.

Raymond P. Kesner and Timothy B. Baker are coauthors of Chapter Four, treating neuroanatomical correlates of language and memory. Kesner is a physiological psychologist and professor of experimental psychology at Utah. His research program deals with a regional neural system analysis of mnemonic information processing and includes neuroanatomical, neurophysiological, neurochemical, and neurobehavioral techniques. In addition to teaching general introductory psychology, physiological psychology, and research methods, he conducts seminars on the neurobiological bases of information processing, including the mechanisms associated with plasticity.

Tim Baker obtained his Ph.D. in clinical psychology at Utah and is now an assistant professor at the University of Wisconsin, Madison. He is interested in substance abuse, particularly alcohol and drug dependence; psychological assessment; and the ontogeny of learning. His teaching interests include abnormal psychology, assessment, behavior therapy, experimental design, neuropsychology, and substance abuse.

Donna M. Gelfand and Donald P. Hartmann are the coauthors of Chapter Five, concerning the development of prosocial behaviors and moral judgments. Both are professors of psychology affiliated with the developmental area at Utah. Gelfand's research interests center on social learning, particularly of prosocial behaviors, and on the prevention of psychological disturbance and physical illness. Her teaching areas are child development and child behavior disorders.

Don Hartmann's research interests include children's prosocial behaviors, methodology, and prevention. He teaches social-learning implications for child development and for assessment, prevention and treatment, methodology, and statistics and design.

Charles W. Turner and David K. Dodd discuss the development of antisocial behaviors in Chapter Six. Turner is an associate professor of social psychology with research interests in theoretical and applied analyses of antisocial behavior and in the cognitive control of emotions and emotional behavior. He teaches social psychology, attribution theory, aggression, field research, psychology and the law, methodology, and statistics and design.

David K. Dodd is a graduate student in social psychology. In addition to the development of antisocial behavior, he is interested in obesity and the prediction of weight change.

ONE

Piaget's Theory of Cognitive Development

Ruth L. Ault and Anne Vinsel[1]

For the past fifty years Jean Piaget, a Swiss psychologist, has studied how children develop their ability to think. Piaget believes that thinking begins in the physical actions a child performs on objects and ends in the capacity to manipulate hypothetical ideas purely mentally. Thus, his theory concerns the development of cognitive or intellectual functioning. Piaget's theory is extraordinarily expansive, covering such diverse topics as children's conceptions of physical causality, space, geometry, and number; the development of language; the formation of moral judgments; and the importance of play, dreams, and imitation (Piaget, 1926/1923, 1930/1927, 1932, 1951/1945; Piaget & Inhelder, 1956/1948; Piaget, Inhelder, & Szeminska, 1960/1948; Piaget & Szeminska, 1952/1941). Since literally hundreds of journal articles and books have been written about various aspects of Piaget's theory, we can only present a detailed examination of a few selected topics.

We begin with a broad outline of his theory without much editorializing. A few key concepts are defined and the four major periods of cognitive development are summarized. This idealized version is intended to provide an overview for those readers who have little familiarity with Piaget's theory. Then we consider three issues which are prominent in the research literature.

The first issue examines the role of stages in Piaget's theory: What does it mean to call his theory a stage theory? We focus on the adequacy of Piaget's theory as an explanation rather than merely a description of cognitive development. This examination, which is primarily logical and philosophical, reveals some fundamental difficulties in trying to test

[1]We appreciate the encouragement, criticisms, suggestions, and help provided by the following people: Richard Ault, Richard Cook, Jorge Martin, Barbara Rogoff, Tom Trabasso, and the graduate students in a seminar at the University of Utah.

Piaget's theory empirically. We conclude that his theory is clearly not explanatory and that no adequate criteria have been proposed for proving that his theory lies somewhere between a true explanation and a mere description.

The second issue considers whether Piaget's stage theory is even an accurate description of cognitive development. We present a sample of research data which considers the universality of the theory for populations both closely resembling and quite different from Piaget's original sample of Genevan schoolchildren. The replication research data with North American and Western European children and adults have confirmed Piaget's description of his first three periods but challenge his description of the fourth period. The universality of the first three periods is also suggested by cross-cultural research and by data on handicapped children, on the elderly, and on animals. The second section ends with Piaget's qualifications and revisions for the fourth period of development, based on the failures to replicate, and with an example (by Riegel) of an alternative formulation for mature intellectual functioning.

Finally, the third issue concerns the role of training studies (also called learning research). Training studies have been quite popular, so that by selectively reviewing them we can present an overview of a large segment of Piaget-inspired research. In particular, we examine how training studies identify various experiential factors which facilitate or retard development. These factors are exemplified by considering the types and success of training one class of Piagetian tasks, conservation. Many researchers believe that successful experimental interventions mirror natural development. The results of training studies have, therefore, been used to suggest alternatives to Piaget's hypothesized mechanisms of development. Other researchers, however, believe that deliberate training does not necessarily mirror the natural acquisition and so they dismiss as inconclusive the entire body of training research.

UNDERLYING ASSUMPTIONS AND DEFINITIONS

Piaget (1970) has said that one cannot understand his theory unless the biological basis of it is examined first. Following his advice, we present some assumptions and definitions on which the rest of the theory is built before we present the stages of cognitive development. The assumptions derive in part from the fact that Piaget, being trained as a biologist, was convinced that intellectual development is just one example of an organism's capacity to develop. Consequently any assumptions one makes about biological growth ought to apply to cognitive development as well.

Biologically Based Assumptions

The first assumption to be addressed is that organisms help determine their own development. With reference to child development, this principle means that it is the basic nature of people to be active. The second assumption is that the biological principles of organization and adaptation provide mechanisms both for stability and change in development. The third biological principle to be considered is that higher processes evolve out of lower ones, thus giving a direction to growth from the simple to the complex. The development of two cognitive structures— schemes and operations—reflect this progression in complexity. Likewise, some cognitive contents are considered more difficult because they can be handled only after the more advanced structures have developed.

Active Nature. Piaget believes that people are naturally *active*. He rejects the stimulus-response model of behavior in which people are viewed as passive recipients of whatever internal or external stimuli happen to impinge upon them at any given moment. Rather, people selectively attend to some features of the environment and selectively ignore others. For example, an infant may look at a fluff of lint or at the edge of the crib but ignore the roar of a passing airplane. The infant's father, on the other hand, may ignore the lint but attend to the airplane which is interfering with his telephone conversation. In addition to selective attention, people are active in the sense that environmental events are classified, organized, and related to other events. The purpose of such cognitive processing of information is to make interactions between the person and the environment more efficient and intelligible. External information is not merely passively copied nor is it interpreted through some maturational structure which unfolds during development. Rather, children construct interpretations of their world by a process which relies on an interaction between the environment and their physical capacities.

Functional Invariants. In order to survive, all organisms must cope with information provided by the environment. Piaget "borrowed" from biology two mechanisms—organization and adaptation—which serve to regulate intellectual coping. Piaget calls these mechanisms *functions* because they express how cognition works and he asserts that they are *invariant* because they occur at all stages of development even though the specific intellectual content processed by these functions will vary with developmental status. Neither organization nor adaptation is directly observable. Rather, each is inferred from activity on some cognitive task.

Organization refers to behaviors or thoughts becoming clustered into systems of related behaviors or thoughts rather than remaining isolated. Organization is therefore inferred whenever behavior seems patterned or clustered rather than random. Being organized has clear advantages over being unorganized. Some problems can only be solved by using many behaviors acting in concert, yet the principle of organization does not preclude other problems being solved with single behaviors. Organiza-

.ion happens spontaneously; it is not something which takes conscious or deliberate effort. Piaget considers organization to be a mechanism in cognition because it is a basic biological principle and because he observed patterns in children's behaviors and thoughts. The particular patterns which get formed through the organization function are the structures of thought. These will be discussed later in this chapter.

The other functional invariant, adaptation, is composed of two complementary components: assimilation and accommodation. *Assimilation* can be thought of as incorporating new pieces of information into already existing mental structures. *Accommodation*, on the other hand, refers to the alteration of existing structures by contact with novel information. Piaget modeled these processes after biological systems such as digestion, in which food is assimilated by breaking it down into a form which the body can use while, at the same time, the body accommodates to the food by actions such as secreting enzymes and moving certain muscles depending on what food is eaten. Piaget (1970) also offers a behavioral example of adaptation in thumb-sucking. An infant who has learned to suck on a nipple will apply this activity to a thumb (thus assimilating the thumb to a previously existing sucking action), but the sucking motions will have to accommodate to the particular shape of the thumb because it is different from the nipple. These two analogies, to digestion and to thumb-sucking, are not quite identical to what Piaget means by cognitive assimilation and accommodation because in each case the structural accommodation is only temporary. The stomach is not permanently altered after each digestive experience nor is one's mouth permanently altered by sucking. But, to the extent that food eventually is used by cells, the cell structures are changed and to the extent that one learns something about thumbs and nipples, the sucking experience has made a permanent change somewhere in the infant. Cognitive accommodations are said to permanently modify cognitive structures.

Assimilation and accommodation can be seen in social interactions as well. Consider the following conversation between two young children.

Bob: Where do you live?

Jane: The house next to the corner hamburger store.

Bob: Oh, you mean next to McDonald's?

Jane: No, not that corner. Next to Burger King.

Jane's first statement was apparently assimilated by Bob into his understanding of one street's arrangement. Jane then had to accommodate to Bob's interpretation and modify it by being more explicit about which corner she had in mind. This example is also not quite identical to cognitive adaptation because the assimilating and accommodating were experienced by two different children. According to Piaget, cognitive assimilation and accommodation always occur together (although the balance between them may change). They are two aspects of one process, not two different or separable processes. Both assimilation and accommodation are necessary concepts because we observe both stability and change in cognitive activity. "Assimilation is necessary in that it assures the continuity of structures and the integration of new elements to these structures" (Piaget, 1970, p. 707). Accommodation guarantees the acquisition of new contents and thus promotes further development.

Assimilation and accommodation are, in a sense, opposing forces. The former tries to maintain the current structure and force change upon the external situation while the latter tries to maintain the external situation and force change upon the structure. Such tension between two forces must reach some balance or the system will fail to thrive. Consequently Piaget proposed a self-regulating mechanism, *equilibration*, which coordinates the actions of assimilation and accommodation, correcting any imbalances between them. Cowan (1978) likens equilibration to a steam engine's governor "which shuts down the engine temporarily when the steam pressure builds up, and then allows the engine to switch on again" (p. 25). This analogy emphasizes that the regulatory mechanism is a property of the system, (hence, self-regulatory) and not something imposed on the system from outside stimulation.

Increasing Complexity. In a cyclical manner, organization and adaptation produce cognitive structures to handle more complex environmental inputs (contents) and the adjustments to these new contents in turn help to produce still more complex structures. Thus both structures and contents reflect the biological principle that growth proceeds from the simple to the complex.

Structures. Piaget uses the term *structure* in a narrowly defined sense. He is not concerned with actual physical structures in the brain such as the temporal lobes or the corpus callosum. Likewise, he is not interested in mapping particular behavior patterns onto physical brain structures. Instead, Piaget uses the term "structure" to refer to the "organizational properties of intelligence" which transcend specific contents (Flavell, 1963, p. 17).

Three characteristics define a group of responses as a structure. First, structures are organized in the sense that elements in a structure are interrelated by certain laws. One element of the structure cannot change without influencing all the other elements. A second property of structures is that they are not static. Structures are continually being transformed via assimilation and accommodation. The third characteristic is their self-regulating ability. Again, through assimilation and accommodation, structures can become components of more complex superstructures, hierarchically arranged.

One other aspect of Piaget's notion of structures needs to be emphasized: structures are said to be constructed by each child. They are not imposed on the child from external stimulation or experience; nor are they merely preformed in one's hereditary make-up, ready to unfold with maturation. Piaget (1970) has said, "The problem then becomes that of understanding how the fundamental structures of intelligence can appear and evolve with all those that later derive from them. Since they are not innate, they cannot be explained by maturation alone. Logical structures are not a simple product of physical experience; in seriation, classification, one-to-one correspondence, the subject's activities add new relations such as order and totality to the object. . . . Thus it seems highly probable that the construction of structures is mainly the work of equilibration" (p. 724–725).

Like functions, structures are not directly observable. They are inferred from sets of behaviors which appear to share some common features. When a theoretical concept (like structures) cannot be measured directly, it is often profitable to model the concept by referring to an analogous system. Piaget makes liberal use of this principle, using abstract algebra, especially group theory, to model his cognitive structures (Brainerd, 1978a). We shall not be concerned with this aspect, although the reader who wants to learn more about Piaget's theory ought to become familiar with his mathematical models.

Contents. Contents are the easiest part of Piaget's theory to understand because they are the observable aspects of the child's behavior. As Ginsburg and Opper (1969) explain it, content "refers to what the individual is thinking about, what interests him at the moment, or the terms in which he contemplates a given problem" (p. 16). Children's answers to the tasks which Piaget devised reveal cognitive contents. Contents are important because they are the raw behavioral data from which structures and functions are inferred. Since they are not very controversial, little space need be given to them.

Structural Development

By oversimplifying a bit, one could say that cognitive development is the development of two particular kinds of structures, *schemes* and *operations*. Piaget has delineated four major divisions in the development of these structures. In the *Sensorimotor Period*, children are said to use only schemes. The *Preoperational Period* is a transition between the predominant use of schemes and the use of operations. Children begin to use such mental representations as symbols and language, but these representations are not true operations. In the *Concrete Operational Period*, children have some true operations, but these operations can only be applied to concrete, physically real situations. Finally, in the *Formal Operational Period*, operations have developed to the point where they can be applied to abstract and hypothetical situations. Since the four periods reflect a transition from schemes alone to schemes and operations, it is necessary to discuss these two concepts in greater detail.

Schemes. Piaget (1970) has written that "a scheme represents what can be repeated and generalized in an action [e.g., the scheme is what is common in the actions of 'pushing' an object with a stick or any other instrument]" (p. 719). No two instances of pushing are ever exactly alike, but each instance bears enough resemblance to the others that an observer would infer a commonality to them. Flavell (1963), using grasping as an example, described schemes[2] in the following manner: "to say that a grasping sequence forms a [scheme] is to imply more than the simple fact that the infant shows an organized grasping behavior. It implies...an organized *disposition* to grasp objects on repeated occasions" (p. 53, italics in the original). When schemes represent overt motor behaviors, they can be called "sensorimotor schemes" (Brainerd, 1978a) and these are the only kind of structures available to infants. Because Piaget also uses the term "actions" to refer to purely mental phenomena, some schemes are said to represent covert mental action sequences. These "cognitive schemes" are approximately the same thing as thoughts (Brainerd, 1978a). Piaget seems to use cognitive schemes as a synonym for cognitive structures, which leads to some confusion. We shall restrict our use of the term scheme to the sensorimotor kind.

Operations. Operations, the second type of structure, are more difficult to describe because they are not directly observable as schemes are. Instead, operations are defined by two characteristics: (1) they are mental, in-the-head representations developed by "internalizing" actions or schemes and (2) they are reversible. The mental quality of operations distinguishes them from schemes which are overt, behavioral, and thus observable directly. Operations are said to develop from schemes through "internalization," which roughly means that a mental representation can be formed when an overt scheme is well practiced and familiar.

The second characteristic of operations, reversibility, refers to the capacity to undo or compensate for one mental action by taking a different mental action and arriving back at the beginning state. Reversibility distinguishes operations from other types of mental activity such as perception and imagining. For example, children can look at a particular blue chair, perceive it as blue and as a chair, and perhaps close their eyes and visualize the same blue chair. All of these are mental activities but because they are static, they cannot be regarded as operations. They cannot be undone or transformed to change the blue chair to any other state. On the other hand, if children think about standing in front of the chair and then sitting down, they can undo this mental action by thinking about standing up again, thus returning to the original state.

---

[2]Early translations of Piaget's work confused the terms "scheme" and "schema." Piaget (1970) distinguished the two terms by defining a schema as "a simplified image (for example, the map of a town)" (p. 719). Therefore, we have substituted the term scheme for schema in the quotation from Flavell (1963).

Children can learn many things from both reversible operations and nonreversible mental activities. For example, from picking up various objects, children can learn that big objects are usually heavier than little objects. This type of knowledge is basically a simple internalization of perceptions. The knowledge stems more from the qualities of the objects picked up than from the organized action of picking them up. In contrast, knowledge arising from operations is based on an internalization of an organized sequence of actions. For example, once a child finds that ten stones are still ten stones regardless of the design into which they are arranged, there is no longer any need to repeat the counting action every time a known number of objects is rearranged. The general principle or knowledge discovered by children is based on their actions upon the objects rather than on any qualities inherent in the objects themselves (Piaget, 1970).

THE FOUR MAJOR PERIODS OF DEVELOPMENT

With this overview in mind, we shall sketch a bit more fully the four major periods of cognitive development. Since we do not have space to provide a comprehensive overview, our discussion will focus on the concepts needed to understand the research reviewed in the second half of the chapter. More extensive summaries of the theory can be found in Ault (1977), Brainerd (1978a), Cowan (1978), Flavell (1977), and Ginsburg and Opper (1969).

The Sensorimotor Period (birth to 1½–2 years)[3]

The Sensorimotor Period is both the shortest period and the one most explicitly charted for temporal sequence, being divided into six stages. Schemes are the predominant structure of this period. Children learn about the world around them by applying their schemes to objects in the environment.

Six Sensorimotor Stages. In *Stage 1* innate reflexes, such as sucking, grasping, and following objects with the eyes, start out being highly stereotyped but become modified through experience. The differential effects of various schemes on objects help the infant to generalize and to differentiate the schemes. Because innate reflexes (a maturational component) are modified by contact with environmental experiences (a learning component), development of new or different schemes is accomplished.

In *Stage 2* children gain more voluntary muscular control over their own bodies and thereby produce random interesting experiences, such as letting their hands dangle in front of their eyes or entwining their fingers in their hair. Once an interesting event occurs, children in the second stage attempt to repeat it, learning new behaviors in the process.

[3]Ages for the periods are rough approximations, serving only as anchors for the sequence.

Further development is seen in *Stage 3* as repetitions are applied to interesting events in the child's immediate surroundings. For example, children may try to reproduce noises they have made by banging their feet against their cribs or sights they have seen by hanging sideways over a chair.

In the first three stages, children are able to gain simple goals by applying one of several schemes. For example, if a child wanted an object that was within reach, all that the child had to do was to exercise the grasping scheme. Or, if the child wanted to move some object, the pulling scheme could be applied. In *Stage 4* schemes such as grasping and pulling are combined into smoothly run, coordinated actions in order to accomplish a goal that could not be achieved by executing any single scheme.

Stage 5 builds on the previous stages. Instead of rigidly repeating an interesting event exactly as had been done before, children now can purposely vary their actions to explore the different results produced by each variation. If a child had previously pushed a piece of food over the edge of a highchair tray, the variations produced in the fifth stage could be releasing the food from shoulder height, throwing the food upward instead of downward, or releasing several pieces of food simultaneously.

Stage 6, which marks the beginning of representational thought, is really a transition to the Preoperational Period because in this stage children begin to exhibit the rudiments of mental representations. In contrast to the learning in the first five stages, which had the quality of trial-and-error groping or even random application of schemes to problems, the problem solving of the sixth stage occurs more efficiently. According to Piaget, children use some form of mental representation to "think" about each of their available schemes, to predict what effect each scheme might have, and then to apply the scheme that has the best chance of being correct. In other words, by using the knowledge gained in the prior stages concerning how objects behave and what characteristics they have, children can anticipate what effects certain schemes might have even though they may never have applied those schemes in a situation resembling the current problem.

Object Permanence.   The overview just presented of the Sensorimotor Period has focused on the inferred underlying structures, that is, on the various schemes of infancy. An alternative way to view the period is to examine one of the more important contents, the development of object permanence. Object permanence can be defined as the knowledge that an object continues to exist independent of one's past and present actions on it, including directly perceiving it, previously finding it in a particular location, or seeing it hidden in one location before it is moved to another location. Piaget identified six stages in the development of object permanence, based on his observations of how children reacted to situations in which a visible object disappeared from view.

In the first stage (from birth to about 2 months), children gaze at an object in their visual field until the object leaves the field, at which point they find something else to watch. In the second stage (2–4 months), children continue looking for a brief time at the location where an object disappeared, as if waiting for it to reappear, but there is no active search for the object. In the third stage (4–8 months), children look where they anticipate a dropped object will land, but this is only true if the children themselves have caused the object to disappear, not if another person has caused it. Stage 3 children will also stop reaching for an object if someone else completely covers it. If the object is only partially covered, they will continue reaching. In the fourth stage (8–12 months), children successfully remove covers that are completely hiding an object and look for objects that other people have made disappear. They are not, however, successful in following a series of visible displacements. For example, if children find an object under their beds two or three times in a row, they subsequently search in that same place even if they have watched the object disappear through the doorway. In the fifth stage (12–18 months), children search for an object where they last saw it rather than where it was usually found. They do not follow a series of "hidden" displacements, though. In this situation an object is placed under one cover, both object and cover are moved behind a second cover, the object is left there, and the first cover is moved back to its original place. Children in the fifth stage look behind the first cover where they saw the object disappear but do not look behind the second cover. Children in the sixth stage (18 + months) look behind both covers.

The stages of object permanence fit into those of the Sensorimotor Period. For example, when infants are merely exercising and refining their reflexes (Sensorimotor Stage 1), looking at objects in their visual field (Object Permanence Stage 1) is the exercise of one reflex. The ability to follow hidden displacements (Object Permanence Stage 6) logically requires children both to form mental representations of the missing object and to mentally anticipate the results of moving the first cover behind the second. Both of these requirements are met as children make the transition to the Preoperational Period (Sensorimotor Stage 6).

The Preoperational Period (1½–2 to 5–6 years)

Symbolic Functioning. The development of the capacity to form and use mental symbols is the major accomplishment of the Preoperational Period. *Symbolic functioning* is the ability to make one thing represent a different thing which is not physically present. We infer the presence of mental representations from the overt behavior of children, especially from delayed imitation, symbolic play, and language. For example, sensorimotor children can imitate a model's actions while the model is acting or immediately after the model has finished. Preoperational children can delay their imitation, waiting hours or days before copying the model's action. It is assumed that children have formed a mental representation of the model's behavior and use that representation to guide their imitation at the later point in time. Similarly, sensorimotor children do not show *symbolic play*, the make-believe or pretend play engaged in by older children. When preoperational children pretend that a stick is an airplane or a rock is a guest at a tea party, they are using the stick or the rock as symbols to represent absent objects. The transition from sensorimotor to preoperational thought corresponds to the time when children begin to use language in one- or two-word sentences. *Language* is almost entirely concerned with symbol manipulation, as the sounds we speak are arbitrarily paired with the objects those words stand for. Further evidence of symbolic functioning is obtained when children start to use their language to talk about past and future events.

Qualitative Identity. We have seen that in the Sensorimotor Period, children develop the idea that an object still exists despite translations of the object in space (e.g., hidden displacements). In the Preoperational Period, children extend their idea about the invariance of an object to take account of changes which are irrelevant to its identity and which are qualitative in nature such as changes in color or shape. For example, DeVries (1969) showed three- to six-year-olds a cat and then placed a mask of a dog over the cat's face. Early preoperational children assert that the cat has changed its identity and has become a dog, whereas older pre-operational children maintain that the animal is still a cat. This *qualitative* identity concept is a forerunner of the conservation of *quantitative* identity concept attained during the Concrete Operational Period.

Figurative Thinking. Despite the advances of preoperational children over sensorimotor children, the thinking displayed by preoperational children is *figurative*, involving a static, "copy" kind of knowledge which is basically a simple internalization of perceptions. In contrast, children who have fully developed operations can both internalize perceptual information and mentally act on that information. This distinction will become clearer in the next section when we compare the performance of preoperational and concrete operational children on various tasks.

The Concrete Operational Period (6–7 to 10–11 years)

Mental Operations. The hallmark of the Concrete Operational Period is the development of mental operations. These operations are mental actions which can be applied to transform an "object" (that is, a thought) in some way. Because mental operations are structures, they are by definition organized into clusters of related operations. In contrast to the organization of schemes, which is visible in spatial and temporal sequencing of movements, the organization of operations is more elusive because operations have no overt component. Instead, operations are said to be organized because they obey certain rules such as reversibility, associativity, and identity (Flavell, 1963). According to these rules, each operation is related to several other operations which do such things as reverse its effect, compensate for it, or leave it unchanged. Reversibility by inversion, for example, involves applying two operations successively, such that the original identity is regained. The most common example is addition and subtraction of numbers. Say that the original state is 1. After adding 2 to obtain 3, one can subtract 2 and return to the original 1. Reversibility by compensation also involves applying two operations in succession, but this time an equivalent state, rather than the original state, is obtained. Cowan (1978) explains this reversibility (which he calls reciprocity) with an example about the area of a rectangle. Say that the original area is its length, L, multiplied by its width, W. If the length were doubled (2L), and the width halved (½W), the area of the new rectangle, 2L X ½W, would be equivalent to the first rectangle, although the two rectangles would not be identical in shape.

Tasks. Since operations are not directly observable, they must be inferred from behavior. To elicit such behavior, Piaget devised a variety of tasks which, he claims, require operations in order to be solved. The best known and most widely researched of these tasks is *conservation*. The basic conservation task involves presenting the child with two objects, both perceptually and quantitatively equal, such as rows of checkers aligned in one-to-one correspondence (number), identical beakers filled with equal amounts of liquid (liquid quantity), or identical balls of clay (mass). An experimenter obtains the child's agreement that the two quantities are equal and then perceptually deforms or transforms one of the two objects; e.g., the experimenter spreads out one row of checkers, pours the contents of one beaker into a shorter, wider container, or flattens one of the balls of clay. The child is asked to judge whether the two quantities are still the same and to justify that judgment. Thus the conservation task deals with *quantitative* invariance in the face of some irrelevant perceptual changes. It is commonly found that preschool-aged children fail these conservation tasks by claiming that the two quantities are no longer equal, while elementary school-aged children pass one or more of them, asserting that the quantities are still the same. These two age groups are the nominal age ranges for the Preoperational and Concrete Operational Periods. Moreover, the verbal explanations that children give for their conservation judgments conform to the rules governing operations. Children demonstrating conservation typically justify their answers with statements such as, "Well, all you did was spread them out and you could put them back together again" (reversibility by inversion rule); "This beaker is taller but it's also thinner" (reversibility by compensation rule); and "You did not add any liquid or take any away" (identity rule).

Four other tasks are popular in the study of concrete operations. *Seriation* tasks test children's ability to arrange a group of objects in order along one of its dimensions, such as placing sticks in order by length. Preoperational children may arrange any two sticks in correct order, but they do not order the entire array correctly. In *transitivity* tasks, children perceive two relationships and then must deduce a third relationship. For example, they perceive a doll named Susan is slightly taller than one named Mary and Mary is slightly taller than one named Jane. Then they must deduce whether Susan is taller, shorter, or the same height as Jane. Preoperational children either answer randomly or guess correctly but cannot give a rational explanation for their choice. *Classification* tasks require children to sort a collection of objects into mutually exclusive categories. For example, if children were shown a single pile of squares and circles of different sizes and colors, their task would be to sort the geometrical forms into two piles, one for squares and one for circles. Early in the Preoperational Period, children make a number of errors, including forming pictures with the shapes and changing the dimension on which a pile is sorted, e.g., from shape to color. In the *class inclusion* task children are asked to compare the size of one collection of objects (say, 12 wooden beads) with members of one of its subclasses (say, 10 blue beads when the other two beads are white). Preoperational children typically state that there are more blue beads than wooden beads. Sometime during the Concrete Operational Period children succeed in performing these tasks correctly. Since the tasks supposedly require reversible manipulations of mental representations, Piaget asserts that children can only solve the tasks if they use mental operations.

Although concrete operational children have operations, they are limited to solving problems which are represented by some physical manifestation (real sticks to move or liquids to pour). By the time children reach the Formal Operational Period, they will be able to apply their operations to purely verbal, abstract, or hypothetical problems.

The Formal Operational Period (11–12 years onward)

The ability to think abstractly is the most important new intellectual skill acquired by formal operational children. Not only can they reason about events based on their personal experiences, they can also reason about events they have never experienced, including both true and false propositions. Brainerd (1978a) refers to this as representing *potential* actions in addition to real actions. Moreover, Piaget claims that formal operational children can coordinate the two types of reversibility (inversion and compensation), whereas concrete operational children could only use each type by itself. This coordination allows formal operational children to reason in two ways: from specific instances to general principles (inductive reasoning) and from general principles to specific conclusions (hypothetico-deductive reasoning). These two types of reasoning are considered further under the section on formal operational tasks after we outline three aspects of formal operational thinking which are direct results of the newfound abilities to coordinate reversibilities and to represent potential actions.

Formal Operational Skills. Both concrete and formal operational children can generate some hypotheses when faced with a problem, but concrete operational children are limited to predicting outcomes they have already directly experienced (hence the label "concrete"). Because formal operational children can represent potential actions, they can generate hypotheses about these potential actions. In addition, from the joint consideration of the two reversibilities, some hypotheses arise which would not be apparent if the operations were considered in isolation. Thus formal operational children are more likely to *generate multiple hypotheses*. To illustrate this more concretely, consider one of Piaget's tasks which resembles a chemistry problem. Children are shown five beakers containing different colorless, odorless liquids and are instructed to combine any or all of the five liquids to produce a yellow-colored solution. Concrete operational children generate some hypotheses, such as combining beakers 1 and 2, or beakers 3 and 4. The formal operational child is more likely to generate all possible combinations, including mixing the beakers three, four, and five at a time as well as in pairs.

A second difference between concrete and formal operational thinking is the *systematic checking of possible solutions*. The chemistry problem also illustrates this principle. Concrete operational children are likely to test their hypotheses in a trial-and-error fashion, randomly mixing beakers, whereas formal operational children plan a systematic approach, for example, combining all pairs of beakers (1 and 2, 1 and 3, 1 and 4, 1 and 5, 2 and 3, 2 and 4, etc.), then combining all triplets and so forth.

Finally, formal operational thinking involves *organizing single operations into higher order operations*. This has also been referred to as "operating on operations," in contrast to operating directly on objects as concrete operational children do. The simplest example comes from arithmetic. Given a problem such as "What number plus 20 equals twice itself?" concrete operational children will use the operations of addition and multiplication on various numbers in a trial- and error-fashion. They might, for example, think of the number 5, insert it in the formula, and decide it was incorrect ($5 + 20 \neq 2 \times 5$). They would continue to try numbers in this manner until the correct one is found. Formal operational children will develop an abstract rule such as $Y + 20 = 2Y$ and solve the formula algebraically, $20 = 2Y - Y = Y$. The separate operations of addition and multiplication would be combined into a higher-order algebraic operation. One of the consequences of the ability to combine operations is that many different aspects of a problem can be dealt with simultaneously. The concrete operational child thinks sequentially, considering only one aspect of a problem at a time. As soon as several aspects can be considered together, in the Formal Operational Period, the logic of a set of statements can be examined. This ability is one of the most important underpinnings in allowing formal operational children to think logically and scientifically.[4]

Tasks. Formal operational thinking must be inferred from children's behavior in the face of certain problems. The two major types of cognitive problems from which formal operations are inferred require hypothetico-deductive[5] and inductive thinking. *Hypothetico-deductive thinking* involves reasoning from a set of premises to a conclusion. Syllogisms are examples of this kind of reasoning. Thus, given the premises: (1) All sheep have wool, and (2) Dennis is a sheep, the formal operational child can correctly conclude (3) Dennis has wool. Concrete operational children are more likely to answer that they cannot say because they have never met Dennis, or that Dennis cannot have wool because he is a person, or that nobody names sheep Dennis. This example demonstrates one of the properties of hypothetico-deductive reasoning: premises are taken as "givens" regardless of whether or not they are true in experience. The ability of formal operational children to separate the process of reasoning from the specific content allows them to work with contrary-to-fact hypotheses. Hypothetico-deductive thinking clearly requires that children be able to deal with more than one aspect of a problem at a time. In the syllogism example above, children must keep in mind both that all sheep have wool and that Dennis is a sheep. In addition, the problem demands that children work with concepts which they have not directly experienced (e.g., a sheep named Dennis).

The second type of problem, using *inductive thinking*, is the complement of tasks using hypothetico-deductive reasoning. While hypothetico-deductive thinking proceeds from general principles to specific predictions, inductive thinking starts with specific instances and proceeds to general laws. An example of an inductive reasoning task is the pendulum problem. The set-up involves a wooden stand, various lengths of string, and several weights. The experimenter suspends, one at a time, different string and weight combinations from the stand and starts the pendulum swinging by pulling the weight back to different heights and releasing it with different forces. Thus specific instances are

---

[4]Concrete operational children can function at an intellectual level comparable to understanding main effects in an analysis of variance research design. Because formal operational children can combine two or more operations, they can understand concepts equivalent in difficulty to interactions in research designs.

[5]Piaget also treats a sixteen-fold propositional logic and a variety of complex "groups" under the rubric of hypothetico-deductive operations. His discussion of these topics is extensive, highly technical, and controversial. To treat these topics adequately would require an entire chapter, so we refer the interested reader to Flavell (1963), Ginsburg and Opper (1969), and Brainerd (1978a).

given in the problem. Once children understand that sometimes the pendulum swings faster than at other times, they are asked to generate the law governing pendulum swinging. The correct response is that the length of the string determines the speed (short strings swing faster). Concrete operational children generally try several combinations of weights and string lengths in a random, unsystematic fashion without proposing or testing hypotheses. Formal operational children, on the other hand, exhibit the three characteristics of scientific thinking outlined earlier. First they isolate the factors which could affect the pendulum's speed, generating multiple hypotheses about the events they have witnessed. Although the solution happens to depend on just one factor (length of string), children must eliminate the possibility that two or more factors in combination affect the pendulum's speed. Thus, they must deal with multiple dimensions simultaneously. Finally, the presence of so many factors and combinations of factors requires children to systematically explore all possible solutions, not just try a few unsystematically.

The Formal Operational Period is the culmination of intellectual development for Piaget. By the time children are 15 or so, they should have all the cognitive structures necessary to do the most intellectually challenging tasks. After formal operations are achieved, Piaget claims that no new kinds of structures develop; intellectual progress after adolescence consists mainly of the accumulation of new contents.

A number of researchers have challenged the notion that formal operational thinking is the pinnacle of development. The fact that many people, even in Western cultures, never reach the formal operational level has led researchers to express dissatisfaction with Piaget's system. Greenfield (1976) comments, "One major criticism of Piaget's theory of development . . . is that his notion of development is really the development of a Western scientist" (p. 324–325). By limiting their research to administering Piaget's tasks, psychologists have failed to consider whether a *different* mature level of development would be possible. Any failure to find formal operational thinking is interpreted as an incomplete rather than a different pattern of development. In effect, researchers have lost sight of the observational method Piaget initially employed so they have needlessly restricted their ability to find a different pattern. As Dasen (1977) summarized the arguments, "Working from within Piaget's theory, and with the usual methodology linked to it, it seems difficult to find anything but data supporting the theory. . . . The demonstration that all individuals are able to reason according to a certain structure does not prove that this is their usual or preferred mode of reasoning" (p. 8).

THREE CRITICAL ISSUES ABOUT PIAGET'S THEORY

What we have just outlined, without much critical analysis, is Piaget's stage theory of cognitive development. The rest of this chapter reviews some critical remarks which have been aimed at three aspects of the theory. The first issue examines the role of stages: What does it mean to call Piaget's theory a stage theory? Earlier, we introduced the term "stage theory" without any formal discussion of what that term meant, but we cannot avoid a thorough examination of it since the concept of stage is at the heart of nearly all criticisms of Piaget's work. Due to common use in the literature, we will use the word "stages" to be synonymous with "periods." The first issue thus focuses on the adequacy of the theory as an explanation rather than merely a description of cognitive development. After concluding that Piaget's theory is not explanatory, we examine, as the second issue, whether the theory even presents an accurate description of development. This examination entails reviewing the replication research in order to assess the universality of the descriptions. Because the evidence suggests that the description is adequate for the first three periods, one is left with the question of what mechanisms account for change from one period to another. One way to look for mechanisms of change is to attempt to change development experimentally. Many researchers believe that training studies can identify experiential factors which facilitate or retard development. Consequently, the third issue concerns the role of training studies.

In order to discuss stage theory concisely, we first need to consider a side issue which recurs in several contexts as a point of criticism of Piaget's stage theory. That issue has been labeled the "problem of diagnosis" by Flavell (1977) or of "measurement sequences" by Brainerd (1978a). Flavell's (1977) excellent discussion uses the transitive inference task as an example of the diagnosis issue. We shall use conservation as the example so that the reader who wants more information can profitably read both sources.

The Problem of Diagnosis.   Accurate measurements are necessary in two situations: (1) when one wishes to place a child at a particular stage of development (or in transition between two stages) and (2) when one wishes to compare the rates of development of two structures, that is to say, that one structure develops before, at the same time, or after another structure. In order to make these comparisons, it is necessary to have a testing procedure which correctly diagnoses a child's potential for performance, neither underestimating nor overestimating the child's level.

Underestimations (also called false-negatives or Type II errors) occur when a test demands skills other than those it was designed to measure. If children cannot meet the extra demands, they will fail the test even though they may have the skill that is of interest to the experimenter. These extra demands are potentially numerous, including having other cognitive skills which enable the child to understand and remember the instructions; focusing attention for as long as the test requires it; having the "proper" degree of motivation or interest; being familiar with the testing materials and a test-like situation with a strange adult so that neither fear nor distraction will lower performance; and, frequently, having the verbal skills to explain the choices made. Children may have the *competence* to pass a test, but their *performance* on a particular test does not reveal that competence because of extraneous testing factors.

Overestimations (or false-positives or Type I errors) occur when children get the right answer for the wrong reason. That is, children can be lucky guessers or they may devise an irrelevant strategy that happens also to yield the correct response (for example, choose the one on the left or the one the experimenter looked at longest or spoke about last). Children may perform adequately without having the hypothesized underlying competence. Table 1-1 summarizes these sources of misdiagnosis.

Table 1-1
Sources of Misdiagnosis

	Underestimation	Overestimation
Synonymous Terms	False-negatives Type II errors	False-positives Type I errors
Test Performance	Fail test	Pass test
Presumed Cognitive Competence	Have competence	Do not have competence
Potential Reasons	Test demands extra skills Subjects fearful or unmotivated	Lucky guesses Irrelevant strategies

It thus becomes crucial to have an accurate test of the child's competence; but, at the same time, we can never be sure that we have such a valid test. Because this situation has not been satisfactorily resolved, the problems in diagnosing a child's capability are frequently invoked as evidence that Piaget's theory can never be empirically demonstrated or that criticisms against the theory are unwarranted. With this issue as a backdrop, we can now return to a discussion of what it means to call Piaget's theory a stage theory.

Stage Theory

In discussing child development, the term *stage* is frequently used by parents, pediatricians, advice books, and psychologists alike as a synonym for chronological age groups. To say "he's in the terrible twos" or "she is going through that awkward stage of adolescence" is to suggest that at certain ages enough children exhibit common behaviors (negativism and awkwardness in our sample stages) to warrant grouping the behaviors together and describing the behavior/age relationship as a stage. These types of stages are *descriptive*, as opposed to explanatory, and their only requirement is that some behaviors change in a systematic way with age. Which behaviors are grouped together at which ages is purely arbitrary.

An *explanatory* stage theory, on the other hand, incorporates all the characteristics of a descriptive theory plus it proposes some mechanism which is responsible for the behavior/age relationship. That is, an explanatory theory must specify why certain behaviors must be grouped together and why the groups occur in the observed sequence. As Kessen (1970) expresses it, "there is some nontrivial reason—some theoretical justification—for collecting these segments together in a chronological line" (p. 58). Similarly, Brainerd (1978*b*) asserts that explanatory stage theories "must posit antecedent variables believed to be responsible for [age] changes that weld the stages into distinct entities.... The behaviors in any given stage go together *naturally* by virtue of their common antecedents" (p. 174, italics in the original).

In the case of Piaget's stage theory, the antecedent variables are the functional invariants (assimilation, accommodation, equilibration). Unfortunately, as a number of critics have noted, Piaget's intended explanations have no independent method of being verified (see Brainerd 1978*b*). The "explanations" are completely circular. For example, Piaget believes that fantasy play expresses a relative predominance of assimilation over accommodation. A girl making pies out of mud ignores the nonedible features of the mud and instead treats it in the same way she would treat dough. We infer the presence of assimilation because we have observed the fantasy play behavior. Yet, Piaget would also like to say that the play occurred *because* the child could assimilate the mud into her schemes for dough. Until antecedent causal variables can be measured independently of the behaviors they are designed to explain, Piaget's theory will be less than an explanatory one.

Accepting the reservation that antecedent variables cannot be measured independently, one can still ask whether Piaget's stages reflect non-arbitrary groupings of behavior. If so, his theory will fall somewhere between a descriptive and an explanatory one. Two sets of criteria, one proposed by Piaget (1960) and one discussed by Flavell (1977) can be examined for this purpose. In the next two sections, we present the broad outlines for each set of criteria and some analysis of how well Piaget's theory fits them.

Piaget's Criteria. Piaget (1960) proposed five criteria which, if satisfied, allow the inference that "objectively certain stages exist" (p. 12). Brainerd (1978*b*) interprets this statement to mean that antecedent variables will "certainly exist if the predictions of the criteria can be verified"

(p. 175). His paper analyzes how well the five criteria imply the existence of some unspecified antecedent variables. Brainerd concluded that four of the five criteria could not be used to demonstrate the existence of antecedent variables. His analysis, however, did not address the question of the nonarbitrary groupings of behavior. We would like, therefore, to examine (1) whether satisfying the criteria will imply a natural, nonarbitrary grouping of behaviors and (2) whether the criteria can be satisfied with empirical data. Our discussion follows the definitions of Brainerd (1978b); alternative terminology and interpretations can be found in Pinard and Laurendeau (1969). The five criteria are (1) cognitive structures, (2) invariant sequences, (3) integration, (4) consolidation, and (5) equilibration.

Cognitive structure. The *cognitive structure* criterion specifies that a unique set of cognitive structures should underlie each stage. These structures determine which behaviors will be observed in the stage, hence they provide an adequate rationale for grouping certain behaviors together. For example, if conservation and class-inclusion performance both depend on the structures of concrete operations, then it is natural to group the performances together in one stage. At the moment, however, there are no empirical data which independently prove the existence of cognitive structures. They are inferred from the same behaviors they are supposed to justify. This circularity prevents any sort of empirical satisfaction of the criterion.

Invariant sequence. The *invariant sequence* criterion predicts a fixed order in the development of the behaviors which define each stage. While an invariant sequence is certainly necessary to a stage theory, its presence is not sufficient to guarantee that nonarbitrary groupings should be made. That the criterion is necessary stems from the connotation of stages as a progression from less mature to more mature intellectual levels. If behaviors developed in a random order for each individual, a stage conception of development would not be appropriate. That the invariant sequence criterion is not sufficient can be exemplified by an analogy to a system with fixed sequences but arbitrary groupings. Temperature, for example, is typically represented by whole numbers such as 32°, 33°, 34°, and so on, but it could as easily be represented by fractions such as 32½°, 33½°, and 34½°. The sequence is fixed in the sense that the numbers increase as temperature rises, but the groupings are arbitrary divisions in a continuous scale. So, finding a fixed behavioral sequence, such as object permanence followed by qualitative identity followed by conservation, is necessary but not sufficient to determine that the behaviors are grouped nonarbitrarily.

Moreover, fixed sequences in development may be produced as an artifact of our measuring instruments instead of being inherent in the cognitive system. As we noted above under the topic of diagnosis, no behavioral test is ever a pure measure of just one skill. Suppose, for example, that conservation of weight "naturally" developed before conservation of number, but our tests show the reverse (number before weight). This situation could arise if the test for weight conservation is very difficult on some irrelevant dimensions, such as requiring knowledge of difficult words, whereas the test for number conservation is very easy. The additional skill required in the weight conservation test produces a fixed sequence of number developing before weight, but this is an artifact of our measuring instrument. It thus appears as if we have no empirical way to verify whether behaviors develop in sequence, simultaneously, or randomly.

Integration. The third criterion, *integration*, requires that each successive stage incorporate the previous ones. Behaviors in one stage are not lost or completely replaced; rather, the higher stage builds upon the accomplishments of the lower stages. While Piaget clearly intended his theory to satisfy this criterion, it seems tangential to the issue of stages. Having a later-developing behavior build upon the skills of an earlier-developing behavior does not help one cut up the stream of development into meaningful divisions. The integration criterion has been interpreted by Brainerd (1978*b*) as being redundant with the fixed sequence criterion. If that is so, it can be dismissed on the same grounds as the invariant sequence criterion. But we do not believe that the integration criterion implies fixed sequences. To use an analogy from foreign-language learning, having a knowledge of verbs will certainly be incorporated into one's later learning of nouns, but the reverse would also be true if nouns were taught before verbs. Integration could be satisfied without the sequence of skills being fixed.

Consolidation. The *consolidation* criterion proposes that each stage contains two phases: an achievement phase in which the behaviors assigned to that stage are fully acquired, and a preparatory phase in which some initial acquisition of the next stage's behaviors are begun. This criterion presents a number of difficulties. On the one hand, it seems to blur the distinctiveness of each stage since behaviors from two stages are present at any one time. This makes it more difficult, not easier, to segment the stream of behavior into natural groups. On the other hand, the consolidation criterion seems redundant with the invariant sequence criterion because it proposes a fixed order for behavior acquisition (achievement of one followed by preparation for the next). The same insufficiencies of the invariant sequence criterion thus may apply to the consolidation criterion as well.

Equilibration. Finally, the *equilibration* criterion refers to an alternation of periods of stability with periods of disequilibrium or change. Additionally, it is expected that the equilibrium times will be long relative to the disequilibrium periods (see Figure 1-1a). If the times of disequilibrium were long relative to the times of stability (see Figure 1-1b), development would seem less like a series of steps (stages) and more like

Figure 1-1a

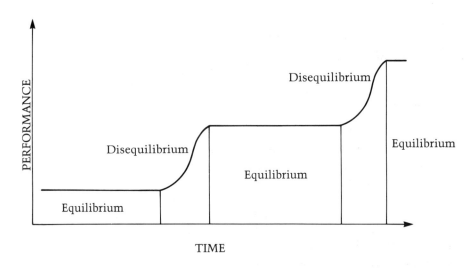

Figure 1-1b

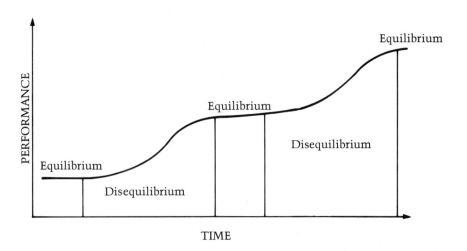

Two models of alternating phases of equilibrium and disequilibrium. In (a) the equilibrium times are lengthy and the disequilibrium times are short. In (b) the equilibrium times are short and the disequilibrium times are lengthy.

a smooth increment. The behaviors acquired together during the phase of rapid change would be a natural, nonarbitrary grouping by which the stage could be defined. Brainerd (1977) believes that this criterion could be subjected to empirical verification. It requires finding alternating periods of behavioral change and stability. He concluded, however, that the data do not confirm the criterion for Piaget's theory. "Smooth behavioral change without noticeable variations in rate seems to be the rule" (Brainerd, 1978b, p. 180). Before accepting this conclusion, however, one must recall that the measurement or diagnosis difficulty applies here as well as to earlier criteria. Depending on one's frame of reference, or the precision of the measuring devices, one can view development as more or less abrupt.

To summarize, it does not appear that Piaget's criteria have immediate applicability in determining the nonarbitrary grouping of his stages. The cognitive structure and equilibration criteria seem conceptually to allow one to make natural groupings into stages, but there are difficulties in finding empirical data to satisfy the criteria. The invariant sequence criterion is necessary, but not sufficient, to form nonarbitrary groups and it, like the integration and consolidation criteria, could be criticized for being subject to measurement or diagnosis difficulties.

Flavell's Criteria. The other major set of criteria which could serve as a standard for measuring a stage theory has been discussed by Flavell (1977). The three criteria are (1) that stages are qualitatively different from one another rather than merely quantitatively different; (2) that the transition from one stage to another is abrupt rather than gradual; and (3) that a large number of related skills or strategies appear concurrently, that is, simultaneously rather than asynchronously. The latter two criteria are slightly modified forms of the equilibration and invariant sequence criteria, so our discussion of these criteria can be much shorter than the criterion of qualitative differences.

Qualitative differences. This criterion states that if certain behaviors are *qualitatively different* from other behaviors, one can assign children to one stage or another on the basis of this meaningful aspect of their abilities. As Flavell (1977) has said,

> Consider the digit span memory test. It would sound silly to say that Mary was in the "three-digit stage" last year but has now entered the "four-digit stage." A stage-type characterization perhaps would not sound so silly if she had used a rehearsal strategy to memorize things last year but then switched over to a wholly different strategy this year, e.g., elaboration (p. 245).

If behavioral changes are only quantitative (from three digits to four digits), segmentation into stages will be arbitrary and will depend on the precision of the measuring device. On the other hand, when a qualitative division can be made (for example, between children who can and cannot use an elaboration strategy), a nonarbitrary grouping suggested, thus making a stage characterization more appropriate. But can any empirical data satisfy the criterion? A number of researchers have claimed that whether a behavioral change looks qualitative or quantitative depends on the level of analyis[6] (Flavell, 1977; McLaughlin, 1963; Pascual-Leone, 1970).

McLaughlin (1963), for example, claims that Piaget's stages are really only quantitatively different when examined at the proper level of analysis. He views cognitive development as an increasing ability to handle objects of thought which are increasingly distant (psychologically) from the subject and to deal with those objects along an increasing number of dimensions. Thus, the objects of thought progress from a concrete object directly perceived by the child (in the Sensorimotor Period) to a concrete object which does not need to be in front of the child (in the Preoperational and Concrete Operational Periods) to abstract or nonreal objects (in the Formal Operational Period). McLaughlin considers this progression a quantitative change in degree of abstractness.

The second quantitative change McLaughlin proposed is a doubling of the number of concepts a child can handle simultaneously. During the time of Piaget's Sensorimotor Period, children are said to process only one concept at a time. The infant cannot compare two objects because two dimensions cannot be handled at the same time. Therefore, object concepts have no distinguishing features. During the Preoperational Period, children can handle two concepts simultaneously. These two concepts are usually an object and its environment. Children will fail the class-inclusion problem, for instance, because they cannot hold in mind an object (such as a white bead), the object's environment (the rest of the pile of wooden beads), and the relationship between the two because that would require a third concept—white wooden beads. Concrete operational children, having doubled the number of concepts to four, can solve class-inclusion problems but they cannot solve problems requiring more than four concepts. For example, in many formal operational tasks the number of all possible alternative solutions exceeds four dimensions. During the Formal Operational Period, children can deal with eight concepts simultaneously. Having so many concepts at their disposal allows adolescents to solve contrary-to-fact syllogisms and to systematically vary all possible factors in an experiment. Concrete operational children can solve syllogisms only if the premises accord with their experiences. If they are acquainted with the premises, they can solve the syllogism in sequential steps. If the premises are imaginary or contrary to fact, they must hold too many dimensions in their minds at once and will fail to solve the problem.

[6]The term "level of analysis" denotes both the size of the unit employed and its generality. Large, broad terms which require many inferences fall toward the abstract end of the level of analysis scale, while molecular units which are close to behavior fall near the concrete end.

McLaughlin's argument, then, is that Piaget has considered his stages to be qualitatively different when, instead, they are only quantitatively different. McLaughlin claims that Piaget has confused the combination of two quantitative dimensions (increasing abstractness of the objects of thought and increasing numbers of concepts the child can handle) with qualitative differences in the ways children think. McLaughlin says that the stages are only quantitatively different regardless of how different the child's behavior looks.

Flavell points out that "what looks like a qualitative change at one level of analysis may not at another" (1977, p. 246). This viewpoint seems to us the most sensible resolution to the dispute. The analyst's frame of reference is important because the closer one gets to a description of day-to-day behavior, the more quantitative the changes look. Piagetian theory, by virtue of being general and abstract, sees more qualitative changes. This does not mean that the quantitative-qualitative debate is a pseudo-issue. Rather, it complicates the reader's evaluative task by requiring a decision about whether the theorist is operating at a level of abstractness appropriate to the data under consideration.

Abruptness. Flavell's second criterion is *abruptness.* As we have said under the discussion of the equilibration criterion, if behavior changes abruptly in a short period of time, all the changes form a natural group by which to define a stage. If behavioral change is slow, it becomes difficult to distinguish meaningful separations. Empirical support for this criterion, however, is in dispute. Although Piaget imparts a "now you see it; now you don't" air to stage transitions, Flavell (1977) believes this presentation is oversimplified. For Flavell, abruptness of stage transitions depends heavily on the definition used to identify a child as either possessing or not possessing a particular cognitive content, which in turn is used to identify a child as being "in" or "not in" a stage. Three definitions can be distinguished: (1) the point at which an item first appears (its evocability); (2) the point at which it becomes a common way of responding (its ease of utilization); and (3) the point at which it is firmly established in the child's repertoire, being used in nearly all appropriate circumstances (its functional maturity.) If the first appearance of an item is used to define the onset of the stage, transitions will probably look quite abrupt. By using either of the other two definitions, the transitions will look less abrupt. For example, many items do not reach functional maturity until several years after their first appearance, so stages appear to overlap. As with Piaget's equilibration criterion, the diagnosis problem remains to be resolved.

Concurrence. The *concurrence* criterion is closely related to Piaget's cognitive structure criterion in the sense that cognitive skills supposedly controlled by a common structure ought to appear together. Yet, the same problem of choosing a definition for the appearance of a cognitive skill makes this criterion hard to satisfy empirically. If the definition of first appearance is used, items may appear nonconcurrently; but if functional maturity is used, synchrony may seen the rule.

Empirical evidence using Piaget's tasks (with their unknown inequalities in task difficulty) reveal consistent *decalages*—Piaget's term for groups of ligically related skills appearing nonsimultaneously. *Decalages* have been particularly noted in the development of conservation, with a consistent finding being that conservation of number develops before conservation of quantity (Brainerd & Brainerd, 1972; Gruen & Vore, 1972) and that quantity develops before weight which develops before volume (Uzgiris, 1964). Since all of these conservations supposedly rely on the same operational structures, it is argued that they should develop together as a unified, tightly knit system. Piaget's explanation for the presence of *décalages* is a version of the diagnosis problem: it is harder to apply some operations in some environmental contexts than in others because of the nature of the environment. While this serves to explain away the lack of concurrence, it makes it difficult to use the concurrence criterion to justify a stage theory.

Summary.   We are left in a disappointing spot. We know that Piaget's stage theory is not explanatory because antecedent causal variables have not been defined independently of the behaviors they are intended to explain. We do not know whether his stage theory lies somewhere between an explanation and a mere description because no set of criteria seems able both to justify natural groupings of behaviors into stages and to be subject to empirical verification. In fact, we still need to examine the question of whether his theory is even an adequate description of cognitive development. We take up this question in the next section.

Universality

Given that Piaget's theory does not meet the criteria for an explanatory stage theory, what may we conclude about its power as a description of cognitive development? Piaget (1972) claims that his theory describes a sequence in the development of cognitive structures. Environmental and cultural influences—such as type of schooling or the availability of toys— may alter the rate of development, but the sequence observed in Genevan children should be universal across different cultures. Clearly, if Piaget's developmental sequence can be shown to be universal, his theory would possess greater descriptive power than if it only applied to middle-class Genevan children.

Piaget (Pinard & Laurendeau, 1969) believes that his theory would be disconfirmed if it were ever found that members of one cultural group developed the structures of a higher level stage before the structures of a lower level stage (stage inversion). (As we have already discussed, since cognitive structures can only be inferred from behavioral contents, perhaps this criterion ought to be rephrased in terms of content rather than structure.) Since the cognitive achievements of Piaget's stages logically depend on acquisitions of the previous stages, it seems unlikely that such evidence could be found. For example, it is difficult to imagine a child who could conserve mass (a concrete operational skill) without already possessing qualitative identity (a preoperational ability). Nevertheless, large inversions in the order of acquisition of cognitive skills would indicate a lack of universality. The second data pattern which Piaget would consider to be disconfirmation is the absence of one stage accompanied by the presence of a later stage (stage skipping).

Piaget's claim that his theory is universally descriptive can be investigated in two ways. First, his results should be replicated on other groups of Western children. In addition, the predicted developmental sequence should appear in children who are very different from those tested by Piaget and his colleagues. In this section we survey both kinds of studies. First we examine replication research using children primarily from the United States and Canada who are very similar to Piaget's subjects. Then we examine studies using subjects who differ from Genevan children in many ways. Specifically, we review cross-cultural research and research with handicapped children, with the elderly, and with animals.

Replication with Western Children.   In general, Piaget's descriptions of the first three periods (Sensorimotor, Preoperational, and Concrete Operational) have been replicated when European or North American children are investigated. The picture is much less clear for the Formal Operational Period, so we review this research in some detail. The major problem with the Formal Operational Period is that children as young as four or five years can pass some formal operational problems, while a majority of adolescents and adults fail some other types of formal operational tasks. Brainerd's (1978a) discussion of implication reasoning, which involves propositional logic, illustrates this difficulty.

In implication reasoning studies, subjects are asked to solve syllogisms like:

Premise 1: If George is a professor, then he is smart.

Premise 2: George is a professor.

Conclusion: George is smart.

The subject is given premises 1 and 2 and is asked to produce the conclusion. *Valid forms* of the implication reasoning problem are phrased in such a way as to test whether the child will draw a correct conclusion. *Invalid forms* test whether the child avoids drawing a plausible-sounding but incorrect conclusion. For example,

Premise 1: If George is a professor, then he is smart.

Premise 2: George is not a professor.

Incorrect conclusion: George is not smart.

Correct conclusion: We do not know if George is smart.

The accuracy of Piaget's description of the Formal Operational Period is seriously challenged by research on valid and invalid implication reasoning. Children who are nominally in the Concrete Operational Period (first, second, or third graders) pass between 77 percent and 90 percent of implication reasoning problems when valid forms are used (Ennis, 1971; Kodroff & Roberge, 1975; Paris, 1973). Some children as young as four or five years can also solve valid forms (Brainerd, 1978a). Thus, one type of formal operational task appears to be relatively easy for concrete operational and even some preoperational children. Research on invalid forms is also difficult to reconcile with Piaget's theory. When concrete operational children are tested on invalid forms, they almost always draw incorrect conclusions. The trouble is, almost everyone else does, too. Adolescents, college students, and college-trained adults pass only 5 percent to 25 percent of invalid form problems, roughly the same percentages as for concrete operational children (Brainerd, 1978a). We will consider what Piaget and others have said about this failure to replicate after we describe the rest of the replication literature.

Cross-cultural Research. Another way to examine the universality of Piagetian theory is to look at children who are very different from Piaget's original subjects, for example, children from traditional or non-Western cultures. Though Piaget's theory has been tested cross-culturally, the possibility of drawing firm conclusions from cross-cultural data is limited in three ways. One is the difficulty we have already discussed as the problem of diagnosis. The same sequence of development might be found across cultures because of the nature of Piaget's tasks rather than because of the nature of cognitive structures. Another problem arises whenever children are tested, but it is especially prevalent in cross-cultural work. Children might not perform well because they are unfamiliar with the testing situation. The third difficulty is that relatively little data have been collected from non-Western or traditional cultures compared to the amount of research with North American and Western European children. So, the research described below should be viewed as suggestive rather than conclusive. With these limitations in mind, Dasen (1977) provided two generalizations about cross-cultural research. (1) The qualitative aspects of Piaget's theory have been observed in all cultures tested. That is, at least the first three major periods (Sensorimotor, Preoperational, and Concrete Operational) appear and develop in the same order, and the stages for particular concepts, such as conservation and object permanence, are the same. Moreover, the explanations given by children for their conservation responses parallel those identified by Piaget. (2) The sequential development of conservation of quantity, then weight, then volume (a *décalage*) is usually verified when data from a sample are averaged, although the order may vary for individual subjects.

Box A. A Cross-cultural Study of Conservation

Armah and Arnold (1977) reported on the ability of young girls from Ghana to perform conservation of liquid quantity and conservation of mass (clay balls). They sampled girls from three age groups (6–7 years, 8-9 years, and 10-11 years) who had either at least one year of schooling or less than one year, and who came either from traditional homes where girls help their mothers in cooking and in making pottery or from nontraditional homes. Armah and Arnold found that the girls from traditional homes did better on the conservation tasks, perhaps because cooking and making pottery gave the girls a lot of familiarity in judging liquid quantities and masses. Formal schooling, on the other hand, had no effect, perhaps because the school curriculum was characterized by rote verbal learning, with little chance to interact with concrete materials.

Much cross-cultural research has taken the form of importing Piaget's conservation tasks to see how well the "other" people performed. (See Box A for an example of a cross-cultural conservation study.) Three factors have been isolated which seem to increase the rate of conservation development:

(1) the amount of Western-type schooling[7]; (2) the amount of contact with members of a Western culture; for example, Australian aborigines who had a lot of contact with the European community performed better than the aborigines who had little contact, even when schooling, urbanization, language, and social class were controlled (Dasen 1974); and (3) the nature of the daily activities in the culture, such as being potters, farmers, or factory workers. In Western cultures virtually all adults achieve conservation. In some non-Western cultures, however, a sizable number of adults do not appear to possess conservation skills (Cole & Scribner, 1974). Piaget would not be too disturbed by this turn of events; those adults would be viewed as simply stopping short of achieving their full potential. On reflection, however, the possibility that functioning adults might not be able to conserve is disturbing. It is difficult to imagine, for example, that one could survive very long in a desert environment believing that the amount of water would increase by pouring it from one container into a taller, thinner vessel. Cole and Scribner (1974) comment that "until we have some better idea of what induces some members of traditional societies to solve conservation problems while their neighbors do not, we cannot be certain about the significance of conservation tests as a tool for understanding the relation between culture and cognitive development" (p. 156).

---

[7]Note that the Ghanaian study summarized above described the school curriculum as emphasizing rote learning and that such schooling did not facilitate acquiring conservation.

Again it should be emphasized that all of these conclusions remain tentative until we solve the problem of making each task as meaningful to the other cultures as it was to the original sample of subjects (Cole & Scribner, 1974). Dasen (1972) points out that most cross-cultural work cannot be evaluated because the experimenter's anthropological sophistication and skill at translating the standard task into the other culture are unknown. A number of cross-cultural studies suffer from not being translated into the native language at all. In addition to translating the test, the testing procedure must be translated to compensate for children's lack of familiarity with being tested, especially by strange adults, and for children's motivation to get the correct answer. The best conclusion is to echo the sentiments of Cole and Scribner (1974):

> We are unlikely to find cultural differences in basic component cognitive processes. While we cannot completely rule out this possibility, there is no evidence, in any line of investigation that we have reviewed, that any cultural group wholly lacks a basic [cognitive] process...(p. 193).

Handicapped Children. Cross-cultural research has demonstrated a basic universality of Piaget's developmental sequence, at least through the Concrete Operational Period, for children who are physically normal. Other researchers have asked just how important physical normality is. Are Piaget's stages so universal as to encompass abnormal (deaf, blind, retarded) children? Deaf and blind children have vastly different environments than normal children, lacking auditory-language experiences and visual-spatial experiences, respectively. To the extent that these experiential deficits change the nature of children's interactions, handicapped children might be expected to have difficulty forming equilibrated structures, that is, in assimilating and accommodating to the environment. Specifically, one might suspect that deaf children would not progress through the Preoperational Period because their symbolic functioning is severely limited when language input is limited. Similarly, one might expect blind children to miss out on parts of the Sensorimotor Period. Because their movement in space is restricted, they are less likely to be successful in searching for hidden objects (attaining object permanence), and they may be less able to control the events they experience such as repeating interesting actions. Would difficulty in the Sensorimotor Period prevent further development in blind children? Fortunately, many deaf and blind children are able to overcome their handicaps. Research has shown that some deaf children are successful on tests of concrete operations, such as conservation of weight (Youniss, 1974), and some deaf adolescents exhibit formal operational skills such as predicting probabilities (Furth & Youniss, 1971), although deaf adolescents perform poorly on tests of symbolic logic (Furth & Youniss, 1971). The sequence of development is the same for deaf children as for normal children, although the rate may be slower by several years.

Similarly, some blind children can achieve normal levels of development, except perhaps for some difficulties with spatial relations (Brekke, Williams, & Tait, 1974; Millar, 1976). Thus Piaget's sequence appears to be universal even in the face of severe handicaps like deafness or blindness.

Mentally retarded children have also been tested for their progress through Piaget's stages. Again, the findings are of a slower rate of development but the sequential pattern is the same as for normals. Gruen and Vore (1972), for example, found the sequence of conservation of number, then liquid quantity, and then weight for both retarded and normal subjects. The retarded children, with IQs ranging from 60 to 78, were about three years behind their chronological age mates. Since the performance of retarded children depended on their mental age level rather than on their chronological age, they could be expected to fall ever further behind their peers. And, of course, many retarded persons never progress very far through the developmental sequence.

The Elderly. Thus far, if Piaget's tasks are used, his description appears accurate. One question which Piaget leaves open is the extent to which his description applies to adult cognitive functioning. Piaget proposes no new qualitative advances in post-adolescent thinking. If his stages are relatively independent of such environmental factors as schooling, cognitive performance should not decline in adulthood (as long as senile brain damage is absent).

The little research that has been done on adults points consistently to poorer performance by older adults compared to middle-aged adults on a variety of concrete operational tasks. Older adults have been found to perform more poorly on tests of egocentrism (Looft & Charles, 1971; Rubin, 1974), perception of part-whole relations (Wapner, Werner, & Comalli, 1960), spatial organization (Comalli, Wapner, & Werner, 1959), and free classification tasks (Denney, 1974a; Denney & Lennon, 1972). Papalia (1972) administered conservation of number, mass, weight, and volume to subjects ranging in age from 6 to 82 years. While the older subjects conserved number, only half of them conserved mass and weight, and few of them conserved volume. Papalia's findings suggest that conservation abilities disappear in the reverse order from their acquisition in childhood.

Several investigators have successfully used training to reinstate adequate performance. For example, Hornblum and Overton (1976) reinstated volume conservation in the elderly by verbal feedback training and Schultz and Hoyer (1976) reduced egocentric performance with practice and feedback training. Denney (1974b) found that middle-aged men and women differed in free-classification tasks, with the women using strategies similar to those used by elderly men and women and by children. When the occupations of the subjects were statistically controlled, the middle-aged women were no different from the middle-aged men. These results suggest that cognitive decrements in the elderly may be due largely to environmental factors such as isolation from educational and environmental demands for abstract thought.

Unfortunately, most of these studies used a *cross-sectional* design, testing different groups of subjects of different ages at one point in time. In order to conclude that the elderly's poorer performance on cognitive tasks indicates a *decrease* from earlier abilities, it is necessary to show that they once were able to perform well. It is possible that older subjects never learned the skills being tested or had less practice in using them (due, for example, to changes in schooling or to occupational patterns). Thus, it is necessary to rule out cohort effects, that is, systematic differences between generations of subjects. Research needs to be conducted using *longitudinal* designs (in which the same people are tested on several occasions) and *cross-sequential* designs (which are combinations of longitudinal and cross-sectional) in order to demonstrate that cognitive abilities actually deteriorate with increasing age.

Animal Research.   Perhaps the most extreme test of the universality of Piaget's stages is to look at the sequence of cognitive development in animals. Of course, only the earliest (prelanguage) steps of development can be tested with nonhuman animals. If Piaget's theory is truly a biologically based one, with cognitive development relatively independent of cultural and environmental factors, animals should show some of the same progressions as human infants.

Cats and primates have been tested for their development of object permanence. Gruber, Girgus, and Banuazizi (1971) have found the first four stages of object permanence in cats, and that these stages develop in the same order as in children. Moreover, different rearing environments affect the rate of development; house cats develop object permanence more rapidly than laboratory-reared cats (Gruber et al., 1971).

Attainment of the fifth object permanence stage (searching for a hidden object after a visible displacement) has been found in some new world monkeys (Mathieu, Bouchard, Granger, & Herscovitch, 1976). The sixth stage (searching for a hidden object after an invisible displacement) has been found in rhesus monkeys (Wise, Wise, & Zimmermann, 1974), in chimpanzees and some new world monkeys (Mathieu et al., 1976), and in squirrel monkeys (Vaughter, Smotherman, & Ordy, 1972). Again, the sequence parallels the one for humans. It should not be surprising that other species besides humans develop object permanence. It is adaptive to be able to find a banana dropped under a leaf or to wait by a hole to pounce on a mouse that disappeared there. Moreover, if chimpanzees can be credited with learning language, they ought to be able to learn a skill which, in humans, in acquired prior to language. The more significant finding is that the developmental sequence is the same across the species that have been tested thus far.

Most of the animal work has been confined to the study of object permanence. Two studies, however, have begun to explore conservation in squirrel monkeys (Czerny & Thomas, 1975; Thomas & Peay, 1976). These studies demonstrated the animals' ability to judge two lengths or two volumes to be equal or unequal, independent of perceptual cues such as color, width, and height. Some methodological difficulties, however, restrict the conclusions that can be drawn from animal research. Verbal explanations cannot be sought from the subjects and obtaining an equality judgment before and after a transformation does not guarantee that the subjects understand any connection between the two presentations. The authors were cautious in interpreting their data as showing skills that might be prerequisites to conservation rather than as being conservation itself.

Summary. The replication evidence we have reviewed in this section looks impressive. The same developmental sequences are found cross-culturally if one uses Piaget's tasks. Deaf, blind, and retarded children follow the developmental sequence of normal children and some evidence points to a similar sequence of sensorimotor development (object permanence) in animals. The rate of development, however, is sensitive to cultural and experiential factors. For example, a decline in conservation performance among older adults seems to be due to a lack of demand for those skills in their everyday life. To return to our original question, then, how universal is Piaget's description of cognitive development? The evidence looks quite good for the first three periods. Only the fourth period, Formal Operations, does not seem to be supported by the replication research.

Piaget's Reformulation of the Formal Operational Period. In partial response to the lack of support for the Formal Operational Period, Piaget (1972) advanced three possible reasons why some children have not yet achieved full formal operations by age fifteen.

1. The rate of development at any stage depends on "the quality and frequency of intellecutal stimulation" (Piaget, 1972, p. 7). If stimulation were lacking, formal operations might not develop until adolescents reached their late teens; in an extremely disadvantageous environment, formal operations might never develop.

2. Children's aptitudes become more diverse with increasing age. That is, development is uniform through the first three periods, but by adolescence only those who become interested in science or philosophy would develop formal operational skills. This option does not imply that some normal adolescents cannot attain full formal

operations; rather, some adolescents simply stop short of their potential.

3. Formal operational skills are more content-bound than those of the first three periods, and formal operational tests are more dependent upon extraneous demands like scientific background.

Piaget favors the third alternative; he has said,

> In our investigation of formal structures we used rather specific types of experimental situations which were of a physical and logical-mathematical nature because these seemed to be understood by the school children we sampled. However, it is possible to question whether these situations are, fundamentally, very general and therefore applicable to any school or professional environment. Let us consider the example of apprentices to carpenters, locksmiths, or mechanics who have shown sufficient aptitudes for successful training in the trades they have chosen but whose general education is limited. It is highly likely that they will know how to reason in a hypothetical manner in their specialty, that is to say, dissociating the variables involved, relating terms in a combinatorial manner, and reasoning with propositions involving negations and reciprocities. They would, therefore, be capable of thinking formally in their particular field, whereas faced with our experimental situations, their lack of knowledge or the fact that they have forgotten certain ideas that are particularly familar to children still in school or college, would hinder them from reasoning in a formal way, and they would give the appearance of being at the concrete level (1972, p. 10).

Formal operations, like other cognitive structures, are supposed to be independent of content areas. However,

> we can retain the idea that formal operations are free from their concrete content, but we must add that this is true only on the condition that for the subjects the situations involve equal aptitudes or comparable vital interests (Piaget, 1972, p. 11).

Thus, both extraneous task demands and lack of motivation may combine to produce an apparent absence of formal operations in individuals who are actually capable of formal thought in their area of expertise.

It is important to note that all three of the above possibilities assume the reality of the Formal Operational Period. Other critics of formal operations (Brainerd, 1978a; Keating, 1979; Cowan, 1978) implicitly favor a fourth alternative: Piaget's Formal Operational Period simply does not describe the way most adolescents think. Instead of just criticizing Piaget's efforts, a few writers (Arlin, 1975; Reigel, 1973) have suggested additions or alternatives to the Formal Operational Period. We will discuss Riegel's criticisms to illustrate one alternative to Piaget's sequence.

Riegel's Alternative Developmental Path. Riegel (1973) argues that adult thought differs from adolescent thought in more than the number and variety of cognitive contents. Piaget, because of his scientific training, saw the scientist as the epitome of cognitive development, operating by testing all possible hypotheses, methodically combining variables, and so on. Riegel argues that (1) scientific reasoning is not necessarily the height of cognitive development and (2) Piaget's formal logical reasoning characterizes what scientists do only when they are not working creatively (or are stuck). "Creative scientific activities are dominated by playful manipulation of contradictions and by conceiving issues integratively which have been torn apart by formal operational thinking" (Riegel, 1973, p. 362). That is, creative thinking is characterized by dialectic thinking in which objects are defined in terms of their often contradictory properties. A dog is neither big nor small; rather, it is big relative to an ant and small relative to an elephant. The hallmark of formal operational thought, in contrast, is that thoughts must be logically consistent; no contradictions are allowed. Piaget's system, with its emphasis on the logic of classes and relations, does not easily incorporate dialectic thinking.

Piaget's tasks do not detect dialectic reasoning because dialectic responses are classified as errors. For example, on a conservation of mass problem, a child who is reasoning dialectically would respond that the clay is both "the same" (the same amount of clay) and "different" (differently shaped).[8] Children's apparent errors on Piaget's tasks need to be examined in light of Riegel's interpretations to see whether dialectic reasoning does occur.

Since dialectic reasoning uses more of the available information about an object than formal operational thinking, Riegel considers dialectic reasoning a more mature, creative form of thought. He does not, however, propose that dialectic reasoning is a fifth stage following formal operational thought. Rather, dialectic thinking can be found at any stage of development and it might coexist with the structures which characterize Piaget's periods. Furthermore, Riegel claims that children originally use dialectic thinking but lose it as they are exposed to formal operationally oriented schooling. To become cognitively mature adults, children must relearn to think dialectically.

Summary. Some modifications in Piaget's original description of formal operational thinking need to be made to account for the striking inability of "normal" adolescents and adults to solve many formal operational tasks. Piaget (1972) has suggested a number of alternative reasons for the performance failure without really changing his conception of the underlying formal operational structure. Others, such as

---

[8]A number of people may respond dialectically when it is inappropriate in the school systems. For example, some very bright students have difficulty with multiple choice tests because they "overinterpret" the questions and can see how several answers could be correct (or how no answer is completely correct).

Riegel (1973) and Greenfield (1976), have argued that Piaget's description of the fourth period is not appropriate for the general adult population and they have called for a new conceptualization of mature intellectual functioning.

Training Studies

Replication studies, testing the universality of Piaget's theory, comprise one large segment of the Piaget-based research literature. The other large segment is composed of training studies. Training studies on Piagetian contents have been conducted for over a decade, primarily in North America, but also recently by Piaget's collaborators. Besides exploring the sheer possibility of teaching Piagetian concepts in a brief period of time, training studies can examine how experience (provided by training) promotes development. We examine training on conservation tasks to illustrate the nature and success of such procedures.

Training as an Index of Experiential Factors. Training studies have been used to suggest possible experiences which facilitate the development of cognitive skills. This has been applied especially to the development of conservation (Kuhn, 1974), so we will present the arguments for that particular case. The logic of using training studies in this fashion is that some skill or knowledge, absent in nonconserving children, is provided by training. If training that skill or knowledge results in subsequent conservation performance, the researcher typically concludes that the development of that skill contributes to the development of conservation. Furthermore, many researchers argue that successful training of conservation mirrors the way conservation is naturally acquired.

Flavell (1977) has delineated the four possible ways in which an experience, supplied during training, can contribute to the development of an ability, say, conservation. (See Table 1–2.)

1. Some experience might be both necessary and sufficient for conservation. If the experience occurs, conservation will arise; if the experience does not occur, conservation will not arise. According to Piaget, such a necessary and sufficient experience would be a cognitive conflict induced by comparing two conflicting judgments.

2. Some experience might be necessary but not sufficient. That is, the experience plus some other factors together might produce conservation. This point is similar to the arguments discussed in the section on diagnosis concerning underestimation. If successful conservation performance requires mental operations plus memory or verbal skills or some other factors, supplying any one of these factors through training will facilitate conservation, but not guarantee it.

3. Some experience may not be necessary, but it could be sufficient. This alternative suggests that there may be several paths to the

development of conservation. Training of one skill may, by itself, produce conservation, but so might providing other experiences.

4. Finally, an experience may be neither necessary nor sufficient, but it could provide some aid to development. For example, watching educational television cannot be necessary for conservation because children develop conservation in cultures where television is not watched. It may not, by itself, be sufficient; perhaps children also need to manipulate objects physically. But television exposure could stimulate activity or teach children something which accelerates the development of conservation.

Table 1-2

Four Possible Connections Between Experiences and Developing Conservation

	Sufficient	Insufficient
	(1)	(2)
Necessary	Have experience → Conservation	Have experience → Conservation OR No conservation
	Lack experience → No conservation	Lack experience → No conservation
	(3)	(4)
Unnecessary	Have experience → Conservation	Have experience → Conservation OR No conservation
	Lack experience → Conservation OR No conservation	Lack experience → Conservation OR No conservation

Flavell argues that the first two possibilities (that some experience is necessary for conservation) can never be demonstrated by training studies because such studies cannot eliminate the logical possibility that other, totally different, routes to conservation exist. Moreover Wohlwill (1973) argues that training studies can never prove the sufficiency of a single experience either, because all studies include multiple factors (especially biological ones) that cannot be ruled out. Hence, the most that training studies can do is to identify plausible experiential factors which aid in the development of conservation.

Types of Conservation Training Studies. The enormous number of conservation training studies testifies to the diversity of opinion about what kinds of experiences can aid in the development of conservation. Kuhn (1974) classifies the training studies in five categories.

1. *Training attention.* The rationale behind this category of training is that children frequently understand the principle of conservation but their attention is distracted by irrelevant cues such as language or perception. If children fail conservation tasks because they focus on irrelevant perceptual features like height or width, then experimenters should train children to ignore those features (e.g., Gelman, 1969).

2. *Providing information.* Children might not exhibit conservation because they might not have had enough information about the results of deforming and transforming the materials used in conservation. Training can provide such information in the form of feedback ("right" or "wrong") after children offer their judgment (e.g., Wohlwill & Lowe, 1962) or in the form of self-discovery, e.g., letting children weigh objects before and after transformations (Smedslund, 1961).

3. *Verbal rules.* Some training studies teach a verbal rule expressing the underlying principle that amount remains the same even though the appearance of an object has changed (e.g., Beilin, 1965; Smith, 1968).

4. *Cognitive operations.* Reversibility and compensation are the two operations most frequently taught in training studies, such as demonstrating that a transformed array can be returned to its original form (e.g., Wallach and Sprott, 1964).

5. *Cognitive conflict.* Studies in this category try to induce conflict between the child's prior beliefs and the reality of conservation. For example, children are asked to predict the height of liquid prior to pouring and then are shown the actual height (Inhelder, Bovet, Sinclair, & Smock, 1966). Other ways to induce conflict are to allow children to argue with each other in a conformity-inducing procedure (e.g., Botvin & Murray, 1975; Miller & Brownell, 1975; Murray, 1972) and to provide models of conserving responses (e.g., Rosenthal & Zimmerman, 1972).

The Success of Training Studies. Numerous conservation tasks (involving number, length, mass, weight, and density) have been successfully trained if, by successful, one means that trained groups pass more conservation items on a posttest than do untrained control groups. (*See* Brainerd & Allen, 1971*a* and Brainerd, 1977 for reviews.) Although not enough comparative research has been conducted to say which training procedure is the most effective, four types have been widely replicated. These four, which Brainerd (1977) called "tutorial," are (1) simple correction by providing feedback and reinforcement; (2) rule learning, especially the inversion rule; (3) observational learning or modeling; and (4) conformity training. In contrast, the self-discovery training done by Piaget's collaborators (e.g., Inhelder, Sinclair, & Bovet,

1974) does not provide as impressive gains in nonconserving children. In self-discovery training, children manipulate the stimuli and are encouraged to make comparisons before and after their manipulations, but no feedback or verbal rules are provided. Brainerd (1977) concludes that data stemming from self-discovery studies are so meager that definitive contrasts between tutorial and self-discovery methods would be premature.

Generalization. Have training studies taught children to make one specific response to one question, or is the knowledge gained broader than that? Within a Piagetian framework, if "real" conservation has been acquired, children should perform conservation tasks correctly using new materials, not just the materials on which they were trained. This type of generalization, called *specific transfer,* has been found in nearly all studies that originally trained conservation successfully (Brainerd & Allen, 1971a). It appears to many researchers that some kind of cognitive reorganization or restructuring has taken place with training because a general principle rather than just a specific response has been taught.

Other researchers counter that cognitive restructuring cannot be inferred unless a second type of generalization, *nonspecific transfer,* is also demonstrated. Nonspecific transfer involves solving a different type of conservation problem that was not trained—for example, passing conservation of length after training on conservation of number. A few instances of nonspecific transfer have been reported. For example, Brainerd and Allen (1971b) found transfer from conservation of density to conservation of volume using clay balls as the stimuli in both cases. However, they did not find transfer to conservation of volume using liquids. (See Box B for a summary of this study.) Gelman (1969) found transfer to conservation of mass and liquid quantity after training conservation of length and number. Nevertheless, Brainerd and Allen's (1971a) review of the literature indicated very little evidence of nonspecific transfer after training. Demanding nonspecific transfer is a very stringent requirement, though, because naturally acquired conservation does not develop concurrently in all contents. That is, *décalage* is more the rule than the exception. Can we expect induced conservation to show nonspecific transfer when naturally acquired conservation does not develop concurrently in all contents? As Kuhn (1974) has said, "How much generalization to nontrained items is necessary to infer genuine structural change? There has been no satisfactory answer to this question" (p. 593).

Box B. Training Density Conservation

The following is a simplified description of a training study conducted by Brainerd and Allen (1971b). We have omitted one of the factors in the design (concerning the order of presenting the training stimuli) and some of the elegant features of randomizing the test questions, with due apologies to the authors.

Hypothesis

The study was conducted to see whether density conservation could be trained and, if so, whether training effects would generalize to volume conservation.

Design

The design was simply to pretest the children on density, solid volume, and liquid volume conservation. Only those who did not conserve any of the concepts were retained in the experiment. Then all children were exposed to a number of density conservation trials. The experimental group received feedback as to whether they were correct or incorrect. The control group answered the same questions and saw the same materials but were not given feedback. Then all the children received a posttest identical to the pretest.

Subjects

The final sample of children, 20 boys and 20 girls, ranged in age from 10 years 2 months to 11 years 7 months. All of them were nonconservers on the pretests.

Pretests

Density. The experimenter showed each child a 50-gram blue clay ball and asked the child to predict whether it would sink or float if the clay were placed in a beaker of water. After the child made a prediction, the experimenter put the ball into the water and pointed out that it sank. Then the experimenter retrieved the clay, dried it, and flattened it into a "raft." The child was asked whether the raft would sink or float (a prediction) and why (an explanation). The clay was not put back into the water. Next the experimenter took about three-quarters of the clay off the raft and asked the child to predict whether this small piece would sink or float and why. Finally even more clay was removed and the sink or float question was repeated.

Solid volume. The experimenter showed each child a 50-gram red clay ball and a beaker about two-thirds full of water. The clay was placed into the beaker causing the water level to rise. The new level was marked by rolling a rubberband around the beaker to the height of the water. Then the ball was removed and rolled into a "sausage." The child was asked what would happen if the sausage was put into the beaker: Would the water rise above, stay below, or come exactly up to the rubberband?

Liquid volume. The experimenter showed each child two identical glasses, 6-cm tall, each half filled with water. After the child agreed that the water occupied the same amount of space in each glass, the water in one glass was poured into a taller, 9-cm glass. The child was asked whether the water in the 9-cm glass takes up the same amount of space or room as the 6-cm glass, or whether one took up more room. The water from the 9-cm glass was then repoured into the 6-cm glass and the child verified that the water in the two 6-cm glasses occupied the same amount of space. Then the water in one 6-cm glass was poured into a 3-cm glass. The same questioning was repeated.

Training

Training consisted of four repetitions of the density pretest, using two green and two brown clay balls. The experimental group watched the experimenter place the clay piece into the beaker after each of their predictions. The control group did not receive this feedback.

Posttests

The posttests for density, solid volume, and liquid volume were identical to the pretests.

Results

Both the predictions and explanations were scored for each child by giving the child one point for each correct prediction and a variable number of points for the explanations based on their articulateness (zero to seven points for density; zero to three points for solid volume; zero to four points for liquid volume). The average posttest scores for the trained group were 7.95 for density, 3.30 for solid volume, and 3.10 for liquid volume. In contrast, the control group scored 2.70 for density, 1.85 for solid volume, and 2.00 for liquid volume. The trained group was significantly better on the density and solid volume tests but not on the liquid volume test.

Conclusions

Simple feedback was an effective training technique for density conservation and the effect generalized to solid volume conservation but not to liquid volume conservation. Thus some nonspecific transfer was found, but only for a task which used the same stimulus materials (clay balls).

Summary. As an indication of the role of some experience in promoting development, training studies can suggest possible alternatives but they cannot prove conclusively how children naturally acquire conservation (Flavell, 1977). We can never know if experimentally induced development uses the same path as naturally acquired development. Given the success of numerous training techniques, many experiences seem to influence the development of conservation. These include learning to ignore misleading perceptual cues, acquiring a generalized rule to express the conservation principle, seeing demonstrations of conservation, being provided feedback, and arguing with conserving peers. Despite the success of these training methods, nonspecific transfer is rarely found. Some researchers (for example, Kuhn, 1974) argue, however, that induced development should not be required to produce more generalization than occurs with naturally acquired development.

CONCLUDING REMARKS

After presenting Piaget's theory of cognitive development in its idealized form, we presented logical arguments and empirical research which both attacked and supported various parts of the theory. It is appropriate at this point to summarize those arguments and see what tentative conclusions can be drawn.

The first issue dealt with the meaning of stages in Piaget's theory. While Piaget clearly intended his theory to be explanatory by proposing the functional invariants (assimilation, accommodation, and organization), the ensuing research tradition has focused on the contents and structures of cognitive development to the virtual exclusion of the functional invariants. Many researchers accept Piaget's application of assimilation and accommodation in the Sensorimotor Period, where they are largely observable, but researchers are less convinced by the applications of the functional invariants in later periods. Clearly, more research is needed which elucidates the explanatory mechanisms (such as assimilation, accommodation, and equilibration) and their relationships with the structures and contents of thought.

The experimental approach of merely administering Piaget's standard tasks to various age groups or populations will not clarify the underlying explanatory constructs because of the circularity involved in defining the constructs. That is, one cannot say that the functional invariants exist as evidenced by successful performance on some task and then attribute the task performance to the functional invariants. In addition, alternative explanatory mechanisms need to be proposed and compared to Piaget's idea. (*See*, for example, the proposal by Trabasso & Riley, 1975, for the development of transitivity.)

The first issue also encompassed a discussion of the problem of diagnosis. Piaget's tasks are frequently criticized for their potential for misdiagnosis (Brainerd, 1978a). Furthermore, the possibility that certain behavioral sequences could arise as an artifact of the measuring instruments reduces our ability to establish empirical criteria for proving the existence of stages. Specifically, Piaget's criteria of invariant sequence, consolidation, and equilibration and the abruptness criterion discussed by Flavell (1977) are all subject to diagnosis problems. Rather than criticize Piaget's theory in isolation, we need more research to enable us to contrast his four-stage division of development with alternative segmentation schemes, such as McLaughlin's (1963) levels.

The second issue addressed the accuracy of Piaget's description of cognitive development. Several investigators have said that Piaget's description of formal operational thinking is seriously flawed (see Brainerd, 1978a). The Formal Operational Period is not widely found across populations and formal operational skills appear more susceptible to "loss" if the proper environmental supports are missing (such as happens with the elderly). These findings have led to skepticism about the Formal Operational Period, with some researchers arguing that the period is a product of Western, scientific training (Greenfield, 1976; Riegel, 1973). A lot of basic investigation remains to be done, especially in the areas of creative thinking (or, as Riegel, 1973, has suggested, dialetic thinking) and intuitive thinking (the process that we have trouble verbalizing).

Yet the bulk of the replication research suggests that Piaget's first three periods are quite universal, extending across a variety of cultures and applying to special populations such as the handicapped and the elderly. Even animal research demonstrates some elements of the Sensorimotor Period, particularly object permanence. Cross-cultural research has, however, reminded us of the distinction between finding that children can perform some task in a particular way and knowing that the performance is their typical or preferred way (Dasen, 1977). The more recent position advocated by cross-cultural researchers and those who study the elderly is to use Piaget's methodology of careful, longitudinal observations to explore various populations without mindlessly transposing Piaget's tasks into other cultures. Returning to longitudinal observations could enable us to find different patterns of cognitive development, if such existed, or alternative descriptions which might be more accurate or more parsimonious than Piaget's descriptions.

Training studies stood at the heart of the third issue which was concerned with the role of experience on development. Training studies were quite popular but have clearly waned in popularity recently. Brainerd and Allen (1971a) attribute the decline in popularity to the fact that training studies were successful. Teaching operations, especially reversibility, led to significantly better conservation performance. Kuhn (1974), on the other hand, thinks that training studies have declined because they proved to be too inconclusive; neither the necessity nor the sufficiency of any experience can be determined by using a training paradigm (Flavell, 1977). In either case, it is clear that experience can dramatically affect the rate of development and that we still need to explore the quantity, quality, and timing of various experiences in both normal and abnormal development.

REFERENCES

ARLIN, P. K. Cognitive development in adulthood: A fifth stage? *Developmental Psychology* 1975, *11*, 602–606.

ARMAH, K., & ARNOLD, M. Acquisition of conservation in Ghanaian children. Paper presented at the meeting of the Society for Research in Child Development, New Orleans, La., 1977.

AULT, R. L. *Children's cognitive development: Piaget's theory and the process approach.* New York: Oxford University Press, 1977.

BEILIN, H. Learning and operational convergence in logical thought development. *Journal of Experimental Child Psychology*, 1965, *2*, 317–339.

BOTVIN, G. J., & MURRAY, F. B. The efficacy of peer modeling and social conflict in the acquisition of conservation. *Child Development*, 1975, *46*, 796–799.

BRAINERD, C. J. Judgments and explanations as criteria for the presence of cognitive structures. *Psychological Bulletin*, 1973, *79*, 172–179.

BRAINERD, C. J. Learning research and Piagetian theory. In L. S. Siegel & C. J. Brainerd (Eds.), *Alternatives to Piaget: Critical essays on the theory*. New York: Academic Press, 1977.

BRAINERD, C. J. *Piaget's theory of intelligence*. Englewood Cliffs, N.J.: Prentice-Hall, 1978*a*.

BRAINERD, C. J. The stage question in cognitive-developmental theory. *Behavioral and Brain Sciences*, 1978, *2*, 173–82 *(b)*.

BRAINERD, C. J., & ALLEN, T. W. Experimental inductions of the conservation of "first-order" quantitative invariants. *Psychological Bulletin*, 1971, *75*, 128–144 *(a)*.

BRAINERD, C. J. & ALLEN, T. W. Training and generalization of density conservation: Effects of feedback and consecutive similar stimuli. *Child Development*, 1971, *42*, 693–704 *(b)*.

BRAINERD, C. J. & BRAINERD, S. H. Order of acquisition of number and liquid quantity conservation. *Child Development*, 1972, *43*, 1401–1405.

BREKKE, B., WILLIAMS, J. D., & TAIT, P. The acquisition of conservation of weight by visually impaired children. *Journal of Genetic Psychology*, 1974, *125*, 89–97.

COLE, M., & SCRIBNER, S. *Culture and thought: A psychological introduction*. New York: Wiley, 1974.

COMALLI, P. E., WAPNER, S., & WERNER, H. Perception of verticality in middle and old age. *Journal of Psychology*, 1959, *47*, 259–266.

COWAN, P. A. *Piaget with feeling*. New York: Holt, Rinehart and Winston, 1978.

CZERNY, P., & THOMAS, R. K. Sameness-difference judgments in *Saimiri sciureus* based on volumetric cues. *Animal Learning and Behavior*, 1975, *3*, 375–379.

DASEN, P.R. Cross-cultural Piagetian research: A summary. *Journal of Cross-Cultural Psychology*, 1972, *3*, 23–39.

DASEN, P. R. The influence of ecology, culture, and European contact on cognitive development in Australian Aborigines. In J. W. Berry & P. R. Dasen (Eds.), *Culture and cognition*. London: Methuen, 1974.

DASEN, P. R. (ED.), *Piagetian psychology: Cross-cultural contributions*. New York: Gardner Press, 1977, *see* Introduction.

DENNEY, N. W. Classification criteria in middle and old age. *Developmental Psychology*, 1974, *10*, 901–906*(a)*.

DENNEY, N. W. Evidence for developmental changes in categorization criteria for children and adults. *Human Development*, 1974, *17*, 41–53 *(b)*.

DENNY, N. W., & LENNON, M. L. Classification: A comparison of middle and old age. *Developmental Psychology*, 1972, *7*, 210–213.

DEVRIES, R. Constancy of generic identity in the years 3 to 6. *Monographs of the Society for Research in Child Development*, 1969, *34*, (3, Serial #127).

ENNIS, R. Conditional logic and primary children. *Interchange*, 1971, *2*, 126–132.

FLAVELL, J. H. *The developmental psychology of Jean Piaget*. New York: Van Nostrand Reinhold, 1963.

FLAVELL, J. H. *Cognitive development*. Englewood Cliffs, N.J.: Prentice-Hall, 1977.

FURTH, H. G., & YOUNISS, J. Formal operations and language: A comparison of deaf and hearing adolescents. *International Journal of Psychology*, 1971, *6*, 49–64.

GELMAN, R. Conservation acquisition: A problem of learning to attend to relevant attributes. *Journal of Experimental Child Psychology*, 1969, *7*, 167–187.

GINSBURG, H., & OPPER, S. *Piaget's theory of intellectual development*. Englewood Cliffs, N.J.: Prentice-Hall, 1969.

GREENFIELD, P. M. Cross-cultural research and Piagetian theory: Paradox and progress. In K. Riegel & J. Meacham (Eds.), *The developing individual in a changing world*. The Hague: Mouton, 1976.

GRUBER, H. E., GIRGUS, J. S., & BANUAZIZI, A. The development of object permanence in the cat. *Developmental Psychology*, 1971, *4*, 9–15.

GRUEN, G. E., & VORE, D. A. Development of conservation in normal and retarded children. *Developmental Psychology*, 1972, *6*, 146–157.

HORNBLUM, J. N., & OVERTON, W. F. Area and volume conservation among the elderly: Assessment and training. *Developmental Psychology*, 1976, *12*, 68–74.

INHELDER, B., BOVET, M., SINCLAIR, H., & SMOCK, C. On cognitive development. *American Psychologist*, 1966, *21*, 160–164.

INHELDER, B., SINCLAIR, H., & BOVET, M. *Learning and the development of cognition*. Cambridge, Mass.: Harvard University Press, 1974.

KEATING, D. P. Adolescent thinking. In J. P. Adelson (Ed.), *Handbook of adolescence*. New York: Wiley, forthcoming Sept. 1979.

KESSEN, W. "State" and "structure" in the study of children. In R. Brown (Ed.), *Cognitive development of children. Five monographs of the Society for Research in Child Development*. Chicago: University of Chicago Press, 1970.

KODROFF, J., & ROBERGE, J. Developmental analysis of the conditional reasoning abilities of primary-grade children. *Developmental Psychology*, 1975, *11*, 21–28.

KUHN, D. Inducing development experimentally: Comments on a research paradigm. *Developmental Psychology*, 1975, *10*, 590–600.

LOOFT, W. R. & CHARLES, D. C. Egocentrism and social interaction in young and old adults. *Aging and Human Development*, 1971, *2*, 21–28.

MATHIEU, M., BOUCHARD, M., GRANGER, L., & HERSCOVITCH, J. Piagetian object-permanence in *Cebus capucinus, Lagothrica flavicauda*, and *Pan troglodytes*. *Animal Behaviour*, 1976, *24*, 585–588.

McLAUGHLIN, G. Psychologic: A possible alternative to Piaget's formulation. *British Journal of Educational Psychology*, 1963, *33*, 61–67.

MILLAR, S. Spatial representations by blind and sighted children. *Journal of Experimental Child Psychology*, 1976, *21*, 460–479.

MILLER, S. A., & BROWNELL, C. A. Peers, persuasion, and Piaget: Dyadic interaction between conservers and nonconservers. *Child Development*, 1975, *46*, 992–997.

MURRAY, F. B. Acquisition of conservation through social interaction. *Developmental Psychology*, 1972, *6*, 1–6.

PAPALIA, D. E. The status of several conservation abilities across the life-span. *Human Development*, 1972, *15*, 229–243.

PARIS, S. Comprehension of language connectives and propositional logical relationships. *Journal of Experimental Child Psychology*, 1973, *16*, 278–291.

PASCUAL-LEONE, J. A mathematical model for the transition rule in Piaget's developmental stages. *Acta Psychologica*, 1970, *63*, 301–345.

PIAGET, J. *The language and thought of the child*, translated by Marjorie Worden. New York: Harcourt, Brace, 1926. (Originally published in 1923.)

PIAGET, J. *The child's conception of physical causality*, translated by Marjorie Worden. New York: Harcourt, Brace, 1930. (Originally published in 1927.)

PIAGET, J. *The moral judgment of the child*, translated by Marjorie Worden. New York: Harcourt, Brace, 1932.

PIAGET, J. *Play, dreams, and imitation in childhood*, translated by C. Gattegno & F. M. Hodgson. New York: Norton, 1951. (Originally published in 1945.)

PIAGET, J. The general problems of the psychobiological development of the child. In J. M. Tanner & B. Inhelder (Eds.), *Discussions on child development*. (Vol. 4). London: Tavistock, 1960.

PIAGET, J. Piaget's theory. In P. H. Mussen (Ed.), *Carmichael's manual of child psychology*. (Vol. 1). New York: Wiley, 1970.

PIAGET, J. Intellectual evolution from adolescence to adulthood. *Human Development*, 1972, *15*, 1–12.

PIAGET, J., & INHELDER, B. *The child's conception of space*, translated by F. J. Langdon & J. L. Lunzer. London: Routledge & Kegan Paul, 1956. (Originally published in 1948.)

PIAGET, J., INHELDER, B., & SZEMINSKA, A. *The child's conception of geometry*, translated by E. A. Lunzer. New York: Basic Books, 1960. (Originally published in 1948.)

PIAGET, J., & SZEMINSKA, A. *The child's conception of number*, translated by C. Gattegno & F. M. Hodgson. New York: Humanities Press, 1952. (Originally published in 1941.)

PINARD, A., & LAURENDEAU, M. "Stage" in Piaget's cognitive-developmental theory: Exegesis of a concept. In D. Elkind & J. H. Flavell (Eds.), *Studies in cognitive development*. New York: Oxford University Press, 1969.

RIEGEL, K. Dialetic operations: The final period of cognitive development. *Human Development*, 1973, *16*, 346–370.

ROSENTHAL, T. L., & ZIMMERMAN, B. J. Modeling by exemplification and instruction in training conservation. *Developmental Psychology*, 1972, *6*, 392–401.

Ross, B. M., & Hoemann, H. The attainment of formal operations: A comparison of probability concepts in deaf and hearing adolescents. *Genetic Psychology Monographs*, 1975, *91*, 61–119.

Rubin, K. H. The relationship between spatial and communicative egocentrism in children and young and old adults. *Journal of Genetic Psychology*, 1974, *125*, 295–301.

Schultz, N. R., & Hoyer, W. J. Feedback effects on spatial egocentrism in old age. *Journal of Gerontology*, 1976, *31*, 72–75.

Smedslund, J. The acquisition of conservation of substance and weight in children: II. External reinforcement of conservation of weight and of the operations of addition and subtraction. *Scandanavian Journal of Psychology*, 1961, *2*, 71–84.

Smith, I. The effects of training procedures on the acquisition of conservation of weight. *Child Development*, 1968, *39*, 515–526.

Thomas, R. K., & Peay, L. Length judgments by squirrel monkeys: Evidence for conservation? *Developmental Psychology*, 1976, *12*, 349–352.

Trabasso, T., & Riley, C. A. On the construction and use of representations involving linear order. In R. L. Solso (Ed.), *Information processing and cognition: The Loyola Symposium*. New York: Halstead Press, 1975.

Uzgiris, I. C. Situational generality of conservation. *Child Development*, 1964, *35*, 831–841.

Vaughter, R. M., Smotherman, W., & Ordy, J. M. Development of object permanence in the infant squirrel monkey. *Developmental Psychology*, 1972, *7*, 34–38.

Wallach, L., & Sprott, R. Inducing number conservation in children. *Child Development*, 1964, *35*, 1057–1071.

Wapner, S., Werner, H., & Comalli, R.E. Perception of part-whole relationships in middle and old age. *Journal of Gerontology*, 1960, *15*, 412–416.

Wise, K. L., Wise, L. A., & Zimmermann, R. R. Piagetian object permanence in the infant rhesus monkey. *Developmental Psychology*, 1974, *10*, 429–437.

Wohlwill, J. F. *The study of behavioral development*. New York: Academic Press, 1973.

Wohlwill, J., & Lowe, R. An experimental analysis of the development of the conservation of number. *Child Development*, 1962, *33*, 153–167.

Youniss, J. Operational development in deaf Costa Rican subjects. *Child Development*, 1974, *45*, 212–216.

TWO

Language Development

David H. Dodd

Lori (three and a half years):   There is no such thing as a dinosaur that
   lives any more.

Father: No, that's right.

Lori: There used to live some dinosaurs when we were gone.

On a daily basis, young children display what they do and do not know
about the world, about ideas, and about language. This girl certainly has
some ideas about those remarkable creatures we call dinosaurs, creatures
no human has ever seen. Her sense of the temporal relation between us
and them seems right, but her use of temporal conjunctions and verb
tense is not quite right. Yet she exhibits a vast amount of language
knowledge in these two sentences.

   This chapter will consider the course of language development from
birth through the preschool years and into the elementary-school years.
We can overview the issues to be addressed here by posing a series of
questions: What is language, that is, what are children acquiring? What
do children learn earliest and what course does language development
take? What kind of language information is available to "teach" language
to young children, and how do they operate on that information? And
what besides language is pertinent to their knowledge of language, that
is, what forms of general knowledge (for example, object permanence) are
important, what kinds of specific facts are necessary (such as knowing
what a dog is)? Obviously these questions are intertwined in complex
ways, but they do help us to structure our discussion. We begin with the
issue which must come first: What is language?

THE NATURE OF LANGUAGE
   Everyone knows that language is the primary basis of communication
among humans, the medium for the transmission of "meaning." This

everyday knowledge is correct enough, though such a perspective captures only a portion of the "what" of language. In this section we will emphasize the distinction between listening and speaking, describe the organization of language at two levels, and describe the four major components of language: sound, grammar, meaning, and function.

The common-sense perspective is certainly congruent with the first point we want to make here. There are two quite different processes in communication: listening and speaking. The listening, or comprehending, part involves making sense out of what is heard, as well as remembering something about it. The speaking, or production, part involves formulating ideas, finding appropriate words and sentences, and articulating the proper sounds. The processes of comprehension and production, although related, are not simply converse. Children may exhibit quite discrepant skills at comprehending and producing language. Throughout we will discuss children's knowledge of each.

Consideration of either of these processes leads to a point central to the study of language: there must be at least two levels of organization of language. The string of speech produced or heard has a particular organization (called surface structure), and the underlying meaning has a related, but different structure. Certainly we can all agree that the string of sounds we speak or hear is organized, that it consists of words which are ordered sequentially and in other ways. The underlying structure is not so easily specified, but it consists of the relations between meaningful elements. In comprehending, we can be said to convert the surface string into an underlying representation that has a different structure. The converse is true of production, namely that underlying representation is converted into a surface structure. The argument that these two levels are organized differently is justified by a number of facts about language, including the existence of ambiguity, synonymity, and discrepancies in elements found at each level. Thus ambiguity is a widespread potential problem if only the elements in the surface string are considered. This is true of both adult's and children's language. Consider the sentence, "Daddy car." It could mean such divergent things as "Daddy's car," "Daddy is in the car," or "Daddy is driving the car." Such different meanings will be indicated in the speech of an older child. But that does not alter the point since ambiguities can be found even in adult language. Similarly, the existence of widespread synonymity also supports this claim. Thus, for a child named Michael, the utterances, "Michael toy," "My toy," and "Mine" will be synonymous in a particular situation. If these two levels of organization were identical or even isomorphic, neither ambiguity nor synonymity should exist. As we shall see in a later discussion of some of the specifics of language development, elements present at either level may be absent at the other level.

The distinction between surface and underlying structure has immense implications for the understanding of children's language. If the surface structure does not map one-to-one against underlying structure in the language heard by children, then children cannot operate as though there were such a simple direct mapping. Indeed, it can be shown that in children's earliest speech the underlying structure—the ideas they are trying to produce—is more complex than the simple language they can use to encode these ideas.

The four major components of language are: sound, grammar, meaning, and function. The sound (or phonological) system is the set of articulations produced and comprehended in a particular language. Every speaker/hearer of a language knows implicitly what sounds (and sequence of sounds) are allowable. For example, in English, the string of sounds made by pronouncing "strab" could be a word, but the pronunciation of "ftab" could not be, even though "ftab" is not inherently unpronounceable. The most important construct in the study of sound systems is the *phoneme*, a term used to designate any set of sounds that is treated as equivalent by users of a particular language. All speakers of English treat the "p" in "pin" and the "p" in "spin" as the same, although they are different. In some languages, these "p's" belong in different phonemic classes. In English "p" and "b" are treated as different sounds (thus "pin" and "bin" are different words in English); but in some languages, "p" and "b" are treated as the same. Children learning the sound system of a language must learn to distinguish *just* those aspects that are relevant to the language they are acquiring and to ignore other discriminable aspects. And, of course, children must also learn how to make all of these sounds within the range of acceptable pronunciation.

The grammar of a language includes those rules that limit how words can be ordered and rules for inflection (for example, the "-s" to mark plurality on nouns). In every language, there are consistent ways of marking the subject of the sentence, the object of the sentence, subordinate clauses, and temporal and durational qualities of the verb. For example, in English, the subject of a clause is generally the noun phrase preceding the verb. In Finnish the subject may precede or follow the verb, but is marked by an inflectional ending on the noun (Bowerman, 1973). The study of grammatical development is concerned with children's acquisition of knowledge allowing them to use order, inflections, and the like to comprehend the utterances of others *and* with the development of their ability to use such devices in their own speech.

The study of meaning in child language has largely focused on two different kinds of language elements—words and sentences. Considerable recent work has centered around the child's earliest understanding of the meaning of words and the gradual refinement of meaning. Children often make revealing errors in their use of words, such as calling all four-legged animals "doggie." The study of sentence meaning has focused on such topics as the variety of meanings encoded in early sentences (for example, causality or location) and the embedding and coordination of clauses.

Finally, the fourth major component is the function of speech, sometimes called "pragmatics." While pragmatics is intimately linked to meaning, it is important to emphasize that language is not simply used for meaning—by adults or by children. While the words and sentences of human speech do *mean* something, a speaker's purpose on a particular occasion may be only indirectly related to what the particular sentence means. For example, "Ooo, it's cold in here" may be used as a request to be snuggled, to close the door, to turn up the heat, or (least likely perhaps) as a statement of fact. It is important to understand how children learn to use language to influence others and to interpret the functional component of others' speech.

Our discussion of the nature of language has emphasized the distinction between comprehension and production and the two levels of language structure: surface and underlying. We have described the four major components of language: (1) sound (phonology), the sounds and combinations of sounds utilized in a particular language; (2) grammar, rules of word order and inflection; (3) meaning, how words and sentences encode particular conceptualizations and relationships; and (4) function (pragmatics), the use of language in context to request, inform, and so on. Next we will consider the methods used in research on language development and the general theoretical orientations followed.

THEORIES AND METHODS OF STUDY

Research on language development has been significantly influenced by theories from psychology and linguistics; yet most of the findings give descriptions of behavior rather than specific confirmation or disconfirmation of theory. Most theoretical development has been at a general level and the methods of study are primarily naturalistic, so that many of the results can be discussed with little appeal to theory. Nonetheless it is useful to consider the major perspectives of the field and to introduce the general orientation to be taken throughout the chapter. First we will briefly discuss the methods used for studying language development.

As we noted, the methods used in this field are primarily naturalistic; a great deal of the earliest research consisted of longitudinal reports on single children, reports that are essentially diaries (see Leopold, 1939-1949; Gregoire, 1937, 1949). These diaries have provided interesting facts for speculation and early theory (Jakobson, 1968) and continue to stimulate some systematic research (E. Clark, 1973). However, the 1960s saw the emergence of more rigorous naturalistic observation in the form of short-term longitudinal studies (from a few months to a few years) of several children with tape-recorded speech samples (cf. Brown, 1973). The tape recordings, together with the observer's notes, formed the basis of various analyses of the development of particular components of the language system. Thus Roger Brown's recordings were used by him and by his students to study temporal reference (Cromer, 1968), sentence negation (Bellugi, 1967), grammatical words and inflections (Brown, 1973), and other specific aspects of development. The inclusion of several children and the systematic samplings of speech over time increased representativeness. Further, the use of audio recording increased reliability and allowed repeated use for different purposes. Nonetheless, most of these studies involved American middle-class children. This approach has since been extended to a range of other languages (Bowerman, 1973; Slobin, 1973). More recently such naturalistic research projects have increasingly utilized videotaping as a means of providing a permanent record of some of the other information important to understanding the child's language. Most of the findings to be reported in this chapter are based on the systematic naturalistic data gathered over the last twenty years.

However, experimental methods have also been applied with increasing success. Experiments have been performed on such aspects as: (1) eliciting plural and past tense inflection to nonsense words (Cazden, 1968), (2) assessing the semantic and/or grammatical bases for interpreting passive sentences (Slobin 1966), and (3) training under various procedures, including reinforcement and elicited imitation (see the review by Dodd & Glanzer, 1974). Such experiments are more important to our understanding of the processes involved in language development. Examples of some relevant experiments will be presented at various points in the chapter. It is probable that future research on language development will be increasingly experimental, reflecting progress in our knowledge of what is acquired and increased interest in the processes by which language is acquired. We now turn to a general discussion of the kinds of theories in the field.

The major theoretical approaches can be partitioned quite roughly into three camps: (1) biological-nativist, (2) empiricist-behaviorist, and (3) cognitive-interactionist. We will summarize each, indicating the kind of evidence central to that approach. The biological or nativist view has emphasized the fact that language is uniquely human and that its development thus depends primarily upon a brain preprogrammed to acquire language. The empiricist or behaviorist view has based all acquisition on experience, minimizing the role of innate contributions. Behaviorism, the modern-day empiricism of psychology, has emphasized the role of association, reinforcement, and/or imitation as forming the basis for acquiring knowledge through experience. The cognitive-interactionist position is, in part, an intermediate position between these two extremes, emphasizing both the nature of the organism and the experiences provided in the environment. Thus biology and environment interact to determine language acquisition. In the particular cognitive point of view taken here, the child's understanding and acquisition of language is held to be determined by a set of strategies, strategies which determine the kind of information extracted from the environment.

Biological-Nativist Views

A nativistic perspective on language development has ancient roots in philosophy, but the current views largely follow Chomsky's (1965) arguments. Young children, who are not intellectually sophisticated, are provided with imperfectly formed speech data by parents and others who are not intent on teaching. Nonetheless, these children learn language rapidly and easily at a time when they are not capable of any comparable mastery of other forms of knowledge. Therefore children must know a great deal to begin with; that is, there must be innate knowledge of what form language could take. Chomsky further suggested that an investigation of features that are universal to languages of the world would likely reveal the kinds of knowledge that are biologically given to the child. While a great deal is now known about such universals (Langacker, 1973), what role they might have in language acquisition has not been well developed except in the form of the kinds of strategies (Slobin, 1973) to be considered under cognitive theory.

A more research-based argument for the biological-nativist view is found in Lenneberg (1967) who has summarized extensive pertinent evidence about the brain and its development. The arguments raised by Lenneberg have been summarized by him (Lenneberg, 1969) in the form of three major points. (1) Every human culture and no nonhuman group possesses a fully developed language; these languages have many features in common, including important constraints on sound systems and grammars. (2) All children start learning language at about the same age and follow a similar course of progress. Language development is highly correlated with age and even more highly correlated with motor development. The course of language development is not particularly influenced by variations in the environment except in extremes of deprivation. Thus maturation of neural structures is probably the controlling factor in language development. (3) Injury to specific portions of the brain can produce specific losses of language, often without other impairment. The age at which the injury occurs is critical; the younger the person so injured the easier language functions can be assumed by other portions of the brain. Thus particular areas of the brain are linked to language and its development.

Unfortunately a specification of how such structures are involved in language acquisition cannot be made; too little is known about the functioning of higher brain centers. While these facts and arguments persuade us that humans are biologically "prepared" to learn language and that language development is linked to maturation, there is no way at present to translate that into specific processes by which children process language information to learn language.

Empiricist-Behaviorist Views

These views center the process of language development in the child's experience. Behaviorism has emphasized associative processes, control of behavior by reinforcement, and/or imitational determination (Staats, 1968). In general, behaviorists have argued that children imitate speech provided by those around them, reproducing sounds, words, and utterances. Further, consequences of particular utterances will modify and strengthen the use of that speech. The traditional version of this claim (Staats, 1968) has classified consequences as positive (reinforcements) and negative (punishments), such that the former strengthen the responses they follow and the latter weaken the responses they follow.

Modern researchers have attempted to validate or invalidate such factors in language development. To summarize such a controversial area in a few brief paragraphs is risky, but we will state some overall conclusions. First, children's imitations are not direct copies of the speech heard by them. There are deletions, substitutions, and alterations of the sounds making words and of the words comprising sentences. These changes from the original are sufficiently regular and systematic within and across children so as to suggest other factors beyond experience. Children's spontaneous imitations exhibit length and complexity limits comparable to limits on their spontaneous productions, that is, children rarely produce imitated sentences longer or more complex than their spontaneous utterances (Bloom, Hood, & Lightbown, 1974; Ervin, 1964).

Secondly, we will consider the nature and possible effects of consequences. There is no simple way to define reinforcement or punishment in language development. With a deliberate experimental intervention, an operational definition of reinforcement is possible. While experiments of this kind have been reported (cf. some articles in Schiefelbusch & Lloyd, 1974), the specialized populations of children, unusual environments, and/or artificial procedures prevent any claim of ecological validity. With normal environments, one way of defining consequences is to call favorable reaction (for example, "Yes," "Good," "That's right") reinforcements and negative reactions (such as, "No," "Don't say that") punishments. Even so, the effects of such reactions are not known, although there is evidence that mothers who correct their children a lot are contributing to slower language development (Nelson, 1973). In any case, such consequences have been linked to truthfulness rather than well-formedness (Brown & Hanlon, 1970). In their study, Brown and Hanlon found that sentences such as "Draw a paper boot" and "Her curl my hair" were approved, whereas sentences such as "And Walt Disney comes on on Tuesday" and "There's the animal farmhouse" were disapproved. Thus ill-formed utterances may be approved because they are truthful and well-formed utterances disapproved because they are not. This result led Brown and Hanlon to wonder how it was that children grow up to be adults who produce a preponderance of well-formed utterances that are, often enough, not truthful when the opposite result should follow from an account based strictly on reinforcement.

A third and final conclusion has to do with more complex consequences that have been called "expansions." These consequences are called that because adults often imitate the child's utterances and expand it into a fully developed sentence. Thus a child who said "Mommy hat" might hear Mother immediately respond, "Yes, that's Mommy's hat." Expansions thus provide the child with a complete and well-formed utterance expressing the idea the child purportedly intended. Despite some controversy in the literature (Dodd & Glanzer, 1974), there is reason to conclude that expansions aid language development (Nelson, Carskaddon, & Bonvillian, 1973). Yet as an experiential variable, expansion is different, and more complex, than behaviorist views have proposed.

These conclusions do not discount experiential effects in language development; rather, they are consistent with the view that children are receptive to language information in particular ways. The effect of experience depends directly on how that experience is processed. That is a major theme of the cognitive-interactionist view.

Cognitive-Interactionist Views

This point of view is not called that by researchers in the field, but some such term is appropriate to many recent claims (Clark & Clark, 1977; Ervin-Tripp, 1973; Slobin, 1973). In its most general form, this view is that language development depends upon the interaction between an organism built with certain ways of organizing experience and the nature of that experience. (Such a view corresponds to Piaget's principle of adaptation.) A child's current knowledge, including knowledge of language, is not simply a result of biological structure since past experience has contributed directly to that knowledge. Yet experience alone is not adequate because the brain organizes and constrains the processing of experience.

At present, no theory adequately specifies the operation of such processes in language development. Piaget's general theory and stages have been suggested as one kind of model (Sinclair-deZwart, 1973). Information-processing theory has also been proposed as an account of cognitive development (Flavell, 1977) and could be applied directly to language development. Yet neither of these views has been linked to the facts of language development in a specific and satisfying manner. The best specification of a cognitive-interactionist view is found in the set of strategies (or operating principles) proposed by Slobin (1973) and in related accounts by Ervin-Tripp (1973) and Bever (1970). In this chapter we will use the term "strategy," a usage somewhat different from its everyday sense. "Strategy" here means a limit, bias, or organizing tendency followed by children in processing experience with language. "Strategy" is *not* meant to be a deliberate or conscious plan to process information in a certain way, only a consistency in how children deal with such information. For example, as we shall see later, the order of language elements is particularly salient to children; although they have no deliberate plan to do so, children learn the order of elements quite readily. The fact that children are especially attuned to order will be termed a strategy.

Ultimately, these strategies need to be incorporated into a more integrated account of language development, presumably as part of a broader account of cognitive development. But it is not clear at present how to elaborate such an account. Hopefully, this account would clarify where such strategies come from by answering questions such as, "Are the strategies innate or do strategies develop," and "Do some strategies operate earlier only to be replaced by others as the child matures?" At present, these questions remain unanswered in the absence of well-developed integrated theory. However, because these issues need serious attention, we will return to them at the conclusion of the chapter when the reader will have an understanding of some of the facts of development and of a number of particular strategies.

In any case, the utilization of this notion of strategy provides a more explicit analysis of language development within the cognitive-interactionist framework. Thus language events (and other events, for that matter) perceived by children are processed in certain ways such that particular information is lost, other information is retained, and all that is perceived is altered. While experience is thus the raw material of language acquisition, the manipulation of that experience determines what is acquired. In this discussion, a list of specific strategies will provide a more explicit account of how information is manipulated or processed; these strategies will be introduced as we discuss some specific facts of language development. We will now turn to a consideration of such facts. We have divided the overall progression into three major periods of time. Early development will focus on the first two years, middle development on the span from two to five years, and later development on the years from five to adolescence.

EARLY DEVELOPMENT

Perhaps the most exciting time to parents and other interested observers is the time of the beginnings of language. Newborns start with nothing in the way of language but by age two or so most children can make a considerable range of sounds, can say a number of words that mean something, can even put together two or three words, and can understand a great deal. This section will look at development during the first two years, with consideration of what the child acquires and how acquisition takes place. Within this period, we will partition development into three phases: prelanguage, first words, and earliest relations.

Prelanguage

A child of ten months looks at a colorful dish of candy on a shelf a few feet away, then looks at Dad, then at the object again. Without moving toward it, she points at it, turns to Dad, and says "Uh." Dad, busy doing something else, ignores her, so the child says it louder. Then, instead of going toward the candy, she crawls toward him, pulls on him while pointing toward the dish, says "Uh" again, and looks into his face imploringly.

By prelanguage we mean that state during which the child does not yet produce anything that could be called a word. For the average child, this would be approximately the first year of life. Of course, even though children at the beginning and at the end of this stage cannot produce a word, there is a vast difference between the newborn and the child of nearly one.

Newborns are only able to communicate in the most limited way— they can cry or not cry. Nor can newborns understand anything said to them, although a soft, high-pitched voice is usually comforting. Recent research (Eimas, Siqueland, Jusczyk, & Vigorito, 1971) has shown that the very young infant's auditory capabilities include discriminating between voiced and unvoiced consonants (for example, "b" is voiced and "p" is unvoiced). This does not mean, of course, that any meaning is attached to any particular sound.

During the first six months, progress is slight. The cries differentiate and more pleasant sounds begin. The earliest speechlike sound is a simple vowel, such as "ah." Then the infant begins to make a consonant-vowel combination in the throat, sounding something like "ga." This is the beginning of what is often called cooing or gooing.

In the remaining six months, progress is more noticeable. Most striking to parents is the babbling. Over a period of several months, the variety of sounds increases until, at nine months or so, many children seem to be speaking a language—a strange, foreign tongue. An interesting feature of this babbling is that the particular sounds made are not dependent upon what sounds are heard in the parents' speech. Thus the babbling of Chinese and American infants is indistinguishable (Atkinson, MacWhinney, & Stoel, 1970). Despite the diversity of sounds produced, the babbling is under voluntary control only in the limited sense that children seem able to control whether or not they babble and to vary the emotional tone of the nonsense produced. But voluntarily producing a particular sound is not possible as evidenced by a failure to imitate an adult's sounds. Parents of an eight-month-old girl may try to elicit imitations and the child may cooperate, but she can only succeed by accident or if the sounds were just previously said by her. It is clear that these early articulations lack the deliberateness of human language. This is further reflected by the fact that the range of articulations produced in the babbling of a nine-month-old contrasts so strikingly with the restricted articulatory skills of children much older. As soon as voluntary speech begins, articulatory control is quite poor; sounds made while babbling may not be voluntarily produced for a year or two or more. Thus the babbling of the prelanguage child is better thought of as articulatory play than as being some form of language.

However, communication is clearly present before language; children "produce" actions equivalent to language before they speak words and they comprehend, in a restricted way, some of what is said to them. As we shall see, prelanguage children operate in terms of pragmatics without knowing much about language in terms of sounds, meaning, or grammar.

Consider first the child's nonverbal productions. Young children are able to make requests before they can speak words. Bates (1976) has called such requests "proto-imperatives" because they are nonverbal precursors to verbal imperatives. Consider the nature of an imperative: the speaker is requesting that the listeners act so as to bring about some goal desired by the speaker. Thus it involves the intention to achieve said goal and to do so through an intermediate action upon another person who is perceived to be capable of acting (and willing to act) so as to achieve that goal. To trace the origins of requests, Bates begins early in the first year of life. At first, actions are not intentionally performed so as to achieve a goal. By about four months, infants begin to use their own actions as a deliberate means to a goal, as, for example, in reaching for an object they see. But children of this age have no conception of using someone else as a means to the goal, such as pointing to something they want someone to get. Only during the latter portion of the first year do children begin to make such requests nonverbally. Bates illustrates a transitional phase with the following account: The child "unable to pull a cat out of the adult's hand, looks the adult intently in the face, and then tries once again to pull the cat" (Bates, 1976, p. 53). This sequence was repeated three times to no avail. But a few weeks later the same child could look at the adult, point to the object, and make vocal noises; all of these actions were designed to influence the adult to act so as to do what the child desired. Subsequently, of course, these nonverbal actions will be replaced by verbal ones which slowly evolve into accepted adult forms. Carter (1975) has described this evolution during the span from about twelve months to twenty-four months. She found that the earliest form is a sound (or word ?), like "ma," which was used as a general object request. Later the names of specific objects are learned and then are combined with the "ma" sound—for example, "Ma ba" ("My ball").

Children also produce nonverbal responses that have declarative functions, in the sense of naming or labelling. Ninio and Bruner (1978) have demonstrated that early responses of pointing, touching, smiling, and babbling are interpreted by mothers to express the intention of labeling or requesting a label. Certainly it is hard to know what children intend in many such cases. Nonetheless, it is clear that they soon learn to get other people's attention by vocalization and nonverbal activity and to direct that attention to particular objects by pointing, looking, and further vocalization. As Ninio and Bruner (1978) argue, it is significant that mothers see their children as having particular intentions, so that the children can at least learn from mother's responses something about what their actions are taken to mean. This brings us to the important point that communication, with or without language, ordinarily takes place interactionally (excepting written texts and, to some degree, lectures). Children must learn to participate in conversations, within which each participant has a turn and many of the turns can only be filled by particular kinds of activity (Snow, 1977); questions must be followed by answers. Consider the following illustrative conversation from Ninio and Bruner (1977, p. 6). In it we see that a child of age one is responding without language and is, to a degree, carrying on one side of a conversation. At the same time, the mother is interpreting these responses as exhibiting appropriate intentions.

Mother: Look!
Child: (Touches picture.)
Mother: What are those?
Child: (Vocalizes and smiles.)
Mother: Yes, they are rabbits.
Child: (Vocalizes, smiles, and looks up at mother.)
Mother: Yes, rabbit.

Although the production aspect is restricted to nonlanguage acts during this first year, comprehension is somewhat more advanced. In children's everyday activities, early nonverbal communication is often associated with some comprehension of the speech of others. Thus, a child's nonverbal request may be translated into a spoken question by Mom: "Do you want a drink?" The child's nonverbal reply may indicate an understanding of something about Mom's utterance—perhaps only the word "drink." To a great degree, comprehension is more advanced than production in the first three or four years, that is, children understand more sophisticated utterances than they can produce (Petretic & Tweney, 1977).

Perhaps this apparent lag in production reflects the fact that the interpretation of utterances is often aided by context, intonation, and nonverbal cues. The child who knows little or nothing about language must utilize these sources of information almost entirely. We will characterize such an approach to understanding the speech of others as a set of three interrelated strategies: (1a) Attend to intonation. (1b) *Attend to nonverbal cues, such as facial expressions and gestures.* (1c) *Attend to context.* Certainly they are central to comprehension at any age; yet in the beginning they are particularly important since they seem to be all the child has to go on. Consider, for example, how a boy of eleven months might correctly interpret the utterance: "Close the door!" Based on these strategies, he can easily be correct without knowing the meaning of a single word. Assume that past experience has given him the simple lesson that commands are couched in a particular intonation. Shatz (1978) has demonstrated that very young children naturally interpret a variety of utterances as commands. The cues of intonation, if attended to, thus signal him that Mom wants him to do something. But what? Well, Mom is looking in a particular direction with an expression that says: "Get busy and do what I tell you." Further, her hand and arm are motioning toward the door. Finally, of course, the door is open and thus the options for acting with respect to it are restricted. Probably "Open the door!" or "Close the window!" would elicit exactly the same response if spoken in the same way and accompanied by the same expression, gestures, and situation. In short, prelanguage children utilize these strategies to make an interpretation of some of the language they hear. Even if an interpretation made this way is incorrect, their failure to react appropriately will generally result in feedback and further information. Given a correct interpretation, they then learn something about the language heard.

First Words

"Mama." (This is a common first word; we will see, though, how it often means something different from a simple name.) At approximately twelve months of age (although the normal range is at least ten to eighteen months), children produce their first word. Identifying the first word is difficult because pronunciation is crude and the meaning may be different from the adult meaning; in fact, what seems to be a word may be only babbling. But, given an approximation to the correct sounds of some word, produced voluntarily, and paired with the appropriate referent, proud parents and language researchers will call it a first word.

We will discuss the child's earliest knowledge of the sound system, then the meaning and function of earliest words, and finally the issue of the process of language learning during this phase of development.

Earlier we mentioned how limited the child's articulatory control is at first; sometimes even very bright children do not really produce first words at this age because they are not able to make even an approximately acceptable string of sounds. The earliest development of articulation is reasonably well characterized by Jakobson's (1968) theory. According to Jakobson, children should begin with the maximum contrast between sounds, namely that between vowel and consonant. Usually, it turns out that this is a consonant followed by a vowel and often the consonant-vowel is repeated, as in "dada." Generally the vowel is a wide vowel (the "ah" of "dada" in the child's speech is not the same as the adult pronunciation of "dada") and the consonant is one that is made at the front of the mouth—"b," "p," "d," "t," or "m." Thus the first word is likely to be "dada," "mama," or "papa." The next phonological developments are in the consonant system. Jakobson predicted that children would next learn the oppositions between nasal and nonnasal and between labials and dentals.[1] In terms of actual words, the nasal feature

[1]Nasality consists of an added quality produced by modulation of air in the nasal cavity; if you say "b," then "m," you should be able to sense that both sounds are formed in nearly the same way except for the nasalization in "m." The difference between labials and dentals is that labials are formed by the lips and dentals by the tongue against the teeth. Contrast your pronunciation of the sounds "b" and "d" as in "bill" and "dill;" notice that "b" involves the lips and "d" the tongue against the teeth.

involves producing such contrasting words as "papa" (nonnasal) and "mama" (nasal), and the labial-dental feature involves producing such differing words as "papa" (labial) and "dada" (dental). The basis of this prediction by Jakobson was the fact that these oppositions are found in every human language. Similarly, Jakobson judged that the vowel phonemes found in all human languages should develop earliest in the child's productions. These predictions are approximately correct, although matters are more complex than this (Dale, 1976).

The utilization of sound differences in comprehension has not been well studied, but recent evidence suggests that the child's comprehension may reflect the child's initial failure to utilize differences that are perceptible. Thus discriminably different sounds such as "p," "b," "m," and "g" were earliest treated as equivalent by Patricia Greenfield's (1973) daughter. Greenfield trained her young daughter to look at Daddy in response to "dada." She then discovered that the child also looked at Daddy when she said, "mama," "baba," and "tata," but the child did not look at Daddy when she said "bye-bye," "bubu," or "dudu." Thus the child's response was based on the vowel, for she distinguished between "a" and at least some other vowels but did not treat the consonant sounds "d," "m," "b," and "t" as functionally different. Of course, the fact that children can discriminate between these consonant sounds means that they can learn to give them functional significance.

The meaning and function of first words is our next topic. Once a string of sounds is used consistently, parents may call it a word even when the child's understanding and intent are not what the parents assume. Greenfield's (1973) daughter learned to say "dada" in response to Daddy's appearance. But when her father tried to use "mama" to announce her mother's appearance, the child responded "dada." For a while, the word "dada" was used for all caretakers including the babysitter. A few days later, after some training on "mama," the girl used it correctly for her mother, but also for the female babysitter. Now she distinguished between "dada" and "mama" on the basis of sex and distinguished both from other people on the basis of a caretaking dimension. Still later, after learning that the babysitter (named Barbara) was "baba," she spontaneously called another woman "baba." Thus these various names are not initially just names for particular people, but for categories.

Nelson (1973) classified the first fifty words of a number of children; nearly two-thirds of these words were names. But only a few of those were the names of particular people or animals; most were general names like "ball," "car," "milk," and "doggie." Thus, a great number of early words are labels for classes of things. As we saw in the case of Greenfield's daughter, even the names of specific people may, in fact, be conceptual. Later, in a general discussion of word meaning, we will consider some issues related to the bases of these categories.

First words sometimes "mean" in a much different way than naming. Many words, such as "hi," "bye-bye" and "my," are clearly not acts of naming. But even the word "mama" may not function as naming at all. Children often use such a word as a generalized request word, saying "mama" whenever they want something. Or they may use "mama" to mean "pick me up." Greenfield and Smith (1976) reported a child who used "mama" for all requests, even of his father. At nineteen months, the boy said: "Daddy, mama, daddy," which meant something like, "Daddy, I want you to pick me up, Daddy." Actually the use of "Daddy" here is not really an act of naming, but a kind of calling Daddy or requesting his attention, sometimes called "vocative." Greenfield and Smith have analyzed the early one-word utterances of several children in terms of the functions of these productions. These functions include naming, vocative, object of demand, negative, and others. Even the earliest words are used for many purposes beyond simple naming.

The last point in our discussion of first words has to do with the related issue of what speech is heard by children and how that information is processed. Recent research has revealed that parental speech to children of twelve to eighteen months is generally simplified, direct, regular, and repetitive (Dodd & Glanzer, 1974; Snow, 1972). Much of that parental speech consists of brief sentences such as, "Look at the *doggie*," "There's a *doggie*," "See the *car*," and "here's your *book*." In such sentences, the focal noun is placed at the end of the sentence and is emphasized. The utterance is brief, simple, and forms a well-defined unit (Broen, 1972). Since the noun is presented in a salient manner the child who hears such sentences should learn about dogs, cars, and books.

Certain kinds of knowledge, some of it quite general, are prerequisite to even the simplest language use. For example, the child may first need to know that the world contains permanent and stable objects, even though those objects come and go and sometimes look a bit different. This is, of course, the concept of object permanence. (See Chapter One.) Piaget has argued that all symbolic representation depends upon the mental permanence of things beyond their immediate sensory impression.

Corrigan (1978) has reported data on the longitudinal linkage between attaining object permanence and language development. She found that, overall, there was no general correspondence between measured stages of object permanence and language development. The onset of first words only roughly corresponded to the final stage (stage 6) of object permanence, when children are first able to retrieve objects that are invisibly displaced from one hiding place to another. But, at the beginning of this stage, children only speak about currently observable objects. At the final rank of object permanence, which is considered the beginning of the preoperational period, there is a large increase in total vocabulary. It is also at this time that children first utilize words to label nonexistence (for example, all gone) and recurrence (more). Corrigan's study is an important contribution in that there is otherwise little data linking such general knowledge and language development.

Some important prerequisite knowledge is unique to language, in particular the knowledge that a language unit can come to stand for, or refer to, an object, event, or relationship. A child must learn that a particular word is related to some other particular kind of environmental stimulation. Perhaps the early slow progress in learning words reflects the child's difficulties with this conception.

Given the appropriate language input and certain prerequisite knowledge, how does the child process the language data in order to learn words? Again, we will refer to these processes as strategies. Strategy 2: *Process and connect what is immediately sensed.* This is, in fact, a general processing limit of very young children. Ervin-Tripp (1973) has argued that, for language learning to take place, the speech event must co-occur with the appropriate referential event. Particular acoustic events (at first very short segments, such as words or syllables) must be paired, often repeatedly, with other events to which the child is attending. Parents usually speak when the child is attending to what they want to name; often they encourage attending by pointing, gazing themselves toward the object, and/or verbalizing first. (Ninio & Bruner, 1978). Ervin-Tripp suggests also that children will probably not learn to name a very novel object, event, or experience. They must first learn about the thing named; they must learn what it does and what it looks like. Thus the earliest words refer to some of the things they already know well— Mom, Dad, the neighborhood dog.

When an utterance is longer than a word, the appropriate acoustic event should be at the end of the sentence since children operate on the basis of strategy 3: *Attend to the end of the utterance.* Probably this reflects the fact that the element(s) most likely to remain in short-term memory is the last word of an utterance. In addition, stressed words and syllables are quite likely to be noticed; strategy 4 is: *Attend to stress.* Thus it is appropriate that parental speech usually follows this form. The sentences on p. 62 are good examples of this. All of them put the critical noun at the end of the sentence with added emphasis and refer to a co-occurring event.

Earliest Relations and Grammar

A boy of nearly two stands by the open front door of his house, looking longingly at the interesting sights outside. As he starts to move out the door, his mother appears and slowly closes the door in front of him. As the bright scene and fascinating noises slowly evaporate, he turns to her and says, "All gone outside."

Sometime between eighteen and twenty-four months, most children begin to make word combinations. From the start, these word combinations are creative, including such novel strings as that in the episode above. By creative we mean that children invent combinations of words they have never heard. A parrot can say "All gone outside" only if that string is first spoken to it. By contrast, children from the start produce novel combinations that must be "created."

Let us begin by discussing what is significant grammatically about such combinations. After that, we can describe the range of meanings encoded in early word combinations. The grammar of two-word utterances is actually quite simple since there are only two possible ways any two words can be combined. What is significant is that children use the order of the two words as a grammatical device; in other words, the order of particular words and kinds of words will be consistent. Certain words will be consistently first in a two-word utterance: "bye-bye" as in "bye-bye Mommy" and "bye-bye, Christmas tree;" "more" as in "more milk" and "more swing." Other words will be last: "it" in "push it" and "off" in "water off." Still other words may be in either position, but that position will be meaningful. For example, the possessor-possession relation will be expressed with possessor first—"Daddy car" meaning "Daddy's car." These consistencies of order are the first-learned grammatical features of human language.

As to the meaning and function of these early sentences, we have already provided some idea in our discussion of the meaning and function of single-word utterances. While many of these functions can be expressed with a single word, the range of possible meanings is greatly extended by combining two or three words. In any case, the explicitness of relations found in two-word utterances is an aid to the listener and is certainly more persuasive to researchers who wonder where the child's intentions leave off and their own inferences begin. For example, possession can be expressed by a single word, as when a girl points to Daddy's coat and says "dada." No one is likely to infer that she is naming the coat "dada." Nonetheless, "Daddy coat" is a clearer indication of the relationship.

The range of early meanings and examples of each are shown in Table 2–1. According to Brown (1973), this set of semantic relationships accounted for nearly all of the two-word utterances produced by children learning a variety of languages. Children everywhere learn to name, to attribute qualities, to greet; at this age, all children speak about location, possession, and action-causal relations (involving agents), and objects. This universality is understandable because these relations expressed by two-word utterances reflect the most basic conceptual relations of human thought.

Again we can ask about the prerequisites to early two-word utterances. The strategies and knowledge described for single-word utterances continue to be applicable. Other early Piagetian concepts are important as well. Many of the sensorimotor concepts (see Chapter One) are encoded in the child's language. As we have already said, object permanence must

Table 2–1

The Major Semantic Relations Expressed in Two-Word Utterances

Relations	Examples
Agent and action	Bambi go.
Action and object	See sock.
Agent and object	Eve lunch (Eve is having lunch.)
Action and location	Sat wall.
Object and location	Baby highchair (Baby is in the highchair.)
Possessor and possession	My Mommy.
Attribute and object	Pretty boat.
Demonstrative and object	There book.
Negation and X (where X is any term)	No wash.
Greeting and name	Bye-bye man.

Note: An agent is any animate being that can perform an action.
  An object is any recipient of an action or thing being named and thus could be animate or inanimate.
  Attribute simply means attributing some quality (e.g., little, fat, pretty) to an object.
  Demonstrative is used primarily to mark naming.

(After Brown, 1973; Copyright © 1973 by the President and Fellows of Harvard College. Reprinted by permission).

set the stage for naming. Attribution is based on knowing that qualities exist independently of specific objects. Some mastery of causality must precede the acquisition of sentences involving agent and action or action and object. The range and quality of more specific information must also increase greatly; the child must learn more and more about objects and events in the world, about what objects might be considered equivalent, about what kinds of things move and cause other things to move, and so on.

Finally, two-word utterances provide us with evidence for a strategy which should be well established for the reader by what we have said already. Strategy 5 is: *Attend to order.* It is clear that young children regularly learn whatever order is consistent in the input (Slobin, 1973). The salience of order as a grammatical feature noticed and copied by children can be demonstrated by many facts of acquisition. For example, children make few ordering errors even in later-learned complex systems such as the English auxiliary system. For example, although the multiple auxiliaries in "He will have been flying by then" are not easily learned, there are rarely any errors of ordering the elements. Nonetheless, there are a few exceptions to this important principle; such exceptions, as will be discussed later, reflect the operation of other general strategies.

Summary

The earliest development of language was partitioned into three phases: prelanguage, first words, and earliest relations and grammar. The prelanguage phase (birth to twelve months) was characterized in terms of the child's inability to produce any meaningful words. But children do acquire precursor skills of requesting and declaring by nonverbal means. Further, children are able to comprehend some aspects of simple adult utterance, primarily through strategies involving intonation, nonverbal cues, and context (1a, 1b, and 1c).

Early in the child's second year, the first words are usually produced. Children begin with simple sounds, producing first words like "dada" or "mama." In comprehension, children may ignore considerable variation in the sounds heard; "mama" and "tata" might be treated as the same. These early words are generally labels for conceptual categories; for example, "mama" may be used for people other than the mother. Further, such an apparent name may have functions other than naming, such as using "mama" to make requests. The process of acquiring early words is often aided by the simple, regular, repetitive nature of parental speech, with nouns emphasized and placed at the ends of utterances. Important prerequisite knowledge includes object permanence and the understanding that a word can stand for an object or event or for classes of either. Strategies associated with acquiring earliest words were: (2) process what is immediately sensed; (3) attend to the end of the utterance; and (4) attend to stress.

Toward the end of the second year children typically begin to put words together. Such combinations exhibit a rudimentary grammar since children utilize consistent orderings of the words providing support for the general strategy: (5) attend to order. The basic semantic relations expressed include agent-action, object-location, possession, attribution, and negation.

MIDDLE DEVELOPMENT

In the early stages of development, acquisition is slow, even during the later months of that first period. But somewhere around two or two-and-a half years, development begins to blossom. The most rapid growth is during the age range from that point to four or five years. For example, vocabulary zooms from 300 words or less at twenty-four months to perhaps 1,000 words at thirty-six months to well over 2,000 words at five years (Dale, 1976; Menyuk, 1971). And the kinds of knowledge represented by these words—an aspect not so easily measured as is total vocabulary—is also vastly increased. The sound system, barely begun at two years, is nearly perfected at five years. During some periods of time, new grammatical features emerge so rapidly that parents feel that progress is at least daily. At two, children's understanding of the complexities of meaning and grammar is quite limited; they seem to have great difficulty expressing many of the ideas they have. But in a very short span of time they reach the point of being able to say almost anything.

Given the rapidity and multiplicity of growth during this span, it is not reasonable to present a chronological account, so we will take each of a series of strands and unravel them for the period from two to five years of age. We will begin with the development of the sound system, proceed to word semantics, then consider some topics related to sentence grammar and semantics, and conclude with a discussion of parental speech and its role in development.

Sound System

Adult: "Johnny, I'm going to say a word two times and you tell me which time I say it right and which time I say it wrong: 'rabbit,' (pause), 'wabbit.' "

Child: "Wabbit is wight, and wabbit is wong." (Dale, 1976, p. 217; changes from phonetic transcription were made for present purposes.)

The development of the sound system is an important, but technically complex, matter; only limited treatment is possible here.[2] Acquisition of the sound system is a significant hurdle for all children; in some cases, the child's mastery of articulation lags so far behind knowledge of words and grammar that outsiders cannot understand anything the child says at the age of three or even older.

The task is not easy, for the sounds of speech are not physically the simple sequences of sounds that we seem to hear. For the older child or adult, "bat" is perceived to contain three distinct sounds, each different than the three distinct sounds in "dog." Further, "brat" has four distinct sounds, three of which are nearly the same as those in "bat." But, for the beginner, any word heard is not so conveniently divided; speech is a continuous stream of sounds, not broken into "b," "r," etc. Further, recent evidence (discussed in Clark & Clark, 1977) has shown how imperfectly the physical signal maps onto the percept, that is, perceptually identical sounds are not physically identical and perceptually different sounds may be physically the same, depending on the context provided by other sounds.

In comprehending, the child has the task of learning what makes a difference and what does not. As we noted earlier, certain sounds are different in ways that do not matter in a particular language. For example, the "p's" in "pin," "nap," and "spin" are different in ways that do not matter in English, so children must learn to ignore the difference. At the same time, they must treat the "p's" in "pin" and "nap" as different from the "b's" in "bin" and "nab." The latter differences are not inherently more salient than the former.

Learning to comprehend these differences must be linked to acquiring some set of words. In essence, if differently pronounced strings of sounds mean something different, then the difference in pronunciation must be

---

[2]The interested reader should look at a source introducing the basics of phonology (Langacker, 1973; Clark & Clark, 1977) and/or phonological development (Dale, 1976).

important. Research with young children is somewhat difficult; imagine asking a child of twenty-four months whether "pin" and "bin" sound the same or different. While, of course, one cannot ask such questions directly, a procedure that is functionally the same was utilized by Eilers and Oller (1976). The procedure and results are summarized in Box A.

Box A. Children's Perception of Differences Between the Sounds of Words.

In Eilers and Oller (1976), the question addressed was whether differently pronounced words really sounded that different to two-year-olds. Children were presented with two toys, one a familiar toy labeled with the correct English word ("cow"), the other a novel toy labeled with a nonsense word ("pow"). After exposure to the names and some practice in naming, the children were told to find some candy hidden under the "cow" or the "pow." Two-year-olds were generally quite successful with this particular distinction ("k" versus "p"), but did somewhat more poorly (on the average) with "rabbit" versus "wabbit" and "block" versus "bock." They did no better than chance with "monkey" versus "mucky" and "fish" versus "thish" ("th" as in "thing") which were presented in the same format. For the two-year-old, some of these differences are so minimal as to *not* make a difference. Yet over the next year or two, "r" versus "w" and "f" versus "th" will be treated differently in comprehension.

Based on their results, as well as other less experimental findings (Dale, 1976), we can thus propose a rather general strategy for the development of the comprehension of sounds. Strategy 6: *Treat as equivalent sounds that are similar.* As stated, this strategy is not particularly predictive since it does not include principles for determining what sounds are similar. But this strategy carries the important implication that children are making abstract categories for sounds rather than beginning with fine discriminations. After all, even one-year-olds may be able to make as many discriminations as adults, but they will tend to ignore most of the perceptible differences in comprehending the speech of others.

The acquisition of the production of sounds has received much greater study; here we will summarize some recent work that looks at the kinds of omissions and substitutions made by children in this age range. Consider the examples given in Table 2–2. Ingram (1974a, 1974b) has shown that alterations of these kinds are found across a wide range of children's words from a variety of languages. Each of the examples in the table illustrates one or more general processes of omission and substitution. In particular, (a)—"elephant–hefant"—illustrates the process of deleting syllables, especially unstressed syllables and adding a consonant (in this case "h") to the beginning of a word or syllable. At first, children cannot produce more than one or two syllables and have difficulty with words beginning with vowels. In (b) and (c), it is apparent that strings of successive consonants—"sp" in (b) and "pl" in (c)—are reduced to a single consonant; usually sounds such as "s" and "l" are dropped and the more striking consonants (such as "p") are retained. The change of "p" to "b" at the beginning of a word—as in (b) and (c) and of "b" to "p" at the end is also consistent with a general bias toward putting certain sounds, called "voiced" (b, n, d, and g) at the beginning of a word and other sounds, called "unvoiced" (p, f, t, and k) at the end. Further, there is an early inability to end a word with a consonant at all—see (e), (f), and (g)—resulting in either its omission altogether or the addition of a final vowel, as is seen in (f). Since the final added vowel is most often an "ee" sound, it is appropriate to the child's productions that parents alter so many words, such as "daddy" instead of "dad," and "mommy," "kitty," "doggie," and the like.

A general strategy for sound production is: 7. *Simplify the production of sounds.* Most words that the young child hears and attempts to duplicate will be beyond his articulatory capabilities; early attempts to pronounce such words will result in simplification, including deletions and substitutions of the kinds illustrated in Table 2-2. Certainly, the development of the child's articulation involves overcoming these early limits and eventually producing the correct sound in the proper place.

Table 2-2

Children's Errors of Production

Target word	Child's Imitation
(a) elephant	hefant
(b) spoon	boon
(c) please	bease
(d) knob	nap
(e) blanket	babi
(f) dot	dati
(g) kiss	ti

(Data from Ingram, 1974*a* and 1974*b*).

Word Meaning

Father (to young daughter playing roughly with cat): "Don't do that to the cat. You'll hurt her."

Daughter's playmate (three and a half years): "Yeah, that would die him."

Word meaning has been a dominant focus in recent research on language development. A resurgence of interest was stimulated, at least in part, by some claims by Eve Clark (1973). While these claims have been challenged on several fronts, they did set the stage for what has happened and they still provide interesting insights into the development of word meaning. Clark (1973) reviewed diary studies of many years, as well as recent experimental evidence, concerned with young children's early use of words. In all of this evidence, children were found to make many naming errors based on the perceptual qualities of physical objects (such as shape, texture, or size); these errors were consistently over-extensions of meaning (for example, calling dogs and all other four-legged animals "doggie"). Table 2-3 presents some examples gleaned from diary reports. The theory Clark used to characterize this range of evidence on word-meaning development she called the *semantic feature hypothesis*.[3] According to this hypothesis, children acquire the meanings of words by gradually adding the specific semantic features which define the concep-tual class being labeled. When first acquiring a word, a child often uses it to refer to a class of objects sharing one or a few general features and thus overextends its use. Gradually the other features are added until the child's concept matches the adult's. Consider, for example, the concept "brother," which involves the more general concept "male" or "boy." If the child begins with this more general concept, then "brother" and "boy" will likely be confused for a period of time in development. When the more specific feature "sibling" is added to the feature "boy," then "brother" will be used correctly. The theory, as presented, is consistent with the diary reports and other evidence amassed by Clark. But recently several criticisms have been leveled at the theory; the two most prom-inent ones will be discussed here.

The first major criticism has come from Nelson (1974), who argued that Clark is wrong in basing her account on static perceptual features such as shape and size. Nelson argued that function and action (move-ment of the object or the child's actions with respect to it) are more central than perceptual features to many early concepts. In fact, exten-sions involving movement and action were included in Clark's examples, and in Table 2-3, but Nelson's claim is that function and action are the core of all early concepts. A ball is a "ball" not just because of its shape, but because it can be rolled, bounced, and thrown. My own child learned early to call a particular ball "football," then called every kind of ball "football." While footballs are not shaped like other balls, they are used in play much like other balls, particularly by very young children. Nelson claimed that children begin with such functional-actional concepts as the core of early semantic knowledge. One kind of evidence for this claim is the fact that children's early concepts are predominantly centered around objects that do something or with which the child interacts—Mom, Daddy, people, cars, dogs, cats, and the like. Static objects are seldom labeled in early speech. This latter argument is sufficiently well-founded

[3]The same theory was used by Clark's husband Herbert Clark (1973) to describe the acqui-sition of spatial and temporal terms.

Table 2-3

Common Overextension of Early Word Meaning

Dimension	Lexical Item	First Referent	Extensions and Overextensions in Order of Occurrence
Movement	Titi	Animals	Pictures of animals, things that move
Movement	Tutu	Train	Engine, moving train, journey
Shape	Mooi	Moon	Cakes, round marks on window, round shapes in books, letter O
Shape	Nenin (French for "breast")	Breast, food	Button on garment, point of bare elbow, eye in portrait, face in a portrait
Shape	Tee	Cat	Dogs, cows, sheep, horse
Size	Fly	Fly	Specks of dirt, dust, all small insects, his own toes, crumbs of bread, a toad
Sound	Sch	Noise of train	Music, noise of any movement, wheels, balls
Taste	Cola (chocolate)	Chocolate	Sugar, tarts, grapes, figs, peaches
Texture	Kiki	Cat	Cotton, any soft material
Action	Our (ouvrir, "open")	In relation to father's door	In relation to piece of fruit peel, in relation to box, in relation to shoes that needed to be unlaced

(From Clark, 1973).

that we can provide the following strategy: 8. *Learn the names of interesting things and events.* While it is not possible to state a set of principles that describe what is interesting to young children, most researchers (and parents) have a sense of what will be interesting: moderate complexity, well-defined contours, bright colors, and movement are among the attributes of interesting visual things.

Actually there is very little evidence for deciding whether children's errors are based on perceptual or functional features, or if either is primary. Bowerman's (1976) report of overextensions by her two daughters indicates that these overextensions were based on perceptual rather than functional features. These children often used shared perceptual features to extend the meaning of a word when the features cut across well-known functional differences. For example, Eva at fifteen months used "moon" for the real moon and for half-grapefruits, slices of lemon, a letter "D" that she stuck on the refrigerator, and other related shapes. One must be cautious in interpreting what children "mean" in making such errors, for it is not correct to conclude that they are unaware of the important differences between the objects involved. Children really do not view the moon, grapefruit halves, and magnetic letters as the same. But the use of a word to label new objects is most often based on what things look like rather than what they are used for. As we shall discuss later, perceptual and functional features are quite often redundant, that is, things that look alike are acted upon in similar ways.

A second major criticism of the semantic-feature hypothesis is more damaging. It is that children do not, as a rule, begin with the most general feature and refine concepts from there. The most persuasive evidence in this regard is the regularity of errors that are *not* overextensions, including errors of underextension, overlap, and complete mismatch. If children always begin with less than an adequate set of features, such errors should not be found. Actually underextensions may be quite common, but go largely unnoticed. Suppose the child says "doggie" only for the neighbor's Collie and says nothing for other dogs, thus underextending the range of meaning. This error is much less noticeable than calling a cow "doggie" because silence can have multiple causes. Overlap actually involves both underextension and overextension since some objects included in the adult concept are not in the child's and vice-versa. An example from Anglin (1977) is a child who used the term "flower" for most flowers but not roses and daisies and, in addition, used "flower" for other plants. Bowerman (1976) reported a striking case of mismatch; her daughter used the word "hi" to refer to any situation in which the hands or feet were covered. This strange error finally made sense when Bowerman discovered that its origin was in her use of a little finger puppet that always said "hi."

Thus current evidence does not support the notion that children always begin with the most general semantic features and add more specific features until the correct meaning is attained; there are too many exceptions to that rule. But the converse is not true either; children do not generally begin with the most specific concepts and move progressively to more general concepts. There are too many examples of overextension for that counterclaim to be reasonable.

So at what level do children begin, and what is the basis of their early errors? Perhaps a concrete example will put these questions clearly, though we will oversimplify in this example. Suppose a young girl sees a neighborhood dog—a rust-colored cocker spaniel. Her father says, "See the doggie." Now she knows to call that particular dog "doggie." But what about a German shepherd? Or a cow? Each is somewhat like a cocker. If the child only calls that particular dog "doggie," she has severely underextended; if only cockers are called "doggie," she has still underextended. If cows and other four-legged mammals are called "doggie," she has overextended. In all of these cases, perceptual features of shape or size may be the basis of error. Alternatively, functional-actional aspects may be operative, such as what the cocker does, especially toward her, and how she interacts with it.

A promising answer to both questions can be found in a perspective particularly associated with the recent work of Eleanor Rosch (formerly Heider), especially in the paper by Rosch, Mervis, Gray, Johnson, and Boyes-Braem (1976). A related argument can be found in Anglin (1977). Roger Brown made a rather similar set of arguments several years previous to either. Brown suggested that children begin at the "usual level of utility" (Brown, 1958) and the "level of probable equivalence" (Brown, 1965). Both of these phrases emphasize the fact that the level of concept involves function, namely that children label as the same those objects that can be dealt with in the same way. In Brown's discussions, this level is determined to considerable degree by parental input, for parents choose from among possible labels those which make distinctions that are appropriate to the child's age. For example, parents usually begin by calling all round objects that can bounce, roll, and be thrown "ball" and all coins "money." Not until a child is ready to play with different balls in specialized ways is it necessary to distinguish "footballs" and "basketballs." Similarly, only when children can count and spend their own money is it important to use the words "penny" and "nickel." Parental choice of label and the level of abstraction where children begin are both at least roughly controlled by the principle of functional equivalence.

Rosch et al. (1976) have extended this argument so that it is more explicit and have provided an array of evidence about what determines the level of equivalence. As we shall see, the evidence also provides some resolution of the argument between perceptual feature and functional-action theories. Rosch and her collaborators find evidence for what they call basic-level concepts—the level of concept which is most generally useful to adults and most likely to be acquired first by children. Consider the hierarchy musical instrument, guitar, folk guitar; in this hierarchy "musical instrument" is certainly the most abstract or general and "folk guitar" the most specific. For reasons we will explain next, "guitar" is in between and is considered a basic-level concept. Table 2–4 presents this and other examples of these levels of concepts. Basic-level concepts are always at an intermediate level of generality. Rosch et al. find that most or all examples of concepts at the basic level look alike (in shape), share most attributes listed by adults, and are reacted to at the motor level in the same way. The superordinate-level concepts have representatives that share very little. Consider the category "musical instruments;" one can say that all musical instruments make musical sounds and are played by the hand and/or mouth. But the range of sounds is extreme, the shapes and sizes quite variable, and the means of playing diverse; guitars, pianos, and trumpets do not look similar and are played in quite different ways. Guitars (basic-level category) generally look similar, have similar

Table 2-4

Examples of Basic-Level, Superordinate, and Subordinate Categories

Superordinate	Basic-level	Subordinate
Musical instrument	Guitar	Folk, classical
	Piano	Grand, upright
Fruit	Apple	Delicious, Mackintosh
	Peach	Freestone, cling
Clothing	Pants	Levi, doubleknit
	Socks	Knee, ankle
Furniture	Table	Kitchen, dining room
	Chair	Kitchen, living room

(From Rosch et al., 1976).

features, and are played in similar ways. At the subordinate level, objects are generally a bit more similar, but the change is only slight. Knowing whether a guitar is classical or folk adds very little in the way of additional information about form, features, or function. While the more specific classification is important, particularly for specialists, most people will say, "She plays the guitar" or "That sounds like a guitar."

Thus one can predict that children will generally begin at this basic level, between very general and very specific. Both overextension and underextension may occur, but the child's concepts will generally begin at the basic level. Some overextensions clearly involve acquiring a basic-level concept but using a more specific term for it, for example, using "football" for all balls. While there may be exceptions to this general characterization and while it does not predict all errors, this view seems to provide a promising beginning in need of further development. A further strategy for word meaning in this period of development is: 9. *Conceptualize at the basic level*, neither too general nor too specific. Based on Rosch's work, we can suggest that the basic level is a level of optimal similarity within categories and discriminability between categories, such that finer categorization adds little new information and more global categorization loses considerable information.

This point of view can also provide a resolution of the argument over whether early concepts are based on perceptual or functional features. Rosch has demonstrated that, for the most part, perceptual and functional information is highly redundant at the level of basic concepts; chairs generally look alike and are acted upon in the same way. Since the perceptual features and functions of objects are related, certain concepts are easier to learn.

The study of word meaning is a complex and rapidly growing aspect of modern research on language development. Here we have only scratched the surface, omitting specific mention of available information on dimensional adjectives (big/small, tall/short), temporal terms, and verbs; for a broader discussion, the reader might consult Clark and Clark (1977) or Dale (1976).

Grammatical Elements

Child (two and one-half years): "I wear Mommy hat."

A child who knows how to express various meanings and combinations in two-, three-, and four-word sentences at the age of two or three years still often produces largely ungrammatical sentences, such as the one above and: "Daddy car," "baby high chair," and "doggy eat food." These utterances are strange and incomplete because the grammatical elements (sometimes called grammatical morphemes) are omitted. By grammatical elements, we mean such words as "is," "in," "the," and such inflections as past tense "-ed," present progressive "-ing," possessive "-'s." With the addition of these elements, the opening example would be transformed into: "I am wearing Mommy's hat" or "I wore Mommy's hat." Similarly "Daddy car" would be "That's Daddy's car" or "Daddy is driving the car." These "little" words and inflections generally play a relatively minor role in understanding utterances, for these elements can often be omitted without loss of meaning so long as the context is known. Indeed, people often send telegrams that are much like the child's speech. Because of the comparability of children's speech and telegrams, such speech has been characterized as "telegraphic" (Brown & Bellugi, 1964). While this term approximately describes what children say at a certain age, the process is certainly not the same. Roger Brown (1973) has chosen to call the grammatical elements the modulators of the basic semantic relations. In some cases, they are simply devices for indicating relations learned earlier by the child, such as possession and location. In other cases, they mark information not necessarily inferred otherwise, such as definite and indefinite articles. In any case, these grammatical elements carry information of lesser semantic significance than the information associated with the basic semantic relations or such information could generally be inferred without the grammatical elements. Table 2–5 provides a list of some of the most frequent grammatical elements in English. These elements are rarely used by children at two years of age, but over the next few years they are slowly acquired and perfected.

Brown (1973) chose to study this particular set because their high frequency of occurrence permitted reliable assessment of the course of acquisition. A major question addressed by Brown was: What determines the relative order in which these different elements are acquired? If some particular element is consistently acquired before some other element, what might be the determining variable? It could be that nothing more is involved than the frequency with which the elements are heard. If some

Table 2–5

Common Grammatical Morphemes in English Listed in Order of Acquisition

Morpheme	Example
Present progressive -ing	I going.
In, on	Mommy in kitchen.
Plural	Cars.
Past irregular	I went.
Possessive	Mommy's coat.
Contractible copula	I'm here.
Articles (a, the)	A gas.
Past regular	Baby spilled.
Third person regular (present indicative)	Mommy drives.
Third person irregular (present indicative)	What is he doing?
Contractible auxiliary	I'm going.

(From Brown, 1973; Copyright © 1973 by the President and Fellows of Harvard College. Reprinted by permission).

element, say the article "the," is heard more often than some other element, say the preposition "in," then the child would acquire "the" before "in." Does frequency determine the order of acquisition? Brown's results provide a clear answer to that question: No! For example, articles are the most frequent in parental speech, occurring about four times as often as the present progressive "-ing," yet the present progressive is mastered first of these fourteen morphemes and the articles are mastered eighth. Similarly, the contractible copula is second in frequency to the articles, occurring at least twice as often as any of the remaining elements, but it is mastered nearly last of the set. Thus the acquisition of these elements is not directly linked to the frequency with which they are heard.

This bears some relation to our earlier discussion of empiricist-behaviorist theories of language development. Such theories have generally taken frequency to be a major factor in the associative and imitational processes (Staats, 1968). Even if reinforcement is taken to be an essential element of such acquisition, as we said earlier, it is difficult to relate to learning about grammatical elements in this context. It is not even clear what element in the sentence is being reinforced. As Brown and Hanlon (1970) demonstrated, reinforcement seems to be completely unrelated to grammaticality. The following discussion will indicate that order of acquisition is a result of something other than frequency or reinforcement.

The order of acquisition actually reflects the syntactic and semantic complexity of the elements. Let us see why the present progressive might be mastered early and the articles late. By present progressive, Brown only considered the addition of "-ing" to the verb; for example, "I am playing" and "doggie barking" would both be counted correct in terms of the presence of the "-ing" even though the latter omits the auxiliary "is." What must children know in order to use this part of the present progressive correctly? First, they must be able to distinguish between action verbs, (such as "run," "give," "eat") and state verbs (such as "want," "know," "like"). The progressive tense is appropriate for action verbs ("I am eating"), but not for state verbs ("I am wanting to go"). Beyond this semantically salient distinction, children have only to add the "-ing" form to the verb stem to form the progressive. There are no problems with irregularities, exceptions, or coordination with other aspects of the grammar. In sum, the present progressive is very simple grammatically and requires semantically only one salient distinction.

In contrast, the acquisition of the article is a considerably more complex problem for the child. First of all, of the three articles ("a," "an," and "the") considered by Brown, "a" and "an" can occur with count nouns (for example, car, dog, tree), but not with mass nouns (such as water, rice, sand), while "the" can occur with either. Secondly, the articles do not usually apply to proper names such as Don, Fido, or Mommy, but they do apply to common names such as cat, or flower. Thirdly, it is important whether the referent named by the noun is definite or indefinite. The definite article "the" is used for those situations where a referent is specific to both the speaker and the listener. In other words, "This is the book" means a particular book that both speaker and listener have in mind. Otherwise, the indefinite article "a," "an," or "some" is appropriate, as in "I want a book" (Brown, 1973). Even though the speaker may well know that the referent is specific to him or her, the referent is not definite unless there is reason to presume that it is definite to the listener also. Knowing what the listener knows or might know involves a level of perspective-taking that children of two or three rarely have. (Chapter One). Thus the proper use of the articles is determined by a number of factors in conjunction; any *one* of these is at least as complex as the action-state distinction necessary for learning the present progressive. Thus it is no real surprise that the acquisition of the articles is relatively late.

In sum, then, this contrast between present progressive "-ing" and the articles illustrates why the order of acquisition is not directly based on frequency of occurrence. An account of language development based only on input variables or direct imitation of forms cannot be adequate. The complexity of the grammatical elements predicts rapidity of acquisition but frequency does not. Children, in learning grammatical elements, are learning complex rules for correct usage, including proper coordination with other elements in the sentence and with referential and contextual facts available to them.

Supporting evidence for the claim that children are learning general rules is found in the widespread occurrence of *overregularization*. Whenever there are regular and irregular varieties of a grammatical element, children will make the irregulars conform to the regular rule at least for a while; this practice is called overregularization. Take, for example, the past-tense inflection in English. While the vast majority of English verbs follow a regular past-tense rule ("-ed"[4] as in "climbed"), there are several irregulars, most of them high frequency verbs, for example, "went," "came," and "made." Children acquire some of these irregulars earliest, but then regularize even the known irregulars as soon as they begin to use regular forms, apparently "unlearning" the correct and frequently heard "went" and substituting "goed" instead. This kind of overregularization is found also with plurals (gooses); it is found in other languages with a range of verb and noun inflections (Slobin, 1973). These errors provide confirmation that children, from a very early age, are learning generative rules.

Based on the common occurrence of overregularization and other facts of development, a particularly wide-ranging strategy can be stated: 10. *Avoid exceptions*. Whenever there are exceptions to some general rule, children will, early in development, apply the general rule to the exceptions. Numerous instances of this strategy have been reported; see especially Slobin's (1973) discussion of several. For example, children invariably begin by putting the auxiliary in questions next to the main verb, which is consistent with the general rule in English; thus sentences like "Where you are going?" are common for a while. Interestingly, this kind of utterance is the rare case of a violation of Strategy 5 (pay attention to order); it is only because the order in questions is an exception to a more general rule that this misordering occurs.

Sentence Variations. Child: "No the sun shining" (age and sex unspecified) (Klima & Bellugi, 1966).

In every language, there are a variety of sentence forms, many of which encode important semantic variations, including questions, negations, commands. By contrast with the simple declarative form, these variations generally involve operations of deletion, addition, substitution, and rearrangement of elements as well as coordination of elements at separate locations in the sentence. Thus, in questions, a wh-word (for

---

[4]This is really an oversimplification since regular past tense in spoken English involves a phonologically conditioned rule. Depending upon the final sound in the verb, either "-d," "-t," or "-ed" is added to form the past tense.

example, who, where) is substituted for the unknown element and the wh-word is placed at the beginning of the sentence. An auxiliary to the verb is compulsory so that if there is none in the comparable declarative form, a dummy auxiliary ("do") is introduced. For example, contrast "I want cake" with "What do I want?" Notice that the auxiliary also precedes the subject noun ("I") in contrast to the usual position after the subject noun.

The coordination of elements can be even more complex. Thus in negations the negative element (such as "no" or "none") is usually placed at the earliest possible point and, in standard English, no other elements can be negated. The elements that can be negated include indefinites, such as "any" (which is negated to "none") and "anywhere" or "somewhere" (which are negated to "nowhere"), and auxiliaries, including "be," "have," "do," and "will," many of which are generally contracted with the negative (for example, "won't"). The task of mastering these various substitutions, deletions, rearrangements, and coordinations is therefore quite complex, especially for the young child.

At two and one-half years or so, the average child begins to differentiate structural variations from the standard declarative form. The semantic intentions are present much earlier; indeed, some parents claim that "no" was their child's first word. The intention to ask a question is marked earliest by intonation. Nonetheless the production of distinct sentence varieties marked in formally different ways must develop over several months. Let us consider a specific account of the development of one of these sentence variations—negation.

The earliest negative is, of course, the single word "no." Then, in the two-word stage, the child begins to attach "no" to other words or sentences. At first it will be simple, like "no spinach," but somewhat later it can be more sentencelike, such as "no like it." In some cases, the child may produce an entirely affirmative sentence and indicate the negation by head shakes, intonation, or some other nonverbal cue. The important point about these early sentential negatives is that the negation is always *external* to the rest of the sentence. The production of a negative always involves attaching a "no" (or "don't") externally to an existing sentence without rearrangement or insertion (Klima and Bellugi, 1966). Examples of these kinds of sentences are given in Table 2–6 under Period 1. Note that these three periods were so labeled for convenience by Klima and Bellugi (1966); while they do follow a clear developmental sequence, no claim of necessary nonoverlapping stages is made here. Although one of the Period 1 sentences is grammatical, the entire set convinces us that such exceptional cases are an accident of a primitive rule being used by the child. Further, the failure to produce sentences with the negative internal to the sentence is matched by a failure to comprehend such sentences. Unless the negation is supported by nonverbal cues or by an additional "no" at the beginning or end, the child interprets the utterance to be an affirmative (Bellugi, 1967). Thus "I don't want you to get any cookies" is likely to be interpreted *incorrectly* by a child of two or so, but "No, I don't want you to get any cookies" will be interpreted correctly. Is it possible that some behaviors of children in the "terrible twos" are linked to miscomprehensions such as this?

In the second period of this acquisition, the negative element *is* within the sentence (see Table 2-6, Period 2). Here the negative often follows the noun phrase, except for many imperatives where the negative is first. While the examples include sentences with "don't" and "can't," these seem to be alternative ways of marking negation rather than being negative auxiliaries as they would be characterized in adult speech. Bellugi argued that the reason they are not auxiliary negative elements is that there are no examples of simple auxiliaries elsewhere in the child's speech; in other words, there are no occurrences of "do" and "can" elsewhere at this age.

Table 2-6

Examples of Children's Negative Sentences at Different Periods of Development

Period 1

No singing song.	No sit there.	No heavy.
No money.	No play that.	No want stand head.

Period 2

I can't catch you.	Don't leave me.	There no squirrels.
I don't sit on Cromer coffee.	That no fish school.	He no bite you.
Book say no.	Touch the snow no.	I no taste them.

Period 3

Paul can't have one.	You didn't caught me.	This not ice cream.
I didn't did it.	I didn't see something.	It's not cold.
Because I don't want somebody to wake me up.	I gave him some so he won't cry.	I not crying.
You don't want some supper.	That was not me.	I not see you any more.
I don't...have some ...too much.	I am not a doctor.	Ask me if I not made mistake.

(From Klima & Bellugi, 1966).

In Period 3 the auxiliaries are now a separate aspect of the child's grammar, because "do," "can," "be," and so forth now occur alone. These sentences are considerably more complex and many use completely grammatical English. But there is a great deal more to be learned beyond this period. The coordination with tense and with indefinites must be accomplished; "You don't want some supper" should probably have the indefinite "any."

Thus the acquisition of sentence negations moves from an earliest period in which the negative element is always sentence external to a phase in which the negative is often inside the sentence without proper use of auxiliaries to a later phase in which auxiliaries are partly worked out but other aspects remain unlearned.

The acquisition of negation provides a general strategy: 11. *Avoid the interruption of elements that belong together.* Since a sentence forms an intact unit, children avoid interrupting that unit when negating it and place the "no" external to it. This strategy is also relevant to children's difficulties with the location of the auxiliary in questions. Since the auxiliary is part of the verb, it should therefore be more difficult to separate it from the main verb, as in "Where are you going?" In the accepted adult form, the noun interrupts the two parts of the verb in questions. This strategy also explains some of the difficulties children have with complex sentences, as we shall see in the next section.

Complex Relations in Sentences. Child: "Why he don't know how to pretend?" (Klima & Bellugi, 1966).

Combinations of semantic relations include the embedding and coordination of more than one sentence. As with sentence variations, these combinations require deletions, additions, substitutions, and rearrangements of elements. In particular, embeddings often involve the deletion or pronominalization of repeated noun phrases (using that, which, or who) and rearrangements such as putting the relative pronoun at the beginning of the relative clause regardless of where it would occur in the same clause alone. Consider, for example, a sentence with a relative clause: "The girl chased the cat that we found." In this sentence "that" has replaced "the cat" in the relative clause and is at the beginning of the clause instead of after the verb; the clause alone would be "we found the cat."

We will illustrate some aspects of the development of complex sentences with a particular kind of subordination—*complements*. A complement is a clause that serves as subject or object of the main clause. Consider one of the sentences given in Table 2–6: "Because I don't want somebody to wake me up." This is a complement construction in which "somebody to wake me up" is the object of "want." The main clause is: "I don't want something," where the something not wanted is that "somebody will wake me up." Thus the something not wanted is a complete sentence (though in its embedded form it is not a sentence that can stand alone).

Such complements first occur as young as two and one-half years of age, but they become more common a year or so later (Limber, 1973). Object complements, like the sentence at the beginning of this section and the example just discussed, are associated with a particular set of verbs—including want, ask, know, expect, tell, watch, and remember. These verbs are acquired in a consistent order; thus, for example, "want" (wanna) is quite early, followed by "gonna" and "hafta," with "remember" and "show" somewhat later (Limber, 1973). Generally, shortly after a verb is first used, it also occurs in a complement construction. Thus when "remember" enters the child's vocabulary, the things "remembered" immediately go beyond "the train" and "your name" to propositions such as "where the duck is" and "how to fix it." (Limber, 1973).

In addition to learning the form of such constructions and the relevant verbs, children face other complexities. For example, negation must be coordinated with embedding. For some verbs, the negation must be attached to the main clause, even though the meaning involves a negation of the subordinate clause. Our earlier sentence might be more appropriately paraphrased as "I want something and that something is that nobody will wake me up," yet the negation can only be in the main clause, that is, "I don't want . . ." For other verbs, the negation may be in either the main clause or the subordinate clause; with those verbs the choice is important to the meaning of the sentence. Consider my daughter at three and one-half years telling me, "Don't tell her to do it anymore," after her mother threw away a broken toy. I had *not* told her mother to throw it away and everyone knew that. What the child meant was, "Tell her not to throw it away anymore." It seems here that the rule of attaching the negation to the main clause (applicable to "want") was overregularized to all verbs. The result was a sentence which would normally be taken to mean something else.

An additional source of complexity is provided for children by the role of the noun phrase preceding the object complement. Normally that noun phrase is the subject of the complement, as in the sentence discussed earlier or in the sentence, "John told Mary to go to the party." In this case it is Mary who will go to the party (if she follows John's orders). However, for a small set of verbs, this rule does not apply.

In the sentence "John promised Mary to go to the party," it is John who will go (if he keeps his promise). Most verbs follow the rule exemplified in the sentence with "told," in which the noun phrase after the verb is the subject of the complement clause. Such a rule is consistent with a more general rule that a verb is most likely to be associated with the nearest preceding noun phrase. But there are exceptions to these rules, including sentences like our second example. Children have difficulty with such exceptions and, in general, with sentences in which the subject and its verb are separated. (C. Chomsky, 1969).

A similar phenomenon is found in certain relative-clause construction, such as, "The boy who chased the cow is fat." It is the boy who is fat, despite the fact that "cow" immediately precedes "is fat." Generally children of three to four years will interpret this sentence to mean that the cow is fat because "the cow" is nearest to the predicate "is fat" (Gordon, 1972). A comparable effect is found in children's productions; even when one presses for imitations of embedded relative-clause constructions, young children change them to conjoined forms in which the interruption is avoided. Consider this exchange from Slobin and Welsh (1973) in which the child's task is to imitate what the adult says:

Adult: "Mozart who cried came to my party" ("Mozart" is the child's bear).

Child (two years and four months): "Mozart cried and he came to my party."

This child consistently avoided the embedded construction, always converting the adult sentence into a form where the noun of each clause immediately preceded the verb.

Such troublesome complement constructions and the relative-clause constructions just discussed provide further examples of two strategies already discussed, namely (10) *Avoid exceptions* and (11) *Avoid the interruption of elements that belong together.*

In all of these cases, the most general rule is one in which elements that belong together are proximate; the exceptions are cases where these elements are separated. Thus both of these rules are consistent with the result that children will have difficulty with such constructions.

Parental Speech

Our discussion of the middle period of development has described what children acquire and some strategies that determine how they process what they hear, but it has not specified what is heard. Now we will summarize what is known about how parents speak to their young children. While parents are not the only source of language data for children of this age, they are certainly the primary one in most cases.

The language of parents to young children learning to speak is a special kind of language. For example, sentences are typically only half as long as those spoken to other adults. Sentences are generally simpler in structure and contain proportionately more questions and imperatives. Further, they are delivered more slowly and carefully. Neither the vocabulary nor the syntax used in speech to young children is as diverse nor as rich as in speech to adults. And virtually every sentence is a clearly distinguished unit. Parents provide clear intonational information and pauses to mark off each sentence as a complete unit. When speaking to adults, it is not unusual to ramble, producing disjointed, incomplete, and strung-together sentences; however, this is quite rare in speech to young children. Providing the child with clearly distinguished sentences is important because the sentence is a fundamental unit in language. The problem of understanding and of learning language would be greatly compounded if there were few clear-cut sentence boundaries.

In addition, sentences spoken to children are nearly always grammatically well formed. Very few errors are found in the speech of parents to young children, both in terms of absolute number and in comparison to the speech of adults to each other. In addition, parental speech to young children involves frequent repetition of certain simple forms, such as, "Look at the light" and "Look at the doggie." While these particular sentences might not occur within a few-minute span, it is not unusual for parents to repeat themselves, literally or functionally, over a short span of time. Perhaps we can best sum up the differences by presenting an example. In Table 2-7 it is quite easy to guess who the mother is talking to in each sample. These samples are both from the mother of a child just under two; they are reasonably representative of the differences between her speech to the child and to the father. In sum, the speech to young children is simple, brief, regular, and repetitive. The language data available to the child is certainly a good set of data from which to build a knowledge of language (this discussion is based on Dodd & Glanzer, 1974). Before putting the matter to rest, though, there is one caveat.

Table 2-7

Speech of a Mother to Her Child of Under Two Years and to the Father

(1) Mother: "So I think probably in another year, he'll be all right, but I really have to . . . keep my eye on . . . them both when they're together." (Note: the "he" referred to is the family dog and the other part of the pair she must keep an eye on is the child.)

(2) (All this takes place while the child is in the bathtub.)
Mother: "You giving the fish a bath, huh?"
  (Short pause.)
Mother: "You giving the fish a bath?"
  (Short pause.)
Mother: "You giving him a bath?"

(Data from author's tapes, 1976).

One must be careful in the kind of interpretation proferred for these facts about parental speech. We do not claim that parents design their speech for teaching purposes. Certainly, there are ways in which this speech is not ideal if it is to be considered arranged for teaching. For example, in teaching a language, it would probably be ideal to present together a number of examples of the same construction rather than continuously mixing constructions together. Yet parents do not follow the optimal teaching design in this regard. Parental speech is not to be taken as a program for teaching language; it is mainly functional, designed to deal with immediate situations in which the listener has limited capabilities. It is concerned with limited topics, such as food and drink, play, and forbidden objects; it cannot be about politics or philosophy. Children have a limited span of attention and a poor ability to understand what is said to them. When children do not react to a request or question in the appropriate way, parents must repeat it more persuasively, more directly, or more simply until children react appropriately. In sum, parents are not speaking the way they do because of an intent to teach language, but because they are trying to communicate in everyday situations with a person who has limited knowledge and communication skills. (This discussion is based on Newport, Gleitman, & Gleitman, 1977; see also other chapters in Snow & Ferguson, 1977.)

Summary

We have described language development during the period from two to five years of age, a time during which progress is very rapid. In our discussion, the sound system, word meaning, and sentence construction were each treated separately.

The development of the sound system was characterized in terms of comprehension and production; for each of these aspects, we learned that children simplify a great deal initially. In comprehension, they (strategy 6) treat as equivalent sounds that are similar, ignoring certain discriminable differences such as "r" versus "w" and "f" versus "th." In production, children (strategy 7) simplify the production of sounds by deleting weak syllables and parts of consonant clusters, ending syllables with vowels, and so forth.

In the acquisition of word meaning, we described children's errors of word meaning, particularly overextensions based on such dimensions as movement, shape, and size. The counterclaim that such errors were founded on functional attributes was discussed and led to one early strategy: (8) *Learn the names of interesting things and events.* Children learn about things that they can interact with, that move, and that are colorful. Children also conceptualize initially at the basic level (strategy 9), where objects are highly similar in form and function; that is, "guitar" would be a category learned before either "musical instrument" or "folk guitar." Because form and function are often redundant at this level, the issue of whether children's errors are based on form or function is often irrelevant.

Grammatical elements (morphemes) are those little words and inflections that make utterances sound like real language. In English, they include prepositions, possessive " 's," past tense, and present progressive "-ing." Children acquire most of these morphemes during this period. The order of acquisition is essentially unrelated to the frequency with which they are heard; rather, order of acquisition reflects the semantic requirements and grammatical constraints on their use. We also discussed the fact that children often overregularize, producing irregulars in accord with the general rule, for example, "goed" and "comed." This fact was expressed as a strategy of wider import: (10) *Avoid exceptions.*

Then we described the development of variations on the basic sentence, focusing particularly on the negative. Initially, children construct negative sentences by attaching a negative element such as "no" to the beginning or end of an existing sentence. This was used as the basis for the general strategy (11) *Avoid the interruption of elements that belong together.* After children have progressed to the point of producing sentences with the negative within the sentence, there are still major tasks in coordinating with the auxiliary system, indefinites, and other language elements. In our discussion of complex sentences, we emphasized the development of complements, particularly object complements where a sentence is the object of the verb. Such constructions are associated with a set of verbs, including "want," "ask," and "remember." Mastery of such constructions supported strategies (10) and (11) since children have difficulty with those few *exceptions* (such as "promise") where the subject of the complement is *separated* from its verb.

Finally, we discussed the nature of parental speech to young children learning language. Such speech is brief, simple, and carefully delivered; in addition, sentence boundaries are well marked and sentences are well formed. However, these facts result primarily from parental efforts to communicate as effectively as possible about immediate circumstances and tasks with a child of limited knowledge and attention span.

LATER DEVELOPMENT

By later development, we mean middle and later childhood, from approximately five years to the beginning of adolescence. Of course, adolescents and adults continue to acquire vocabulary, skill at comprehending complex ideas, and competence at building long strings of spoken and written discourse. Most of the current research literature has focused on development before five years, at least in part because this is the time of the most dramatic changes. The consideration of later development up to adolescence has been mostly concerned with grammatical development, word meaning, and pragmatics. Later grammatical development will be concerned with how children overcome difficulties with certain kinds of sentences that "violate" general strategies and with how grammatical knowledge can form the basis of acquiring new information about language. The section on word meaning will describe children's acquisition of more abstract terms (such as "furniture") and their understanding of the various properties and interrelatedness of concepts. Pragmatics will highlight children's continuing acquisition of more complicated rules of conversation, including taking into account the listener's point of view.

Later Grammatical Development

Two different matters are discussed here: (1) some particular aspects of grammar which are difficult even at nine or ten years of age; and (2) how effectively children can apply what they know about grammar to aid in the interpretation of new sentences with unknown words.

First, particular constructions are difficult for children of six or seven years and even older. Such sentences are especially interesting because they seem so simple to us. Consider the sentences "The wolf is happy to bite," "The duck is fun to bite," and "The wolf is nasty to bite" (Cromer, 1970). The first is actually the easiest since the subject of "bite" is given and precedes the verb. In the second, however, the duck is only superficially the subject; that is, the duck is not the creature that will bite, but the one to be bitten. The third sentence is ambiguous, for it could be comparable to either the first or second, that is, the wolf could either bite or be bitten. While the second seems simple enough to adults, it is a problem for children because it is an exception to a very general rule that subjects precede, and objects follow, verbs. "The duck" is the surface subject, but the semantic object, of "bite."

In studies of children's understanding of such constructions, Chomsky (1969) and Cromer (1970) have asked children to act out sentences with puppets. Their enactments show that, up to about age seven, children consistently misinterpret sentences like our second example and always take sentences like the third example to mean that the subject of the sentence does the action indicated by the verb.

In accounting for this difficulty, we can certainly call on strategy 11 "Avoid exceptions," since sentences of this type are exceptions to a general rule. Yet the rule (to which these are exceptions) is so general in English that we might state it as a strategy; comparable rules might be stated for other languages. The rule, for English, is that any verb will have as subject the nearest preceding noun unless marked otherwise; for example, passive sentences are marked by the "by phrase" and "to be" form. This strategy can be stated as: 12. *Connect as semantic subject the noun phrase immediately preceding the verb of a clause* (Fodor, Bever, & Garrett, 1974). This strategy is somewhat different from the earlier ones in that it is unique to a language (or class of languages) and it is clearly learned. Children certainly learn a number of specific ways of coping with the possible complexities of the language that they hear. As adults, we utilize a number of simplifying strategies to make sense out of what we hear. These strategies in comprehension lead to a correct interpretation most of the time, but result in error on occasion as well as often determining our interpretation of what might otherwise be an ambiguous sentence. Thus it seems reasonable that children would begin to use similar operations for making sense of the language they hear. (See Clark & Clark, 1977, for a description of a number of such strategies used by adults.)

This particular stragegy applies also to another structure studied by Carol Chomsky (1969). The sentences "Ask Joe what to feed the doll" and "Tell Joe what to feed the doll" differ only in terms of the verbs "ask" and "tell." Yet the meaning is quite different since in the "tell" sentence it is Joe who will feed the doll and in the "ask" sentence it is the asker who will. Notice that "Joe" is the nearest noun to the verb phrase "feed the doll." Based on the strategy above, then, the prediction would be that young children will correctly interpret the second sentence, but that they would interpret the first as meaning the same thing. That is exactly what Chomsky (1969) found. With younger children, both sentences are likely to result in the child going over to Joe and saying "The hot dog." Thus children, by five years, have learned that the subject of a clause is the immediately preceding noun; with this strategy they can correctly interpret most English sentences. Their errors allow us to see that they do follow such a strategy; during middle childhood, most children learn the exceptions to this rule.

This discussion has anticipated our second topic, which has to do with how children can use knowledge already acquired to make sense of new information. Early in the study of language development, Brown (1957) demonstrated this fact. In his study, children (three to five years of age) were shown a picture in which a pair of hands were performing an action (like kneading) on a mass of confetti-like material in a container. The three critical elements in the picture were: the container, a countable kind of thing, which is normally named by a count noun; the confetti-like material, which cannot be counted and is thus likely to be named by a mass noun ("milk" and "sand" are mass nouns); and the action of kneading, which would likely be named by a verb. As they were shown this picture, children were told one of the following: (1) "In this picture is a sib" (count noun); (2) "In this picture is some sib" (mass noun); or (3) "In this picture you can see sibbing" (verb). Afterward, all children were given a choice of a set of three pictures, one of which depicted the same container, one the same substance, and one the same action. Children generally chose the element consistent with the sentence about the first picture. For example, if told "In this picture you can see sibbing," children selected the picture in the subsequent set that depicted the kneading action. Thus, even by three or four years, children can begin to use grammatical information to know what someone else could be talking about. When a word fits in the sentence as a verb, then young children can infer that the person using it is talking about an action.

Inflections, prepositions, articles, and a variety of other grammatical elements provide indicators about the part of speech (and thus the likely semantic category) of new words, phrases, and even clauses. As children master more and more of the language system, that knowledge further aids new mastery. Ervin-Tripp (1973) has emphasized this point. Clark and Clark (1977) have provided a number of specific processing strategies used by adults for comprehending language. Obviously children are moving toward such adult skills in the period from five to ten years, and even earlier. We will here give one of the Clarks' strategies as applicable to children of this age, although others might also be included. That strategy is: 13. *Use grammatical elements to determine part of speech and kind of phrase or clause.* This is exactly the kind of strategy followed by children in Brown's experiment, who could only know that "sibbing" is a verb because of the "-ing" inflection and who also knew that verbs most often refer to actions.

Word Meaning

A child is asked how dogs and cats are alike.

Child: "Dogs bark and cats meow" (Lippman, 1971).

Obviously children in later development continue to acquire new concepts and words and to refine old concepts. What is perhaps most important and interesting about later development of word meaning is the growth in the child's understanding of the interrelationships of words, including hierarchies of concepts and the various properties and functions of things and people.

Probably the most widely researched aspect of relationships between words is the association task, in which children are asked to give an associate to a word given by the tester. Research using this task has consistently revealed a shift in the type of response made during the period between five and nine years of age. Before five, children give words that are from grammatical classes other than the stimulus word. These responses are called *syntagmatic* because the stimulus word and the response word might be found in a syntactic sequence. For example, a common syntagmatic response to "table" is "eat" and to "soft" is "pillow." During the next few years, children *shift* to making primarily *paradigmatic* responses—that is, giving words that come from the same grammatical class, such as "chair" to "table" and "hard" to "soft." A conclusion often made is that the younger children link words to other words that are related situationally and the older ones produce associates based on similarity of form or of function or because the words are at coordinate or superordinate-subordinate locations in a hierarchy (for example, dog/cat or dog/animal).

Nelson (1977) recently reviewed the evidence on the syntagmatic-paradigmatic shift and discussed the complexities of finding a completely satisfying explanation for the shift. Children who have clearly mastered hierarchical relations in some domain may nonetheless fail to utilize those relations in the association task. Thus the shift must involve the salience to the child of particular relations; given a free choice of words, the younger child may not draw on known coordinate terms (such as cat/dog). Classroom tasks may increase the salience of certain relations in the child's memory. School may also teach children about the nature of such tasks. Further, the younger children may not understand the free association task in the same way as older ones, interpreting it in some way not congruent with the experimenter's plan, for example, as a playful situation. School teaches children about doing tasks, about following instructions, and about trying to discover what the taskgiver wants.

Thus the study of word associations does not provide any direct and easy answers to questions about the development of word meaning. The syntagmatic-paradigmatic shift is a striking and interesting discovery that reflects important developmental changes, but the changes are not only in the child's knowledge of word meaning. As Nelson (1977) concludes, the word association task is only one of many tasks that can inform us about the organization of semantic information. We will consider some recent evidence based on quite different and informal procedures.

Anglin (1977) has reported data based on interviews in which children between two and six and one-half years were asked a series of questions about a set of familiar words. The words included "dog," "food," "flower," "animal," "collie," "rose," and "plant." Thus Anglin included words at several levels in different hierarchies; "dog" is subordinate to "animal" and superordinate to "collie." In the interview, the series of questions about each word included: (1) What is a ____? (2) Tell me everything you can about ____. (3) What kinds of ____ are there? and (4) What kind of thing is a ____? The entire set of questions was designed to elicit a range of knowledge, including what these things look like, how they act, what uses they can be put to, and subordinates and superordinates. Anglin found that the youngest children (three and one-half years) gave about as many total properties as the older ones (around six years), but that the older children gave many more subordinates and superordinates.

Contrast these two transcripts:

E: "What's a dog, Andy?"

Andy (male, three years, ten months): "Ruff."

E: "Ruff? OK, tell me everything you know about dogs."

Andy: "They bite us. They bite."

E: "Um hum. What else? What do they look like?"

Andy: "They look black."

E: "What do dogs do?"

Andy: "They walk."

E: "What kinds of dogs are there?"

Andy: "Black."

E: "What kind of a thing is a dog?"

Andy: "Uh, I don't know." (From Anglin, 1977, p. 200.)

Then the examiner gave an example of "what kind of thing" a child is, namely a person, and tried again, with no success, to get Andy to suggest what kind of thing a dog is. An older child, however, responded quite differently:

E: "What is a dog?"

Eric (male, five years, seven months): "A dog is a animal."

E: "OK, can you tell me...everything you know about dogs?"

Eric: "Well, they bark."

E: "Uh huh."

Eric: "And they chase you, and cats."

E: "What does a dog look like?"

Eric: "A dog looks like, kinda like a cat . . . and a bit different. Um, cats have real big ears and dogs have kinda curved ears. (From Anglin, 1977, p. 212.)

Later Eric listed different kinds of dogs: German shepherd, beagle, bloodhound, and Dalmatian. Finally he responded to the question "What kind of thing is a dog" by saying that it is an animal. This transcript also illustrates the older child's ability to compare two kinds of things (dogs and cats) on the basis of similarity and difference, a rather sophisticated operation involving dealing with coordinate categories ("dog" and "cat") in terms of a shared feature (in this case, "ears") that are distinguishably different ("big" versus "kinda curved").

Anglin used the same procedure with three undergraduates who gave still more extensive information, particularly in terms of subordinates and superordinates. Adults almost invariably gave some of each, for terms at any level of abstraction. Children, however, gave only subordinates for the most general terms (such as "animal," "plant"); even the oldest children gave superordinates primarily to the most specific terms (for example, rose would elicit flower). Thus these children by the age of six years have barely begun to exhibit mastery of the complex interrelations involved with even everyday concepts. As a final aspect of this complex problem, let us summarize some comparable results with a radically different culture and language.

Brian Stross (1973) has provided an interesting account of the acquisition of plant names by children learning to speak a Tzeltal dialect in the state of Chiapas, Mexico. In this culture, plants are particularly important socially and economically, as they are the major source of food, medicine, tools, and danger (poison). Children in this culture begin learning plant names at around two years of age, though the first names are typically for the products rather than the plants (for example, banana). By four years of age, a child's plant vocabulary will easily exceed 100 and the child can indicate uses of many of these plants, primarily food. At this age, children know many generics ("banana," "bean") without knowing any terms for species; they also have some rudimentary sense of how to apply superordinate (suprageneric) names to unknown plants.

Between four and twelve years, new names are added to such an extent that the child of twelve approaches the adult mastery of over a thousand plant terms. But what happens goes beyond adding new names; among the other knowledge exhibited by children later in childhood (nine to twelve years) is increased knowledge of specific names (the particular kind of banana or bean). Further, the older children make identification of plants with less reliance on contextual cues, such as the location of a particular plant, and are able to take into account the full range of forms and growth stages. Most of all, older children (especially twelve-year-olds) can provide a vast stock of subsidiary information about the plants, including uses, dangers, how it is prepared, where it grows, when it bears fruit, and how to distinguish it from others. Stross writes:

> As an example, where the six-year-old can recognize the name a "catul uk" "black sapote" and also indicate that it bears edible fruit, the twelve-year-old is able to additionally point out that the unripe fruit can be mashed and thrown in the river to stupefy fish for catching, that the tree will grow to a particular height relative to other trees, and that it bears fruit toward the end of the rainy season (Stross, 1973, p. 138).

Thus the child's acquisition of more specific plant terms and the overall sense of taxonomic relations and properties, as well as the more elaborate lore of these plants, does not develop until later in childhood.

Children acquire a vast amount of complex information, especially during this period, and it makes little sense to restrict a discussion of word meaning to the acquisition and refinement of meaning of isolated words. The conceptual relations acquired by children are rich and diverse; unfortunately we have no adequate theoretical description of such relations. Currently there is a great deal of active research on such relations with adults; this research is currently called "semantic memory" (Collins & Loftus, 1975). Perhaps this work will contribute to a more integrated account of the acquisition of word meaning.

Pragmatics

Telephone rings and child answers.

Child (five years):   "Hello."

Caller: "Is your mommy there?"

Child: "Yes."

Pause.

Caller: "Uh, can I talk to her?"

Child: "Yes."

Pause.

Caller: "Please bring your mommy to the phone." (After Ervin-Tripp 1977.)

It is probably in the area of language function that mastery takes the longest even though function is central from the earliest. This is because function is often complex and subtle, involving social constraints, beliefs about what others know, sequencing of discourse, possible or probable inferences from what is said, and indirect ways of acting with language. Thus the development of pragmatic skills is linked to the development of social skills, to the loss of egocentrism, and to understanding when and why people are indirect. Consideration of this range of issues is beyond us here, but we will touch a few major points, particularly where there is current evidence.

First, the issue of explicitness or directness has received research attention, mostly in terms of children's understanding of indirect requests. Children, as the opening example on the telephone illustrates, can have considerable difficulty with indirect requests. Notice that the caller makes two initial efforts to ask the child to bring the mother to the phone, but those are ignored by the child. These requests are really indirect since they are questions, questions correctly answered by the child. Yet adults, in discourse with each other, quite commonly make requests in the form of questions. Ervin-Tripp (1977) has provided an insightful discussion of how children deal with the variety of forms of request. Table 2–8 provides examples of several types; each could be uttered as a request to "bring me the truck." The direct forms of request include simple imperatives and embedded imperatives which are comprehended correctly by younger children. However, the indirect (or nonexplicit) forms such as question directives and hints are more troublesome. The reason these nonexplicit forms are more difficult is that they are ambiguous as to function. A question, such as those in the telephone example, can simply be interpreted as a question, even by an adult. Thus, in reply to "Is that truck fun?" one can simply say "Yes." These nonexplicit forms do not "refer to the act or object desired..." (Ervin-Tripp, 1977, p. 166), so that the listener is left to infer what the speaker intends. In the more explicit forms, the act and/or object are specified directly. Young children do not produce the nonexplicit forms as requests and do not understand someone else's intent in using them (Ervin-Tripp 1977).

Table 2–8

Request Types with Examples

Request Type	Example
Imperative	Get me the truck.
Embedded imperative	Could you get me the truck?
Question directive	Is that truck fun?
Hint	That truck belongs here.

(Based on the discussion by Ervin-Tripp, 1977).

In related work, Garvey (1975) has reported that hints can be found in children's speech but only as adjuncts to explicit requests. For example, "That's where the iron belongs. Put it over there" (Garvey, 1975). Ervin-Tripp claimed that children as old as ten may fail the "Is your mommy there?" request on the telephone. Certainly much younger children may succeed with that particular request since "training history" in certain routines may teach the proper response on the phone. Also, children may exhibit apparent understanding of nonexplicit requests when certain "activity sets" are evoked; in other words, any form of request may elicit naming if a book of pictures is being viewed. On the whole, however, it is clear that these indirect forms are hard to interpret and less likely to be produced before five years. Thereafter, children will begin to understand

and use such forms, but full acquisition, including the ability to respond without redundant context and cues, extends well into the elementary school years.

A second general issue is the acquisition of rules of sequence in discourse. For example, in a normal dyadic conversation, a question by person A is followed by an answer (or refusal to answer) by person B. Similarly, a summons to conversation ("Hey, John") normally demands some response ("What?"), which in turn requires that a topic of conversation be introduced by the summoner (Schegloff, 1968). Yet such sequences are among the simpler ones managed by adults in normal conversation where discourse constraints pertinent to setting, listener, and previous speech (including jokes, stories, and lectures) operate in more complex ways.

Children begin to master some of these sequence rules quite early. Dore (1977) has analyzed the answers to questions of children between approximately three and three and one-half years of age. Questions asked of these children were usually answered, and answered appropriately. With wh-questions (those involving who, what, where, when, and why), about half were answered in the most direct and appropriate way—a where question answered by the specification of a location. Yet many other kinds of answers are appropriate, such as "I don't know." Further, even the questions not answered (about 27 percent of the time) were dealt with in such a way as to reflect a deliberate nonanswering in at least 83 percent of those cases. Finally, some of the answers observed by Dore indicate sophisticated knowledge of the presupposed information provided by many questions. Consider the following exchange:

Q: "Did you do that?"

R: "Tasha did it." (From Dore, 1977.)

The child does not answer with a simple "Yes" or "No" to this question, but rather implicitly accepts the presupposed claim that somebody did "that" (whatever it is) and tells who did it. Dore concludes that even children this young have mastered certain subtleties of the conversational game.

Similarly, children begin reasonably early to deal with the summons-answer sequence (Nofsinger, 1975). By four years, they can demonstrate their mastery of this sequence by deliberately violating the rules. A favorite entertainment is to summon someone, then deliberately not provide any conversation following the response. My daughter, at three and one-half years, had learned the following exchange. Although she was mimicking older children, she understood full well what it accomplished:

Lori: "Y'know what?"

Me: "What?"

Lori: "That's what."

After parental complaints about the endless barrage of that exchange, she spontaneously modified it to provide a minimum of information to constitute a conversation. So after she was four it became:

Lori: "Y'know what?"

Me: "What?"

Lori: "That's what. [Pause] And I love you."

Yet even among these sequences, the simplest to learn, there are many special cases that would be well beyond the skills of a child of four. Consider the person who answers the phone by not answering it, saying: "Just a minute, please." A child will not know how to deal with this (hopefully excusable) delay in answering a summons. Or adults often answer a question by asking another first, as when someone asks if you are going to a party and you ask what time it starts, then answer after they answer. These and other aspects of conversational sequences have not been studied developmentally, but the study of children's mastery of discourse will be prominent in research in the near future.

A third aspect of pragmatics, and one which has been the target of a great deal of research, is knowing what your listener knows and being able to take that into account in speech. One prominent approach to studying children's skills in this area is the work of Glucksberg and Krauss (1967), who used a special communication game. In it, two people are seated on opposite sides of a table with a screen between them. In front of each person is a set of blocks with different line drawings on each; the blocks are easily distinguished from each other, but are difficult to name (two examples are shown in Figure 2–1). One person must tell the other which of the blocks was selected by the experimenter and can do so only by describing it. Since neither person can see the arrangement of the other's blocks, it can be a difficult task, at least for children. Young children can play such a game successfully with familiar and namable objects (such as animals), but they are not successful with figures of the kind in Figure 2–1. Young children tend to produce short, idiosyncratic, and relatively uninformative messages (for example, "mother's dress") to characterize the figures. These descriptions are meaningful to the child

Figure 2–1

Examples of the Kinds of Figures Used in the Glucksberg and Krauss (1967) Communication Game.

Reprinted by permission of the authors and the *Merrill-Palmer Quarterly of Behavior and Development*.

who makes them, for a child can later select the same figure if his or her message is repeated back to him or her. But children are largely unaware that these idiosyncratic messages cannot be used by someone else. Failure to communicate in this game is quite high, even with children up to twelve years of age. Certainly this failure to take into account what someone else could see, know, or understand is closely tied to the egocentrism of young children (see Chapter One).

These somewhat disparate points about the acquisition of pragmatics have been provided to illustrate the range of knowledge necessary to use language to interact appropriately and effectively with others. Children begin in all of these aspects quite early, but generally continue to have some difficulties at least through most of the childhood years. It should be no surprise that language mastery of this kind is difficult, for pragmatic achievements involve sophisticated cognitive accomplishments and advanced social skills.

Summary

Later development (five years to adolescence) of language has not been as extensively studied as has earlier development. In this chapter we have emphasized certain aspects of grammatical development, word meaning, and pragmatics. The description of grammatical development focused on two main points. The first of these involves the difficulties that children have with sentences that are exceptions to the general strategy: 12. *Connect as semantic subject the noun immediately preceding the verb.* Such exceptions include: "The duck is fun to bite" or "Ask Joe what to feed the doll." The second point concerns how children utilize already acquired knowledge to aid in the interpretation of new information, particularly how they can use strategy (13): *Use grammatical elements to determine part of speech and kind of phrase or clause.*

The discussion of word meaning emphasized the range of knowledge children acquire during this period, knowledge of superordinate-subordinate relations, of properties, functions, actions, and uses. Finally, our consideration of pragmatics centered on children's use and understanding of indirect requests, simple discourse sequences, and their ability to plan utterances that take into account what others know.

CONCLUSIONS

Is there any doubt that acquiring language is a complex task demanding considerable knowledge and requiring diverse skills? Yet children everywhere master the task with apparent ease and in a moderately short period of time, succeeding whether their parents know anything about teaching or not. To account both for the complexity and diversity and for the ease of acquisition is not simple; the best conclusion that can be provided here involves a sense of what is acquired and how the child proceeds. To make the matter a bit more concrete, imagine that a mother has just told fifteen-month-old Johnny, "Honey, it's time to take your bath." What can he learn from this relatively simple utterance? What must he know beforehand, what must be available in the context, to allow him to make any interpretation? How can the mother's subsequent reactions aid the process? What strategies might be applicable, and how might they function as part of his overall processing of language data?

First, it must be clear from the development discussed in this chapter that Johnny will not at this age understand the entire utterance; he will selectively build his knowledge. There is a developmental progression such that some aspects are learned early; those aspects form the building blocks from which other aspects are acquired. At the age of fifteen months, probably only one word (and perhaps but a portion of that word) will be utilized. Later that one word might be known information from which other knowledge can be built. Thus, we would expect Johnny to begin with the simpler aspects of such an utterance, simpler aspects of sound, grammar, meaning, and function.

But, of all the information that is there, what determines what aspect in particular will be noticed and acquired? If Johnny knows nothing about any of the words and nothing about what his mother is intending, there is not much reason to believe that he will learn anything. We can predict, based on the *strategies* (see Table 2-9) that certain aspects of the context and of the utterance will be attended to. In particular, he can reach some interpretation if the utterance is spoken in conjunction with being brought into the bathroom and the tub being filled with water (strategies 1(c) and 2). Also, he should attend to stressed words (strategy 4), the end of the utterance (strategy 3), which is where "bath" is; however, only a simplified version of "bath" may be actually coded (strategy 6). Certainly, his subsequent imitation of that utterance will probably be restricted to "ba" (strategy 7).

Table 2-9

A Summary List of the Strategies

1. (a) Attend to intonation.
   (b) Attend to nonverbal cues, such as facial expressions and gestures.
   (c) Attend to context.
2. Process and connect what is immediately sensed.
3. Attend to the end of the utterance.
4. Attend to stress.
5. Attend to order.
6. Treat as equivalent sounds that are similar.
7. Simplify the production of sounds.
8. Learn the names of interesting things and events.
9. Conceptualize at the basic level.
10. Avoid exceptions.
11. Avoid the interruption of elements that belong together.
12. Connect as semantic subject the noun phrase immediately preceding the verb of a clause.
13. Use grammatical elements to determine part of speech and kind of phrase or clause.

Even when he is three years old, a full understanding of that utterance is unlikely. However, by then more will be known and other strategies may be applied. The strategies are also developmental; they must be differentially relevant as a function of any child's knowledge about situations, facts, and likely meanings, as well as the structure and vocabulary of the language being acquired. It is not even plausible to suggest that fifteen-month-old Johnny might pay attention to the order of elements (strategy 5) across the whole utterance when those elements are unknown, nor could he be sophisticated enough to connect the nearest preceding noun phrase to the verb (strategy 12). However, that is not to say that early strategies are never used after a certain stage in development. "Pay attention to intonation, nonverbal cues, and context" (strategy 1) continues to function into adulthood.

One critical question that has been neglected thus far is where these strategies come from. A complete answer to that question would require a fully developed theory well beyond what exists now. Yet some of the strategies do fit current conceptions of the nature of human cognition. Thus several of these strategies can be linked to the notion of short-term memory (see Ervin-Tripp, 1973, in particular). The fact that children first attend to the ends of sentences follows, in part, from the limited capacity of short-term memory and the fact that the most recent input endures in short-term memory. Strategy 2 (process and connect what is immediately sensed) also can be linked to the limited permanent knowledge possessed by the child, so that only events sensed within the time span (perhaps as much as thirty seconds) of short-term memory are readily linked. Also, particular information is selectively retained by short-term memory; for example, stressed words and, within words, stressed syllables can be held for a brief duration. When a child is able to retain a longer sequence, it will be retained, and even rehearsed overtly, in the order of input, somewhat like a tape recording of brief duration; this seems to fit children's attention to order. The kind of information stored in more permanent memory must, at first, be especially limited by what can be held in short-term memory.

Johnny's interpretation will determine, at least some of the time, what he does or says next, which will most certainly affect what his mother does next. If he does not understand anything, his mother will proceed to prepare the bath and will likely repeat this utterance with variations such as, "Look, here's your bath." Perhaps he will then at least repeat "ba." This interactional nature of language development is critical; based on Johnny's response, particular responses by the mother will follow. Her response may ultimately elicit an appropriate verbal or nonverbal response which will, in turn, elicit some feedback from the mother. Interactions about baths, food, toys, and so on will be repeated, often on a daily basis, as Johnny becomes an increasingly skilled participant. Thus language development must depend significantly on these interactional events; "Honey, it's time to take your bath" might never become sensible if it were isolated from all other discourse of any kind.

While it may still seem a miracle that a fifteen-month-old can make any sense out of the language input available, these general points provide a sense of how acquisition can take place. Our understanding of this rich process is quite incomplete, but there has been a rapid increase during recent years in our knowledge about language development. None of this has diminished the miracle of language development; increased understanding deepens our awe at what all children accomplish.

REFERENCES

ANGLIN, J. M. *Word, object, and conceptual development.* New York: Norton, 1977.

ATKINSON, K., MACWHINNEY, B., & STOEL, C. An experiment on the recognition of babbling. *Papers and reports on child language development,* Committee on Linguistics, Stanford University, 1970, No. 1.

BATES, E. *Language and context: The acquisition of pragmatics.* New York: Academic Press, 1976.

BELLUGI, U. The acquisition of negation. Unpublished doctoral dissertation, Harvard University, 1967.

BEVER, T. G. The cognitive basis for linguistic structures. In J. R. Hayes (Ed.), *Cognition and the development of language.* New York: Wiley, 1970.

BLOOM, L., HOOD, L., & LIGHTBOWN, P. 1974. Imitation in language development: If, when, and why? *Cognitive Psychology,* 1974, 6, 380–420.

BOWERMAN, M. *Early syntactic development: A cross-linguistic study with special reference to Finnish.* Cambridge, Mass.: Cambridge University Press, 1973.

BOWERMAN, M. Semantic factors in the acquisition of rules for word use and sentence construction. In D. M. Morehead & A. E. Morehead (Eds.), *Normal and deficient language.* Baltimore: University Park Press, 1976.

BROEN, P. A. The verbal environment of the language-learning child. *ASHA Monographs,* 1972, No. 17.

BROWN, R. Linguistic determinism and the part of speech. *Journal of Abnormal and Social Psychology,* 1957, 55, 1–5.

BROWN, R. How shall a thing be called? *Psychological Review,* 1958, 65, 14–21.

BROWN, R. *Social psychology.* New York: Free Press, 1965.

BROWN, R. *A first language: The early stages.* Cambridge, Mass.: Harvard University Press, 1973.

BROWN, R. & BELLUGI, U. Three processes in the child's acquisition of syntax. *Harvard Educational Review,* 1964, 34, 133–151.

BROWN, R., & HANLON, C. Derivational complexity and order of acquisition. In J. R. Hayes, (Ed.), *Cognition and the development of language.* New York: Wiley, 1970.

CARTER, A. L. The transformation of sensorimotor morphemes into words: A case study of the development of "more" and "mine." *Journal of Child Language,* 1975, *2;* 233–250.

CAZDEN, C. B. The acquisition of noun and verb inflections. *Child Development,* 1968, *39,* 433–448.

CHOMSKY, C. *The acquisition of syntax in children from 5 to 10.* Cambridge, Mass.: M.I.T. Press, 1969.

CHOMSKY, N. *Aspects of the theory of syntax.* Cambridge, Mass.: M.I.T. Press, 1965.

CLARK, E. V. What's in a word? On the child's acquisition of semantics in his first language. In T. E. Moore (Ed.), *Cognitive development and the acquisition of language.* New York: Academic Press, 1973.

CLARK, H. H. Space, time, semantics, and the child. In:, T. E. Moore (Ed.), *Cognitive development and the acquisition of language.* New York: Academic Press, 1973.

CLARK, H. H., & CLARK, E. V. *Psychology and language: An introduction to psycholinguistics.* New York: Harcourt Brace Jovanovich, 1977.

COLLINS, A. M., & LOFTUS, E. F. A spreading-activation theory of semantic processing. *Psychological Review,* 1975, *82,* 407–428.

CORRIGAN, R. Language development as related to stage 6 object permanence. *Journal of Child Language,* 1978, *5,* 173–189.

CROMER, R. F. The development of temporal reference during the acquisition of language. Unpublished doctoral dissertation, Harvard University, 1968.

CROMER, R. F. Children are nice to understand: Surface structure clues for the recovery of a deep structure. *British Journal of Psychology,* 1970, *61,* 397–408.

DALE, P. S. *Language development: structure and function.* (2nd ed.) New York: Holt, Rinehart and Winston, 1976.

DODD, D. H., & GLANZER, P. D. Environmental factors in early language acquisition. *JSAS Catalog of Selected Documents in Psychology,* 1974, *4,* 75.

DORE, J. "Oh them sheriff": A pragmatic analysis of children's responses to questions. In S. Ervin-Tripp & C. Mitchell-Kerman (Eds.), *Child discourse.* New York: Academic Press, 1977.

EILERS, R. E., & OLLER, D. K. The role of speech discrimination in developmental sound substitutions. *Journal of Child Language,* 1976, *3,* 319–329.

EIMAS, P., SIQUELAND, E. R., JUSCZYK, P., & VIGORITO, J. Speech perception in infants. *Science,* 1971, *171,* 303–306.

ERVIN, S. M. Imitation and structural change in children's language. In E. H. Lenneberg (Ed.), *New Directions in the Study of Language.* Cambridge, Mass.: M.I.T. Press, 1964.

ERVIN-TRIPP, S. Some strategies for the first two years. In T. E. Moore (Ed.), *Cognitive development and the acquisition of language.* New York: Academic Press, 1973.

ERVIN-TRIPP, S. Wait for me, roller skate! In S. Ervin-Tripp & C. Mitchell-Kerman (Eds.), *Child Discourse.* New York: Academic Press, 1977.

FLAVELL, J. H. *Cognitive development.* Englewood Cliffs, N. J.: Prentice-Hall, 1977.

FODOR, J. A., BEVER, T. G., & GARRETT, M. *The psychology of language: An introduction to psycholinguistics and generative grammar.* New York: McGraw-Hill, 1974.

GARVEY, C. Requests and responses in children's speech. *Journal of Child Language*, 1975, *2*, 41–63.

GLUCKSBERG, S., & KRAUSS, R. M. What do people say after they have learned to talk? Studies of the development of referential communication. *Merrill-Palmer Quarterly*, 1967, *13*, 309–316.

GORDON, A. Psychological and linguistic complexity in child language. Unpublished doctoral dissertation, Stanford University, 1972.

GREENFIELD, P. M. Who is "Dada"? . . . Some aspects of the semantic and phonological development of a child's first words. *Language and Speech*, 1973, *16*, 34–43.

GREENFIELD, P. M., & SMITH, J. H. The structure of communication in early language development. New York: Academic Press, 1976.

GREGOIRE, A. *L'apprentissage du language* (Vols. 1–2). Paris: Droz. 1937, 1949.

INGRAM, D. Phonological rules in young children. *Journal of Child Language*, 1974, *1*, 49–64 *(a)*.

INGRAM, D. Fronting in child phonology. *Journal of Child Language*, 1974, *1*, 233–241. *(b)*.

JAKOBSON, R. *Child language, aphasia, and phonological universals*, trans. A. R. Keiler. The Hague: Mouton, 1968.

KLIMA, E. S., & BELLUGI, U. Syntactic regularities in the speech of children. In J. Lyons & R. J. Wales (Eds.), *Psycholinguistics papers: Proceedings of the Edinburgh Conference.* Edinburgh: University of Edinburgh Press, 1966.

LANGACKER, R. W. *Language and its structure* (2nd ed.). New York: Harcourt, Brace Jovanovich, 1973.

LENNEBERG, E. H. *Biological foundations of language.* New York: Wiley, 1967.

LENNEBERG, E. H. On explaining language. *Science*, 1969, *164*, 635–643.

LEOPOLD, W. F. *Speech development of a bilingual child: A linguist's record* (Vols. 1–4). Evanston, Ill.: Northwestern University Press, 1939-1949.

LIMBER, J. The genesis of complex sentences. In T. E. Moore (Ed.), *Cognitive development and the acquisition of language.* New York: Academic Press, 1973, pp. 109–185.

LIPPMAN, M. Z. Correlates of contrast word associations: Developmental trends. *Journal of Verbal Learning and Verbal Behavior*, 1971, *10*, 392–399.

MENYUK, P. *The acquisition and development of language.* Englewood Cliffs, N.J.: Prentice-Hall, 1971.

NELSON, K. Structure and strategy in learning to talk. *Monographs of the Society for Research in Child Development*, 1973, *38* (1–2, Serial No. 149).

NELSON, K. Concept, word, and sentence: Interrelations in acquisition and development. *Psychological Review*, 1974, *81*, 267–285.

NELSON, K. The syntagmatic-paradigmatic shift revisited: A review of research and theory. *Psychological Bulletin*, 1977, *84*, 93–116.

NELSON, K. E., CARSKADDON, G., & BONVILLIAN, J. D. Syntax acquisition: Impact of experimental variation in adult verbal interaction with the child. *Child Development*, 1973, *44*, 497–504.

NEWPORT, E. L., GLEITMAN, H., & GLEITMAN, L. R. Mother, I'd rather do it myself: some effects and non-effects of maternal speech style. In C. E. Snow & C. A. Ferguson (Eds.) *Talking to children: Language input and acquisition.* Cambridge, Mass.: Harvard University Press, 1977.

NINIO, A., & BRUNER, J. The achievement and antecedents of labelling. *Journal of Child Language*, 1978, *5*, 1–15.

NOFSINGER, R. E., JR. The demand ticket: A conversational device for getting the floor. *Speech Monographs*, 1975, *42*, 1–9.

PETRETIC, P. A., & TWENEY, R. D. Does comprehension precede production? The development of children's responses to telegraphic sentences of varying grammatical adequacy. *Journal of Child Language*, 1977, *4*, 201–209.

ROSCH, E., MERVIS, C. B., GRAY, W. D., JOHNSON, D. M., & BOYES-BRAEM, P. Basic concepts in natural categories. *Cognitive Psychology*, 1976, *8*, 382–439.

SCHEGLOFF, E. A. Sequencing in conversational openings. *American Anthropologist*, 1968, *70*, 1075–1095.

SCHIEFELBUSCH, R. L. & LLOYD, L. L. (Eds.) *Language perspectives—acquisition, retardation, and intervention.* Baltimore: University Park Press, 1974.

SHATZ, M. On the development of communicative understandings: An early strategy for interpreting and responding to messages. *Cognitive Psychology*, 1978, *10*, 271–301.

SINCLAIR-DEZWART, H. Language acquisition and cognitive development. In T. E. Moore (Ed.). *Cognitive development and the acquisition of language.* New York: Academic Press, 1973.

SLOBIN, D. I. Grammatical transformations and sentence comprehension in childhood and adulthood. *Journal of Verbal Learning and Verbal Behavior,* 1966, 5, 219–277.

SLOBIN, D. I. Cognitive prerequisites for the development of grammar. In C. A. Ferguson & D. I. Slobin (Eds.), *Studies of child language development.* New York: Holt, Rinehart and Winston, 1973.

SLOBIN, D. I., & WELSH, C. A. Elicited imitations as a tool in developmental psycholinguistics. In C. A. Ferguson & D. I. Slobin (Eds.), *Studies of child language development.* New York: Holt, Rinehart and Winston, 1973.

SNOW, C. E. Mothers' speech to children learning language. *Child Development,* 1972, 43, 549–565.

SNOW, C. E. The development of conversation between mothers and babies. *Journal of Child Language,* 1977, 4, 1–22.

SNOW, C. E., & FERGUSON, C. A. *Talking to children: Language input and acquisition.* Cambridge: Cambridge University Press, 1977.

STAATS, A. W. *Learning, language, and cognition.* New York: Holt, Rinehart and Winston, 1968.

STROSS, B. Acquisition of botanical terminology by Tzeltal children. In M. S. Edmonson (Ed.), *Meaning in Mayan languages.* The Hague: Mouton, 1973.

THREE

Information Processing and Developmental Memory: An Overview[1]

Marigold Linton

An infant sees a brightly colored mobile and moves vigorously. Are these sights and movements stored permanently? Infants and young children show pleasure when their mother is there and discomfort when she is gone. How early do infants begin to recognize and remember faces? Children sometimes seem programmed to learn verbal materials. A rarely heard profanity appears discouragingly permanent and television jingles may become household pests after a few spirited prime-time renditions. Why then is it so difficult for the child to remember to say "please"? And why do multiplication tables take so interminably long to learn? A 5-year-old boy may forget where he left his jacket, may forget to put his toys away, or forget the time he is to return home from play. But it is a rare child who forgets a promise. Is this simply a matter of interest or of effort? Filled with enthusiasm the young child begins to describe an event or tell a story. After listening in puzzlement to such an account the parent will often plead, "Start again at the beginning!" These events or story sequences may lack organization, and children's efforts at recall may omit "important" elements while enshrining trivial features of the incidences. Do children remember events so differently from adults?

When we consider the memory of either children or adults, it is often prodigious capacity or unusual content that intrigues us. Indeed, memory feats involving specialized or esoteric knowledge may be compelling. However, the substantial array of information that is shared by virtually all members of a society is perhaps more impressive. Considered from this standpoint, most children attain truly remarkable memorial competence. A listing of children's knowledge—facts about their world, facts about themselves, rules for social relationships and interactions, rules for games, and rules about acquiring knowledge—can be expanded almost

[1]I wish to thank C. R. Neale for his invaluable assistance in the writing of this chapter.

without limit. But again the most cursory discussion with a group of children reveals remarkable diversity in both interests and knowledge. One child can name all the baseball players in the National League together with the current standings of the teams, while others can name the flowers in a spring garden, can be a whiz at "concentration," or can recite dozens of stanzas of a favorite poem.

As humans move from infancy to adulthood the amount they know increases prodigiously. Even infants, however, possess a small number of adaptively significant behaviors (or skills) which permit them to interpret their environments and react efficiently. With remarkable speed this original cognitive base is modified and expanded by experience and after a relatively brief period the young child's behavior is dominated less by the original capacities than by accumulated experience. While rudimentary cognitive skills are found in infants and very young children, knowledge relevant to conducting our lives and solving our problems expands, is reorganized, and matures throughout our lives.

In this chapter I describe both children's information processing and their memory, using theories of adult information processing as a partial framework. The probable continuity of cognitive processes in children and adults argues for trying to understand all human memory from a common framework. Such an effort will be particularly useful if, as has been suggested by a number of psychologists, "most of these processes probably undergo no significant development with age" (Flavell & Wellman, 1977). In the first section, I briefly describe a composite theory of adult information processing. In the second section I turn to a description of infant capacities. During infancy and early childhood information processing differs so markedly from that of later childhood and adulthood that it can scarcely be described in adult terms. In the third section I examine short-term memory in young children; in the fourth section I look at the acquisition of memorial strategies in childhood. In the final section I assess the adequacy of the adult model in summarizing research on children's memory.

MODELS OF MEMORY

Although memory has attracted the attention of thinkers since the time of the ancient Greeks, the systematic study of memory as part of a complex information-processing system came into its own during the late fifties and early sixties. Information-processing theories provide a framework in which memorial processing plays a critical role in the acquisition, organization, retrieval, and use of knowledge. These theories focus on the successive processing steps that information entering an organism undergoes. As you read the words on this page, for example, you are acting as an information processor. Words are perceived and attended to, patterns are recognized, meanings are accessed/retrieved, and some material is stored. Throughout such normal processing, information must be stored, sometimes only for a few moments (so that further processing can occur) and sometimes relatively permanently. When material is held, however briefly, we speak of "memory." In the last fifteen years several memory models have dominated research on adult information processing. Although each of these general models can be criticized for oversimplification and omissions, collectively they provide an excellent framework for summarizing our knowledge about information processing and storage. In the following pages I present a blend of the traditional models with selected features of the newer models. Because the theoretical distinctions among them are not crucial for our purposes, these differences will generally be blurred.

Memory Models

The typical memory model can best be characterized by a description of the stages from transitory to relatively permanent store through which information is thought to move and of the classical experiments that define these hypothetical stages. Figure 3-1 provides a typical summary of this model. The model postulates three discrete stages of memory. The first of these, the sensory information store(SIS),[2] is crucially involved in encoding material and is assumed to hold sensory information during the brief period required for further processing. Such information is either lost from SIS or enters the short-term store (STS) through the active processes of attention and pattern recognition. STS, a longer lasting but still brief store, holds information for immediate use or for further processing. STS contains a mechanism (auditory rehearsal) for recycling information temporarily back into the store, but information may also be encoded into a more permanent form and enter long-term store (LTS). LTS with its very persistent traces most closely conforms to the popular notion of memory. Some researchers have suggested that information in LTS leaves indestructible traces. Such a contention, however, is difficult to demonstrate and it seems more satisfactory to assume *relative* permanence of information stored in this memory. Let us turn now to a more detailed examination of the operation of memory.

Sensory Information Store (SIS)

Information impinging on our receptors enters the information-processing system and is held momentarily by the brief store, the SIS. Representation in this store is thought to be a relatively complete, literal copy of the physical stimulation that lasts about one second.

What evidence leads us to believe that such a remarkably brief memory store exists? Although a sensory store was first posited almost a century ago, the first persuasive evidence of this store's existence was obtained by Sperling in 1960. In a typical experiment, a twelve-letter

---

[2]Also called the sensory register, the icon (visual store), or the echoic (auditory) store.

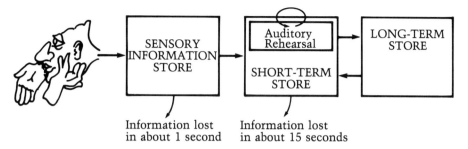

Figure 3-1

Information from the environment is picked up by our senses, is processed in the brief sensory information store, undergoes further analysis in the short-term store, and finally, under optimal conditions, becomes a part of our permanent knowledge in long-term store.

array (there were four letters in each of three rows) was presented tachistoscopically for a very brief period and the adult viewers called out as many items as they could from the array. Typically adults were unable to report all twelve letters. Was this simply a perceptual limit? Could the viewer simply not *see* twelve letters in so brief a time? Significantly, participants felt they had seen many more items than they could report. It seemed to them that letters from the end of the array were forgotten during the time it took them to report the earlier letters. But if you forget a letter in a matter of milliseconds, how can you show that you ever saw it? To the "whole report" method just described, Sperling added a "partial report" procedure. As before, an array of letters was presented. However, instead of reporting the whole array, viewers reported only the particular row of letters signaled by a tone presented shortly after the visual display ended. Because the viewers did not learn the identity of the crucial row of letters until after the physical array was removed, they could not "beat the task" by reading only the target row while the array was exposed. Participants typically could report most letters in whatever row was signaled, thus we *infer* that the entire array must have been available at least temporarily. The number of letters viewers could report depended on how quickly the signal occurred. The earlier the signal, the better the accuracy. If the signal was delayed just one second after the array had ended, partial report performance was as poor as whole report performance. On the basis of these studies Sperling argued that viewers had seen all the items and that the information was retained in a transitory store that could hold large amounts of material for processing by the system. He estimated that in adults this store lasts about one second before vanishing.

Additional evidence suggests that this transitory store holds raw and unprocessed information. To describe material as "unprocessed" means that the material is not yet interpreted, for example, that the identities of the constituent symbols are not yet known. To explore this feature of the store Sperling (1960) presented two rows of intermixed letters and numbers, for example, 3KN6, M2R7. In this case two tones might be used to signal first or second line, respectively, or two tones might signal recall from the whole array of just the letters or just the numbers. If the symbols in the array were already processed, the letters or numbers could be readily picked out; therefore, partial report performance for the letter-number condition should be similar to that when the first or second row was reported. Partial report involving letters versus numbers, however, was as poor as report of the whole array. The explanation is that symbols in SIS are indeed in a raw, unprocessed state. When a signal to report a single row occurs the viewer presumably begins to encode material in the appropriate row and can complete processing of the target letters before the store fades. However, when the signal to report letters or numbers occurs, there is no shortcut to determining the identity of the symbols. The viewer must begin with the first and process all of the symbols through to the end, reporting only the letters or numbers as the signal indicates. In short, the processing requirements for reporting numbers versus letters are identical to those for the whole report condition. In both conditions every symbol must be processed and while this encoding occurs the other symbols in the array are being forgotten.

A further series of elegant studies examined the characteristics of processing in SIS. How long does it require to encode a single symbol in SIS? Sperling (1963) found that up to about forty to fifty msec one additional symbol was encoded every ten msec (or one about every hundredth of a second). But for longer durations, with increases up to 200 msec (or about four times as long), virtually no additional symbols were encoded. The question then arises, what causes the abrupt changes in encoding rate? Although a number of explanations for this phenomenon were suggested it seemed likely that the encoding processes themselves became refractory after a limited amount of material is processed. The results of an ingenious study (Sperling, Budiansky, Spivak & Johnson, 1971) confirm this hypothesis. It appears that adults require about eight to ten msec to process each symbol but that only five to seven symbols can be encoded before the system becomes refractory.

In short, there has been found for adults a very brief holding store in which raw, unprocessed information is held for less than a second while the material is being encoded. Symbols are encoded very rapidly (eight to ten msec each), but the system works in short bursts before becoming momentarily refractory. We shall return later to consider how children encode material.

Short-Term Store

According to the memory models, newly encoded material is stored in a second temporary store. As early as 1890 William James argued that information was held briefly in primary memory (our STS) and only later proceeded on to secondary memory (our LTS). This argument for a temporary store separate from LTS was ignored for many years, but the results of studies in the late fifties argued persuasively for an intermediate memory lasting about fifteen seconds.

Peterson and Peterson (1959) believed that newly acquired information was held in a transitory store from which information faded rapidly. This rapid loss of information from the temporary store was not noted in most situations because it was masked by rehearsal. Peterson and Peterson, therefore, attempted to control rehearsal. In one condition college students were presented with a single consonant trigram (for example, DQB). The consonants were remembered with little difficulty—accuracy was usually 100 percent—even after brief delays. In a second condition, however, students engaged in a demanding simultaneous task. Immediately after the trigram was presented, students heard a three-digit number (for example, 947) from which they counted backwards by threes or fours (947, 944, 941 . . .) until a signal to recall the trigram was given. This difficult task effectively prevented rehearsal and permitted an examination of STS durability in the absence of rehearsal. After as few as eighteen seconds, students in this rehearsal-preventing task performed at chance level. This experimental outcome thus supported the hypothesis that incoming information was held in a temporary store whose duration was about fifteen to eighteen seconds, if rehearsal was prevented.

Just as STS differs from LTS in durability, it also differs in capacity. In a classic paper, Miller (1956) argued that the amount of information that can be held in STS is of the order of seven plus or minus two "chunks" of information. Adults can, for example, remember about seven newly presented letters or numbers. If the letters are recoded into words the number of letters recalled increases dramatically but there is a comparable restriction on the number of words recalled. Similarly, if the words are recoded into phrases or sentences the number of words we can recall is greatly expanded. Miller called these organizational units "chunks" of information.

A number of additional lines of research have been regarded as critical in distinguishing STS and LTS. These include (1) studies that suggest that verbal short-term memory is phonetic while verbal long-term memory is semantic; (2) examination of variables that produce differences in the early or late items in free-recall (see the section on serial position curve); and (3) investigation of the phenomenon of acquisition amnesia. Acquisition amnesia is a rare memory abberation (usually produced by brain trauma) that results in apparent inability to retain information permanently. For example, a victim of this disorder would be able to greet you by name for a minute or so following an introduction but would be unable to recall having met you some minutes later or after a brief interruption. To pursue the lines of research that were crucial in establishing the existence of STS would take us far beyond the scope of this chapter.

Adult short-term memory has indeed been so extensively studied that it is impossible to provide an adequate summary of the methods and findings. However, three classes of studies that have yielded results of particular significance for both adults and children will be covered briefly. *Rehearsal* studies permit us to examine the effects of repetition of materials in "refreshing" information in the STS and in moving it into LTS. *Memory scanning* studies permit us to estimate how and how rapidly we access information held in our STS. Studies that focus on the free recall of items from varying *serial positions* in lists have been useful in distinguishing between short-term and long-term store.

Rehearsal. Rehearsal is assigned two major functions by typical memory models. It is responsible for refreshing information in STS and it is a major mechanism for transferring material from STS to LTS. Without rehearsal newly acquired material may be lost permanently from memory. The effects of rehearsal have been extensively studied. Not surprisingly, it is typically found that items rehearsed most often are most likely to be recalled. More detailed analysis of rehearsal, however, has distinguished two varieties: maintenance and elaborative rehearsal (Craik & Lockhart, 1972). Maintenance rehearsal (for example, repeating or holding material for some immediate use) renders material immediately available but does not increase subsequent availability. Elaborative rehearsal (organizing or categorizing the material), intended to make material permanent, does have the expected effect.

Numerous studies (Hellyer, 1962; Rundus, 1971; Rundus & Atkinson, 1970) have demonstrated that under ordinary circumstances where learners know that recall will be required at a later time, rehearsal increases both the immediate and delayed availability of material. Under these circumstances adults engage in a wide variety of organizational and other memorial strategies to retain the material. We thus have clear evidence for elaborative rehearsal. A recent series of studies, however, has shown that rehearsal may effect the immediate availability of material without increasing recallability after a delay. In an illustrative study (Craik & Watkins, 1973), adults presented with a series of long lists of words were required to keep track only of the last word that had begun with some particular letter, for example, "g." Lists systematically varied the intervals between successive words beginning with the target letter. Thus the duration that a word was held and, presumably, the amount of rehearsal that each target word received was varied. Although all subjects readily give the appropriate "last word" at the end of the list, a later surprise recall test of the target words from all lists indicated that recall was not related to time the items had been held. Targets held longest in the original lists were not more likely to be remembered than words held only briefly. We may conclude that although rehearsal plays a significant role in recall, recall under varying circumstances demands different kinds of rehearsal.

Memory Scanning.   S. Sternberg (1966) wished to determine how we access the material held in STS. For example, suppose you have just been introduced to six people. Was one of them named "David?" In your search of the STS to determine the presence of a single target item, do you go through the stored items one at a time (serially) or are all of the items searched simultaneously (in parallel)? Sternberg's ingenious technique provided a test of this question. Adult participants learned sets of numbers containing one to five items. An example of a five-item set might be 75481. After a number set was learned, a single "probe" number, for example, 3, was presented. Participants indicated whether the probe number matched a previously learned number by pressing a "yes" or a "no" button. In this example, of course, a person would press "no." If the hypothesis of parallel processing is correct, that is, if a person simultaneously examined all numbers of a small set, the reaction time would be about the same regardless of size of the original set. Thus the parallel processing hypothesis requires that the reaction time function be a flat line when plotted against set size. On the other hand, for the serial-processing hypothesis (that set numbers are examined one at a time) to be correct, response time must increase as set increases. These predictions are summarized in Figure 3–2a and b. Sternberg found that processing time increases as the number of items in the set increases (Figure 3-2c), supporting the hypothesis that information in STS is accessed serially. Figure 3-2c also shows that decisions are made equally rapidly in negative sets (those in which the target did not appear) as in positive ones (those in which the target did appear). This finding is somewhat surprising since in a negative set every item must be searched (only after each item has been examined can you be sure that the target is absent) while with the positive sets it would be possible to end the search when the target item has been found (such a search is called "self-terminating"). The fact that positive and negative searches take the same amount of time implies that an equal number of items are searched, hence that both searches are "exhaustive"; thus in positive sets all items are examined, even if the item has already been found. Sternberg's research, therefore, suggests that scanning of short-term memory is both serial and exhaustive. This stands in marked contrast to the functioning of our long-term memory whose enormously large contents can be accessed so rapidly that we may readily infer that neither serial nor exhaustive searches are possible.

Serial Position Curve.   Finally, let us consider the serial-position effect in free recall. You have just joined a group and been introduced in rapid succession to twenty people. It is not unusual under these circumstances to remember none of the names you have just heard. If you do recall some of the names, however, they are likely to be the first or the last names that you have heard. The names you heard in the middle of the sequence are very often forgotten. Similarly, when adults attempt to recall a list of words they just heard they begin by recalling words from

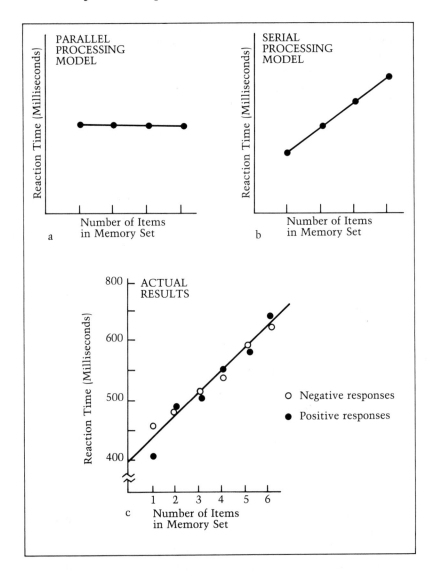

Figure 3-2

In Sternberg's memory-scanning task, reaction time is plotted as a function of the size of the memory set (number of items learned). (a) A flat function is predicted by the parallel processing model. (b) An increasing function is predicted by the serial processing model. (c) Actual results of the scanning task conform closely to the prediction of the serial processing model.

From "High-Speed Scanning in Human Memory," Sternberg, S., *Science*, August 1966, *153*, 654–656. Copyright © 1966 by the American Association for the Advancement of Science. Adapted from Roberta L. Klatzky, *Human Memory: Structures and Processes*. W.H. Freeman and Company, Copyright © 1975. Reprinted by permission.

the (just-presented) end of the list and then proceed to the beginning of the list. Again the words in the middle of the list are likely to be forgotten. The classic U-shaped function of free recall (see Figure 3–3) reflects the tendency of items at the beginning (primacy) and at the end (recency) of lists to be recalled better than items from the middle of the list. This pervasive memorial phenomenon has been documented repeatedly under a wide variety of circumstances in the laboratory and is readily observable in real-world settings. The models assume that these early items are better encoded or better rehearsed and thus are more likely to be stored in long-term memory. Furthermore, the items from the end of the list are well recalled because they occurred so recently that they still reside in STS.

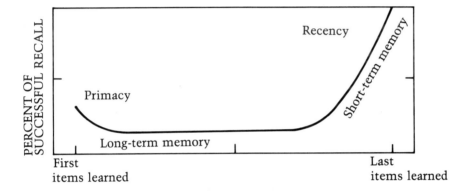

Figure 3–3

The classic U-shaped free-recall function results when well encoded materials are recalled from LTS (primacy) and relatively recent materials are recalled from STS (recency).

In summary, STS appears to be a relatively brief store that permits small amounts of partially encoded material to be held briefly for immediate use or for further processing which may result in more permanent storage. Although the unassisted duration of this memory is rather brief, rehearsal can be employed to maintain information in the store as long as it is required. Some forms of rehearsal are useful in transferring information to LTS. Although we have focused in this discussion on processing of information that enters newly from the outside, another related and invaluable function of STS involves holding information drawn from LTS, or intermediate steps in our own cognitions. When we attempt mental multiplications (such as 23 x 54) we find ourselves seriously taxed by the requirement of holding the original numbers as well as the intermediate and final products. This aspect of the STS has been called "the working memory" (Baddeley, 1976).

Adults make efficient use of their STS and most have good functional knowledge of the store's restrictions and limits. Are these limits similar for young children? What knowledge do they have about their STS, and how adequately do they work with this system? We shall return to these questions later.

Long-term Store

LTS is by far the most complex of the three memory stores. Indeed, LTS is almost synonymous with the functioning of the mind. Information already stored in LTS guides the processing of incoming information; categories and rules of storage representing past memories guide both deliberate and nondeliberate storage patterns. Of course, LTS (in the sense of memory most familiar to all of us) is the node from which specific representations of past events are retrieved.

Research on long-term memory, almost as varied as the store itself, can be summarized according to a number of different schemes. Perhaps the most comprehensive perspective is provided by an analysis of encoding, storage, and retrieval processes. Encoding and recoding go on continuously at all levels of memory. A number of encoding issues were discussed in the context of SIS and STS; one of these, rehearsal, as indicated earlier, is a process by which information may be moved from temporary to permanent storage. Other deliberate strategies for encoding information include organization of material relating it to other information already in memory, and a variety of mnemonic devices, for example, learning a rhyme ("Thirty days hath September, April, June, and November . . .") to help us recall the number of days in the months.

One of the most formidable questions facing the cognitive psychologist concerns the organization of information in our LTS. The amount and variety of information that can be accessed, the range of cues that provide effective prompts, and the speed with which most transactions take place all impose constraints on any explanatory model we might construct. Both the speed of access and the relatively rare errors that the system makes have provided some general cues about the organization of memory. Memories do not appear to be stored in the form that seems most reasonable to us, for example, as words or images. It seems likely, instead, that information is stored "propositionally"; that is, we hold in memory, for example, units more basic than words—a number of features that represent the word visually and auditorily, as well as the explicit and implicit significance of the words or ideas. In addition, it seems likely that information in the system is highly organized. It is probable that a variety of organizational schemes exist for different classes of materials and that a single set of memories may receive multiple representation, thus making access under different cue conditions convenient. Evidence for organization of some memories in a hierarchical array will be presented later.

Finally, we know something of the way in which material is retrieved from LTS. Both internal and external cues are effective in reactivating memories. The more explicit and complete are the memory prompts, the more likely we are to produce a precise piece of target information. If rather general cues are employed to elicit memories, we speak of *recall* (for example, you might be asked what happened in school today, what happened the evening of September 8th, or what factors led up to the Civil War). If more specific cues are used we speak of *cued recall* (for example, "What is Don's last name? It begins with 'K' "). If the proposed information itself is presented we speak of *recognition* ("Was it Endel Tulving who established the distinction between semantic and episodic memories?"). Recognition is more accurate than is recall, while cued recall lies somewhere between.

Among the wide range of long-term memory topics only a few can be touched in this brief coverage. The issues I have chosen are (1) the distinction between episodic and semantic memories, (2) the problem of accessing semantic information, and (3) reconstructive memory.

Episodic and Semantic Memory. Our memories differ in strength, and in when and how we acquired them. Tulving (1972) labels as "episodic memories" representations of specifically encoded incidents or events that are associated with a particular time. Thus any specific memory, such as memory for the last telephone call you received, is an episodic memory. By contrast, semantic memories are relatively independent of particular incidents or events. They are built up over time, on the basis of repetitions of the information, and are held as generalized world knowledge. Your knowledge about answering telephones or your knowledge about a familiar caller comprise semantic information. Other examples of episodic memories are getting a traffic ticket last week, buying a new outfit, or learning a particular list of nonsense syllables in a laboratory. To a surprising extent, though, we are creatures of our semantic memories. For example, we know the route by which we go to work each day even when we cannot recall driving to work yesterday. We may recognize a melody without remembering any specific instances of hearing it earlier. Our knowledge of grammar, our knowledge of etiquette, our knowledge of the likes and dislikes of our friends, and our understanding of their unique personalities are other instances of semantic information.

Although the implications of the distinctions between episodic and semantic memories are not yet fully understood, it is likely that their encoding, storage, and retrieval characteristics differ. Episodic information is acquired during a limited time frame, and it seems likely that unless the information is striking or exceptional most episodic information become nonretrievable after a brief period (R. Brown & Kulik, 1977; Linton, 1975). Semantic memories emerge from individual episodic memories and are acquired over a relatively long time period.

Accessing Semantic Information.   Probably the best known study exploring speed of accessing semantic information is Collins and Quillian's 1969 study which examined speed of responding "yes" to true statements such as "a canary is yellow," "a canary has skin," and "a canary breathes." Response speed was shortest when the descriptors were specific to the canary (such as "yellow") rather than generally characteristic of birds ("flies") or animals ("breathes"). Thus "the canary is yellow" was affirmed most rapidly, "the canary has feathers" required more time, and "the canary breathes" required the longest time (see Figure 3-4). On the basis of these and related findings a hierarchical

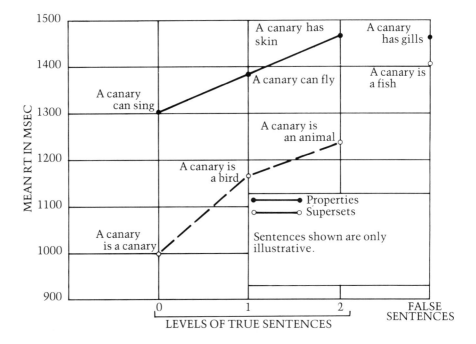

Figure 3-4

It takes longer to access information stored at a higher than at a lower level in our hierarchically organized memories.

From "Retrieval Time from Semantic Memory," A. Collins and M. Quillian, *Journal of Verbal Learning and Verbal Behavior*, 1969, 8, 240–247. Reprinted by permission.

organization of semantic information was inferred (see Figure 3-5). It is assumed that our most general concepts are at the top of the hierarchy and that descriptive information that applies to all elements in the hierarchy are stored at this level. Descriptors true of the lower levels in the hierarchy but not true of higher ones are stored at the appropriate lower levels. This system is "economical" because general information

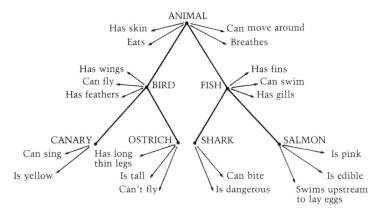

Figure 3-5

Information in long-term memory is thought to be hierarchically stored with general concepts and descriptions stored at the top of the hierarchy and more specific information lower in the hierarchy.

From "Retrieval Time from Semantic Memory," A. Collins and M. Quillian, *Journal of Verbal Learning and Verbal Behavior*, 1969, 8, 240-247. Reprinted by permission.

is stored only once in the system rather than repetitively with each specific instance. To answer "yes" to "the canary is yellow," you access information that is specific to canaries and is directly available. To answer "yes" to "the canary has feathers" you must know that canaries are birds and that birds have feathers. Because general information is stored at higher levels and must be accessed indirectly, it requires longer access times. These semantic-accessing studies, in short, provide us a simple heuristic for how memory materials may be organized. Because systems evolve and change, however, it would be simplistic to assume that all information is organized according to this scheme.

Reconstructive Memory.   A card file into which we delve for desired information and a moderately reliable video-tape recording are "models" that sometimes seem plausible when we think casually about our memories. One clear finding from long-term memory research is that information in LTS is not held in the form of intact global memories that can be accessed like file cards or replayed from some stored tape. It seems likely that fairly basic elements that may be called "attributes" (Underwood, 1969) or "propositions" (Norman & Rumelhart, 1975) are stored and that our global memories are reconstructed from these memorial elements. Because the reconstructive processes involve combining separately stored elements, plans, and rules to create the final product, it is not surprising that errors in memory occur either through omission of some original elements or through improper inclusion of erroneous elements in recall. Even individual words or names are apparently stored and accessed in terms of separate attributes. R. Brown and McNeill's (1966) tip-of-the tongue study indicated that even when a sought-for word is not immediately remembered, the number of syllables, some features of how it sounds, and other attributes may be separately available. The reconstructive nature of memory is also evident when more complex bodies of information are retrieved. Bartlett (1932) presented detailed protocols illustrating systematic changes in prose material resulting from the addition and deletion of information to produce recall that was simpler and better formed. Other researchers (Bransford, Barclay, & Franks, 1972; Franks & Bransford, 1972) have shown that when people are asked to identify material as new or old, they are relatively insensitive to changes that do not affect meaning and accept as old a variety of recombinations of old information. Loftus (Loftus & Palmer, 1974; Loftus & Zanni, 1975) has explored some of the conditions under which extraneous or incorrect information may be incorporated into existing memory structures. In short, these studies indicate that recall involves a reconstructive activity in which a wide variety of relevant and irrelevant information is employed to reconstruct a memory.

As we have seen, LTS holds the vast array of information we have accumulated over our lifetimes. We have noted particularly that memories may be stored (in elemental form, as attributes and propositions), that they may be organized (hierarchically), and that memories are probably reconstructed rather than recalled more globally.

Contemporary Themes

According to contemporary theory there is considerable flexibility in the kinds of analyses performed on incoming information. Information may be encoded at lower phonetic and graphic levels or it may be encoded at higher semantic or meaning levels. For example, analysis of a typical verbal input depends on the context in which input is imbedded with phonetic, syntactic, and semantic analyses proceeding concurrently. Theorists such as Rumelhart (1977) suggest that these analyses are coordinated by a central processor[3] that uses immediate information about ongoing analyses from all parts of the processing system to direct processing capacity to the most useful analyses at any time. This model implies that while promising domains may be extensively processed, less promising domains receive more cursory analysis.

One particularly attractive feature of contemporary models is that information encoding and storage relies heavily on individuals' past experiences and their unique perception or understanding of the occurrence. For example, as a young girl reads her first primer she may well

---

[3]The concept of a central processor is rejected by some psychologists who feel that careful analysis of how information is encoded is sidestepped by creating this "homunculus," a little person in the head whose essential tasks are to perceive, remember, and make decisions for us.

carefully spell out each letter, taking time to verify that the first letter of *dog* is a "d" rather than the potentially confusing "b." She may also use the context provided by the adjacent pictures of "Spot" to assist in this interpretation. After she has completed a sentence she may have to return to extract the meaning of the passage. The older child is much less likely to analyze the letters and will tend to focus on the word/meaning of the communication. Indeed, adults often fail to observe the omission of letters or even words in passages from which the meaning has been extracted with considerable efficiency.

Thus, speed of analysis is thought to depend on the familiarity of the material. Unfamiliar material is likely to be processed slowly and deliberately through all the steps. Highly familiar, meaningful stimuli which match the cognitive framework guiding the analyses may be more rapidly processed to a deep semantic level than are less meaningful stimuli. Rapidly processed material may be retained better, however, highly practiced material may be processed so rapidly and automatically that relatively little trace remains. Consider, for example, the wide range of verbal and motor routines we nonattentively run off each day. We often cannot remember whether we have turned off the car lights, set the brake, or removed the key from the ignition because these acts are not distinctively encoded in our memories as they occur. These new dynamic models give us a glimpse of a new family of active flexible information-processing theories that are potentially capable of incorporating individual differences, past experiences, and idiosyncratic strategies employed in encoding information.

Information-processing models are the product primarily of studies based on adult memory. We can then ask how the encoding, storage, and retrieval processes of children (from infancy to adolescence) compare to those of adults. In the following sections I consider (1) infant capacities, (2) develomental changes in SIS and STS, and (3) the development of memorial strategies in childhood.

INFANT CAPACITIES

We may assert quite confidently that a fully developed memory system does not exist in the infant or young child for neither the neurological nor the cognitive elements essential to the mature memory are present.[4] But the infant is unexpectedly difficult to study because not even the newborn enters the experimental setting with a *tabula rasa* (the philosophers' unmarked tablet). Infant flexibility in learning and memory tasks depends more on inborn disposition than on as yet limited experiences (for example, infants are predisposed to suck and readily modify their

[4]Sherashevski, the remarkable mnemonist described by Luria (1968), reported memories that he attributed to the first days of his life. Considering on the one hand Sherashevski's remarkable memory as an adult, and on the other the physiological constraints placed on such recall, it is interesting to speculate what the lowest limit for such recall may be.

behaviors to facilitate this important reflex). As infants mature, their capacities are increasingly dominated by their experiences and the semantic structures they have acquired, and much less by physiological restrictions. Finally, learning in older children and adults depends heavily on skills previously acquired and very little on built-in associations.

In studying the very young infant, the challenge has been to develop methods that demonstrate consistent evidence for retention. Other questions—for example, those about the store in which information might be held, the level to which information has been processed, the durability of memories, or the time sequence for emergence of the memory stores —have been raised but not answered. In this section I shall first consider several paradigms[5] that are useful in examining processing and transitory information store in infants: stimulus preference and habituation (which bear on the retention of materials), and classical and instrumental conditioning (which may provide, in part, an index of associative capacity). Then we consider Piaget's concepts of object permanence and the development of schemata that provide the bare beginnings of long-term and semantic memories in the infant.

Transitory Memories

Stimulus Preference. Stimulus preferences and habituation paradigms examine the responsivity of infants to the stimuli about them. Stimulus preference denotes an increased responding to a stimulus while habituation refers to a decreased responding to a stimulus. Responsivity depends on the age (and sometimes gender) of the infant and on both the stimulus' complexity and the infant's degree of experience with it. Alert infants respond to environmental stimuli; for example, they fixate visual stimuli. Up to about eight weeks of age infants appear to be "captives of visual stimuli." How long they look at stimuli depends on stimulus characteristics, with moving or high-contrast stimuli receiving more attention than static or low-contrast stimuli. Parents' knowledge of this relationship is reflected in their choice of objects to be placed near the crib. Very young infants' viewing time does not depend on experience with stimuli for they do not respond differently on the basis of familiarity. That is, they neither show preference to nor habituate to old stimuli. Wetherford and Cohen (1973) have found that six- or eight-week-old infants presented with a repeated stimulus intermixed with novel stimuli

---

[5]It is immediately apparent that these paradigms, constituting the major tools for examining memory functioning in young infants, did not appear in the discussions of adult literature despite their suitability for adult research. Although information-processing models have blurred the distinctions between perception, learning, and memory, classical and instrumental conditioning simply have not played a significant role in its recent development. Nevertheless, exploring these paradigms makes it possible for us to examine children's memory from the earliest days.

increasingly prefer to look at the familiar stimulus (over trials fixation of the familiar stimulus increases while fixation of novel stimuli decreases). The development of a preference for familiar stimuli in these young infants demonstrates rudimentary retention because, given proper controls, differential responding cannot occur without some memorial trace. By ten weeks of age, however, infants reverse their preferences and over trials fixation of familiar stimuli decreases while fixation of novel stimuli remains relatively constant.

Thus, preference for familiar stimuli is replaced by a preference for novel stimuli (indicated by habituation to the familiar stimuli); it is to the phenomenon of habituation we now turn. The brief summary that follows relies heavily on Jeffrey and Cohen's (1971) comprehensive review of infant habituation.

Habituation. If a stimulus is repeated, most organisms, including older infants, become less responsive to it. This responsiveness has been indexed by a variety of measures, usually by changes in heart rate and visual fixation. Several early studies found evidence for habituation in three- to eighteen-month-old infants with fixation time and heart-rate responses to visual stimuli (Kagan & Lewis, 1965; Lewis, Bartels, Fadel, & Campbell, 1966; Lewis, Goldberg, & Rausch, 1968). Methodological problems, however, prevent us from concluding unambiguously that habituation did occur in these studies.

Lewis, Goldberg, and Campbell (1969) performed a study across a wide age range: three-, six-, nine-, thirteen-, eighteen-, and forty-two-month-old infants were included. Infants viewed a matrix of lights in which the center light blinked on and off for thirty seconds. No habituation was found for three-month-old children; however, habituation increased regularly between six and eighteen months with no further increases in the forty-two-month-old group. The failure of Lewis et al. (1969) to find habituation in three-month-old infants when Wetherford and Cohen (1973) found habituation in ten-week-old infants may be attributed to stimulus differences in the two studies. Wetherford and Cohen employed a rather simple set of stimuli in comparison with the complex stimuli used by Lewis et al. The more salient, lively, active, or complex the stimuli the longer habituation requires and presumably the later the age at which habituation occurs.

In one very careful study, Pancratz and Cohen (1970) presented a single stimulus to four-month-old male and female infants for ten trials. On six subsequent test trials the familiar pattern was alternated with three novel stimuli. The stimuli were four colored geometric figures whose use was counterbalanced across conditions. Familiarization trials lasted fifteen seconds, and intertrial intervals were five seconds. Under these conditions, male infants habituated fairly rapidly but female infants did not. Since males showed habituation but females did not, it is not surprising that in the test phase male infants responded differentially to the familiar and the novel stimulation (fixation times of 2.4 and 6.9 seconds, respectively), but that female infants did not (fixation times of 5.3 and 5.5 seconds, respectively). Similar sex differences were reported by Cohen, Gelber, and Lazar (1971).

The picture is complicated, however, by an interaction between novel and familiar stimuli and novel and familiar environments. Jeffrey and Cohen (1971) summarize a study by Weizmann, Cohen, and Pratt (1971) by stating: "The pattern of results that emerges is that beyond two months of age, male infants display a more consistent preference for novelty when in a familiar environment but female infants prefer novelty more consistently when in a novel environment" (pp. 88-89). Another important pattern pointed out by Jeffrey and Cohen is that studies employing relatively simple geometric stimuli have shown good habituation while those using more complex stimuli have not.

In summary then, we find evidence of memory functioning in children six to eight weeks of age through their preference for old (familiar) items. Infants as young as ten weeks, but clearly by three or four months, show preference to novel stimuli and habituation to repeated visual stimuli. Finally habituation and responsivity to stimuli generally depend on the infant's age and gender and on the complexity (and familiarity) of the stimuli. Looked at broadly, these data suggest that gender is influential in determining how infants process information. If habituation is an adequate measure of memory, then the implication is that even in infants, memory is dependent on "meaningfulness" and stimulus complexity.

Conditioning. We can see evidence of retention in the very young infant but memory involves considerably more than holding information for brief periods of time. The duration of memories does increase but perhaps as importantly, associations begin to develop between isolated memory representations. Associations are studied in adults in a number of different ways; perhaps the most familiar of these are the induced associations among verbal materials in paired-associates learning, but associations may also be examined in other paradigms including classical (respondent) and instrumental (operant) conditioning. Unlike verbal association paradigms, these latter paradigms may be employed for very young children. Classical conditioning is assumed to involve the association between the existing response systems and new, previously unassociated stimuli. Operant conditioning is thought to involve creating of associations between existing response systems and reinforcement contingencies. Classical conditioning has been found in a wide variety of organisms and in a wide range of response systems in complex organisms. Because of its pervasiveness classical conditioning would seem to qualify as a very elementary form of learning. It therefore seems reasonable to expect to observe classical conditioning in very young infants. A debate continues, however, about the existence of classical conditioning in neonates (Sameroff, 1972). For example, despite a number of efforts to demonstrate such learning, neonates cannot be conditioned to associate a tone with a sucking behavior or a tone with a head-turning response. Two observations from classical conditioning studies are especially germane to infant processing capacities. (1) In the young infant conditionability depends on a complex interaction between the plasticities of the sensory and the response systems. By six months of age, however, there is a decrease in the domination of the infant's sensory/response systems by built-in associations and a variety of classically conditioned responses are possible. (2) Infants and young children apparently require (or tolerate) much longer CS-UCS interstimulus intervals than do adults. Successful infant conditioning studies frequently have employed periods as long as ten to twelve seconds rather than the .5-second interval traditionally used with animals and adults. The justification for the use of the longer intervals has been that neonates require more time to "absorb" stimuli (Fitzgerald & Brackbill, 1976), a concept that would seem to imply that encoding or processing times for infants is greater than for older children or adults.

Finally, let us consider instrumental conditioning in neonates. To what extent can an infant learn the association between responses and reinforcements? A variety of behaviors, including sucking and specific components of the sucking response (Sameroff, 1968), can be modified in newborns using an instrumental conditioning paradigm. In such studies, however, conditioned sucking occurs almost immediately on the first trials rather than showing the gradual increments in responding or extinction that are ordinarily associated with instrumental conditioning. These rapid changes may provide evidence for the plasticity of the sucking response rather than strong evidence for conditionability per se.

Why is it difficult to demonstrate classical conditioning if we can apparently obtain instrumental conditioning in the neonate? Sameroff (1972) argues that the two paradigms differ in their requirement of an association between a new stimulus and a response. In the instrumental conditioning paradigm the continguity between response and reinforcer strengthens an already existing response. Classical conditioning requires a response to be learned to a previously nonassociated stimulus. Sameroff argues that "the newborn's inability to be conditioned" is the result of "an inability to form associations to a new stimulus" (p. 191). According to him, the infant is "prepared" to make a variety of biologically significant responses which can come to be associated with a range of stimuli. The effectiveness of stimuli in conditioning stituations, however, depends on the infant's experiences with them. Conditioning can proceed only after a variety of experiences with the stimuli has been accrued.

Summary
The paradigms that are the most effective in informing us about infant capacities provide only meager answers to questions suggested by information-processing models. Despite this there are important lessons

to be learned about how infants incorporate new information. It is clear that in infants, far more than in children or adults, a dynamic interplay exists between physiological predispositions and the incipient memorial capacities (see especially Sameroff, 1972). If built-in representations exist in the infant—for example, how to execute sucking or head-turning responses—these responses may be increased providing that the infant is not required to *encode* a new set of stimuli to be associated with them. We have also encountered some provocative hints at the temporal course of infantile processing. The conditioning literature suggests that relatively long interstimulus intervals may be optimal for infants, perhaps a reflection of the longer time required to "absorb" or process information. In addition there is some suggestion that habituation proceeds best when intertrial intervals are very short—on the order of a half to five seconds. At least one researcher (Watson, 1967) has argued that the duration of the STS for young infants is not longer than 5 seconds or a period less than one-third that estimated for adults.

There appears to be little evidence for relatively permanent effects of habituation—one study that reports habituation measurable after twenty-four hours for neonates (Keen, Chase, & Graham, 1965) has not been replicated. We do, however, encounter evidence for the dependence of memorial processes on stimulus complexity and familiarity. Indeed, the differential responding by infants in a familiar versus a novel environment speaks of a relatively permanent memorial acquisition, although the parameters of learning and forgetting such "semantic" information have not been spelled out. Although there is no persuasive evidence that we are dealing here with the same memory processes we hypothesized for adults, the possible communality of these processes has considerable appeal.

Long-term Store: Beginnings of Semantic Memories

Object Permanence. The development of complex thought is dependent on a kind of bootstrapping operation. Semantic memories on the one hand are the products of past episodic memories but, on the other, once formed they guide the encoding and retrieval of later information. Craik and Lockhart (1972) emphasize that the form and durability of memory traces depends on the processing information receives—processing that is guided by semantic memories. Piaget and Inhelder (1973), similarly believe that memory follows the course of the cognitive stages; what can be remembered depends on the child's current cognitive level.

Let us return to the beginnings of semantic memories. As A. Brown (1975) has pointed out, the distinction between episodic and semantic memories proposed by Tulving (1972) closely resembles Piaget's distinction between "memory in the strict sense" and "memory in the wider sense" (Piaget & Inhelder, 1973). Piaget and Inhelder associate "memory in the strict sense," the equivalent of Tulving's episodic memory, with a "memory that is both particularized and also (roughly) localizable in time" (p. 5). They associate "memory in the wider sense," the equivalent of Tulving's semantic memory, with the development of schemata.[6]

Let me illustrate Piaget's general theme by recounting his well-known observations on object permanence. Piaget presented an object visually to his infant offspring. Before the age of four months (Stages 1 and 2 of the Sensorimotor Period) his daughter would respond actively to the stimulus, fixate it, or smile. When the object was abruptly removed there was no further response, neither signs of displeasure at the object's removal nor evidence of search for it. She simply shifted her attention to another object. By Stage 3 of the Sensorimotor Period (four to eight months) her response to the removal of an attractive object was a brief search, usually in the same modality as the stimulus presentation (for example, a visually presented object would be looked for but not felt for). By Stage 4 of the Sensorimotor Period (eight to twelve months) there was a full-blown multiple-modality search for the lost object or evidence of discomfort that the object was gone. Piaget interprets these results to mean that the infant has gradually acquired an internal representation of the object, or has, in his terms, developed object permanence. Almost by definition object permanence must be acquired before other, more complex, functions of memory may appear. That is, a plausible sequence of memorial development is (1) internal representation of objects present in the environment, (2) internal representation of objects that continues briefly after the object has been removed from the environment, and finally (3) internal representation of objects that can be reinstated after prolonged absence of the object from the external environment.

It is clearly premature, nevertheless, to assume that there is "no memory" (in the sense of no internal representation) prior to four months. Although Piaget failed to find evidence of responding to missing objects, the responses employed to index memory functioning are themselves complex behaviors that mature over time. Bower (1974), employing heart-rate acceleration and eye movements, found changes to missing stimuli at eight weeks of age, an estimate of the acquisition of object permanence that is considerably earlier than that obtained with Piaget's complex responses. In the following section we encounter evidence that lowers the estimate of the acquisition of object permanence to the first days of the infant's life.

Memory for Faces: Development of a Particular Schema. The evolution of memory for faces provides an alternative vantage point from

---

[6]These structures, according to Phillips (1975, p. 12) "form a kind of framework onto which incoming sensory data can fit—indeed must fit if they are to have any effect; but it is a framework that is continually changing its shape so that as many data as possible *will* fit."

which to view semantic memory development in infants. Findings on infants' responses to faces, however, present us with additional evidence that the information processing of the infant is extraordinarily complex. Until recently it was believed that the child was several months old before it began to respond differentially to faces. Carpenter (1975), however, has shown that as early as two weeks of age, babies presented with their mother's or a stranger's face looked at their mother more frequently than at the stranger. Perhaps more surprisingly, between twelve and twenty-one days of age, infants are able to imitate the facial gestures of an adult (Meltzoff & Moore, 1977). This latter behavior suggests the existence of an enormously complex information-processing system since a visual representation (the adult's facial gesture) must be identified with a proprioceptive representation (the child's facial gesture). Meltzoff and Moore (1977) hypothesize "that this imitation is based on the neonate's capacity to represent visually and proprioceptively perceived information in a form common to both modalities. The infant could thus compare the sensory information from his own unseen motor behavior to a 'supramodal' representation of the visually perceived gesture and construct the match required" (p. 78). Of particular interest is the fact that young infants can produce the matches on the basis of stimuli that are terminated prior to the beginning of their imitation. This ability to imitate following a delay strongly implies that very young infants (Meltzoff & Moore report imitations from one sixty-minute-old newborn) can respond to absent objects providing that both the object and the response are compatible with those special capacities that the infant possesses. The human face and imitative responses to it are apparently special in the sense that there are built-in predispositions linking the two.

The older literature demonstrates much less precocious development of facial schema. One reason for this difference may be a failure of other experimental methods to capitalize on the special associations between facial stimuli and certain classes of responses. Researchers (Kagan, 1970; Lewis, 1969) hypothesize that the young infant slowly develops a schema for the face. In these studies, as in the stimulus preferences and habituation studies, differential fixation of a face is assumed to indicate the degree to which a schema has developed. Very young infants do not respond differentially to normal and to disordered (scrambled) faces. At about three months infants begin to fixate regular and cyclops (one with a single eye in the center of the forehead) faces longer than schematic and scrambled faces, thereby indicating that a face schema is emerging (Lewis, 1969).

By four months of age the eyes are the most salient portion of the face and are responded to as a unit in the upper half of the face. It is not until the fifth month that a schema emerges in which eyes, nose, and mouth stand in a "particular relationship to one another" (Caron, Caron, Caldwell, & Weiss, 1973). Thus between the third and fifth months of life, there develop rudiments of a facial schema, a crude guide used in encoding and remembering faces. Although a functional schema has emerged, considerable additional refinements in the schema take place over time. Dirks and Gibson (1977), comparing responses of five-month-old infants to real faces versus photographs in a fixation time paradigm, found that these young infants "used only rather gross physiognomic features" to determine similarities between faces. By six months of age the infants recognize unique faces (Gibson, 1969) and can identify the faces of their caretakers.

Several months after the capacity to identify unique faces (and to develop specific attachments) emerges, infants begin to develop stranger anxiety (a discomfort with unfamiliar people which emerges in infants raised in the United States at about eight months of age [Rheingold & Eckerman, 1973]). It has been observed, however, that in societies where childrearing practices place the child in more continuous contact with the face of the caretaker, discrimination of faces (as indexed by stranger anxiety) occurs many months earlier than in the United States. Although careful cross-cultural studies of facial-schema development have not been done, it is reasonable to expect that infants would develop facial schemata most rapidly in societies which provide the most early experience with faces.

Summary

In this section I have attempted to characterize the earliest stages in the development of the infant's information-processing system. Comparing infant behavior with that of older children and adults is complicated by the use of very different experimental methods and paradigms. The picture is complex but I would like to summarize these studies in the unifying framework of the information-processing model: What do we know about the infant's sensory store? It seems likely that initial encoding of stimuli takes longer in infants than in older children. Slower processing is not surprising and would be expected both because of the physiological immaturity of the system and because the cognitive structures (or schemata) that ultimately come to guide information processing are, in the infant, only in incipient stages of development.

What have we learned about the infant's short-term store? Piaget suggests that in the very young infants there is no object permanence. Translated literally this implies "no memory" of absent objects. This conclusion, however, is apparently specific to the particular responses that Piaget employed as his criteria. For example, Bower (1974) found heart-rate changes in response to the removal of an object in children as young as two months. Furthermore, delayed imitations of facial gestures imply that very young infants can hold information for brief periods before acting on it. Watson (1967) estimates STS duration at five seconds. Finally, Sameroff (1972) suggests that although infants may be able to modify a response when an appropriate reinforcer is presented, infants may not be capable of associating two previously nonassociated events, implying that the creation of new associations is a developmentally more advanced cognitive operation than simply strengthening existing associations.

LTS whose operation is dependent on the adequate functioning of the short-term stores would be expected to emerge later; there is evidence for permanently stored material by about six months. The schemata that guide the processing system are present in inchoate form for such environmentally significant objects as faces, but these semantic representations are still undergoing refinement.

SHORT-TERM STORES

As we begin to deal with children in middle childhood, questions generated from the perspective of adult information-processing models are easier to answer. I begin by examining the early development of the two short-term stores, SIS and STS.

Sensory Information Store

Let us begin the examination of SIS by asking how the sensory store might change developmentally. First, the durability of the store (the persistence of the memory) may change with age. Second, children may differ from adults in the time required to encode (process) symbols in SIS or in the maximum number of symbols that can be processed before the system becomes refractory. It is theoretically possible for advantages in durability, processing speed, and processing maximum to favor either the adult or the child. To anticipate our story a bit, most research has shown that children process information more slowly than adults, but the picture is more complicated than that. Children's slower information processing may result from factors that influence memory indirectly, such as attention and incentive.

SIS Capacity. A series of studies have examined children's SIS duration.[7] If there are differences in sensory-store duration, how might such differences be demonstrated? Pollack, Ptashne, and Carter (1969) devised an ingenious method to test the duration of such spans. Let us consider their reasoning. If a brief dark interval separates two light flashes, what controls your ability to detect the dark period? One factor is the durability of the image created by the first flash. If the image persists for a sufficiently long time it may simply mask the dark interval. Pollack et al. found that adults detected shorter dark periods than did children. According to their reasoning, older individuals' increased capacity to detect brief intervals implies that children possess a more durable icon. This sugges-

---

[7]Because the results from the visual system are considerably more stable than those from the auditory system, all of the SIS research I describe for both adults and children involves the visual system.

tion of differences in sensory-store durability is only tentative, but let us examine another study that leads us to a more compelling, albeit still incomplete, answer to the question of relative duration of adult's and children's SIS.

Gummerman and Gray (1972) explored both the duration of SIS and the speed of transfer of information from the store. Second-, fourth-, and sixth-grade children and adults identified one of two simple shapes (a rotated T) under one of two masking conditions. On experimental trials the stimulus was followed by a patterned mask which "erased" the material presented earlier and thus rigorously held SIS duration constant by immediately interrupting processing of the SIS information. On the control trials the test stimulus was followed immediately by a white mask (a brightened field) which was assumed not to affect SIS duration. If performance improves with age in the patterned-mask (fixed SIS duration) condition, we may assume that processing speed increases with age since, with the SIS duration held constant, differences must be produced by variations in processing speed alone. If this result occurs a more complex prediction is necessary for the white-mask condition. If young children's performance is better in the white-mask condition than in the erasure condition, we may assume that their sensory stores are more durable, because only a more persistent store could compensate for the slower processing times.

With the patterned mask (hence stores of equal duration), Gummerman and Gray found that second and fourth graders performed less well than did sixth graders and adults. However, in the white-mask condition, children performed as well as adults (in fact, sixth graders performed better than college students). Since accuracy increased with age when SIS duration was artificially controlled, we may conclude that young children encode information less rapidly than older children and adults. The comparability of children and adults when SIS varied freely implies that the young children's stores are sufficiently durable to offset their slower processing times. In short, in most naturally occurring situations children should be able to extract as much information from a briefly presented display as can adults.

Several studies have examined processing speed of children and adults employing more complex arrays. These studies estimate both processing speed and the maximum number of symbols processed before the system becomes refractory. Haith, Morrison, and Sheingold (1970) tachistoscopically (150 msec.) presented geometric figures in arrays of two, three, or four symbols to five-year-olds and to college students. Students indicated the forms they had seen by pointing to the figures on a display (so that naming wasn't necessary). While college students recognized more symbols as array size increased, five-year-olds recognized approximately 1.6 symbols regardless of array size. These data suggest that young children process information less rapidly than adults and that a relatively low number of symbols are processed in a brief period. Blake (1974) confirmed that young children (four-year-olds) process SIS material less rapidly than do older children and college-age adults. In her study all subjects processed single-item arrays equally rapidly, but as array size increased (up to four items) the youngest children became progressively slower.

Eidetic Imagery. A discussion of the durability of children's visual store is not complete without at least brief mention of the controversial topic of eidetic imagery in children (Gray & Gummerman, 1975; Haber, 1969). Most of us envy those who seem to have "photographic" memories. Presumably those who have this capacity can perform such feats as glancing at a printed page and reading it back from a printlike visual memory when it is needed. Eidetic imagery, long thought to be a kind of photographic memory, has been reported with high frequency among nonliterate people and among children. Unfortunately, the research on eidetic imagery yields very ambiguous results. The studies that most strongly support the existence of eidetic imagery are the older ones that rely on individuals' self-reports about the persistence of an image. In these self-report studies, children were usually asked whether an image still existed and were not required to give additional independent evidence of the image's quality. Although children report persistent images, these reports are not related to the quality of subsequent memory. The perfect test for eidetics is one that requires them to report, after a delay, something that is unpredictable from their viewing of the visual scene. Using a sophisticated methodology, researchers have presented two figures in the same location separated by a brief delay. When these two figures are superimposed, they produce a figure unpredictable from either. The assumption is that if the image from the first figure is retained briefly then the second image will be superimposed on it, and then the unexpected combination of the two figures will be seen. This methodology has not solved the problem, however, because these studies have also been the subject of considerable criticism. Can we conclude that the eidetic image, if it exists, is a phenomenon related to the sensory store? This interpretation seems unlikely. The image described is too highly processed and too durable to be associated with this early memory store. Despite the intuitive appeal of observations on eidetic imagery there are few sound conclusions we can draw concerning this phenomenon. We know only that some children do have excellent memories and some do report holding these memories in visual form. Although the study of eidetic imagery may one day contribute to our understanding of children's coding processes, we must wait for paradigms that solve the methodological problems plaguing this research.

Summary
The studies examining children's SIS have extended our understanding of the early stages of young children's information-processing systems.

The observation that a child's SIS operates less efficiently than an adult's has been refined. It appears likely that the SIS system changes developmentally in the following ways: (1) the icon becomes less durable as children mature (Pollack et al., 1969); (2) encoding speed in SIS, especially for complex materials, increases developmentally; and (3) the apparent ceiling on the amount of information processed in a given time increases with age. Further, there is no evidence linking eidetic imagery reported for young children to functioning of SIS. Encoding information involves complex processes which become more efficient as the child matures. Do similar changes occur in STS, the temporary store in which newly encoded information is placed?

Short-term Memory

A consideration of adult memory models suggests four major ways in which STS may change developmentally: (1) in the amount or kind of *rehearsal*[8] that occurs; (2) in the *amount of information* that may be held in the store; (3) in the store's *durability* in the absence of rehearsal (the amount of time that information lasts); and (4) the speed with which information in STS can be *accessed* (the Sternberg paradigm).

Rehearsal. Children's recall increases with age; for example, memory span improves from ages two and a half to sixteen years. Not only does the amount recalled increase with age, but there are dramatic changes in the pattern of recall. These improvements are probably related to children's gradual acquisition of rehearsal strategies. Before considering the effects of rehearsal on the pattern or magnitude of recall, let us examine how rehearsal develops.

In an earlier section I distinguished two kinds (or functions) of rehearsal. Maintenance rehearsal reenters into STS material of subspan length, but its effectiveness in moving information into permanent long-term storage has been the subject of controversy.[9] Elaborative rehearsal may make material permanent, presumably by moving information from STS to LTS. In what sequence do these rehearsal strategies emerge developmentally? Maintenance rehearsal, which requires simple verbal repetition of items, makes relatively few cognitive demands, and might be expected to emerge relatively early to supplement less active ways of holding material. Elaborative rehearsal refers to more complex ways of encoding material. Rather than simply repeating "beeswax," a child may imagine bees or a honeycomb or think about the consistency of chewed wax or about taunting someone, "none of your beeswax." Each of these comprises elaborative rehearsal of the word/concept the child is trying to

---

[8]Rehearsal is a process closely linked to the strategies integral to both STS and LTS functioning. For convenience I discuss most aspects of rehearsal here, leaving until a later section the rehearsal-training literature.

[9]For example, recent evidence (J. Brown, 1976) indicates that maintenance rehearsal may increase probability of recognition, but not probability of recall.

remember. Because elaborative rehearsal is more complex than maintenance rehearsal it should develop later and require longer to become fully established.

One important way of examining the development of children's strategies and storage processes is through evidence of overt rehearsal such as explicit lip movement or pointing. One of the earliest studies on rehearsal (Flavell, Beach, & Chinsky, 1966) simply addressed the question of whether maintenance rehearsal increases from kindergarten to fifth grade. The experimenter randomly arranged before the child seven pictures depicting easily recognizable and nameable objects and pointed to three of them. After the pictures had been rearranged, the child was asked to point to the same three pictures in the same order. Accuracy and order of recall should depend on the amount of rehearsal. Pronunciation of the object names required conspicuous mouth movements; thus by observing the children's lips it was possible to determine whether they were using overt rehearsal. Of twenty children the number engaging in overt rehearsal increased from two to twelve to seventeen for kindergarten, second-, and fifth-grade children, respectively. Children who reported they rehearsed increased from two to sixteen to twenty for the three grades. It is somewhat surprising that fifth-grade children still used overt rehearsal (moving of lips) rather than the adult pattern of silent rehearsal. This study provides direct evidence that the use of overt (presumably maintenance) rehearsal increases with age. Moreover, a subsequent study showed that first-grade children who rehearse spontaneously recall more information than children who do not (Keeney, Cannizzo, & Flavell, 1967).

Conrad (1971) examined the occurrence of rehearsal among young children using a more subtle approach. Children were presented with picture sets containing objects whose names varied in acoustic (sound) similarity. Conrad (1963) had earlier demonstrated that adults recall acoustically similar sets less well than acoustically dissimilar sets. The most plausible explanation for this discrepancy is that adults rehearse the names of the objects and that there is more opportunity for interference among the items with similar than with dissimilar names. He reasoned that if children rehearsed verbally using common labels (the picture names) they would show poorer recall for the acoustically similar sets characteristic of adults. On the other hand, if children did not use verbally mediated rehearsal, recall of the two sets should not differ. For children under five, recall was similar for both stimulus sets. As this explanation requires, moreover, relative difficulty of remembering sets with similar names increased with age. From this Conrad concluded that children under five neither label pictures nor rehearse their labels. It should be pointed out that Conrad's study, and those of Flavell previously cited, do not preclude the possibility that children may use nonstandard labels or that they may engage in direct rehearsal of the pictures by thinking about them.

Several studies (Cuvo, 1975; Ornstein, Naus, & Liberty, 1975) have examined the course of rehearsal and free recall in older children. Cuvo (1975) examined rehearsal in fifth- and eighth-grade children and in adults. He did not expect the number of overt repetitions to increase over this age range, but he expected improved free recall, presumably mediated by improved elaborative rehearsal. Cuvo presented his participants with twenty moderately common words. Following each word participants were instructed to rehearse aloud any of the previously presented words for a four-second period. After several words had been presented rehearsal might include several repetitions of the last word or a review of earlier words. For example, following the word "horse" in the middle of a list one child may say "horse, horse, horse, window, horse"; another child might say "horse, yellow, window, paper, dress." Overt rehearsal (number of words repeated during the interval) did not increase with age, but amount of recall increased systematically. In combination with the earlier results, this finding suggests that maintenance rehearsal increases only to about the fifth grade. Cuvo also explored several features of elaborative rehearsal; for example, he found that the number of different items included in rehearsal sets (the variety of words rehearsed in any particular interitem interval) increased systematically with age. His findings suggest that elaborative rehearsal continues to change even after maintenance rehearsal is firmly established and that improved elaborative rehearsal produces better recall.[10] Cuvo, moreover, found that the words any particular child rehearsed most were most likely to be recalled. Since Rundus (1971) had shown a similar finding for adults, we may conclude that for all ages the amount of rehearsal of individual items is an effective predictor of recall. Thus amount of rehearsal allocated to particular items continues to predict within—but not between—individual variations in recall into adulthood.

As children mature they acquire a wide range of elaborative rehearsal strategies. As we have seen, they move from sheer repetition of words to skilled reentry of old items into the rehearsal set. They may reorganize materials into more easily recalled units. As long as there are demands for memory skills, individuals' proficiency with elaborative techniques is likely to increase. Although we shall not pursue elaborative techniques further, one need merely allude to the vast literature on the implementation and effectiveness of mnemonic devices with adults to illustrate that improvements in elaborative rehearsal do not end in childhood.

Interference Paradigms in Short-term (or Working) Store. As indicated earlier the interference (Peterson-Peterson) paradigm examines

[10]It is unlikely, however, that improved recall and modified strategies are attributable solely to maturation. Particularly when comparisons involve grade-school children and college students, it is probable that the populations differ on a number of characteristics including intelligence. Belmont and Butterfield's (1969) summary shows that intelligence, like age, is a good predictor of recall.

STS durability when subsequent interfering material is processed. The everyday prototype of this experience is recognized as a problem even by young children (Kreutzer, Leonard, & Flavell, 1975). You have just looked up an unfamiliar telephone number but are briefly interrupted before you can dial. The number is virtually irretrievable after only a few seconds. But the ability to hold information in the face of interference is not a phenomenon restricted to telephone numbers. Such difficulties are commonplace in our efforts to carry on conversations and to transact our daily business. With age individuals become more adept at being able, for example, to carry on complex conversations with increasingly large groups of people. But the young child's working store is particularly susceptible to interference. The child runs enthusiastically into the house: "Guess where we're going tomorrow at school?" "Honey, be careful, you're tracking mud all over the floor!" There is a dutiful tidying, then the almost inevitable reproach: "You made me forget what I was going to say." The studies examining interference developmentally suggest that children's rehearsal styles are partially responsible for the differences in susceptibility of children and adults to interference.

Rosner and Lindsley (1974) explored children's short-term memory in a paradigm derived from adult interference studies. The study examined five-year-olds' recall of word triplets under conditions of no delay, with simple (unfilled) delays, or with interference (filled) delays. In the task's game context children were to remember the three words and to transmit them to a moon man who could not get the information directly. To make the interference procedure more age appropriate during the interference delay, children did not count backward from some arbitrary number (as required in the 1959 Peterson & Peterson study) but simply repeated numbers presented by the experimenter. Recall that adult performance was essentially perfect with no-delay and simple-delay conditions but that performance was impaired following interference delay. In contrast, because young children rehearse inefficiently or not at all, performance after the simple delay should be poorer than after the no-delay condition although both should be superior to the interference delay condition. Rosner and Lindsley, in fact, obtained these results. The mean percent of items correctly recalled under the no-delay, simple-delay, and interference-delay conditions were sixty-seven, forty-five, and eighteen, respectively. Thus children's short-term memory, like adults', is susceptible to interference from concurrent stimuli but additional decrements result from inefficient rehearsal strategies.

Memory Span. The memory span task is one of the most familiar short-term memory tasks. A small number of items are presented (visually or auditorily) and the learner must repeat them in correct serial order. The memory span is the longest set of items that the person can correctly repeat. Evidence from a wide range of studies indicates an increase in span over the developmental period from two and a half years to young adulthood. For two-and-a-half-year-old children, the span is about two items; for five-year-olds, about four; for six- to eight-year-olds, about five; for nine- to twelve-year-olds, about six; and for college students, about eight. We observe that Miller's (1956) magical number of seven plus or minus two does not hold for very young children.

What factors are responsible for this improvement in memory span with age? Crowder (1969) provided a partial answer with a running-span procedure. He compared span lengths obtained under two conditions. In the first condition, spans were estimated from a series of nine-item sequences. Since item number remained constant at nine, the number of items to be remembered was predictable. In the second condition the critical nine-item sequences were imbedded among longer, variable-length sequences (running span); thus the number of items to be recalled on any trial could not be predicted. With running-span procedures, span was reduced for adults. In comparison with an estimated span of about eight under predictable span conditions, span was four to five items under running-span conditions. The running-span estimate is thought to provide a relatively strategy-free measure of short-term memory, while the recall *difference* between predictable-span and running-span conditions may indicate the strategic contribution to short-term memory. If this argument is correct, that is, if the acquisition of strategies is responsible for increases in predictable span then, unlike predictable span, running span should remain constant across childhood.

In their study of children's span Frank and Rabinovitch (1974) found the usual increase in memory span for third, fifth, and seventh graders under predictable-span conditions. Running span, which provides the strategy-free measure of STS, showed an improvement from third to fifth grade but leveled off for seventh-grade children. Studies of predictable span confirm that strategies continue to improve throughout childhood, but the studies of running span indicate that other changes, perhaps in encoding, which affect efficient use of STS also occur during this period.

Memory Scanning Paradigm. Hoving, Morin, and Konick (1970) employed the Sternberg paradigm to determine the speed of memory search in kindergarten, fourth-grade, and college students. Memory sets of two, three, and four items (line drawings of very common objects such as hammer and dog) were employed. Students from kindergarten to college required the same amount of time to search items; however, average encoding and reaction times were shorter for older individuals. These data suggest that children as young as five search their memories as rapidly as adults and that the search is serial and exhaustive. However, children encode material differently than adults, an issue that is examined further in some additional studies.

In the study just described simple line drawings were employed, and further research has indicated that the speed of memory search depends on the kind of materials employed. Apparently the invariant search time for subjects of different ages holds only if relatively simple materials—such as digits, letters, or pictures of common objects—serve as members of the stimulus sets. Baumeister and Maisto (1977) employed either familiar figures or random forms as members of their memory sets. With familiar forms they found very similar rapid memory search times for preschool, third-, and fifth-grade children. They found slower searches with unfamiliar than with familiar objects for all children, but the preschoolers' scanning was most impaired. This finding (in combination with several arguments not considered here) implies that preschool children hold complex information in STS less efficiently than do older children. To test this hypothesis, Baumeister and Maisto (1977) instructed half of their preschool children to use verbal labels for the random shapes while the other half were not so instructed. The use of the verbal labels speeded the scanning times but increased encoding times. Apparently children require considerable time to generate verbal labels, but children can use those labels effectively to considerably increase rate of memory scanning.

It has been suggested by Cavanagh (1972) that it requires about 250 msec. to scan all information stored in STS. According to his hypothesis the retrieval speed for any class of stimuli depends on the amount of "space" that the particular material occupies in STS. It seems reasonable then that preschool children can store familiar material like digits, letters, and common objects about as efficiently (in about the same space) as can older children. Unfamiliar objects, however, are stored less efficiently by preschool children than by older children who presumably spontaneously use labels and other mediators to reduce the storage space required in STS. Under instructions to use verbal labels, however, preschool children, too, are able to take advantage of the space-saving efficiency and they, too, show increases in retrieval speed.

Summary

If we return to consider the four issues raised at the beginning of this section we can summarize our findings as follows. (1) The distinction between maintenance and elaborative rehearsal appears valid for young children. Maintenance rehearsal in children increases from preschool to about fifth grade. Development of elaborative rehearsal begins at about the same time and continues over a much longer period of time. Rehearsal effectively increases the amount of recall. (2) Memory-span data suggest that amount of information held in STS may increase slightly from age two and a half to sixteen; however, it appears likely that only a small portion of this is attributable to changes in the system's capacity per se. Increased encoding efficiency and improved rehearsal strategies with age appear the most likely candidates for explaining the improved performance. (3) Although children are particularly susceptible to interference, their "less durable" short-term stores appear (again) to be attributable to inefficient rehearsal strategies. (4) Simple information can be rapidly encoded and accessed by young children, but more complex information takes considerably longer to encode and to access for children than for adults. Children can use verbal labels effectively to improve access times. To a surprising extent, the differences between the memories of children and adults appear to depend on differences in strategies for encoding information and for rehearsing information being held temporarily.

PROBLEMS OF LONG-TERM MEMORY: STRATEGIES

"All improvement of memory consists, then, in the improvement of one's habitual methods of recording facts" (William James, 1890, p. 667).

Before beginning a systematic discussion of children's long-term memory I would like to turn to a question that is in the minds of many readers: "What about my own childhood memories?" Many adult conceptions of children's retentiveness are colored in part by their own memories of childhood events. We each cherish our own "first memories." (My own first memory, at twenty-five months, is of some burnt cereal served me by my father on the day my younger brother was born.) We each remember significant events from early childhood as well as occacional bits and pieces that have been retained for no apparent reason. Does our ability to recall these items mean that children's memory must be good? Unfortunately, it is not clear precisely what our early memories mean because there is rarely a scientifically acceptable way to verify these memories. Theoretically we must contend with the reconstructive nature of memory (which I examine later in this section). In most cases we simply cannot determine the accuracy of the descriptions of childhood events we obtain. Furthermore, if such an account is independently verified, it is possible that recall is based on someone's later description, a picture, or some other factor. Research on adult recollections of childhood events has faltered because scientists could not judge the true age or credibility of these supposed early memories.

It is especially clear when we consider long-term memory that the memory does not develop in a vacuum separate from other cognitive skills. Comprehension of materials and memory for them generally increase with age and are perhaps inextricably related. Piaget (Phillips, 1975; Piaget & Inhelder, 1973) and A. Brown (1975), among others, propose a parallel development of cognitive structures and efficient memory strategies (ways of encoding material). Although the adult theories have been less concerned with strategies, one dynamic processing conception that fits well with conceptions of strategy acquisitions of young children is that of the "executive" (for example, Rumelhart, 1977). The executive is an active agent that plans action, allocates attention appropriately, and determines the order in which cognitive tasks are to be undertaken. It could, presumably, select among existing known methods for learning memorial materials. One can imagine a developing executive acquiring increasing knowledge about its world and devising increasingly complex strategies and plans.

Piaget and Inhelder (1973) are particularly concerned with active processing. In describing the acquisition and recall of schemata (semantic memories), for example, they talk about active construction of meaning, through assimilation and accommodation. Other researchers, probably those who have employed tasks focusing on the acquisition of more restricted memories, have commented on children's passivity or inefficiency. In this section we trace the development of young children as effective active encoders of the material they wish to retain.

When young children are confronted with nonsalient materials that demand active processing (for example, when they are required to learn a list of words), their lack of strategies for absorbing and retaining information becomes apparent. They sometimes seem not to comprehend themselves as memorial organisms. In the language adopted by A. Brown (1975), the maturing child must come to "know about knowing" and "know how to know." Examination of children's memorial strategies has followed two lines. (1) Researchers may look at what children say about their memories. Called "metamemory" by Flavell (1970) or "knowing about knowing" by A. Brown (1975), this knowledge or awareness may tap any verbalizable aspect of information storage and retrieval. (2) Children's use of strategies and the impact of such strategies on recall performance has also been examined. Such studies may focus on naturally occurring strategies or on how children acquire the skills they lack and their subsequent success in using them. These methods complement each other, yet for some tasks surprising inconsistencies are found between children's descriptions of their memories and their recall performance.

I begin this section by exploring what children say about their memories. Here I am concerned with (1) the strategies children consider appropriate for particular memorial situations and (2) children's success in monitoring their memories' contents and appraising their memories' effectiveness. In a later section I examine the strategies children actually use, the effect of changing strategies on performance, and the prospects of training strategies that do not presently exist. Finally I consider the effects of organizations on children's recall.

Metamemory: Knowing about Knowing

Kreutzer, Leonard, and Flavell (1975) list the following six memorial tasks confronting young children. (1) They must recognize themselves and others as mnemonic beings. (2) They must recognize that self-initiated mental activity is critical in allowing them to learn and remember things. (3) They must develop intuitions about the capacities, limitations, and peculiarities of the human memory system. (4) They must understand the relationship between properties of the stimulus material and prospects for retaining it (for example, that familiar material is recalled better than nonfamiliar material). (5) They must recognize situations where purposeful activity is required *now* if the material is to be accessed in the future, and they must learn to judge the amount of effort required to permit later recall. (6) They may acquire an almost limitless repertoire of deliberate and conscious memory strategies—planful storage activities that aim at facilitating future retrieval.

Kreutzer et al. (1975) performed unusually thorough interviews of kindergarten, first-, third-, and fifth-grade children, exploring their strategies for dealing with a variety of memorial situations. Answers to most queries suggested that children's memorial competence increases with age. The oldest children often dealt with the questions in the same way as adults. Some children at every age from kindergarten on showed surprising competence in describing their memorial worlds, but older children were more likely to respond appropriately. Young children more often than older ones misunderstood the problem situation and its memorial consequences and, when deliberate memorial strategies were sought, they more often could describe no strategies or only inefficient ones.

Variables Affecting Performance: Person. When children were asked to assess their own and others' memories, Kreutzer et al. found older children more likely than young to recognize that individuals differ in their memorial capacities and that situations vary in their memorial demands. They were more likely to qualify their memorial competence and, for example, recognize that they sometimes forget, that they sometimes were good rememberers, and that sometimes their friends remembered better than they. Children demonstrated their growing understanding of memory development by attributing better memories to older individuals and assigning simpler memorial schemes to younger children.

Variables Affecting Performance: Task. More older than younger children appreciated the negative effects of retroactive interference. (Which child would remember the names of more children from a party, the one who went directly home after the party or the one who played with some other children he did not know following the party?) Children as young as kindergarten recognized that savings occurred in relearning information learned earlier and then forgotten, but older children were more likely to provide "savings-type" explanations. With increasing age, more children recognize that imbedding recall items in a story format aids memory. Similarly, older children are more likely to know that related words (opposites like boy-girl, hard-easy, black-white) are learned more easily than are arbitrary pairs. Younger children's difficulty with this judgment is poignantly captured in the performance of one four-and-a-half-year-old who continued to maintain that related pairs were more difficult even after she had learned a list and had gotten all the opposites (but not the arbitrary pairs) correct.

Sensitivity to the Need to Put Out Special Effort. Children were presented with the following situation: "If you wanted to phone your friend and someone told you the phone number, would it make any difference if you called right away after you heard the number or if you got a drink of water first?" (Kreutzer et al., 1975, p. 9). More older than younger children were aware of the problem of forgetting from short-term memory. Only the oldest children appeared to recognize the effectiveness of rehearsal in preventing short-term memory loss (an age difference we encountered earlier) and suggested they would rehearse the material. Many children at every age suggested using external memorial aides—for example, writing down a telephone number that had to be remembered or placing objects where they could not be missed when needed.

Perhaps the most striking features of these observations on children's metamemories is the relative sophistication of their verbalizations of memorial relationships in the world in comparison with their implementations of strategies. In the next section we look more closely at the relationships among memory appraisal, mnemonic strategies, and recall performance.

Memory Appraisal: Knowing What You Know

Tasks Producing Overestimation. Kreutzer et al. (1975) suggest that older children are more realistic in estimating their capacity to remember material. The interview data, however, do not tell us exactly how children's understanding of their memory and their memory capacities change with age. A number of studies have assessed concurrent changes in their ability to estimate and in their memory capacity. Descriptions from the literature and anecdotes from researchers indicate convincingly how difficult it is for young children to appraise the contents of their memories. "Learn these pictures," the young boy is instructed. He glances briefly at them, perhaps repeats their names out loud, and then insists he knows them. When the materials are removed, he is baffled that he cannot recall the names.[11]

In their early seminal study, Flavell, Friedrichs, and Hoyt (1970) examined changes in children's estimates of the longest word list they could correctly recall. Children four to nine years of age were given easily nameable pictures in sets of increasing size: one, two, three, and so on, up to ten. For each list length, children were asked whether they thought they could recall a list that long. Following this memory appraisal task, children's actual list-learning capacity (memory span) was determined. They were verbally presented with word lists whose length varied from

[11]Judgments of how well material is known continue to be difficult even for adults. College students, if their reports to professors are to be believed, experience similar difficulties in knowing when they have learned class materials. Even after they feel they have learned the material to a reasonable level, some students "draw a blank" when faced with questions on an examination.

one to ten items. Memory span (the number of items correctly recalled after one repetition) increased with age. Although all children overestimated the longest list they could recall, older children overestimated less than younger ones. Flavell et al. found that a surprising 60 percent of the preschoolers but only 25 percent of the fourth graders predicted they could recall the longest (ten-item) list.

Young children's overoptimistic memory appraisal has been explored in a number of additional studies. For example, Markman (1973) found that memory appraisal improved with repetition of the task and that training readily improved appraisal accuracy for some five-year-old children. Yussen and Levy (1975) examined the effects on appraisal performance of: (1) information from peer norms and (2) feedback (indication of success or failure) from their own performance. Surprisingly, the feedback condition (failure versus success on the demonstration trials) had no effect on the children's memory-span estimates. Several preschoolers predicted memory spans of nine or ten (although they had just been shown that they could not remember lists that long). These predictions were accompanied by comments such as: "If you gave me a different list like that, I could do it" (Yussen & Levy, 1975, p. 507). Coming to use feedback from your own performance to improve future estimates appears surprisingly difficult. Similarly, preschool children did not modify their estimates on the basis of information about their peers' performance. Third graders in the peer norm condition, however, substantially lowered their estimates indicating their sensitivity to information on their probable memory limitations.

A Task Producing Accurate Estimation. Kelly, Scholnick, Travers, and Johnson (1976) examined children's assessment using the Atkinson, Hansen, and Bernbach (1964) picture-location task. Children were presented with a series of from three to ten pictures and then were asked to indicate the original picture locations by placing duplicate pictures in the same order. Thus, unlike the appraisal tasks which depend on verbal recall of item content (and hence on verbal encoding and retrieval), the present task requires only that the child retrieve the location of the item.[12] This item-location procedure permits particularly flexible examination of appraisal and recall. Both the number of items placed correctly and the longest list perfectly recalled increased from kindergarten to fourth grade. How well could children predict their own specific performance under these conditions? In this study, comparisons of each

---

[12]Young children's recall of item location, while not as accurate as that of adults, is good (see Kosslyn, Pick, & Fariello, 1974). This task may be different from other tasks we have considered since external cues, which young children used effectively (Kreutzer et al. 1975), may predominate over internal cues. Furthermore, the item-location task depends on reconstruction rather than pure recall, thus the child need only retrieve the memory scheme rather than generate the scheme unaided. An argument may be made that ordering items is easier than serial recall and that difficulties in memory-estimation tasks are linked somehow to the child's difficulty in estimating accessibility of memories (Kelly et al. 1976).

child's predictions with actual recall on the same list indicated 75 percent accuracy. Appraisal accuracy in this item-location task was far superior to that found in the earlier list-learning studies.

Factors Leading to Overestimation. Monroe and Lange (1977) attempted to determine the stimulus factors leading to overestimates in young children's memory assessment. Kreutzer et al. (1975) had observed that young children thought they would remember colored items better than black and white ones, but they did not examine actual recall performance. If children overestimate on the basis of salience, Monroe and Lange reasoned that the youngest children would overpredict their recall of physical objects more than pictures. Their preschoolers predicted that they would remember objects better than pictures, unlike older children who did not *predict* differential recall for pictures and objects. However, like second and fifth graders, preschoolers recalled an equal number of objects and pictures. Finally, in a series of results that suggest additional complexities in the relationships among prediction (assessment), recall, and age, Monroe and Lange found that preschoolers used order of items rather than organization as the basis of their predictions, but that their performance, like that of older children, was influenced by categorization schemes. Thus, children's accuracy in estimating their memory capacity depended on the compatibility of the memory task with their characteristic basis for making predictions.

The ability to appraise memory's contents is a complex skill whose evolution is somewhat independent of the changes that take place in the child's ability to recall information. Early studies that asked for global estimates of memory ("could you recall a list as long as this?") yielded overoptimistic memory estimates from young children. Recent studies that have concretized the task (by requesting item-by-item information) have shown that young children can estimate the contents of their memory quite accurately. Finally, young children do not recognize the specific characteristics that make material memorable for them. For example, they overemphasize physical salience and item order and do not yet appreciate the significance of organization.

Memory Appraisal and Memory Strategies. We might expect that children with good memory-appraisal skills would also show good recall. That is, it is plausible that "knowing how to know" and "knowing" should be related. We can perhaps better understand children's verbal estimates if we examine the relationship between estimates and children's memorial strategies. At least one researcher (Markman, 1973) found that training memory-appraisal skills did not improve memory span. Kelly et al. (1976) explored how children apply their memory appraisal skills to improve performance in memory tasks. In a recall task involving superspan lists children were asked to reproduce the original order in which items had occurred. Following the recall task they made judgments of item accuracy and then chose the items they wished to study on the next trial. Younger children studied all items more than did older children, presumably because the items were more difficult for them. Moreover, all children studied the items they missed more frequently than the items they already knew. Niemark, Slotnick, and Ulrich (1971), too, noted that at every age some children segregated out items missed on earlier trials. Masur, McIntyre, and Flavell (1973), however, found that older children focused their review on items they had previously missed while first graders were equally likely to study items previously missed and those successfully recalled. Moreover, young children benefited equally from reviewing both kinds of items. Older children identified missed items more accurately than did younger ones and also benefited more from studying and reviewing missed items.

At least some of these studies suggest that young children review items relatively superficially and that unlearned (missed) items receive only slight emphasis. College students refresh their memories, but in addition they retest their recall and are more likely to adopt strategies such as breaking the list into subsections for intensive study or using cumulative rehearsal. Young children do not use even those appraisal skills they have to produce useful strategies (see Flavell et al., 1970). As a result, children do not prepare themselves for recall as well as adults, even when their appraisal skills are equal. Not surprisingly then, memory-appraisal skills have not been found to be related to other memorial skills such as recall readiness, study strategy, and actual recall.

Difficulties in selecting the most relevant material for study do not end in middle childhood. Computer-directed rehearsal is better than self-selected rehearsal for college students precisely because the computer drops out material the learner already knows and presents material the learner does not know (Atkinson, 1968). Left to their own resources, college students, like young children, tend to spend too much time rehearsing items they already know and too little time on items not yet learned.

Rehearsal Training

In an earlier section I discussed the developmental sequence in which rehearsal strategies were acquired. A question that arises naturally (both from theoretical and from practical educational concerns) is whether strategies that hasten information acquisition can be taught. In this section, therefore, we consider the extent to which rehearsal strategies can be deliberately trained.

A number of studies have investigated the effectiveness of training rehearsal in children who are not skilled rehearsers. Keeney et al. (1967), whose investigation of spontaneous rehearsal was mentioned earlier, also attempted to train rehearsal. They asked: (1) Can children who do not rehearse be easily trained to rehearse? (2) Do children trained to rehearse recall as well as those who rehearse spontaneously? (3) How permanent is rehearsal training? That is, will a child trained or required to rehearse continue to rehearse when the requirement is eliminated?[13]

First-grade children were asked to indicate the three items in a seven-item display that the experimenter had previously indicated. On the basis of their performance two extreme groups, a group of rehearsers and a group of nonrehearsers, were selected. On the training trials, all of the nonrehearsers and half of the rehearsers were instructed to rehearse. Following trials on which rehearsal was required, there were rehearsal-optional trials. Children were easily trained to rehearse, and following training their performance was comparable to that of the natural rehearsers. However, given the option to rehearse or not, ten of seventeen original nonrehearsers showed no overt signs of rehearsal and performed less well on the final trials. In this case a task was selected that in some first-grade children did not elicit spontaneous rehearsal strategies. These children benefited from rehearsal instructions but they reverted to a nonrehearsing mode when the rehearsal requirement was eliminated.[14]

Organization

In an earlier section it was noted that organization begins to influence children's recall some time before its value in improving recall is appreciated. Let us return now to a fuller examination of organization in recall.

Why should organization be so effective in improving recall? Organizing materials, clustering them, and categorizing them aid memory because these processes require more active and thorough encoding of materials. Furthermore, accessibility of memories is increased through organizational strategies, especially those that use the naturally occurring hierarchical organization of the memory system.

Although it has generally been found that free recall increases with age (Jablonski, 1974), the relationship between age and organization (for example, the arrangement of items into categories) is not clear. It has generally been assumed that as organization increases, recall also increases; however, the relationship among these variables is somewhat in question (Jablonski, 1974).

Weist and Crawford (1977) assumed that if organizational strategies were reflected in rehearsal or recall of young children that their form

---

[13]Flavell (for example, Keeney, Cannizzo, & Flavell, 1967) has adopted the language of "production" and "mediation" deficiencies (and inefficiencies) to describe the failure to employ strategies and inability to profit from use of the strategies, respectively.

[14]This description at least superficially parallels the behavior of adults who learn and then do not use specialized mnemonic techniques (mnemonic techniques are any of a variety of deliberately learned and applied memorial strategies). Such mnemonics do not ordinarily occur spontaneously in adults. Persons who use mnemonics often show remarkable improvements in recall (furthermore, adults are probably more aware of the advantages of these techniques than are children). Despite successful experiences, however, many adults report difficulty in continuing to use these partially assimilated techniques.

might be relatively simple. Their analysis, therefore, searched for the most elementary organization; they determined whether each adjacent pair of items in recall did or did not come from the same category. They required first-, third-, and fifth-grade children to learn twenty-four words, four from each of six categories, combined into four sublists that contained one word from each category. Under free recall conditions about 24 percent of all first-grade children's two-word combinations were categorical combinations. For fifth-grade subjects, 70 percent of the combinations were categorical combinations. Thus, in comparison with fifth-grade children, spontaneous categorical organization occurred relatively infrequently in the recall of first-grade children.

But if organization does increase, what effect does this have on recall? Niemark et al. (1971) attempted to determine whether organization and clustering are related developmentally to increased recall. That is, are organizational and clustering strategies significant ones in the development of improved mnemonic skills among young children? Children from grades one, three, four, five, six, and college students comprised the target population. The students were presented with twenty-four pictures which could be organized into four classes of six pictures each. They were given three minutes of study and were permitted to reorganize the pictures if they wished. Recall increased regularly from first grade to college. The amount of clustering, however, changed less markedly than did recall. There were no differences in clustering among first-, third-, and fourth-grade children, although these young children clustered less than did fifth and sixth graders, who in turn clustered less than did college students.[15]

Moely, Olson, Halwes, and Flavell (1969) wished to know (1) whether children could categorize items, (2) whether they used categorization to improve recall, and (3) whether clustering promoted recall. Kindergarten, first-, third-, and fifth-grade children were asked to learn the names of twenty-four pictures of common objects belonging to four conceptual categories. One group of children merely named the items and then were permitted two minutes to reorganize the items in any way that would facilitate recall. Following three trials with the same twenty-four pictures, children were asked to sort them into the four categories. Moely et al. (1969) formed a ratio of the amount of clustering done in preparation for the recall task with that done in the simple categorization task. The lower the values, the less the children actually used available clustering skills in the memory task. (Even smaller ratios would be obtained if children's clustering in memory preparation were evaluated relative to the

---

[15]However, Denney and Ziobrowski (1972) observed that first graders cluster more than adults on lists where stimulus words comprise complementary pairs (such as pipe and tobacco), while adults cluster more than first graders when the lists are made up of similar items (such as king and ruler). These differences suggest that young children may have different bases for clustering than do adults.

total amount of clustering possible.) The ratios obtained for kindergarten, first-, third-, and fifth-grade children, respectively, were .07, .16, .19, and .60. An examination of the data of only those children who performed perfectly on the postrecall categorization trial provided additional evidence of younger children's inability to deploy strategies efficiently. The number of children who perfectly categorized the items in the categorization trial were one, five, nine, and fourteen for the four ages, respectively. Considering only these students who categorized perfectly on this trial, the mean clustering score preceding the recall task was three times as large for the fifth-grade children as for the younger children.

How easily clustering strategies may be trained in children who lack them provides another index of the availability of these strategies. Although fifth-grade children engaged in a fair amount of clustering behavior when left to develop their own strategies, the younger children generally did not do so. Third graders, but not the younger children, engaged in considerable clustering in response to the suggestion to categorize items and label the categories. In the younger children only a very strong teaching manipulation induced clustering behavior in the memory-preparation task. Thus more direct and forceful manipulations are required to elicit clustering behavior in younger children.

Finally, how effective are strategies when they have been induced? The general striking finding was that as amount of clustering (either spontaneous or induced) increased there was a parallel increase in the level of recall. Hence in this situation, too, strategies that were not used spontaneously did enhance recall.

Summary

As children move from early to middle childhood their understanding of their memories increases. They learn what strategies are effective, and they develop skill in employing these strategies. But any mnemonic strategy is itself a complex set of rules—and children do not acquire and implement all elements at the same time. For example, we find that children accurately identify items that need further study considerably before they use this information to formulate adequate rehearsal strategies.

During the course of early and middle childhood children learn to organize materials in rehearsal and recall. They become progressively more like adults in this organization. It apparently takes considerable time, however, for children to consistently employ the organizational skills they have in the service of improved recall. Improved organization is at least generally related to improved recall and, as we have seen with other training manipulations, induced organization (like spontaneous organization) is effective in improving recall. Improvements continue, but even in adulthood we find frequent echoes of these problems of managing memory.

CONCLUSIONS

There are several ways to evaluate the adequacy of the information-processing model to summarize the cognitive development research reviewed in this chapter. First, how well does the model fit as a function of age? Second, how well does the model fit each hypothesized memory stage? In addition to these questions of fit, we may consider some problems and prospects for using information-processing models in real-world applications.

Evaluating the Fit

Age. Information-processing models describe a mature system that responds flexibly to incoming information. It is, consequently, inadequate for infants and very young children. The model becomes more adequate for older children and by middle childhood the fit is good. The sources of difficulties in applying the model to very young children are threefold. First, information-processing models arise primarily from research on adults and generally are silent concerning the emergence of encoding processes and memory stores. Second, methodological difficulties, formidable at any age, are especially acute in research with infants and young children. It is difficult to devise tasks that are equally suitable or comparable for individuals across a wide age span. Lastly, substantial difficulties inhere in understanding the functioning of very young infants. An adequate model of infant processing must be able to describe a system that is initially dominated by built-in encoding capacities and stimulus-response connections. Can the neonate process complex stimuli? The answer is both "Yes" and "No"! The preprogrammed stimulus-response connections are responsible for surprisingly sophisticated performance in young infants. Thus, remarkably complex encoding and responses may be possible, but only for a narrow range of stimuli. The complex interactions that occur as this system moves from a dependence on a limited number of built-in processing capabilities to become, in a matter of a few brief months, a highly flexible processor have thus far eluded systematic interpretation. Imposing challenges confront the researcher in discerning stimulus-response connections of sufficient evolutionary significance to be built in, in selecting behaviors sensitive to changes from the fixed to a flexible mode, and in conceptualizing changes (often apparent regressions) in performance as steps toward increased flexibility. Only gradually does the child's information-processing system come to be guided by the organized system of semantic memories that is typical for adults. Unfortunately, at present we know little about the emergence of this dynamic and flexible system.

Memory Stages. How adequate is the information processing model in describing the young child's memory? Although the evidence for several kinds of memory are quite persuasive for adults, these distinctions have little descriptive value for the memories of infants and very young children. A complex memory structure may emerge before school age, but little research has been done on information processing capacities of preschool children, and the issue remains open. By school age, however, children's memories can be generally described in the same terms as adults'. How, then, do the successive stages of memory of children and adults compare? The memories of adults are generally superior to those of children, but strategic differences are probably responsible for adult superiority, particularly in the long-term store. Changes in long-term memory in childhood appear almost completely attributable to changes in encoding, storage, and retrieval strategies. The older child and the adult encode material more carefully, process it more deeply, organize it more richly, and can retrieve it with a richer set of cues. Some differences in STS also appear to be strategic, for young children are less likely than older children and adults to rehearse materials. At least partially as a result, children hold verbal materials in the STS less well than do adults. SIS, however, may be more durable for young children than for adults, with this advantage for young children offset by their less efficient encoding, especially for complex or difficult materials. That encoding itself probably includes strategic elements is suggested by the improved encoding that occurs when children are provided effective codes for summarizing complex materials. Thus, the immature strategies selected by young children may be responsible for their poorer performance even for this brief memory store.

In short, the adult information-processing framework provides a heuristic for children's memory but does not provide an adequate model for the complex interplay we encounter in the infant as the information-processing system moves from neurological immaturity to maturity and from a built-in to a learning-based system. Although the model ignores most issues associated with the acquisition of strategies, the general semantic information that an individual has accumulated (and this clearly includes strategies and knowledge about memory) guides the processing of new information, at least in some versions of the model. Although this mechanism is not ordinarily described in developmental terms, progressive changes in this semantic information base must occur as the individual develops.

Problems

One issue alluded to in passing in this chapter deserves explicit mention: the "ecological validity" of the paradigms considered. To be ecologically valid, the studies must be grounded in real-world, nonlaboratory observations, or else generalization from laboratory into nonlaboratory settings must be clearly possible. Little of the research reported in this chapter and relatively little basic research has focused upon ecologically valid paradigms. The significance of such studies for understanding information processing, particularly in very young children, is underscored by research on recognition of mother's face and imitation of facial gestures as indices of infant memory. Information processing cannot be understood in a framework independent of the material to be processed and the particular system doing the processing. The infant is surprisingly competent when stimuli relevant to his or her existing systems are employed. Just as the salmon may "home" when internal and external conditions are right, and the honey bee may demonstrate surprising memory for map locations, so may the infant, under optimal conditions, engage in sophisticated information processing and responding.

A closely related issue is the lack of concern with information-processing variability among individuals in these models. The general assumption is that processing modes are reasonably similar for all individuals and that the focus of research should be on the similarities rather than the differences among individuals. However, an approach emphasizing individual differences might be more congenial with the kinds of developmental changes we have seen in infancy and childhood. In the final section we shall see some of the potential advantages of combining an information-processing approach with concerns for individual differences.

Finally, this chapter has focused largely on standard memory models, which have the advantage of relative simplicity and clarity and a large amount of associated experimental research. It is likely, however, that some more contemporary models may be more sensitive to, or provide richer heuristics for, research on children.

Prospects (Applications)

A model's applicability to real-word phenomena provides an alternative index to its value and potential. In the brief discussion that follows I shall focus on two closely related educational issues, measurement of intelligence (IQ) and cognitive training (or remediation), that I believe are beginning to be importantly influenced by information processing models. Most people are surprised to learn that learning and memory theories historically have had little impact on intelligence testing. Furthermore, most efforts at cognitive training or remediation have lacked a theoretical information-processing basis. Both intelligence testing and those educational efforts we can label "cognitive training" emerged at about the same time as the early research on learning and memory; but these movement developed in relative isolation from each other.

In the very recent past, however, there have been a number of efforts to provide an information-processing base for measuring intelligence (Hunt, Frost, & Lunneborg, 1973; Hunt & Lansman, 1975; Pellegrino &

Glaser, 1978; R. Sternberg, 1977). Although these approaches differ considerably, they are all concerned with understanding the make-up of intellect in terms of encoding, storage, and retrieval processes. They are concerned with individual differences that may exist in these fundamental processes; it may be useful to describe as more intelligent individuals who encode information more rapidly than others, store material more durably, or retrieve it with greater efficiency. A measurement of intelligence that assesses an individual's particular impairment has greater value as an educational tool than the quantitative estimates of ability that intelligence tests provide. Most work examining the information-processing basis of intelligence has been done on adults; however, it seems likely that important work on children's intelligence employing this framework will follow.

Training cognitive skills (cognitive remediation)—like measuring intelligence—has been guided less by theoretical considerations than by the use of strategies or materials that appear effective. The evidence for the effectiveness of cognitive remediation remains an open issue (for example, the effectiveness of the Head Start programs are a matter of controversy), but, at least in some cases, efforts to improve general cognitive skills, especially in young children, have been effective. The comparison between using general versus specific knowledge about improving cognitions may be similar to the differences between old and new methods of training athletes. At one time little more was done with athletes—for example, football players—than to assure proper weight, reasonable fitness, and proper practice for the particular position they played. As knowledge about the body increased, the kinds of drills and exercises necessary to strengthen particular sets of muscles have been determined much more precisely—leg, back, or arm muscles may be strengthened very efficiently. Furthermore, it is recognized that athletes with long, loose muscles require different classes of exercises to optimize their fitness than do athletes with short, tight muscles.

Analogously, we may expect improved returns when we understand the structure of intellect sufficiently well that we can target a particular narrowly focused cognitive difficulty. Suppose that we find that John is deficient in encoding skills. Our prospects for improving his intellective skills are far better than if we know only that ''he isn't very intelligent.'' Not enough work has been done for us to know for sure, but it seems likely that strategic skills are teachable. Strategies, however, may be more trainable than the relatively automatic functioning of the system. It remains an open and exciting question whether, given the appropriate (yet-to-be-developed) methods, we can improve the basic capacity of the information-processing system to respond.

REFERENCES

ATKINSON, R. C. Computerized instruction and the learning process. *American Psychologist*, 1968, 23, 225–239.

ATKINSON, R. C., HANSEN D. N., & BERNBACH, H. A. Short-term memory with young children. *Psychonomic Science,* 1964, *1,* 255–256.

BADDELEY, A. D. *The psychology of memory.* New York: Basic Books, 1976.

BARTLETT, F. C. *Remembering: A study in experimental and social psychology.* London: Cambridge University Press, 1932.

BAUMEISTER, A. A., & MAISTO, A. A. Memory scanning by children: Meaningfulness and mediation. *Journal of Experimental Child Psychology,* 1977, *24,* 97–107.

BELMONT, J. M., & BUTTERFIELD, E. C. The relations of short-term memory to development and intelligence. In L. P. Lipsitt & H. W. Reese (Eds.), *Advances in child development and behavior* (Vol. 4). New York: Academic Press, 1969.

BLAKE, J. Developmental change in visual information processing under backward masking. *Journal of Experimental Child Psychology,* 1974, *17,* 133–146.

BOWER, T. G. R. *Development in infancy.* San Francisco: Freeman, 1974.

BRANSFORD, J. D., BARCLAY, J. R., & FRANKS, J. J. Sentence memory: A constructive versus interpretive approach. *Cognitive Psychology,* 1972, *3,* 193–209.

BROWN, A. L. The development of memory: Knowing, knowing about knowing, and knowing how to know. In H. W. Reese (Ed.), *Advances in child development and behavior* (Vol. 10). New York: Academic Press, 1975.

BROWN, J. (Ed.) *Recall and recognition.* London: Wiley, 1976.

BROWN, R., & KULIK, J. Flashbulb memories. *Cognition,* 1977, *5,* 73-99.

BROWN, R., & MCNEILL, D. The "tip of the tongue" phenomenon. *Journal of Verbal Learning and Verbal Behavior,* 1966, *5,* 325–337.

CARON, A. J., CARON, R. F., CALDWELL, R. C., & WEISS, S. J. Infant perception of the structural properties of the face. *Developmental Psychology,* 1973, *9,* 385-399.

CARPENTER, G. Mother's face and the newborn. In R. Lewin (Ed.), *Child alive: New insights into the development of young children.* London: Temple Smith, 1975.

CAVANAGH, J. P. Relation between the immediate memory span and the memory search rate. *Psychological Review,* 1972, *79,* 525-530.

COHEN, L. B., GELBER, E. R., & LAZAR, M. A. Infant habituation and generalization to differing degrees of stimulus novelty. *Journal of Experimental Child Psychology,* 1971, *11,* 379-389.

COLLINS, A. M., & QUILLIAN, M. R. Retrieval time from semantic memory. *Journal of Verbal Learning and Verbal Behavior,* 1969, *8,* 240-247.

CONRAD, R. Acoustic confusions and memory span for words. *Nature,* 1963, *197,* 1029-1030.

CONRAD, R. The chronology of the development of covert speech in children. *Developmental Psychology,* 1971, *5,* 398-405.

CRAIK, F. I. M., & LOCKHART, R. S. Levels of processing: A framework for memory research. *Journal of Verbal Learning and Verbal Behavior,* 1972, *11,* 671-684.

CRAIK, F. I. M., & WATKINS, M. J. The role of rehearsal in short-term memory. *Journal of Verbal Learning and Verbal Behavior,* 1973, *12,* 599-607.

CROWDER, R. G. Behavioral strategies in immediate memory. *Journal of Verbal Learning and Verbal Behavior,* 1969, *8,* 524-528.

CUVO, A. J. Developmental differences in rehearsal and free recall. *Journal of Experimental Child Psychology,* 1975, *19,* 265-278.

DENNEY, N. W., & ZIOBROWSKI, M. Developmental changes in clustering criteria. *Journal of Experimental Child Psychology,* 1972, *13,* 275-282.

DIRKS, J., & GIBSON, E. Infants' perception of similarly between live people and their photographs. *Child Development,* 1977, *48,* 124-130.

FITZGERALD, H. E., & BRACKBILL, Y. Classical conditioning in infancy: Development and constraints. *Psychological Bulletin,* 1976, *83,* 353-376.

FLAVELL, J. H. Developmental studies of mediated memory. In H. W. Reese & L. P. Lipsitt (Eds.), *Advances in child development and behavior* (Vol. 5). New York: Academic Press, 1970.

FLAVELL, J. H., BEACH, D. R., & CHINSKY, J. M. Spontaneous verbal rehearsal in memory task as a function of age. *Child Development,* 1966, *37,* 283-299.

FLAVELL, J. H., FRIEDRICHS, A. G., & HOYT, J. D. Developmental changes in memorization processes. *Cognitive Psychology,* 1970, *1,* 324-340.

FLAVELL, J. H., & WELLMAN, H. M. Metamemory. In R. V. Kail, Jr. & J. W. Hagen (Eds.), *Perspectives in the development of memory and cognition.* Hillsdale, N. J.: Erlbaum, 1977.

FRANK, H. S., & RABINOVITCH, M. S. Auditory short-term memory: Developmental changes in rehearsal. *Child Development,* 1974, *45,* 397-407.

FRANKS, J. J., & BRANSFORD, J. D. The acquisition of abstract ideas. *Journal of Verbal Learning and Verbal Behavior,* 1972, *11,* 311-315.

GIBSON, E. J. *Principles of perceptual learning and development.* New York: Appleton-Century-Crofts, 1969.

GRAY, C. R., & GUMMERMAN, K. The enigmatic eidetic image: A critical examination of methods, data, and theories. *Psychological Bulletin,* 1975, *82,* 383-407.

GUMMERMAN, K., & GRAY, C. R. Age, iconic storage, and visual information processing. *Journal of Experimental Child Psychology,* 1972, *13,* 165-170.

HABER, R. N. Eidetic images. *Scientific American,* 1969, *220,* 36-44.

HAITH, M. M., MORRISON, F. J., & SHEINGOLD, K. Tachistoscopic recognition of geometical forms by children and adults. *Psychonomic Science,* 1970, *19,* 345-347.

HELLYER, S. Supplementary report: Frequency of stimulus presentation and short-term decrement in recall. *Journal of Experimental Psychology,* 1962, *64,* 650.

HOVING, K. L., MORIN, R. E., & KONICK, D. S. Recognition reaction time and size of the memory set: A developmental study. *Psychonomic Science,* 1970, *21,* 247-248.

HUNT, E., FROST, N., & LUNNEBORG, C. Individual differences in cognition: A new approach to intelligence. In G. Bower (Ed.), *The psychology of learning and motivation.* New York: Academic Press, 1973.

HUNT, E. & LANSMAN, M. Cognitive theory applied to individual differences. In W. K. Estes (Ed.), *Handbook of learning and cognitive processes*, Hillsdale, N. J.: Erlbaum, 1975.

JABLONSKI, E. M. Free recall in children. *Psychological Bulletin*, 1974, *81*, 522-539.

JAMES, W. *The principles of psychology* (Vol. 1). New York: Dover, and Co., 1950. (Originally published by Henry Holt & Co., 1890.)

JEFFREY, W. E., & COHEN, L. B. Habituation in the human infant. In H. W. Reese (Ed.), *Advances in child development and behavior* (Vol. 6). New York: Academic Press, 1971.

KAGAN, J. The determinants of attention in the infant. *American Scientist*, 1970, *58*, 298-306.

KAGAN, J., & LEWIS, M. Studies of attention in the human infant. *Merrill-Palmer Quarterly*, 1965, *11*, 95-127.

KEEN, R. E., CHASE, H. H., & GRAHAM, F. K. Twenty-four hour retention by neonates of an habituated heart rate response. *Psychonomic Science*, 1965, *2*, 265-266.

KEENEY, T. J., CANNIZZO, S. R., & FLAVELL, J. H. Spontaneous and induced verbal rehearsal in recall tasks. *Child Development*, 1967, *38*, 953-966.

KELLY, M., SCHOLNICK, E. K., TRAVERS, S. H., & JOHNSON, J. W. Relations among memory, memory appraisal, and memory strategies. *Child Development*, 1976, *47*, 648-659.

KOSSLYN, S. M., PICK, H. L., JR., & FARIELLO, G. R. Cognitive maps in children and men. *Child Development*, 1974, *45*, 707-716.

KREUTZER, M. A., LEONARD, C., & FLAVELL, J. H. An interview study of children's knowledge about memory. *Monographs of the Society for Research in Child Development*, 1975, *40* (1, Serial No. 159).

LEWIS, M. Infants' responses to facial stimuli during the first year of life. *Developmental Psychology*, 1969, *1*, 75-86.

LEWIS, M., BARTELS, B., FADEL, D., & CAMPBELL, H. Infant attention: The effect of familiar and novel visual stimuli as a function of age. Paper presented at the meeting of the Eastern Psychological Association, New York, April 1966. Described in W. E. JEFFREY & L.B. COHEN (1971).

LEWIS, M., GOLDBERG, S., & CAMPBELL, H. A developmental study of information processing within the first three years of life: Response decrement to a redundant signal. *Monographs of the Society for Research in Child Development*, 1969, *34*, No. 9.

LEWIS, M., GOLDBERG, S., & RAUSCH, M. Novelty and familiarity as determinants of infant attention within the first year. Unpublished manuscript, 1968. Described in W. E. JEFFREY & L. B. COHEN (1971).

LINTON, M. L. Memory for real-world events. In D. A. Norman and D. E. Rumelhart (Eds.), *Explorations in cognition*. San Francisco: Freeman, 1975.

LOFTUS, E. F., & PALMER, J. C. Reconstruction of automobile destruction: An example of the interaction between language and memory. *Journal of Verbal Learning and Verbal Behavior*, 1974, *13*, 585-589.

LOFTUS, E. F., & ZANNI, G. Eyewitness testimony: The influence of the wording of a question. *Bulletin of the Psychonomic Society,* 1975, *5,* 86-88.

LURIA, A. R. *The mind of a mnemonist.* New York: Basic Books, 1968.

MARKMAN, E. Factors affecting the young child's ability to monitor his memory. Unpublished doctoral dissertation, University of Pennsylvania, 1973.

MASUR, E. F., McINTYRE, C. W., & FLAVELL, J. H. Developmental changes in apportionment of study time among items in a multitrial free recall task. *Journal of Experimental Child Psychology,* 1973, *15,* 237-246.

MELTZOFF, A. N., & MOORE, M. K. Imitation of facial and manual gestures by human neonates. *Science,* 1977, *198,* 75-78.

MILLER, G. A. The magical number seven, plus or minus two: Some limits on our capacity for processing information. *Psychological Review,* 1956, *63,* 81-97.

MOELY, B. E., OLSON, F. A., HALWES, T. G., & FLAVELL, J. H. Production deficiency in young children's clustered recall. *Developmental Psychology,* 1969, *1,* 26-34.

MONROE, E. K., & LANGE, G. The accuracy with which children judge the composition of their free recall. *Child Development,* 1977, *48,* 381-387.

NIEMARK, E., SLOTNICK, N. S., & ULRICH, T. The development of memorization strategies. *Developmental Psychology,* 1971, *5,* 427-432.

NORMAN, D. A., & RUMELHART, D.E. Memory and knowledge. In D.A. Norman & D.E. Rumelhart (Eds.), *Explorations in cognition.* San Francisco: Freeman, 1975.

ORNSTEIN, P. A., NAUS, M. J., & LIBERTY, C. Rehearsal and organizational processes in children's memory. *Child Development,* 1975, *46,* 818-830.

PANCRATZ, N., & COHEN, L. B. Recovery of habituation in infants. *Journal of Experimental Child Psychology,* 1970, *9,* 208-216.

PELLEGRINO, J. & GLASER, R. Components of inductive reasoning. Paper presented at ONR/NPRDC Conference, March 6-9, 1978, San Diego, California.

PETERSON, L. R., & PETERSON, M. J. Short-term retention of individual verbal items. *Journal of Experimental Psychology,* 1959, *58,* 193-198.

PHILLIPS, J. L., JR. *The origins of intellect: Piaget's theory.* (2nd ed.). San Francisco: Freeman, 1975.

PIAGET, J., & INHELDER, B. *Memory and intelligence.* New York: Basic Books, 1973.

POLLACK, R. H., PTASHNE, R. I., & CARTER, D. J. The effects of age and intelligence on the dark-interval threshold. *Perception and Psychophysics,* 1969, *6,* 50-52.

RHEINGOLD, H. L., & ECKERMAN, C. O. Fear of the stranger: A critical examination. In H. W. Reese (Ed.), *Advances in child development and behavior* (Vol. 8). New York: Academic Press, 1973.

ROSNER, S. R., & LINDSLEY, D. T. The effects of retention interval on preschool children's short-term memory of verbal items. *Journal of Experimental Child Psychology,* 1974, *18,* 72-80.

RUMELHART, D. E. *An introduction to human information processing.* New York: Wiley, 1977.

RUNDUS, D. Analysis of rehearsal processes in free recall. *Journal of Experimental Psychology*, 1971, *89*, 63-77.

RUNDUS, D., & ATKINSON, R. C. Rehearsal processes in free recall: A procedure for direct observation. *Journal of Verbal Learning and Verbal Behavior*, 1970, *9*, 99-105.

SAMEROFF, A. J. The components of sucking in the human newborn. *Journal of Experimental Child Psychology*, 1968, *6*, 607-623.

SAMEROFF, A. J. Learning and adaptation in infancy: A comparison of models. In H. W. Reese (Ed.), *Advances in child development and behavior* (Vol. 7). New York: Academic Press, 1972.

SPERLING, G. The information available in brief visual presentations. *Psychological Monographs*, 1960, *74* (Whole No. 498), 1-29.

SPERLING, G. A model for visual memory tasks. *Human Factors*, 1963, *5*, 19-31.

SPERLING, G., BUDIANSKY, J., SPIVAK, J., & JOHNSON, M. C. Extremely rapid visual search: The maximum rate of scanning letters for the presence of a numeral. *Science*, 1971, *174*, 307-311.

STERNBERG, R. *Intelligence, information processing and analogical reasoning: The componential analysis of human abilities*. Hillsdale, N. J.: Erlbaum, 1977.

STERNBERG, S. High-speed scanning in human memory. *Science*, 1966, *153*, 652-654.

TULVING, E. Episodic and semantic memory. In E. Tulving & W. Donaldson (Eds.), *Organization of memory*. New York: Academic Press, 1972.

UNDERWOOD, B. J. Attributes of memory. *Psychological Review*, 1969, *76*, 559-573.

WATSON, J. S. Memory and "contingency analysis" in infant learning. *Merrill-Palmer Quarterly*, 1967, *13*, 55-76.

WEIST, R. M., & CRAWFORD, J. The development of organized rehearsal. *Journal of Experimental Child Psychology*, 1977, *24*, 164-179.

WEIZMANN, F., COHEN, L. B., & PRATT, R. J. Novelty, familiarity, and the development of infant attention. *Developmental Psychology*, 1971, *4*, 149-154.

WELSANDT, R. F., JR., ZUPNICK, J. J., & MEYER, P. A. Age effects in backward visual masking (Crawford paradigm). *Journal of Experimental Child Psychology*, 1973, *15*, 454-461.

WETHERFORD, M. J., & COHEN, L. B. Developmental changes in infant visual preferences for novelty and familiarity. *Child Development*, 1973, *44*, 416-424.

YUSSEN, S. R., & LEVY, V. M., JR. Developmental changes in predicting one's own span of short-term memory. *Journal of Experimental Child Psychology*, 1975, *19*, 502-508.

FOUR

Neuroanatomical Correlates of Language and Memory: A Developmental Perspective

Raymond P. Kesner and Timothy B. Baker

INTRODUCTION

The purpose of this chapter is to examine the relationship of the maturation of a biological system (the brain) to the emergence of two faculties that are extremely important to humans—language and memory. There are many levels at which one can examine child development; these include studying overt behavior, cognitive styles or strategies, psychophysiological responses, neuroanatomy, or neurochemistry. Psychologists often study different types of overt behavior emitted by a child as he or she develops. This does produce important information on the behavioral topography of developmental changes. However, crucial information can be lost if one restricts the analysis of developmental changes to a single informational level. For instance, discovering the pattern of speech emergence in children cannot provide a scientist with a complete view of human language acquisition. This is because speech emergence transpires in the context of tremendous maturational (neuroanatomical-neurophysiological) changes that are intimately linked to language learning and usage. Ignoring either behavioral or biological information precludes a complete understanding of child development. This chapter represents a synthesis of neuroanatomical and behavioral information as they relate to the development of language and memory.

This chapter has a definite organization and it may be of heuristic value for the student to understand this organization before he or she proceeds. First, we present basic neuroanatomical information on the structure and function of neurons and major parts of the brain. We do not intend for the student to memorize such information. We merely feel that it provides a necessary context for learning about the relationship of brain maturation and the development of language and memory. It suggests both the complexity of the brain as well as the interrelatedness of its parts. After presenting a brief overview of human neuroanatomy we describe the general trends in brain maturation. Next, we look for evidence linking language and memory to particular areas of brain tissue. As we shall see, we are more successful in this regard with language than with memory. Our next concern is this: If there are neuroanatomical areas associated with language and memory, what is the relationship of their biological maturation with the emergence of those functions? Finally, we seek to determine the extent to which environmental manipulations or conditions can affect the relationship between neuroanatomical maturation and language and memory development.

BASIC NEUROANATOMY

Cellular Organization

It has been assumed by many scientists that the development of complex, highly organized, long-term memory and language systems is associated with structural changes in specific neuroanatomical systems. It is, therefore, necessary to present the basic cell types and anatomical subdivisions of the brain in order to understand which components of neurons or which brain regions are critically related to the development of memory and language. The central nervous system consists mostly of two types of specialized cells, *neurons* and *neuroglia*. The number of neurons and neuroglia in the human brain has been estimated to be 10 billion and 90 billion, respectively. Although neurons come in many shapes and varieties, they consist of at least four major components (*dendrites, soma* or *cell body, axons,* and *terminal buttons*) separated on the basis of function, but maintaining one continuous cell membrane. A schematic diagram of a neuron is shown in Figure 4–1. The dendrite is a specialized process that acts as a receptive region for the neuron. There are many varied dendritic arrangements with many branches (often called "dendritic trees") associated with neurons. On the surface of many dendrites are little buds known as "dendritic spines," which contain the receptive membranes of neurons where messages are received from other neurons. The cell body contains the nucleus and the machinery to keep the neuron alive. The size (5–100 microns) and shape of neurons vary greatly.

The axon is a process that originates from a morphologically distinct part of the neuron, the *axon hillock*, and specializes in the conduction of nerve impulses and transportation of chemical substances generally over a considerable distance. Nerve impulses representing information are usually conducted away from the cell body to the terminal buttons, but transportation of chemicals (axoplasmic transport) goes in both directions. The axon is a long, slender tube and is covered by a discontinuous *myelin sheath*. Myelin covers and insulates the axon from surrounding

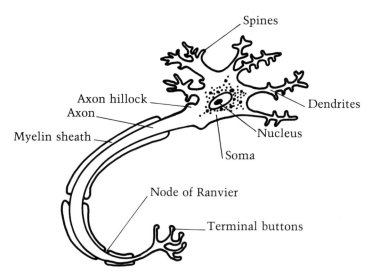

Figure 4-1

Schematic representation of a neuron showing the interrelationships of its components.

tissue except for small spaces between segments of myelin called *nodes of Ranvier*. Not all axons are covered by myelin, but those that are covered conduct nerve impulses more rapidly via a mechanism called "saltatory conduction."[1] There is only one axon per neuron in contrast to possible hundreds of thousands of dendrites per neuron. As an axon approaches another cell (such as a neuron, muscle, or other type of cell), it divides and branches a number of times. At the end of each of the branches are little knobs known as "terminal buttons." These buttons make contact with other cells (mostly neurons) and thus constitute the presynaptic membrane of synapses. The presynaptic membrane is where chemical messages are released from one neuron to travel to another.

A *synapse* is a junction between the membranes of a terminal button at the end of an axonal branch of one cell and a dendritic spine (axodendritic) or soma (axosomatic) of another cell (see Figure 4–2). Since information is transmitted in only one direction, the terminal button membrane is referred to as the "presynaptic membrane" and the dendritic spine membrane as the "postsynaptic membrane." The space separating these two membranes is about 200 A° (10^{-7}mm) wide and is called the "synaptic cleft." Within the presynaptic membrane are found synaptic vesicles, which contain neural transmitter substances. These neural transmitters are released by nerve impulses and in turn activate

---

[1]"Salto" means "jump" in Latin. In saltatory conduction nerve impulses jump from one node of Ranvier to the next—rather than maintaining their usual wavelike progression across the length of the neuron.

receptors located in the postsynaptic membrane. Activation of the postsynaptic membrane will produce either an increase or decrease in the probability that the activated neuron will produce a nerve impulse.

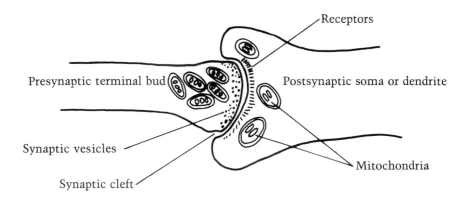

Figure 4-2

Essential features of a synapse.

In contrast to neurons, neuroglia cells provide a variety of supportive functions. Different types of neuroglia cells surround neurons and synapses, transport substances from the blood supply to neurons, regulate the chemical composition of fluid surrounding neurons, produce myelin, and digest dead neurons. The role of neuroglia in the development of neuronal processes as well as the formation of long-term memory and language is at present undetermined and therefore will not be considered in future sections.

From a developmental perspective, cell bodies mature first followed by growth and branching of dendrites and axons. Next, there is the establishment of contacts (synapses) between neurons followed by growth of neuroglia cells and myelinization of axons.

Structual Oganization

The *central nervous system* (CNS) is composed of the brain and spinal cord. The brain is that portion of the CNS located within the skull while the spinal cord is that portion of the CNS located in the spine. We will briefly review the structure and functions of the major areas of the brain; we will begin with that area closest to the spinal cord.

Brain Stem. The brain stem is that neural region lying between the spinal cord and the cerebellar and cerebral cortices. The major parts are the medulla and pons. The brain stem increases in size from the spinal cord to the cerebrum and contains large neural fiber tracts (groupings of axons) going to and from the brain.

The *medulla*—the most caudal (meaning "toward the tail") portion of the brain stem (see Figure 4-3)—contains not only important fiber tracts leading to and from the brain but also major nuclei (groupings of neurons). It contains centers for vital functions such as control of the cardiovascular system and gastrointestinal activity.

The highest, or most rostral (meaning "toward the head"), portion of the brain stem is the *pons* (see Figure 4-3). The nuclei of a number of cranial nerves connect with the pons, including those important for salivation and facial expression. Also, centers for control of respiration are located in the pons.

Midbrain. This area is located just above the brain stem (see Figure 4-3) and shares many interconnections with it. The midbrain contains the *superior* and *inferior colliculi* on its dorsal (back) aspect, and cranial nerves controlling eye movement on its ventral (front) aspect. The inferior colliculi represent an important relay for acoustic (hearing) information, while the superior colliculi represent an important relay for visual information. It is interesting that in animals that depend heavily on acoustic feedback (for example, the bat, which uses echo-location) the inferior colliculi are the larger of the two sets of colliculi, while in animals chiefly dependent on visual feedback (for example, the monkey, which is dependent upon a sensitive visual system for brachiation) the superior colliculi are larger. This is just one example of how a particular neuroanatomical feature—size—bears a relationship to function.

Inside the brain stem (medulla, pons) and midbrain, toward the ventral surface, lies the *reticular formation*. This is a dense network of neurons that plays an important role in determining the onset of sleep, dreaming, and state of arousal or wakefulness (cf. Jouvet, 1967; Lindsley, 1958). Damage to the reticular formation often results in alterations in consciousness.

Cerebellum. The cerebellum is a rather large convoluted mass of tissue that overlies the pons (see Figure 4-3). The principal functions of the cerebellum are the control of fine motor movement and maintenance of muscle tone and posture. It receives sensory feedback from the inner ear; such feedback is probably vital to the cerebellum's achievement of postural control. A clue to the cerebellum's function can be garnered from the behavior of patients who have suffered damage to that structure. Depending upon the exact location of the cerebellar damage, patients may suffer impairment of either balance or posture. Some patients may therefore develop an unsteady ("ataxic") gait that has a characteristic jerky appearance, or patients may have an "intention" tremor that occurs at the initiation of a motor movement. Patients with such a tremor often exhibit poor hand-eye coordination and tend to over- or under-reach desired objects.

Thalamus. The thalamus (see Figure 4-3) is a vital sensory integration center that is responsible for conveying most of the sensory information that reaches the cortex. Most of the sensory information traveling

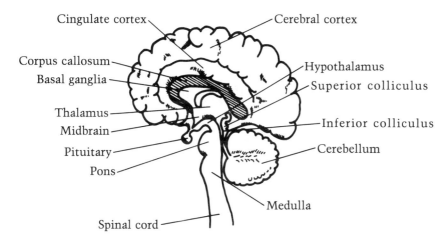

Figure 4-3

Diagram of human brain seen from medial plane (split down the middle). The major features described in text are labeled in the figure.

through the brain stem and spinal cord synapses in the thalamus. From the thalamus such sensory information is diverted to the appropriate region of the cerebral cortex (for example, visual information is routed to the visual cortex). Another important function of the thalamus is to relay messages from one area of the cerebral cortex to another. Thus, the thalamus has been considered the "switchboard" of the brain, since it conveys so much important information to various brain regions.

Hypothalamus. The hypothalamus lies at the base of the brain—just under the thalamus ("hypo" is "under")—and is located just above the roof of the mouth. The hypothalamus is a region that contains numerous groups of nuclei that play a principal role in affecting the operations of the endocrine glands. It is not surprising that the pituitary gland—the "master gland" of the endocrine system—hangs from a slender thread of tissue just under the hypothalamus (see Figure 4-3). The hypothalamus also plays an important role in the regulation of blood pressure, body temperature, sexual responses, eating, and drinking.

The hypothalamus is connected to many other areas of the brain besides the pituitary gland. Some of these areas—the *septal area*, the *amygdala*, the *hippocampus*, and the *cingulate cortex*—are thought to form an integrated neurophysiological circuit called the *limbic system* (see Figure 4-4). These structures are implicated in emotional reactions, goal-oriented behaviors, and memory. For example, damage to the amygdala can lead to a marked reduction in violent behavior. The relevance of the hippocampus to memory will be discussed in detail later.

Basal ganglia. The basal ganglia surround the thalamus; in turn, they are surrounded by the cerebral cortex. They are composed of the *globus*

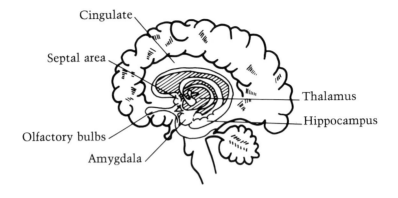

Cingulate

Septal area

Olfactory bulbs

Amygdala

Thalamus

Hippocampus

Figure 4–4

Diagram of the major components of the limbic system.

pallidus, the *putamen,* and the *caudate nucleus.* These structures appear to be involved in the expression of motor movement. Damage to the basal ganglia has been implicated in several human diseases, the symptomatology of which usually involves motoric dysfunction. In Parkinson's disease, for instance, deterioration of the basal ganglia and substantia nigra is frequently observed upon autopsy. Primary Parkinson's features are a tremor at rest, a loss of associated movement (such as arm swinging while walking), and rigidity. Another clinical condition, Huntington's Chorea, is associated with damage to the globus pallidus and the putamen. Patients with this condition move with jerky, unpredictable motions ("chorea" means "dance" in Greek). Animal research has also implicated the basal ganglia in the production or control of motor movements (Buchwald & Hull, 1967; Wilburn & Kesner, 1974).

Cerebral Cortex. The cerebral cortex covers most of the brain and is the most recently evolved brain area. Lower animals such as the rat and rabbit have relatively smooth cortices. As you ascend the phylogenetic scale the advanced primates (such as rhesus monkeys, chimpanzees, and gibbons) have large and heavily wrinkled cortices similar to humans. The human cortex is about 2 mm thick and its wrinkled structure gives it about three times the amount of surface area it would have if it were flat. The cerebral cortex of humans is so large and complex that about three-fourths of all brain neurons are located there. There is a general concurrence among scientists that the greater amount of cerebral cortex a species has relative to its body mass the greater its ability to learn new behaviors and adapt to varying environments. If this supposition is correct, it is easy to see why humans have become the most dominant animal on earth.

The cerebral cortex is divided into four major areas—or lobes—by heavy wrinkles on the cortex surface. The depressed portion of a wrinkle on the brain's surface is called a *fissure* or *sulcus,* while the raised hilly portion of the wrinkle is called a *gyrus.* The major brain lobes—the temporal, parietal, occipital, and frontal lobes—and the sulci and gyri that divide them are depicted in Figure 4-5.

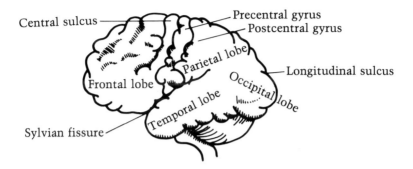

Figure 4-5

The lobes of the cerebral cortex and the major sulci.

While much of the cortex is thought to be "association" cortex—for which specific functions are not known—some cortical areas are linked to particular functions or behaviors. For instance, the *occipital* cortex located in the occipital lobe is known to be directly involved in vision and the processing of visual information. The strip of cortex just anterior (in front of) to the central sulcus (the *precentral gyrus,* see Figure 4-5) is sometimes called the "motor strip" and appears to control many of our voluntary movements. The portion of cortex just posterior (behind) to the central sulcus (the *postcentral gyrus,* see Figure 4-5) is sometimes referred to as the "sensory strip"; and, appropriately enough, it is the area of the cerebral cortex most closely related to touch. If this area is removed, sensation of touch is almost completely lost. Therefore, this area is called the primary sensory area for touch. The primary sensory area for hearing is located in the auditory cortex, which is part of the temporal lobe.

As can be seen in Figure 4-5, the cortex is divided into right and left sides by a sulcus that runs right down the middle of the brain surface. This *longitudinal fissure* descends into the neural tissue until it reaches the top of a thick group of white nerve fibers called the corpus callosum (see Figure 4-3). While this group of fibers is now known to be very important, only a short time ago scientists were unaware of the purpose of these fibers. After examining cases where the corpus callosum had been severed, one scientist humorously concluded that the only purpose of the corpus callosum was to hold the two halves of the brain together (Lashley, 1950). Sperry (1962), who helped discover the function of the corpus callosum, has suggested that this fiber bundle allows for an integration of the information coming to each cerebral hemisphere. When a patient has had the corpus callosum severed (a "commissurotomy" is usually performed to prevent epileptic seizure foci from spreading from one side of the brain to the other), the right hand can literally not know what the left hand is doing! The corpus callosum is very important in allowing one side of the brain to communicate with the other. This important function will be discussed later when we examine how brain functions may become associated with only one cerebral hemisphere—a process called "lateralization."

Perhaps the oldest and most widely accepted principle of cerebral maturation is that of *neurophylogenesis*, which posits that the central nervous system matures in a caudal to rostral sequence that is, from tail to head). Except for an occasional exception (for example, some segments of the spinal cord), this principle seems fairly valid. Although there are other theories of cerebral or CNS development, most have at least one tenet in common—the cerebral cortex is the last, or one of the last, neural structures to attain maturity (Himwich, 1971). This has great importance for the emergence of memory and language.

Some fundamental facts of neuroanatomical development appear to be true of almost all mammalian species. The brain increases in weight, volume, and length as it develops. Brain fluid (mostly water) is gradually replaced by neural tissue—lipids and protein—and these changes, in keeping with neurophylogenesis, usually occur in a caudal to rostral fashion. Furthermore, in most species the nervous system tends to be precocial relative to other organ systems in that it shows greater early development. In humans, the brain's weight at birth is 25 percent of its adult weight, while it is 75 percent at 2½ and 90 percent at 5 years (Achenbach, 1974). These numbers are considerably higher than for most organ systems at the same ages.

The brain structures that tend to show the earliest development are those most strongly implicated in the organism's survival. For instance, the pons, medulla, and midbrain—all responsible for such vital functions as respiration—show very early development, both in terms of their myelinization and in their size. Later, the cerebellum and thalamus show increasing development, with the cerebellum achieving considerable growth by age one. The cerebral cortex, especially the association cortices, are among the last brain structures to attain maturity.

ANATOMICAL CORRELATES OF LANGUAGE

Now that we have reviewed the cellular and structural aspects of human neuroanatomy, we will examine in more detail the role of specific peripheral, global, and discrete neuroanatomical systems that might subserve language. Following that, we will do the same for memory function.

Peripheral Correlates

One way of discovering the anatomical correlates of language is to ascertain what language-related anatomical features are peculiar to humans. Although impressive gains have been made in teaching symbolic communication strategies to infrahumans (cf. Fouts, 1975; Premack, 1971; Rumbaugh, von Glasersfeld, Warner, Pisani, & Gill, 1974), no infrahuman has yet been found to have anywhere near the same level of biological preparedness for speech as do humans (cf. Limber, 1977). Descartes observed that language was a characteristic aspect of being human over 300 years ago.

> For it is a very remarkable thing that there are no men, not even the insane, so dull and stupid that they cannot put words together in a manner to convey their thoughts. On the contrary, there is no other animal, however perfect and fortunately situated it may be, that can do the same. And this is not because they lack the organs, for we see that magpies and parrots can pronounce words as well as we can, and nevertheless cannot speak as we do, that is, in showing that they think what they are saying. On the other hand, even those men born deaf and dumb, lacking the organs which others make use of in speaking, and at least as badly off as the animals in this respect, usually invent for themselves some signs by which they make themselves understood. And this proves not merely animals have less reason than men but that they have none at all, for we see that very little is needed to talk (Descartes, 1637, cited in Limber, 1977).

Not only did Descartes point out the universality of language among humans and its absence among other animals, but he also observed that language is distinct from the ability to make words. This introduces the question of whether human articulatory skills are important or necessary for the use of language. Thus, in our search for anatomical correlates of language we will start with those structures most obviously linked to the production of speech—the vocal tract.

Some scientists have claimed that one reason that higher primates such as the chimpanzee do not acquire language is because their vocal tracts cannot produce the sounds required by human speech (Lieberman, Klatt, & Wilson, 1969). While these scientists do not propose that this is the sole reason for apes' linguistic deficits, they view vocal tract differences as a contributing factor. Lieberman and his associates, for instance, have shown that the ape vocal tract is incapable of executing vowel sounds. Could the presence of a specialized vocal tract be an adequate explanation for human language capability? It has been suggested that without the ability to produce sounds one cannot receive the feedback necessary for language.

It is doubtful that the preceding assertion is correct. It is certainly not necessary for humans to have an intact peripheral[2] vocal system to acquire language. Cases have been reported where persons have lost their entire larynx and/or tongue prior to their acquisition of language and yet

---

[2]Peripheral here means outside the central nervous system. The larynx, tongue, and lips would be parts of the peripheral vocal system.

those individuals were able to learn and use language (Limber, 1977). In one case, a young girl born without a tongue—in addition to other vocal tract defects—was able to produce and use speech by flexion of the facial and mouth floor musculature (Drachman, 1969). In another case, a person born with a profound inability to speak, could understand spoken language quite well (Lenneberg, 1962).

Central Brain Correlates: Global

If peripheral structures are not necessary for language, then central structures must be. A simplistic, but legitimate, hypothesis is that humans possess language since the human brain is so large compared to that of other animals. This simple postulate, of course, does not explain why animals having brains larger than humans' (for example, whales) do not have language. Or, on the other hand, this explanation does not reveal why nanocephalic[3] dwarfs—whose brains often weigh less than those of chimpanzees—often acquire language.

A more sophisticated hypothesis posits that humans have language since the human brain is large relative to the human body mass. This explanation would account for the linguistic capabilities of nanocephalic dwarfs since they have brain/body weight ratios similar to normal adolescents. This explanation does not account for the lack of language in chimps or rhesus monkeys, however, as those species can have the same brain/body weight ratios as humans at various times in their developmental histories.

Perhaps more important than the absolute size of the brain or the size of the brain relative to body weight is the organization of the human brain and its unique development after birth. For, while other animals have larger brains or similar brain/body weight ratios, none have the same brain organization and none have similar neural developmental histories. As Lenneberg (1967), a noted neuropsychologist studying language, observed: "Apparently the organization of the brain is more important for language than its mass, and the entire matter must be discussed in the light of developmental processes and growth" (p. 71). Both the human brain's specialized structure and its developmental history will be principal subjects for much of the rest of this chapter.

Central Brain Correlates: Discrete

In the following two sections we will demonstrate that an important feature of the brain's specialized structure is that language as well as

---

[3]Nanocephalic dwarfism is a rare condition in which adults achieve a height of about 2½ to 3 feet. These dwarfs differ from other dwarfs in that they have the same body proportions as normal adults. As Lenneberg observes:

> The fully mature have a brain/body weight ratio well within the limits of a young teenager. Yet their head circumference and estimated brain weight barely exceed those of a newborn infant. . . . Intellectually, these dwarfs show some retardation for the most part, often not surpassing a mental age level of five to six years. All of them acquire the rudiments of language including speaking and understanding, and the majority master the verbal skills at least as well as a normal five-year-old child (Lenneberg, 1967, p. 70).

memory is principally mediated by a few relatively discrete brain regions. Before showing this, though, we would like to issue a warning. While we search for neuroanatomical regions that are especially involved in language as well as memory, we must not forget that such areas are parts of an integrated unit. Therefore, their functions can never be wholly separated from functions of other parts of the brain. This is because the brain is organized as an integrated unit with a tremendous amount of communication and feedback from one section to another. The integrated nature of human brain function and structure has important implications for topics covered in this chapter. Also, when we make phylogenetic comparisons between humans and infrahumans, we must remember that ad hoc comparisons of structural changes may be unjustifiably simplistic. While interspecies comparisons of brains may reveal modest structural changes, far more important differences may go unnoticed. For instance, a change in an operational principle (such as a method of communication among neurons) or the way structural components interact might render gross structural comparisons superfluous. Lenneberg (1967) observes:

> A brain is an integrated organ, and cognitions result from the integrated operation of all its tissues and suborgans. Man's brain is not a chimpanzee's brain plus added "association facilities." Its functions have undergone reintegration at the same pace as its evolutionary development" (p. 395).

A second implication we can derive from the brain's structural and functional integration concerns our induction of brain functions from conditions where brain parts have been removed or damaged. If brain parts are highly interdependent, then damage to a brain part might affect a function or behavior that the brain part does not directly control. One oft-noted analogy is that if almost any part of a radio or television were damaged, that electronic beast would commence howling. Are we then to assume that all such parts have as their function "howling suppression"?

Richard Thompson (1975) states:

> Mnemonic abilities, complex behavioral processes, and consciousness do not live in particular pieces of neural tissue. They are the end result of the interrelated activities of the human brain, the most complex machine in the universe and seemingly the only machine that has ever attempted to understand itself (p. 106).

Despite these theoretical reservations we have decided that the neuroanatomical bases of language and memory will be revealed only by an examination of specialized structures of the human brain and its developmental history. First we will examine structures peculiar to the human brain that are probably related to human linguistic abilities; in a later section we will discuss human mnemonic abilities.

As noted earlier, the "association cortices" are those areas of the cortex for which specific functions are not known. However, there is evidence that one such cortical area is involved in the integration and synthesis of information transmitted to the brain by the sensory systems (for example, touch, vision). The association areas are thought to be involved in such sophisticated "higher" functions as thought and language. Therefore, we would expect humans to possess a relatively greater amount of this cortex than other animals. This, in fact, is the case. As one ascends the phylogenetic scale the ratio of prefrontal cortex (phylogenetically, the most recently developed area of association cortex) to the rest of the cortex steadily increases. The proportion of total cortical area occupied by the prefrontal cortex is 11 percent in the macaque, 17 percent in the chimpanzee, and 20 percent in humans.

There are other neuroanatomical indices that show their greatest development in the human brain (cf. Milner, 1976). Most of these indices reflect cortical changes. For instance, the proportion of association to sensorimotor cortex changes drastically across species. The rodent has 90 percent sensorimotor and 10 percent associational cortex, the cat 70 percent and 30 percent, the monkey 40 percent and 60 percent, and the adult male 15 percent and 85 percent, respectively. The number of discrete cortical areas (areas having distinct cellular arrangements) also shows a similar increase. The albino rat has about 13, the adult cat 36, and the human 52. Other neuroanatomical indices showing steady increases as we ascend the phylogenetic scale are the thickness and number of cortical layers, the number and depth of fissures, and the number of unmyelinated cortical layers at birth.

While such progressive changes in size and complexity are suggestive, none are tied directly to language. There are more suggestive data, however, because the human brain is larger and more complex in a specific place—the cerebral cortex—and the association cortex in particular. We will attempt to show that there is a special relationship between specific cortical association areas and language. Evidence for this relationship comes from three different areas: aphasia, electrical brain stimulation, and neuroanatomy.

Aphasia. Aphasia is a language disturbance in which previously acquired language skills are lost due to brain damage. Aphasia per se does not imply a motoric or sensory deficit related to language expression or reception. Language disturbance due to aphasia is the direct result of the brain's inability to use the symbolic logic we call language. The hearing and speaking systems of aphasic persons are intact, but they do not know how to acquire information from the former or express themselves through the latter. Since the aphasic's communication disorder derives from such a high level language disturbance it evidences itself in every vehicle of expression. Not only is the global aphasic's speech production and comprehension disturbed but the ability to read and write is also compromised. If the aphasic was deaf prior to the aphasia, whatever sign language he or she had used for communication would be rendered useless. Aphasia is a "linguistic deficit that includes problems of symbolic and integrative functioning that cross all language modalities'' (Johns & LaPointe, 1976, p. 172).

One of the most frequently noted characteristics of aphasia is that it is more likely to result from left hemisphere damage than from damage to the right hemisphere.[4] A gross neuroanatomical examination would show that the right and left cerebral hemispheres are almost identical in appearance—yet one is seemingly much more involved with language than the other. Not only do the hemispheres appear to be differentially involved in language, but their involvement is related to a person's handedness. About 99 percent of right-handed persons have language located almost exclusively in their left cerebral hemispheres, while about 75 percent of left-handed persons (about 10 percent of the population, Hardyck & Petrinovitch, 1977) have significant left-hemisphere language mediation (Penfield & Roberts, 1959). This finding has been confirmed over and over again in studies of brain-damaged patients. Right-handed patients almost always have language problems with left-hemisphere lesions, while they rarely do with right-hemisphere lesions. The predominance of left-sided language (the "lateralization" of language) provides at least some information on the location of language-related neural tissue.

Aphasia is not a monolithic entity that is invariant in its course or characteristics. Indeed, every case of aphasia has its idiosyncracies and the aphasic patient must always be viewed as an individual with problems that are specific to his or her case. However, there do appear to be broad classes or types of aphasia; an examination of these classes reveals additional information about the relation of linguistic function to its neuroanatomical substrate.

There is no universal agreement as to the proper classification of different types of aphasia (Johns & LaPointe, 1976). However, certain major types have been advanced which can adequately describe a great many aphasic patients—at least with respect to the major symptomatology. Many patients will conform, in general, to one of the major types of aphasia; but few will do so perfectly.

The first type of aphasia to be described and attributed to a particular neuroanatomical lesion was *Broca's aphasia*. This condition has been implicated with lesions in Broca's area in the frontal lobe (see Figure 4-6). In the early 1860s Paul Broca had under his care a patient by the name of Leborgne. This patient became known to neurologists as ''Tan'' since that was the only word he could utter. This first case of Broca's aphasia points out a cardinal feature of that condition. Broca's aphasics have extremely small vocabularies and expend a great deal of effort to

---

[4]Aphasia is usually caused by one of the following conditions: intracranial occlusion and infarction (about 40% of hemisphere vascular lesions result in language disturbance), trauma, tumors, and abcess.

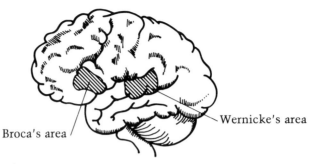

Broca's area

Wernicke's area

Figure 4-6

Primary language areas of the human brain are located in the left hemisphere. Broca's area lies adjacent to the motor cortex. Wernicke's area lies in the temporal lobe.

express themselves in even the simplest of ways. They are essentially nonfluent, using few words, and most of these are simple nouns or action verbs. They are often mute, and when they do talk tend to repeat the few words they can use over and over. Hughlings Jackson, a prominent early neurologist, termed the few simple words mastered by Broca's patients as "stock" or "recurring" utterances (Alajouanine, 1956). The French poet Baudelaire, who had Broca's aphasia, retained the words "cre nom"— probably a residual of "sacre nom de Dieu." Alajouanine (1956) reports of one patient who could only pathetically reiterate "Bonsoir, les choses d'ici-bas"—"Farewell, things of this world." This paucity of verbalization allows grammar of only the most basic sort. The inability of Broca's patients to express themselves extends into every facet of symbolic communication. Broca's patients cannot write or use any sign language to communicate since the ability to use language itself is disturbed. As Hughlings Jackson (1932, in Mohr, 1976) observed:

> Speaking is propositionizing—that the speechless patient cannot propositionize *aloud* is obvious—he never does. But this is only the superficial part of the truth. He cannot propositionize internally...the proof that he does not speak internally is that he cannot express himself in writing....He can say nothing to himself, and therefore has nothing to write (p. 225).

Jackson's observation strikes at the heart of the differences between Broca's aphasia and other types of expressive disorders, like *dysarthria* and *apraxia* of speech. Dysarthria occurs when patients know what they want to say and write their message normally. However, due to faulty innervation of the mouth musculature, they cannot pronounce words well. An apraxia of speech differs from dysarthria in that speech apraxic patients cannot speak even though they have no notable paresis (weakness), paralysis, or incoordination of the mouth musculature (as does the dysarthric patient); they just cannot use such musculature for speech. (An *apraxia* is an inability to perform purposive movements or complex acts, although motivation, motion, sensation, and coordination are preserved.) Apraxic patients *can* use the mouth musculature for nonlanguage purposes (such as yawning or whistling). Johns and LaPointe (1976) note that "Quite simply then, in the absence of any problem of symbolic nature or paralysis or incoordination of the speech musculature adequate to account for the speech disorder, a patient with a 'pure' apraxia of speech knows exactly what he wishes to say but he cannot say it" (p. 172). Like the dysarthric, the speech apraxic can read and write.

What is the purpose of making these elaborate distinctions between different types of communication disorders? Only this: it is important to demonstrate that aphasia produces an interference with language itself and not with some related but nonessential process. If we are to use aphasia to study language, we must know their relationship. A "pure" Broca's aphasia interferes with language itself; dysarthria and apraxia of speech merely disrupt one mode of its expression.

This brief review of Broca's aphasia has stressed the problems of language expression or production. There is a reason for this: while the Broca's aphasic often has some problems with language comprehension, such problems are less severe than are his or her expression difficulties. Since the effects of aphasia transverse language modalities, the Broca's aphasic can read better than he or she can write, and he or she can understand spoken material better than he or she can produce it. This dichotomy between mastery over language comprehension and expression serves as a focal point for separating the two major types of aphasia—Broca's and *Wernicke's aphasia.*

Wernicke's aphasia—often called jargon, receptive, or fluent aphasia—is characterized by a normal or high output of speech but with very poor comprehension. This condition has usually been associated with lesions in Wernicke's area in the temporal lobe (see Figure 4–6). The Wernicke's patient appears to have little difficulty in emitting a great deal of verbal material, but the meaning is often obscure. Such patients frequently begin a sentence that appears to be progressing in some normal, logical fashion, only to deteriorate into a "word salad" as their speech continues. One explanation for this is that Wernicke's aphasics know what they want to say and they begin to do so, but their tremendous comprehension deficit interferes with their monitoring of their own speech. Thus, after an initial utterance, they do not know what they have said or what they are saying, and they lapse into disturbed meaningless speech. Such patients also have a tendency to use *paraphasic* speech—they tend to substitute an inappropriate but similar word for a normal word or term. For instance, one patient seen by the second author referred to the hospital barbershop as the "station haircut room" and substituted "peoples' exchange" for the hospital canteen store.

Thus, Wernicke's aphasia is the mirror image of Broca's aphasia. Wernicke's patients produce words with considerable facility but have great difficulty in comprehension—regardless of communication modality. Like Broca's aphasia, Wernicke's aphasia occurs in the absence of any strict sensory or motor deficits that could account for such language problems. Therefore, these patients can hear speech and can see to read perfectly well, they just cannot decipher such sensory input. One recovered Wernicke's aphasic patient once explained that when he was aphasic he felt like he was listening to a foreign language that he could never learn. As the reader may surmise, having either Broca's or Wernicke's aphasia may be one of the most frustrating and emotionally painful experiences a person could ever have.

As stated earlier, some aphasics cannot be classified into either of the two types described above. *Global* aphasics for instance, have severely disturbed comprehension *and* expression. Such patients are either totally mute or merely repeat nonsense syllables or grunt. The reason that we have concentrated on Broca's and Wernicke's aphasias, however, is that these conditions reveal information on the location of neural tissue critical to language functions.

Lesions in Broca's area were implicated in expressive disorders by Paul Broca in the 1860s, while Karl Wernicke linked comprehension disorders with lesions in Wernicke's area at about the turn of the century. Many scientists have obtained similar results since those times. Some scientists have speculated that these two areas serve as speech centers and that speech is actually produced in these chunks of neural tissue. As we have previously noted, there are some conceptual problems that accompany such a strict "localizationist" point of view. D. O. Hebb, a well-known modern neuropsychologist, models an excellent approach to the relation of the function and neuroanatomical location.

> No psychological function can exist within a segment of the cortex by itself. We commonly say that vision is located in the visual area, a part of the occipital lobe; but this does not mean that the whole process of seeing (or even of visual imagery) can occur in the occipital lobe. What it means is that an *essential part of the process occurs there, and only there.* Speech is "localized" in the cerebral cortex on the left side (for most persons). This again does not mean that the mediating processes of speech can occur in that tissue alone; it does mean that their organization depends on it (Hebb, 1958, in Mohr, 1976).

Some controversy exists concerning exactly where a lesion must occur to produce different types of aphasia. Mohr (1976), for instance, suggests that a lesion of just Broca's area produces a transient and mild language disturbance that is strikingly different from the severe and intractable syndrome known as Broca's aphasia. True Broca's aphasia, according to Mohr, usually stems from an infarction of the left middle cerebral artery and involves considerably more tissue than just Broca's area. Whether or not Mohr is correct, there is considerable agreement (Benson & Geschwind, 1976) that expressive language disturbance is associated with a lesion just above and anterior to the Sylvian Fissure (Broca's area) and receptive language disturbance results from a lesion below and posterior to that fissure (Wernicke's area; see Figure 4-6). Finer distinctions than this are not necessary for our purposes; and besides, individual variation would probably render such a fine-grained analysis invalid.

By way of review, what we have discussed thus far are the following points. (1) Human language is *lateralized*; that is, it tends to occur in the left cerebral hemisphere. (2) Aphasia is a language disorder resulting from brain lesions and appears to interfere with language itself. (3) Broca's aphasia, an expressive language disorder, results from lesions just above and anterior to the Sylvian Fissure (in or near Broca's area). (4) Finally, Wernicke's aphasia, a receptive or comprehensive language disorder, results from lesions just below and posterior to the Sylvian Fissure (in or near Wernicke's area). Next, we will briefly review other evidence that affords additional support for the notion that particular neural areas are especially involved in language.

Electrical brain stimulation.   Penfield and his associates (for example, Penfield & Roberts, 1959) obtained interesting data by electrically stimulating the brains of patients while they were undergoing neurosurgery. Since the brain has few pain receptors,[5] such operations can be performed with only a local anesthetic while the patient is conscious. Cerebral cortical stimulation involves applying an electrode to the cortex surface and passing an electric current into a patient's brain at sufficient intensity levels to obtain a behavioral response. The current used is very low and therefore quite innocuous. Penfield and his associates found that stimulation to particular temporal-parietal lobe areas was quite effective both in causing vocalizations (usually brief, single-vowel, monotonic cries) and also in abruptly curtailing patients' vocalizations. These researchers felt that such a cessation in vocalization and speech was analogous to a clinical aphasia. Interestingly, the cortical areas that produced speech arrest subsequent to their electrical stimulation had very similar locations to those that are implicated in Broca's and Wernicke's aphasias (see Figure 4-6). The cortical areas that Penfield and Roberts found were most associated with language are those just above and anterior to the Sylvian Fissure and just below and posterior to that fissure.

Not only do such electrical-stimulation results agree with aphasia cases with respect to the particular cortical areas involved in speech, but they also provide further evidence for lateralization. Penfield and Roberts found that ''when stimulation produces aphasic arrest, it is clear that the hemisphere exposed is dominant for speech, for we have never been able to produce such an effect from the nondominant hemisphere'' (Penfield & Roberts, 1959, p. 111).

---

[5]Most intracranial pain receptors are not located in neural tissue itself, but rather in the meninges (the connective tissue surrounding the brain) and vascular tissue.

Neuroanatomy. A final type of information that provides additional evidence concerning the neuroanatomical correlates of language comes from the histological examination of neuroanatomical features. Shortly after Broca and Wernicke postulated that language functions were mediated above and below the Sylvian Fissure, it was discovered that that fissure was longer and had a different slope on the left hemisphere than on the right (Cunningham, 1892). Furthermore, Cunningham found these cerebral asymmetries existed in the brains of very young infants. His data suggest that the hemispheres are different from birth and that they are possibly designed for different functions.

Later, in a well-known study, Geschwind (Geschwind & Levitsky, 1968) discovered that the planem temporale, an area located near the Sylvian Fissure in Wernicke's area, is significantly longer in the left hemisphere than in the right. As Mohr (1976) noted, one reason this finding generated so much interest was that "in a statistically significant number of adult brains . . . the region of maximum Sylvian Fissure asymmetry corresponds with the region where left-sided lesions are most likely to result in Wernicke's aphasia, a profound and long-lasting disruption of all elements of language" (p. 507). Thus, Geschwind's finding provided evidence of a morphological correlate for both the lateralization of language and its specific location within the left cerebral hemisphere. Importantly, Geschwind's findings with respect to the greater length and area of the left planem temporale have been replicated in the brains of adults, newborns, and fetuses (Wada, Clarke, & Hamm, 1975; Witelson & Paille, 1973). Recently, Rubens (1977) confirmed that the left Sylvian Fissure is longer than the right and that this, in turn, results in a longer left planem temporale and parietal operculum. However, he noted that such gross morphological asymmetries are only suggestive of neuroanatomical specialization for function.

We have provided fairly compelling evidence that particular neuroanatomical areas are critically involved in language. Now that we have described the neuroanatomy of language, we will explore the specific brain regions that might be associated with memory.

ANATOMICAL CORRELATES OF MEMORY

Central Brain Correlates

The complexities of mnemonic information processing have been discussed in detail in the previous chapter. We will concentrate only on the operations of long-term memory and its neurobiological foundations.

In recent years it has been proposed that there are two classes of information stored in long-term memory—episodic and semantic (Tulving, 1972). Examples of episodic memory are specific personal experiences that have occurred at particular times in particular places. For example, one's ability to remember what one ate for yesterday's breakfast, lunch, or dinner represents an episodic memory. Most forgetting involves such specific information stored within episodic memory. This forgetting is probably due to the interference of other similar personal experiences. For example, one's inability to remember what one ate for breakfast, lunch, or dinner two weeks ago might be due to all the other intervening meals since that time. In contrast, information contained within semantic memory constitutes knowledge of the world and need not be tied to specific spatiotemporal events. For example, the facts that caffeine is an important ingredient of coffee or that there are twelve months in a year are examples of semantic memories that are probably recalled by most of us without reference to a particular place or time. Two major neural regions of the brain subserve processes associated with the storage and retrieval of information within episodic and semantic long-term memory (Kesner, 1980; Rozin, 1976), namely, the hippocampus (see Figure 4-4) with episodic memory and the cerebral cortex (see Figures 4-3, 4-5, 4-6) with semantic long-term memory. While other neural regions are also important in processing mnemonic information, most of the data point to the hippocampus and cerebral cortex as critical neuronal substrates.

The hippocampus and episodic memory. The association of the hippocampus with episodic memory derives from cases where humans have had their hippocampi removed surgically, where viral encephalitic conditions affect the hippocampus, where prolonged alcohol intoxication produces damage to the hippocampus, and where blood flow to the hippocampus has been temporarily reduced. All of these conditions produce an amnesic syndrome involving a failure to recall events of the recent past even though immediate and short-term memory are relatively normal. In addition, patients so affected cannot relate recent experiences to past experiences. For these patients, the past remains elusive and unfamiliar. The best-known case (Milner, 1970) is that of H.M., who was subjected to bilateral removal of parts of the temporal lobes including the hippocampus in order to control epileptic seizures. Immediately following the operation, he did not recognize the hospital staff nor could he remember or learn his way around the hospital. He had vague memories of events that occurred within three years prior to the operation (retrograde amnesia). For example, he could not remember that his uncle died three years prior to the operation but he could remember a few more recent trivial memories. However, his early memory was intact and clear and his speech, short-term memory, and semantic memory appeared to be normal. For example, Milner (1970) reports that on one occasion the patient was asked to remember the number 584. After sitting quietly for fifteen minutes he correctly recalled the number and when asked how he did it, said "It's easy. You just remember 8. You see, 5, 8, and 4 add up to 17. You remember 8, subtract it from 17 and it leaves 9. Divide 9 in half and you get 5 and 4, and there you are: 584. Easy." Immediately afterward he was quite unable to remember 584 or his train of thought.

H.M.'s main problem after his operation was and is his inability to recall any new event once it becomes unavailable to short-term memory. For example, six months after his operation his family moved to another house on the same street, but he continued to go to the old house because he did not remember the new address. Each time he was told of the death of his uncle, he would become very emotional and then promptly forget. H.M.'s condition has not changed over the twenty years since his operation. His intelligence remains above normal. He works at a job assembling cigarette lighters and cardboard frames, but he cannot describe the job. He has been able to learn some new motor skills and has learned something about the spatial environment in which he lives. He remembers that President Kennedy was assassinated, but otherwise he has not learned anything new during these past 20 years. His own description of his inability to remember his past experiences is very apt: "Every day is alone in itself, whatever enjoyment I've had, and whatever sorrow I've had. . . . Right now, I'm wondering have I done or said something amiss? You see, at this moment everything looks clear to me, but what happened just before? That's what worries me. It's like waking from a dream. I just don't remember" (Milner, 1970).

Similar deficits have been reported in humans with viral infections involving the hippocampus or those with a history of repeated episodes of alcohol intoxication (Butters & Cermak, 1975; Victor, Adams, & Collins, 1971). This latter condition is known as Korsakoff's psychosis and is characterized by an inability to learn and remember new experiences. In addition, there is an inability to organize past experiences into a coherent narrative of the past. This deficit can result in extensive confabulation (making up of events that have not occurred) as Korsakoff's patients apparently attempt to fill in the gaps in their sketchy recollection of past events. Lastly, such patients are frequently disoriented with respect to time and place. The following is a description of a patient with Korsakoff's psychosis quoted by Barbizet (1970) from Delay (1942, p. 28).

Victor, aged fifty-nine, is suffering from alcoholic psychopolyneuritis. He has extensive memories of his past and can, for example, give a detailed account of his military service in Indochina in 1903 during the Annam campaign and of the conditions of his service during the 1914–1918 war. For more than a year, however, Victor has been progressively forgetting everything he has just perceived or accomplished. He can carry on a conversation, but as soon as one leaves him he states that he has seen nobody; if his questioner returns, Victor does not recognize him and this behavior is repeated each time Victor sees him. After some months at Sainte-Anne he is unable to recognize either the doctors or the nurses; he loses his way in the hospital wing, of which he cannot recall the geography any more than the the name of the ward or the number of his bed. He reads the paper but immediately forgets what he has read and will show the same surprise he originally showed upon reading the same news again. Victor cannot recognize his place at table and cannot remember if he has actually eaten what has only just been served to him. He plays cards, but as soon as the game is over he forgets that he had been playing. His amnesia extends with the same intensity to all perceptions: visual, auditory, and tactile, and even the polyneuritic pains provoked by the pressure of the calf muscles are immediately forgotten.

It is important to note that in Korsakoff's psychosis, extent of neural damage often involves regions other than just the hippocampus. Such diffuse damage could account for the more extensive clinical problems such patients present when compared to those with discrete hippocampal lesions (such as H.M.).

Disturbance in storage and/or retrieval of information within episodic long-term memory can be transitory due to a temporary occlusion of the blood supply to the hippocampus or the presence of epileptic activity emanating from foci (small lesions) within the hippocampus. During such an attack persons might suddenly not remember events that happened hours or even days before the attack. For example, they may be surprised at seeing an object in a place where they themselves had placed it on the previous day. In spite of their amnesia for recent events, however, they are capable of engaging in conversation and simple daily activities. After the attack, which may last from minutes to hours, there is complete recovery of memory for experiences prior to the attack, but events that occurred during the attack are lost. This syndrome, known as "transient global amnesia," can also be produced by seizure-inducing electrical stimulation of the hippocampus in humans (Bickford, Mulder, Dodge, Suien, & Rome, 1958), and animals (Kesner, Dixon, Pickett, & Berman, 1975). All these cases have in common a disturbance of normal function of the hippocampus and a loss of episodic memory. They produce a failure to recognize or recall recent events (especially new events) in the presence of relatively normal short-term memory, intelligence, and ability to learn some simple motor skills. In the case of Korsakoff's psychosis there may also be confabulation and disorientation.

Large hippocampal lesions in animals, especially monkeys, also produce learning deficits when complex tasks are used (for example, concurrent pattern discrimination, delayed matching-to-sample, sequential ordering of responses [Iverson, 1976]). Also, temporary and reversible disruption of normal hippocampal function induced by electrical stimulation of the hippocampus immediately after a learning experience will disrupt subsequent long-term memory while short-term memory remains intact (Berman & Kesner, 1976; Kesner & Conner, 1974).

Finally, Penfield (1970) has demonstrated that electrical stimulation of the temporal lobe including the hippocampus of humans can often elicit memorylike experience. For example, stimulation of a patient who was a secretary elicited the following response: "Oh, I had a very, very familiar memory, in an office somewhere. I could see the desks. I was there and someone was calling me, a man leaning on a desk with a pencil in his hand" (Penfield, 1970, p. 113). It is possible that such memories do not represent the normal memory recall process, but nevertheless they suggest that the hippocampus might have access to specific information probably stored in the cerebral cortex.

The cerebral cortex and semantic memory. The cerebral cortex has been implicated with semantic memory for a variety of reasons. First, its size and the complexity of its neuronal organization render it a likely candidate for the storage and processing of one's wealth of semantic memory. Second, as we have discussed in the previous section, language is principally mediated by the cerebral cortex. Since human semantic memory is largely comprised of language-related information, it is probable that the cerebral cortex is also important for semantic memory. Lastly, diffuse damage to the cerebral cortex from such degenerative presenile dementias as Alzheimer's and Pick's diseases results in a marked decrease in mental status characterized by a loss of long-term memory. Dementia patients show deficits in many areas of intellectual functioning—including memorization, learning, problem solving, verbal abilities, reasoning, and abstract thinking. However, in tests of memory, their primary deficits are in long-term, rather than short-term, memory.

The sequence of decay of cognitive function in presenile dementia starts with failure of memory for recent events while old memories remain largely intact. For example, a dementia patient is unable to adapt to a new situation and has difficulties in ordering recent events chronologically. His memories of early events become increasingly impoverished in that he shows disorganization in the formulation of plans and fails to recognize familiar places. These problems are followed by a loss of organized recall of specific recent experiences. Examples of this are not remembering the news shortly after a news broadcast and repeating the same story to the same audience in rapid succession. Eventually there will be a loss in personal skills (such as playing a piano or knitting) followed by a loss in social habits and automated routines (for example dressing and normal speech). At this stage patients often become depressed. Finally, the patient loses awareness of the problem, becomes mute, refuses to eat, and engages in very stereotyped behaviors. It is of interest to note that the loss of function parallels, in reverse order, the development of complex cognitive functioning including the development of semantic memory. Alzheimer's disease is representative of disease states that produce symptoms of dementia. It is characterized by gross atrophy of the brain, loss of cells in the cerebral cortex and other neural regions (such as the hippocampus), degeneration of nerve cells, and the occurrence of senile plaques. Other types of dementia like Pick's disease and Creutzfeldt-Jakob disease also produce diffuse disturbances of the cerebral cortex. Thus, semantic memory is probably subserved by the entire cerebral cortex. At present no specific location within the cerebral cortex has been found to be associated with specific memories, although it is possible to access specific memories via stimulation of the hippocampus (Penfield, 1970).

ONTOGENY OF LANGUAGE AND MEMORY

The purpose of this section is to present the salient maturational features of both memory and language development. Initially we will discuss the difficulty in selecting an appropriate neuroanatomical index of maturation. We will then attempt to show the existence of some degree of correlation between neuroanatomical indices of maturation and language and memory development.

Assessing the maturation of the CNS necessarily involves an important decision concerning the particular index or indices to be used. A caveat to keep in mind is that different maturational indices may produce very different developmental histories. One maturational index may suggest a particular neural structure to be completely mature, while another index reveals considerable immaturity. Another problem encountered in the selection and acceptance of maturational indices is that those factors critical to the functioning of neural systems may not be the ones available or selected for scrutiny. While scientists can observe and measure such factors as neural weight and myelinization, the truly critical development processes may involve such difficult-to-quantify processes as neurotransmitter synthesis or intracellular growth patterns.

The method usually used to select a neurophysiological or neuroanatomical index of a function is to examine as many indices as possible and select the one(s) that best predicts or correlates with the emergence or alteration of that function. There can be considerable variation in the relationship of different behaviors or functions and the various indices of neuroanatomical maturation. The emergence and development of language, for instance, most often appears to be compared with neuronal myelinization while dendritic arborization ("arbor" means "tree" in Latin) or branching is currently the most frequently used indicator of memory development. The use of these indices to assess language- and memory-related neuroanatomical maturation is probably due to precedent or convention since, as we will soon see, they both yield similar developmental histories. One potential use of the relationship between a neuroanatomical index and a function is that such relationships might reveal the particular neuroanatomical substrates of functions. The fact that myelinization and dendritic arborization are both correlated with language and memory emergence suggests that those functions might emerge through the general maturational development of relevant neuroanatomical areas. The congruence of these two indices also affords us greater confidence in our discussion of the association between language and memory and neuroanatomical maturation.

Maturation and Language Development

Before examining the correspondence between neuroanatomical indices and language emergence, we will briefly depict the normal progression of language acquisition. (See Chapter Two for a more detailed presentation.) From about 0–6 months the infant (from Latin, meaning "without speech," Nash, 1970) mostly cries, fusses, and coos— primarily the former. Then, from about 6–12 months babbling and cooing become more prominent, and crying less so (Ervin-Tripp, 1966). Also, there is a gradual progression at this time from vowel to consonant sounds, and the variety of sounds becomes greater. A child's first words usually appear anywhere from 12–18 months and these are usually simple nouns. While children usually have very small vocabularies at this time, they make the most of their few words through the use of expressive intonation. Also, there is considerable evidence that language comprehension surpasses speech during this early period of development. Some scientists speculate that children first produce true language at the next stage of language acquisition, 18–24 months of age. This is when children produce their first simple sentences. Such sentences may only be a few words in length and may employ inappropriate syntax, but they nevertheless reflect the child's use of a limited vocabulary to meet his or her particular needs in particular situations. The child uses words that he or she once merely imitated and creates new—sometimes unique—sentences that reflect his or her desires. Such sentences are not parroted and thus do not represent explicit imitations of modeled adult language. Lastly, from the ages of 30–48 months the child's language skills and vocabulary develop tremendously. Vocabulary size triples or quadruples, sentences become longer, and grammar grows more complex. It is no accident that in most countries formal education begins only after this stage of dramatic language acquisition is past. By the time the average five-year-old child in the United States enters school, he or she has a vocabulary of about 2,500 words.

The progression from one language period to the next is remarkably consistent and invariant. This regularity appears in the face of a large variety of cultures (Slobin, 1966) and environmental hurdles (such as those facing deaf children born of deaf parents [Lenneberg, 1967]). Such consistency in the face of tremendous environmental flux suggests that there is a genetic predisposition for language emergence (Chomsky, 1965, 1972) and that language emergence is tied to maturation. We will now examine this latter proposition by investigating the relationship of neuroanatomical maturation and the unfolding of language.

Myelinization is a process in which neurons are sheathed by a layer of lipid (fat). Myelinization occurs both pre- and postnatally and the process is probably not complete until puberty (Nash, 1970). Myelin insulates neurons and therefore aids in the transmission of nerve impulses. While neurons can conduct impulses prior to myelinization, they are much more efficient when they are mature (myelinated). Another reason that myelinization is a good maturational index is that it is temporally correlated with other important developmental changes: an increase in the number and size of nerve cells, the pigmentation of particular brain structures, and the development of axons and dendrites. Perhaps more important for our purposes, myelinization appears to be correlated with function or use. For instance, if one eye of a newborn cat is deprived of light, this will reduce the myelinization of the optic tract leading from that eye.

As our discussion of aphasia and cortical stimulation would suggest, a search for neuroanatomical correlates of language eventually leads to the cerebral cortex. Myelinization is an important index of cortical maturation because, while cortical neurons themselves lack myelin, the axons leading to and from cortical areas are myelinated. As previously noted, the myelinization of such axons can be related to the development of the corresponding cortex.

In a heroic series of studies that spanned about twenty-five years, Conel (1939–1967) examined the maturation of the cerebral cortex. He not only employed myelinization as a developmental assessment but used a variety of other measures as well. Some neuroanatomical developmental trends of the cerebral cortex noted by Conel are these: (1) width and thickness of every cortical layer increase, (2) the density of nerve cells decreases as nerve cell size increases, (3) axons and dendrites increase in length and width, and (4) exogenous fibers (that is, fibers coming to the cortex from other brain regions) increase in size and number (Milner, 1976). Using such indices Conel was able to map a pattern of cortical development.

At birth, human infants differ very little from other mammalian species with respect to the mature portions of their CNSs. They differ from the young of other mammalian species only in terms of their *potential* for a greater and longer developmental process. In accordance with the principle of neurophylogenesis, the behavior of newborn infants is directed primarily by the brain stem and midbrain. Only after about one month do the primary motor and sensory cortical areas and the visual cortex begin to function.

The primary motor and sensory cortices show the earliest and most rapid development of any of the cortical areas. Within these areas, the tissue closest to the central sulcus develops the earliest—perhaps because of the ample blood supply to this area. Next, areas adjacent to primary sensory and motor areas develop at slower rates. Then, association areas in the temporal, occipital, and parietal cortices mature even more slowly. The prefrontal cortex is the last to begin the maturational process, and that process transpires most slowly (Turner, 1948, 1950).

The preceding constitutes the order of maturation of large sections of cortical tissue. Such a progression is of little interest to us, however, unless it can be related to the emergence of language. There is evidence that a progression in language skills is temporally linked with the general maturation of cortical areas known to be important for language. For instance, while the frontal lobes are the fastest growing cortical areas between 15-24 months of age (a period when language is first emerging), only two areas are receiving increased numbers of myelinated fibers coming from other parts of the brain. One is the area of the primary motor strip that controls mouth movements and the other is Broca's area. Unfortunately, a comparison of such global attributes is not very convincing and merely reveals that the two measures are temporally correlated. Body weight is, no doubt, also positively correlated with language emergence. Yet this fact does little to elucidate the morphological correlates of language. We must, therefore, examine the maturation of particular cortical layers and their relationship to the emergence of language in order to construct a stronger case for the neuroanatomical correlates of language. In order to understand the possible developmental relationships between different cortical layers and language, it is necessary to describe briefly the six cortical layers of the human cerebral cortex.

The six cortical layers are numbered 1 through 6 according to how a neuroanatomist or neurosurgeon comes upon them (see Figure 4-7). Thus, the top cortical layer, layer number 1, is on the outside of the brain while the inside layer is number 6. The layers can briefly be described as follows.

> *Layer 1: The molecular layer.* This layer is composed primarily of ascending axons and dendrites coming from lower layers. It contains relatively few cell bodies and these are typically horizontal Cajal cells and granule cells.
>
> *Layer 2: The external granular layer.* Contains mostly small pyramidal cells and granule cells, both of which have axonal and dendritic processes ascending to the molecular layer.
>
> *Layer 3: The external pyramidal layer.* This layer is very similar to Layer 2 except that it has a higher percentage of pyramidal cells.
>
> *Layer 4: The internal granular layer.* This layer consists chiefly of small granule cells.
>
> *Layer 5: The deep pyramidal layer.* Layer 5 is composed of medium and large pyramidal cells which send axons down to the white matter below the cortex and long apical dendrites to higher cortical layers.
>
> *Layer 6: The fusiform layer.* This lowest layer contains granule and pyramidal cells. These have a myelinated axon rising to higher cortical layers while dendrites branch both vertically and horizontally.

There is some evidence and much speculation that higher developmental functions in humans are dependent upon the top three layers of cortex (layers 1-3) which are together called the *supragranular layer*. These three layers are uniquely human and Ramon Cajal, the Nobel laureate and renowned neuroanatomist, has suggested that the sophisti-

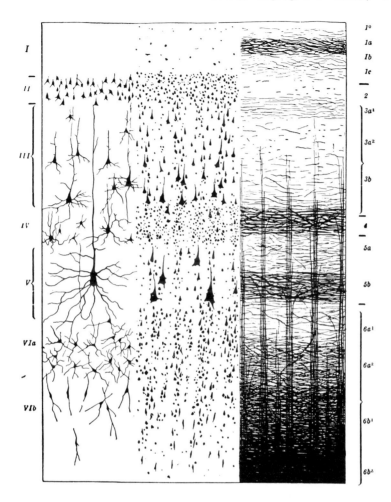

Figure 4-7

Schematic histological characteristics of the six layers of the cerebral cortex. A few examples of typical nerve cells are shown on the left, the distribution of cell bodies in the middle, and the distribution of fiber processes on the right.

From S.W. Ranson and S.L. Clark, *The Anatomy of the Nervous Systems*, 9th ed. (Philadelphia, Penn.: W.B. Saunders, 1953), p. 323. Reprinted by permission.

cated thought processes of humans are mediated by these supragranular layers (cited in Milner, 1976).

Milner (1976) has mapped the stages of cortical maturation that accompany the emergence of speech. She reports that cortical layers 5 and 6 of Broca's area begin to mature at about 1 month after birth—the same time that meaningful vocalization begins (that is, vocalization that communicates inner states). At about 9-12 months, when infants begin uttering intelligible words, cortical layer 3 begins to be myelinated. From 1-2 years, when childrens' vocabularies are expanding, the third cortical layer of Broca's area is almost completely myelinated as are the third layers of other association areas involved in speech production. When children have their greatest burst in language capabilities (from 2-4 years) all of the third cortical layers of speech and language areas are myelinated. Support for the relationship between Broca's area maturation and language emergence can also be gleaned from an examination of dendritic arborization or branching. While there are few or no dendritic interconnections at birth, their number increases dramatically during the first two years of life. Figure 4–8 depicts the rapid development of dendritic interneural connections around Broca's area before and during language acquisition. As Figure 4–8 reveals, the greatest increase in dendritic arborization around Broca's area occurs during the time when language is first emerging (about 12-24 months).

Thus, a comparison of the maturation of discrete cortical areas and language emergence reveals an even more intimate association between neural maturation and language than was obtained from global cortical assessment. Knowledge of the relationship between specific brain areas and language might aid in the elucidation of neurodevelopmental concepts such as critical or sensitive developmental periods, neurolocalization of function versus equipotentiality, and lateralization.

Maturation and Memory Development

There are two salient features that characterize memory development in both animals and humans. First, there appears to be a relatively rapid development of episodic memory compared to the more gradual development of semantic memory. For example, in humans tasks involving recognition of pictorial material tap episodic memory almost exclusively and, therefore, show either no developmental changes at all or just small ones early in life. In contrast, tasks requiring recall from semantic memory (for example, spontaneously retelling a previously heard story or integrating the meanings of sentences) show marked age-related changes in the efficiency of performance (Brown, 1975; Olson, 1976; Reese, 1976). It must be recognized, however, that age-related changes in learning and memory may often be due to alterations in development of sensory, motor, motivational, or attentional processes. It is necessary to dissociate specific age-related changes in learning and memory from these other contributing variables.

Second, there is an increasing development of new and more effective encoding and retrieval strategies, such as verbal labeling, rehearsal, clustering, categorization, higher-order organization, use of imagery, and adoption of plans. For example, early in development children do not rehearse, they learn simply by repetition. During that time they go through a period in which instructions to use a particular strategy like

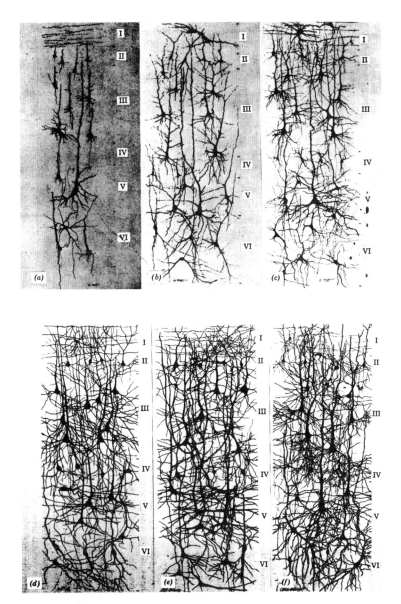

Figure 4-8

Postnatal development of human cerebral cortex around Broca's Area (FCBm); camera lucida drawings from Golgi-Cox preparations. a: newborn; b: 1 month; c: 3 months; d: 6 months; e: 15 months; f: 24 months. Inspection of original sections shows an even more dramatic increase in density of neuropil between 15 and 24 months.

rehearsal have no benefit. Later in development children can learn to use simple strategies like rehearsal, but they do not use them spontaneously. During this time specific instructions to use a mnemonic strategy might improve performance. Finally, a developmental point is reached in which children can select from a number of available strategies, but they do not necessarily select the appropriate one for the task (Brown, 1975; Flavell, 1977). Even though it is more difficult to assess the use of strategies in animals, it appears that young animals are less efficient than older animals when encoding and retrieval strategies are required to perform complex tasks such as a 14-choice-point maze (Arenberg & Robertson, 1977), delayed-response learning (Fox, 1971; Medin, 1969; Riopelle & Rogers, 1965), passive-avoidance learning (Feigley & Spear, 1970), or taste-aversion learning with long taste-illness delays (Baker, Baker, & Kesner, 1977). In contrast, no age differences occur in acquisition of simpler learning tasks like a 2-choice-point maze (Arenberg & Robertson, 1977), active avoidance, or taste-aversion learning with little delay between taste and illness experiences (Baker et al., 1977). However, in these easier tasks differences do occur on subsequent retention tests, implying either a deficiency in strategies to encode information into semantic memory or a deficiency in the development of appropriate retrieval strategies with a subsequent accelerated forgetting. For example, Campbell and Campbell (1962) showed that when 18- and 100-day-old rats were conditioned to fear a specific compartment of a shuttle box and then tested for retention of fear immediately, 21 or 42 days later, there was almost perfect retention for both age groups when tested immediately after training, but the 18-day-old rat showed no retention on tests 21 and 42 days later. In contrast, 100-day-old rats showed excellent retention (no forgetting) at all retention intervals. Similar results have been reported for active avoidance, T-maze escape learning, and appetitive-discrimination learning situations (Campbell, Jaynes, & Misanin, 1968; Kirby, 1963; N. Smith, 1968).

Campbell and Spear (1972) have suggested that young rats forget specific information faster than adults; they suggest that this condition is akin to infantile amnesia. A different interpretation (the one we prefer) suggests that younger animals have excellent retention based on episodic memory capacity but have not acquired appropriate strategies to organize information into semantic or organized memory and thus cannot retain information for long periods of time. Thus, infantile amnesia may be due to an inefficient use of processes necessary to organize information into semantic memory.

A third salient feature of memory development has only been described for humans. It appears that knowledge and awareness of one's own memory capability (metamemory) increases over time. For example, one of the facts about one's memory that has practical consequences for mnemonic behavior is a cognizance of the rapid decay of information from short-term memory. To test for knowledge of this fact a child was asked,

"If you wanted to phone your friend and someone told you the phone number, would it make any difference if you called right away after you heard the number or if you got a drink of water first?" Children in the first through fifth grades invariably said that one should phone immediately, while kindergartners said one could phone or get a drink of water with almost equal frequency (Kreutzer, Leonard, & Flavell, 1975). More detailed information substantiating all three of these developmental characteristics of memory in humans can be found in the previous chapter.

In summary, it appears that retention of a variety of experiences in both animals and humans is a function of the degree to which information is organized in semantic memory. During early stages of development the lack of use of mnemonic strategies (reliance on repetition) and lack of awareness of one's memory capabilities contribute to inefficient encoding of specific experiences into an organized memory system. This entails an increased probability of forgetting and infantile amnesia. With age, the increasing use of appropriate means to organize information increases the probability of retention and decreases the probability of forgetting.

Are the above mentioned developmental changes in memory due to neural maturational processes? A partial affirmative answer to this question was provided by Campbell, Misanin, White, and Lytle (1974). They compared retention capabilities of young and adult guinea pigs and rats. The guinea pig is a precocial animal—it has a 65 day gestation period and is born with a fully developed central nervous system. Myelinization is nearly complete and dendritic and axonal growth is at a level that a rat achieves 20–30 days after birth. Campbell et al. (1974) showed that, in contrast to rats, the young guinea pigs do not show rapid forgetting–perhaps because of their use of encoding or retrieval strategies. Thus, the guinea pig's capacity for encoding information into an organized memory appears to be fully developed at birth while the rat's is not, suggesting that the poor retention by the neonatal rat is primarily due to the immaturity of its nervous system rather than its lack of experience.

Are there maturational changes that could serve as indices of critical events during memory development? In order to answer this question it will be necessary to describe specific neural maturational changes that occur in the hippocampus and cerebral cortex during postnatal development in both animals and humans. We will emphasize mostly dendritic differentiation, which includes growth and branching of dendrites with the formation of spines and simple and complex new synaptic connections. This choice is based on the findings that animals reared in impoverished or enriched environments show not only alterations in memory development but also marked changes in dendritic differentiation. It should be realized, however, that many other neuro-anatomical as well as physiological and neurochemical changes might also relate to the development of learning and memory. In addition, because of the paucity of data available on humans, the most extensive studies have been undertaken with rats and cats. Extrapolation to the human situation must, therefore, be approached with caution. In order to interrelate measurements of specific anatomical changes among species Himwich (1973) has proposed a system whereby the time between an animal's conception and maturity is divided into equal periods. All measurements are then expressed as a percentage of an adult value, thereby minimizing the interspecies time-scale differences. For example, this system suggests that the changing weight of the human brain between 15½ and 20 months after birth corresponds to a similar proportion of development in the rat between 13 and 17½ days after birth. Pyramidal-cell development of the cerebral cortex in the human brain at 2 to 4 years of age appears similar to the same level of neural development of the 25-30-day-old rat. Obviously the time-scale of comparison will vary with the specific neuroanatomical measure.

Hippocampus. There are two basic cell types that comprise the hippocampus. The *pyramidal cell*, located in Ammon's Horn, and the *granule cell*, located in the dentate gyrus region of the hippocampus (see Figure 4-9). The axions of pyramidal cells provide for interconnections with other neuronal structures. In contrast, axons of granule cells interconnect with pyramidal cells and other cells within the hippocampus. In humans, the pyramidal and granule cells are well developed at birth and mature with changes in dendritic growth and arborization (Conel, 1939–1967). In cats, mice, and rats the pyramidal cells are also well developed at birth. In the rat only a few granule cells are present at birth, but they differentiate rapidly to a total of 87 percent between 0 and 16 days and reach adult levels by 8 months of age (Altman & Bayer, 1975).

Synaptogenesis (development of synaptic connections) of pyramidal cells or granule cells has not been studied in humans, but synaptogenesis of dendrites emerging from granule cells has recently been studied in detail in rats (Cotman, Taylor, & Lynch, 1973; Crain, Cotman, Taylor, & Lynch, 1973). They found regular increases in the number of simple and complex synapses starting about 4 days after birth until adulthood.

Cerebral Cortex. The cerebral cortex, as shown in Figure 4–7, has many layers whose major components show a high degree of constancy of arrangement. In humans the cerebral cortex is completely stratified at birth. Of the many types of cells in the cerebral cortex there are two cell types of major interest, the pyramidal cell located mostly in layers 2, 3, 5, and 6, and the granule cell located mostly in layer 4. Examples of pyramidal and granule neurons are shown in Figure 4–10.

In humans, it has been found that at birth pyramidal cells are well developed. Most growth changes of the dendritic plexus in terms of

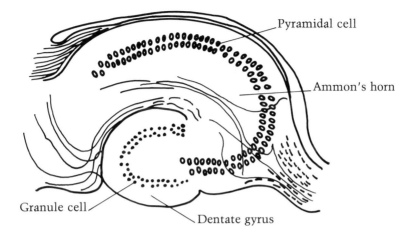

Figure 4-9

Schematic drawing of the hippocampal formation showing the location of Ammon's Horn with pyramidal cells and dentate gyrus with granule cells.

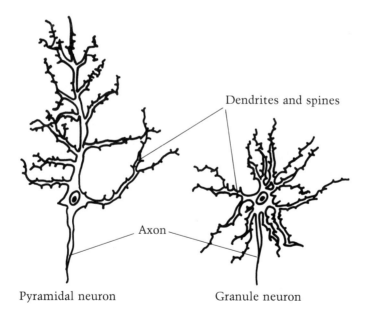

Figure 4-10

Two types of neurons from the cerebral cortex. The pyramidal cells have long axons leaving the cortex (projection fibers), whereas the granule cells are locally distributed. Large numbers of these granule cells are responsible for the voluminous cortex of primates, especially humans.

increase in size and branching pattern have taken place before the age of two years. Even though further growth occurs, there is a marked decrease in the rate, taking at least another two years to reach the dendritic complexity seen in adults (see Figure 4–8). In contrast, the time course for development of dendritic complexity in the rat takes about 25-40 days to complete (Eayrs & Goodhead, 1959; Schade & Van Groenigen, 1961).

The granule cells develop after birth and appear to grow their dendritic arborizations somewhat slower than do pyramidal cells. Neuronal input into the cerebral cortex is also well developed at birth in humans, but axons continue to increase in density after birth.

Myelinization of afferent axons and intracortical axons occurs very late in humans. For examples, in humans myelinization of the corpus callosum starts about the fourth month postnatally, but is not complete until seven years of age. Also, it has been estimated that intracortical or intrinsic connection within cortical association areas continues to develop until the second and third decade of life (Yakovlev & Lecours, 1967).

With respect to synaptogenesis only a few axodendritic synapses are seen at birth in both rats and cats. Axosomatic synapses appear at the end of the first week in the cat and at the end of three weeks in the rat. Unfortunately, comparable results on formation of synaptic junctions in humans are not yet available. Most types of synapses continue to increase, especially in conjunction with development of dendritic spines. These changes in number of synapses have been quantified using both Golgi and electron-microscope techniques[6] by Eayrs and Goodhead (1959) using the somatosensory cortex of the rat; Aghajanian and Bloom (1967) using layer 1 of the parietal cortex of the rat; and Cragg (1975) using visual cortex in the cat. Their results are shown in Figure 4–11. In all three cases marked increases in the number of synapses can be seen starting about the twelfth day postnatally and increasing at a phenomenal rate until ages 26-30 days, at which time adult levels were reached, except in the case of the cat's visual cortex, where this increase was followed by a decrease in the number of synapses. The observation by Cragg (1975) implies that during maturation more synapses may be produced than are necessary and furthermore suggests the possibility that experience could function not only by adding new synapses but also by preserving old synapses.

In summary, of the many neuroanatomical changes that occur within the hippocampus and cerebral cortex during maturation, the growth and

---

[6]The Golgi technique represents a neuroanatomical method in which neural tissue is immersed in an osmium-dichromate solution followed by impregnation with diluted solutions of silver nitrate. The value of this Golgi staining procedure rests upon the fact that only 10 percent of neurons appears stained dark brown against a yellow background. It is, therefore, possible to identify individual cells with their axons, axonal ramifications, dendrites, and dendritic spines (see Figure 4–8). The electron-microscope technique represents a neuroanatomical method in which neural elements including synapses and cellular constituents (such as ribosomes, mitochondria, and vesicles containing neurotransmitters) can be identified because of tremendous magnification.

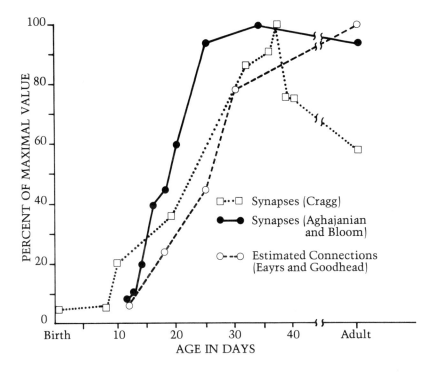

Figure 4–11

Changes in number of synapses in visual cortex of the rat (Cragg) and parietal cortex of the rat (Aghajanian and Bloom) and changes in number of estimated connections in somato-sensory cortex of the rat (Eayrs and Goodhead) as a function of age. The number of estimated connections or synapses is expressed in percent of maximal value.

branching of dendrites with the formation of spines with simple and complex new synaptic connections constitute the most important changes. Furthermore, it is clear that dendritic differentiation of pyramidal and granule cells within the hippocampus and neocortex mature in parallel with improvements in the organization of memory function. Although the degree to which these neuroanatomical maturational changes relate to memory development is not known, this type of information might aid in the elucidation of specific means by which new experiences can affect development of an extensive episodic and semantic memory system.

LANGUAGE DEVELOPMENT: EXTENT OF PLASTICITY

Before we discuss the role of plasticity of the nervous system during the development of language and memory, it is of importance to define what is meant by plasticity. Unfortunately, plasticity has multiple meanings and thus definitions will vary greatly. Most often plasticity is defined as the tendency of the nervous system to adjust to environmental influences during development and maturity and to establish or restore functions hampered by pathological or experimental conditions. This definition does not infer the mechanisms involved nor their adaptive value. In the present chapter we will discuss the extent of plasticity of specific neural elements based on either recovery of normal function following neural damage incurred at different ages or based on differential environmental experience.

At this point in the chapter we have accumulated a substantial amount of knowledge attesting to the lateralization of language and its mediation by fairly discrete areas of the cerebral cortex. Such information will enable us to appreciate the profound interplay between maturational processes and the capacity for language acquisition. One way to expose this interplay is through the examination of the effect of age on the potential for aphasia recovery (see Lenneberg, 1967; Searleman, 1977, for excellent reviews of relevant literature).

An adult with "true" Broca's or Wernicke's aphasia usually has severe language disabilities that persist until the end of his or her life. While Broca's aphasics may utter words or phrases (often unintelligible), these are mere remnants of a previously normal adult language. Wernicke's aphasics only understand a modicum of the language they had previously mastered. The most important point to note here is that not only do aphasics fail to recapture their previously acquired language skills, but they also fail to relearn language. That is, if their former language ability is gone and their aphasia persists, they are irrevocably bereft of language.

A normal infant—and even most abnormal infants—will progress from a nonlanguage to language state with no apparent specialized training or education. In contrast, even with specialized language training and therapy, patients with long-standing aphasia do not relearn language even over many years. Lenneberg (1967) has pointed out that aphasics show a learning deficit only for language. Such persons readily acquire concepts or information that does not require linguistic mediation. (This is true except in those cases where the pathological process or agent that produced the aphasia results in more general neurological, and hence cognitive, dysfunction.)

There are two possible explanations for an aphasic adult's inability to acquire language. First, language reacquisition may be impossible because the specific tissue, destroyed by whatever factor caused the aphasia (for example, trauma, aneurysm, cerebral occlusion, or infarct), was necessary for language. In other words, there are specific cortical tissues that must *always* be present for language to occur. A second explanation is that an adult cannot learn language simply because he or she is an adult (that is, no longer growing).

When adults become aphasics they do not really lose language per se. It would be erroneous to assume that language was somehow contained in the neural tissue that is destroyed by the aphasia-producing lesion. In an earlier section we stated that long-standing aphasia was usually intractable (resistant to change). Some cases of aphasia, however, do improve—and this usually happens within half a year of aphasia onset. Improvement (remission) of adult aphasia is of great importance. Adult aphasics do not relearn language when their aphasia remits; rather, they suddenly begin to be able to use their old preaphasic language skills. We know that language is not relearned since it reappears quite rapidly and the adult passes through none of the characteristic stages that normally accompany language acquisition (such as babbling, one-word utterances, and simple grammatical structure). Thus, language per se is not lost in aphasia—just the ability to use it.

One question that arises at this point concerns why some adult aphasics show remission and others do not. If transient aphasia and intractable aphasia are qualitatively different, it might not be accurate to draw inferences from one to the other. This contention is probably incorrect. Persons who recover from aphasia do so when one of the following conditions exists. (1) The damage leading to aphasia can be repaired by the body (Luria, 1970). For instance, glial cells can help remove clotted blood that is exerting pressure on a brain area important for language. (2) The aphasic person is left-handed. Such persons have greater bilateral representation of language than other persons (Hardyck & Petrinovich, 1977; Roberts, 1969). Thus, if these persons sustain a unilateral lesion which results in aphasia they have a better chance of recovery due to their transhemispheric language representation (Botez & Crighel, 1971; Luria, 1970). Therefore, there is simply less chance that a lesion will damage *all* the language-related tissue. The important point to note in both of these cases is that the difference between intractable and transient aphasia is a quantitative difference and not a qualitative one.

Adult and childhood aphasia[7] are sequelae of similar agents or processes. The most notable difference in their etiologies is that young children become aphasic from right-hemisphere lesions more frequently than adults (Searleman, 1977). This is merely due to the fact that language is less completely lateralized in children than in adults. Both adult and childhood aphasias exert similar effects on language. Children who had acquired language before they became aphasic lose their language abilities just as adults do. An important difference in the two conditions is their long-term prognosis.

It is relatively easy to depict the aphasia-recovery prognosis for children (Lenneberg, 1967). If a very young child (20–36 months) suffers a lesion to cortical areas that would produce aphasia in adults, he or she

---

[7]The term "childhood aphasia" will be used in this chapter mainly for convenience. Some authorities (for example, Benson & Geschwind, 1976) contend that it is inappropriate to use the term aphasia with children since they feel the term should be reserved for instances where language has been completely acquired prior to the aphasia-producing lesion.

becomes unresponsive, mute, and loses what little language he or she had. Yet, shortly thereafter the child will begin to relearn language just as he or she had initially. The child will pass through all the regular stages of language acquisition that normally precede adult language. If a slightly older child (3-4 years) sustains a similar lesion the effect is even less dramatic than in a very young child. This is because at this time children are experiencing a tremendous burgeoning of language and the lesion effects are superimposed upon this curve of rapid language acquisition. Thus, these children will evidence a temporary hiatus or pause in language use and acquisition, but after a few weeks steady improvement is obtained. Lastly, in older children (4-10 years), lesions produce the same aphasic symptoms as in adults. The only difference resides in the prognosis. Aphasia in 4-10-year-old children almost always subsides. Furthermore, when aphasia in this age group subsides, it does not do so in a few months, as happens with cases of transient adult aphasia. Rather, it shows steady improvement for a number of years—and all improvement ceases at puberty. In essence, the older the child, the less chance of recovery. Teenagers have the same aphasia-recovery prognosis as adults.

What does the age-dependent nature of aphasia-recovery reveal about the relationship of neuroanatomical development and language acquisition? First, adults do not relearn language after aphasia. When they recover from aphasia it is simply because their preexistent language skills are restored. Such restoration occurs rapidly and resembles the patient "remembering" past language knowledge. Children do relearn language after aphasia. The closer aphasia occurs to the time of greatest language acquisition in normal children (3-4 years old), the more rapid and complete the reacquisition. This age-dependent pattern of aphasia recovery provides compelling evidence that the ability to learn language is dependent upon growth processes. This suggests that there is a critical period[8] for language acquisition (about 2-10 years) and that language cannot be acquired outside this time frame. Further evidence for the proposition that there is a critical period for language acquisition emerges from studies of disturbances of lateralization.

While there are morphological differences between the left and right hemispheres at birth and while most children show preferences for right-side functions (which are mediated by the opposite left hemisphere) very shortly after birth (Turkewitz, 1977), the two hemispheres appear to be equipotential for later language acquisition (Basser, 1962; Kinsbourne, 1974; Kohn & Dennis, 1974; Lenneberg, 1967). Damage to either the right or left hemisphere before the age of two will likely result in delayed speech onset in equal numbers of cases (Alajouanine & Lhermitte, 1965;

[8]"Critical period" implies that an organism passes through a developmental stage or period during which it is especially sensitive to particular environmental influences or stimuli. After this developmental period, however, the organism is insensitive to these environmental influences.

Lenneberg, 1967). This is because language in very young children is probably equally represented in both hemispheres. As the child grows older, however, language function becomes more and more inextricably linked to a single hemisphere—almost always the left (except in about 3 percent of adults).

One way we know that language functions tend to be increasingly relegated to the left hemisphere as a child matures comes from childhood-aphasia data. As previously noted, there is an equal likelihood of speech disturbance, albeit temporary, from injuries to the left and right hemispheres before two years of age. However, later on in life left-hemisphere injuries are much more likely to produce speech dysfunction (although, if the child is young enough, such dysfunction will not be permanent).

Another indication of the positive correlation of left-hemisphere language mediation and age stems from cases of massive unilateral cerebral damage or cerebral hemispherectomy. Cerebral hemispherectomy is the removal of one of the cerebral hemispheres—often because of tumors or uncontrollable epilepsy. If unilateral damage or hemispherectomy occurs before puberty, language is transferred to the remaining hemisphere and no aphasia results—regardless of which hemisphere is removed (Basser, 1962). On the other hand, should a hemispherectomy be required later in life (after 10 years) the emergence of aphasia *is* a function of which hemisphere is removed. If the left hemisphere is removed at this time it is a virtual certainty that speech dysfunction will result (Burklund, 1972; A. Smith, 1966). If the right hemisphere is excised, chances are slight that long-term aphasia will develop.

Hemispherectomy, like aphasia, presents valuable opportunities for us to learn about the neuroanatomical substrates of language. Since this operation allows scientists to isolate one hemisphere from the other (at least to a certain degree), it results in an excellent route to the study of lateralization of function. As already noted, the left hemisphere is the principal mediator of language. The right hemisphere is by no means dormant, however; it is thought to be the principal mediator of nonverbal visuospatial tasks (Gazzaniga, 1970; Levy, 1974). Does this mean that the right hemisphere is completely devoid of language, or "word-blind," as Geschwind (1965a, b) has suggested? Probably not.

Even after a complete hemispherectomy of the left cerebral hemisphere most patients can at least utter expletives, rote phrases, and occasionally rudimentary speech (Gott, 1973; Zangwill, 1967). Not only is such simple expressive speech intact in patients with dominant (usually left) hemispherectomies, but evidence suggests that their comprehension surpasses their expression (Gott, 1973; A. Smith & Burklund, 1966; Zaidel, 1976). Interestingly, one type of verbal expression that such patients excel at is singing (Gott, 1973; Smith & Burklund, 1966)! This may be due to the fact that the right hemisphere is especially important for musical abilities and functions (Bogen & Gordon, 1971; Kimura, 1964; Luria, 1966; Milner, 1962). Thus, even though the right hemisphere is grossly deficient in language skills when compared to the left, it never-theless can comprehend simple verbal stimuli and mediate primitive utterances. There is some speculation, in fact, that what little language ability aphasics do possess comes from their healthy, intact, right hemi-spheres, rather than from their impaired "dominant" hemispheres (Nielson, 1946; Zangwill, 1960; cf. Searleman, 1977). Therefore, the only language skills aphasics may have access to are those that were acquired by their right hemispheres prior to lateralization (Searleman, 1977; Zaidel, 1976, 1977).

To review, Lenneberg (1967) succinctly summarizes the relationship of age-related aphasia and lateralization in this way: "The outlook for recovery from aphasia varies with age. The chance for recovery has a natural history. This natural history is the same as the natural history of cerebral lateralization of function" (p. 153). Apparently a child may learn language only when his or her CNS is growing and maintains plasticity. As long as one hemisphere can assume the functions of the other, no permanent dysfunction will result. In childhood both hemispheres begin to acquire language. It is only with increasing age that the great majority of language functions are mediated through the left hemisphere. When the shift of language functions to the left hemisphere is nearly complete and an individual's CNS ceases growing, language can no longer be learned or "shifted" to the right hemisphere.[9] It is at this point that a person becomes susceptible to intractable aphasia.

One question at this point might be: "What is the specific develop-mental change that renders the right hemisphere incapable of assuming language functions?" The answer to that question undoubtedly involves some as-yet-unknown process of physiological maturation. Knowing that answer, however, would not reveal why language begins to lateralize to the left hemisphere in the first place. Even while a child is still capable of acquiring language with his or her right hemisphere, that hemisphere becomes increasingly uninvolved with language. This decreasing involvement, or lateralization, begins very early in life. Dichotic listening tasks (where different auditory stimuli are presented to both ears simultaneously) have shown that the right hemisphere is less responsive to verbal stimuli than the left (Kimura, 1967). This effect occurs in children starting at about 3–5 years (Borowy & Goebel, 1976; Kimura, 1963; Knox & Kimura, 1970) and occurs irrespective of sex or race (Borowy & Goebel, 1976). One interesting aspect of language lateral-

[9]The exact age at which lateralization is complete is in dispute. While most authorities have contended that the process is not complete until puberty (Basser, 1962; Lenneberg, 1967; Zangwill, 1960), Krashen (1972, 1973) has compiled evidence suggesting that most language lateralization is complete by five years of age. While Krashen presents important evidence to support his view, it is likely that language functions are lateralized at different rates (cf. Zaidel, 1977), and for some functions the lateralization process continues until puberty (Satz, Bakker, Teunissen, Goebel, & Van der Vlugt, 1975).

ization is that it may be more complete in middle-class children than in lower-class children (Borowy & Goebel, 1976; Geffner & Hochber, 1971; Kimura, 1967).

Since the right hemisphere becomes less involved in language learning at a time when it is still capable of such learning, some scientists have speculated that an area in the left hemisphere actively inhibits language acquisition in the contralateral hemisphere (see Zaidel, 1976). Unfortunately, this is speculative; the actual reason for lateralization is still unknown. While reasons for language lateralization are of great interest, that question is not of primary concern in this chapter. The most important effect of maturation on language does not concern the mechanism or likelihood of transference of hemispheric function but rather the inability of an individual to acquire a language after a certain age (about 10–13 years).

It is rare to see the age limitation set on language acquisition in normal persons since all the major characteristics of language are acquired considerably before puberty. However, in children with Down's syndrome[10] all steps in language acquisition are drastically slowed or "retarded." These children go through the normal sequence of stages of language acquisition, but at a greatly slowed pace. When these children reach puberty, however, all language ceases. Down's syndrome children usually acquire only rudimentary language skills (very simple grammatical structures and small vocabularies) before puberty and therefore have language deficits for their entire lives. This illustrates an important point. It is not the lesion in childhood aphasia or hemispherectomies and the resultant need for lateralization that sets an age limit on language acquisition. Rather, it happens to all of us. It is simply not noticeable in most people since they acquire language well before the critical period has expired.

The fact that people can learn second languages late in life does not compromise the age-limited language-acquisition hypothesis. For if one is learning a *second* language this necessarily implies that an initial language has already been learned and that the necessary neuroanatomical and neurophysiological conditions for language are present. It is only if such conditions are altered after puberty that the language-learning ability is lost. Human languages have many similarities and learning a particular language should pose no great problem, insofar as language can be learned at all.

---

[10]Down's syndrome or "mongolism" is the most frequent identifiable cause of mental retardation. It is responsible for about 10–20 percent of all moderately to severely retarded children. Down's syndrome children usually have I.Q.s below 50 and are characterized by an unusual physical appearance consisting of eyes which are slanted up and out, a vestigial third eyclid, flattened or blunt facial features, misshapen teeth, a large tongue, protruding abdomen, underdeveloped genitalia, and short extremities. It is caused by a chromosomal abnormality in which chromosome pair number 21 fails to separate before meiosis and thus mongoloid children have 47 rather than 46 chromosomes (a trisomy of chromosome 21).

The existence of a critical period for language acquisition explains a great many clinical observations, such as why dominant hemispherectomy permanently disrupts language as a function of age. There is little information that is antagonistic to the notion of a critical period for language. One notable exception, however, is the case report of Genie (Fromkin, Krashen, Curtiss, Rigler, & Rigler, 1974). Genie was a girl who was raised in profound isolation for the first thirteen years and nine months of her life. Her parents, at least her father, were psychotic and maintained Genie in an isolated, restrained condition for much of her childhood. Genie's mother reported that Genie's father and brother never spoke to Genie—although they did bark at her like dogs.

When Genie was discovered, or rescued, from this pathetic situation she was malnourished, unable to stand erect, incontinent, and mute. Although Genie was reportedly unresponsive and apathetic after her ordeal, she did not appear to be autistic or psychotic. A cardinal feature of her behavior, however, was her almost absolute silence. Evidently Genie's father punished her severely if she made any sound. Thus, upon her admittance to the Children's Hospital of Los Angeles in 1970 after almost fourteen years of profound social and sensory isolation, Genie appeared to have no language.

Within a few weeks after her hospital admission Genie began to imitate words used in her presence; after five months she began to spontaneously produce words herself. Comprehension tests administered to her initially showed a meager vocabulary and little appreciation of grammatical structure. A slow but steady improvement in Genie's performance was noted on such tests over the next two years. She appeared to progress from a state of little (if any) language to mastery of the linguistic concepts of singular/plural nouns, negative/affirmative sentences, possessive constructions, comparative and superlative adjectives, and others. Simultaneously, she added numerous words to her vocabulary.

Does this case study invalidate the critical-period hypothesis with respect to language acquisition? No—for a variety of reason. First, we can never be absolutely sure about Genie's early exposure to language. One version of her history, for instance, indicated that she had acquired some language when she was quite young. There is a possibility that she was not as mistreated and deprived when she was quite young as when she was older. She was, for example, occasionally taken to the doctor until she was a little over 3½ years old. Such an early beginning of language during her critical period for language acquisition may have provided a necessary basis for any language she later used. This possibility is consistent with ratings of her linguistic skills two years after her rescue. Although she showed greatly improved language expression and comprehension at this time, her language skills were nevertheless rated as appropriate for a child of between 1½–3 years of age.

Other problems encountered with accepting this case history at face value are that we cannot be sure how her psychological condition per se affected her language use and her reaction to language tests. Lastly, it must be stressed that even if she did acquire some rudimentary or primitive language skills during adolescence, this by no means constitutes normal language acquisition.

A fascinating parallel to human language, with its lateralized neuroanatomical substrate and critical period for acquisition, can be found in certain songbirds. Marler (1972), for instance, has shown that male white-crowned sparrows have critical periods for species-specific song acquisition (10-50 days of age). Nottebohm, along with other scientists, has provided convincing evidence that not only do songbirds such as the white-crowned sparrow and the canary have critical periods for song learning, but also that these birds show cerebral hemispheric lateralization of language functions[11] (Nottebohm, 1970, 1971, 1977). Further, not only do canaries show evidence of lateralization, but apparently song functions are lateralized to the left hemisphere—just as human language is usually mediated via the left hemisphere. The similarity does not stop here, however. Song retention in canaries is impaired as a function of lateralization of the lesion just as humans show aphasia as a function of laterality of trauma. What's more, canaries' left and right hemispheres are evidently equipotential for song acquisition early in life; specialization occurs only during their critical periods for song learning. While such correlatives are tremendously suggestive, Harnad and Doty (1977) warn against viewing the canary as a close analogue of the neuroanatomical representation of language in people. They note that (1) humans and songbirds are phylogenetically remote, (2) some vocal (and in fact, garrulous) birds do not show signs of lateralization (for example, the parrot), and (3) some relatively nonverbal birds appear to show some evidence of laterality. Finally, birdsong can in no way be considered a language. Thus, we should not rely too heavily on a songbird analogue—no matter how suggestive the neuroanatomical correspondence.

We have reviewed those neuroanatomical changes that appear to correspond with language acquisition in the young. An equally legitimate query asks what neuroanatomical developments are correlated with an inability to learn language. Again Lenneberg has surveyed the appropriate literature and has arrived at the following list. Perhaps one of the most important changes concerns the number of neurons per unit of cerebral cortex—neurodensity. Neurodensity is a very important index of maturation since the more space there is between neurons, the more room there is for dendritic interconnections to form. While there are few or no dendritic interconnections in the cerebral cortex at birth, the number grows quite rapidly during the first two years of life (see Figure 4-8). Such interconnections are largely responsible for the fact that the cerebral cortex increases in weight by 350 percent during this time. Apparently

---

[11]In fact, data suggest that canaries' lateralization of song may be even more complete than lateralization of language in humans.

such growth is necessary for the acquisition of a complex function such as language.

Not only does the brain increase in weight and arborization during the first two years, but this increase continues throughout the period during which language may be acquired (albeit at a reduced rate). So what happens to these processes at that time when language acquisition can no longer occur? Just about in the middle of puberty both dendritic arborization and weight increase cease. We have previously seen that a certain level of neuronal maturity and growth is necessary for language acquisition to begin. This latter information suggests that active neuronal growth is necessary for language acquisition to continue. Once the period of very rapid dendritic arborization and brain weight gain is over, so is the period of language learning. While this temporal association is only correlative, it is nevertheless compelling. It makes sense that the brain could make maximal adjustments to the environment at a period of time when it has its greatest potential for growth.

Even myelinization bears the same relationship to language acquisition as do dendritic arborization and brain-weight gain. Myelinization, as previously noted, shows rapid increases in cortical areas related to language just prior to the emergence of language. However, the process of myelinization continues throughout life. This would seem to be contrary to a process that is correlated with language-learning ability. In a finer analysis, however, it was discovered that only certain components of myelin continued to be manufactured at high rates after puberty, while others (cholesterol and cerebrosides) did not (Folch-Pi, 1952, 1955, cited in Lenneberg, 1967). Thus, a general pattern emerges after an examination of neural development and language acquisition. When those neuronal growth processes associated with initial language acquisition stop, the aptitude to learn language is gone. Such a neuroanatomical analysis coincides nicely with the previously noted language-learning capabilities of aphasics and the mentally retarded.

Such maturational factors as dendritic arborization or myelinization do not *cause* language. Language is an extraordinarily complex facility that derives from no single factor. The relationship these developmental processes share with language is that they define the neuroanatomical environment in which language learning can occur. Such factors define the biological boundaries within which psychological or experiential events can influence the language-acquisition process.

MEMORY DEVELOPMENT: EXTENT OF PLASTICITY

If dendritic differentiation, which includes dendritic spine development and axodendritic synaptogenesis, is the most important correlate of memory development, then it should be possible to demonstrate that experiences that alter memory also affect dendritic differentiation. Indeed, it has been shown that rearing animals in the dark, or placing animals in impoverished environments, conditions of malnutrition, and mental retardation result not only in deficiencies in memory development but also in decreases in development of dendritic differentiation.

For example, Coleman and Riesen (1968) raised cats in the dark from birth to 100 days. They found a reduction in dendritic length and branching of stellate cells in the visual cortex, while pyramidal cells in layer 5 of the visual cortex were not affected.

Valverde (1967, 1971), using the Golgi technique, examined growth of dendritic spines in the visual cortex of mice reared in darkness for 22–25 days and found a 35 percent decrease in spines of apical dendrites of pyramidal cells from layer 5. When mice reared in darkness are exposed to light twenty days after birth, there is an increase in the number of dendritic spines per unit length of the apical dendrites of pyramidal cells in layer 5 of the cortex. Furthermore, he found that the number of spines varied with the duration of light exposure. After four days of exposure, spine frequency was not significantly different from that of the light-reared controls.

Fifkova (1970a, b), using the electron-microscope, studied the visual cortex of rats following unilateral lid suture. She found a 20–30 percent decrease in both axosomatic and axodendritic synapses in layers 2–5, with an increase in axodendritic synaptic size of 7.5 percent.

Purpura (1974) studied pyramidal cells of motor cortex of mentally retarded children between the ages of three months and twelve years using the Golgi method. He found two types of dendritic-spine abnormalities, namely a loss in number of dendritic spines and the presence of very thin spines that resemble spines of primitive developing neurons. The degree of dendritic-spine loss and abnormality appeared to be related to age and to the severity of mental retardation. Similar deficiencies in dendritic development were found by Huttenlocher (1974), who studied pyramidal cells in the frontal cortices of five severely retarded children under the age of five.

With respect to malnutrition, Cragg (1972), using the electron-microscope, reported that malnourished rats had 38–41 percent of the number of pyramidal-cell synapses as normal rats. Similar results were found by Salas, Diaz, and Nieto (1974) and by Escobar (1974). They reported that postnatal undernourishment in rats reduced the number of dendritic spines, the number of pyramidal cells in the cerebral cortex, the number of cells in the hippocampus, and retarded the development of myelinization.

In contrast, it has been shown that excessive sensory stimulation, enriched environments, and formal training in specific learning tasks result not only in improved memory development but also in increases in dendritic differentiation.

For example, enhanced sensory input by subjecting infant rats to thirty-five days of continuous visual stimulation results in increases in dendritic spines in the visual cortex (Parnavelas, Globus, & Kaups, 1973). Similarly, Shapiro and Vukovich (1970) demonstrated increased spine density in visual cortex following eight days of repeated handling, stroking, presentation of loud noises, flashing lights, and electric shocks.

Using a somewhat different approach, a number of investigators (Greenough, Wood, & Madden, 1972; Hebb, 1947; Rosenzweig, 1971) have placed weanling animals in enriched environments typically consisting of many play objects and group housing. The effects of these experiences are usually assessed relative to animals that are housed in individual cages (isolation condition) or simply grouped together (social condition). There is a great deal of evidence that rats raised in enriched environments learn mazes and other complex tasks more readily, explore novel environments more freely, and behave differently from rats raised in isolated environments. Early work using these procedures demonstrated that rats raised in enriched environments had thicker cerebral cortices, larger cortical neuronal cell bodies, more glial cells, and differences in brain enzyme activities compared to rats raised in isolation or in social environments (Rosenzweig, 1971; Rosenzweig, Bennett, & Diamond, 1972). In more recent work using the Golgi technique, it has been shown that rats raised in enriched environments show an increase in the number of dendritic branchings within the visual cortex and hippocampus, but that there are smaller increases in the temporal cortex and no changes in the lateral frontal cortex compared to rats raised in isolated or social environments (Holloway, 1966; Greenough & Volkmar, 1973; Greenough, Volkmar, & Juraska, 1973). Globus, Rosenzweig, Bennett and Diamond (1973) also reported a higher frequency of synaptic spines in the visual cortex in animals raised in an enriched (relative to an isolated) environment.

In summary, these experiments suggest that dendritic differentiation as a function of differential experiences may represent possible mechanisms for encoding of specific experiences. However, these changes may simply reflect responses to environmental stimulation rather than the mechanism of differential storage of information within an episodic or semantic long-term memory system.

Nevertheless, it appears that the major neuronal element that changes during development as a function of maturation and experience is the differentiation of dendrites with changes in growth and synaptogenesis, suggesting that they might represent a correlate of long-term memory development.

SUMMARY AND DISCUSSION

We will briefly review some of the major points we have made with respect to the interplay between development and the neuroanatomical substrates for language and memory.

Language

There is no simple explanation for humans' extraordinary language abilities. Peripheral systems (such as the vocal tract) are not primarily responsible for human's language skills, nor are simple global brain attributes (for example, size or weight). Rather, language acquisition is dependent upon the development and interaction of specialized regions of the human brain as they are affected by experience.

We can identify brain structures implicated in language through the occurrence of aphasia or through procedures like brain stimulation. Aphasia is a condition in which language abilities are lost through brain damage. The use of language is not lost because of sensory or motor deficits, but rather simply because the aphasic has lost the ability to use a symbolic communication strategy.

Aphasia and brain stimulation have shown that tissue in the association cortex in one's left hemisphere is especially involved in language. Broca's area, located in the parietal lobe, is involved in expressive language, while Wernicke's area, located in the temporal lobe, is involved in receptive language. Interestingly, the child is apparently prepared for language lateralization at birth since areas important for language (for example, the planem temporale) are larger in the left than in the right hemisphere.

Not only are discrete areas of the cerebral cortex associated with language, but maturation of these areas is correlated with language acquisition. Broca's area, for instance, shows its greatest development in terms of myelinization and dendritic differentiation when language is first emerging. There is a strong relationship between the growth and development of certain areas of the cerebral cortex and the emergence of language. This relationship between brain growth or maturation and language acquisition can be more firmly established by examining the age-related course of aphasia.

Young children can relearn language quite well after aphasia. This is true even if they have suffered permanent damage to brain areas important for language use (such as the left-hemisphere Broca's area). A child can recover because his or her CNS has great plasticity and can adjust to environmental insults or changes. Plasticity is apparently related to growth. When the CNS is undergoing tremendous growth, different parts of it can assume different roles or functions depending on the need. An adult, however, has a mature CNS with relatively little growth potential and, hence, little plasticity. This results in poor aphasia recovery.

Not only is a growing CNS necessary for complete aphasia recovery but, more importantly, it is necessary for language learning to occur at all. This can be seen from cases where there is slow or retarded language acquisition (as with Down's syndrome). Language learning ceases in such cases when the CNS achieves maturity—even though the language acquired at that point may be woefully rudimentary. The period of time between the start of the maturation of language-related areas and the time when the CNS is largely mature (about 2–10 years) constitutes a critical period for language acquisition. Such a time frame agrees well with the period of maximal CNS growth as assessed by myelinization of fibers leading to the cortex and by dendritic differentiation.

Memory

Information contained in long-term memory can be classified as episodic and semantic. Episodic memory consists of specific personal experiences that are linked to particular places and times. Semantic memory contains general information of the world that is not necessarily associated with any particular place or time.

The most important brain areas for long-term memory performance are probably the hippocampus and the cerebral cortex. The hippocampus appears to be especially implicated in episodic memory. Information on the role of the hippocampus in long-term memory derives from patients who have had their hippocampi removed surgically, viral encephalitic conditions affecting the hippocampus, Korsakoff's psychosis, and transient global amnesia. While the hippocampus seems to be principally involved in long-term episodic memory, the cerebral cortex is implicated in long-term semantic memory. This has considerable intuitive appeal since semantic memory is largely comprised of language-mediated information and the cerebral cortex is critically involved in language.

In normal human memory development, semantic memory shows greater developmental changes than does episodic memory. The substantial improvement seen in semantic memory might not be due to brain maturation per se, but instead might also be due to children's learning to use effective encoding and retrieval strategies (mnemonic schemes). Young children frequently use no memory strategies at all; this may be due to the fact that they have not learned the likelihood or consequences of forgetting. Older children begin to use mnemonic schemes spontaneously, but they do not always use them appropriately. Eventually, children make extensive use of strategies such as rehearsal and labeling and employ them appropriately. Thus, one reason that young children show poor long-term semantic memory performance is that they simply have not learned the value of, or techniques for, memorization.

At present, memory cannot be linked as closely with a discrete brain region as can language. However, there is evidence that dendritic differentiation, an important neural development process, is closely related to memory performance. Conditions affecting dendritic differentiation affect memory processes as well. For instance, rearing animals in the dark, placing animals in impoverished environments, malnutrition, and mental retardation result in decrements both in dendritic differentiation and memory performance. Mentally retarded children, for example, have been found to have a reduced number of dendritic spines and the spines they do have are very thin.

The correlation between dendritic differentiation and long-term memory capability gains credibility from the fact that the relationship is bidirectional. Poor memory is associated with reduced dendritic differentiation, while good long-term memory performance is associated with high levels of differentiation. Thus, copious sensory stimulation, enriched environments, and training in learning tasks all result in improved memory performance in rats in the presence of high levels of dendritic differentiation.

Integration

This chapter has examined the neuroanatomical substrates of two different functions—language and memory—from a developmental perspective. It may help the student assimilate some of the foregoing information if we compare and contrast those two functions.

One important and obvious difference between language and memory has tremendous implications for their study. While the processes of language are readily available for public scrutiny, memory processes must always be inferred. This does not rule out the existence of underlying, unobservable language processes. Instead, it merely notes that at some level language per se can be directly observed. Memory, on the other hand, is always an inferred process that we use to explain how humans and animals maintain information over long periods of time. There is no observable memory process. There is only an end product—a remembrance.

Since language is more observable, scientists can make fine discriminations between its stages and components. It is much more difficult to achieve a similar degree of resolution with respect to memory. This undoubtedly is why we have a fairly clear understanding of the normal stages of language acquisition (for example, one-word utterances, two-word sentences, and so on), but only an imprecise notion of memory stages. Indeed, our current knowledge suggests that there are hardly any stages to episodic memory acquisition at all. This could largely be due to the difficulty encountered when studying memory rather than because of the nature of episodic memory itself.

Since memory has less well-defined developmental stages than language, it is much more difficult to correlate its development with discrete maturational changes. That is why we were not able, for instance, to link different memory stages to the maturation of particular cortical layers. As a consequence of these differences between language and memory, certain neurodevelopmental concepts (such as critical periods) can more readily be applied to language than to memory.

We have defined plasticity as an organism's capacity to respond or adjust to environmental influences and to establish or restore functions hampered by experimental or pathological conditions. In this context we can view a critical period as a time of maximal plasticity followed by a time of minimal plasticity. Thus, the critical period for language acquisition is from 2–10 years when children: (1) quickly respond to environmental language stimuli and rapidly acquire language, and (2) possess the potential for restoration of language processes interrupted by pathological conditions (such as aphasia) through neuroanatomical re-representation of language functions.

Because of their plasticity, children can pass from a nonlanguage to language state by *acquiring* (learning) language. Adults, of course, cannot. Language may be *restored* in adulthood, but not acquired. Further, adults cannot shift their lateralization of language in the event they suffer trauma. Does human memory development have any phenomenon analogous to a critical period or a circumscribed period of plasticity?

An examination of human memory reveals considerable plasticity throughout life. While old age is often accompanied by decreased mental status, this phenomenon is not universal; most elderly people can still remember a considerable amount of information. The only evidence suggesting a lack of memory plasticity after childhood stems from cases like H.M., where a bilateral hippocampectomy in an adult resulted in a permanent lack of long-term memory. While we cannot be certain what the effects of a similar operation would be in a young child, it would probably be less debilitating since memory functions might be mediated by alternate brain structures. In any event, it appears that the notion of critical periods is much less germane to the acquisition of memory than it is to language. This underscores the point that child development consists of the acquisition of a variety of different functions, all of which may have unique developmental histories.

One traditional question in neurology and physiological psychology concerns the extent to which we can localize the mediation of functions to particular brain parts (Hebb, 1958). The relationship between language and memory and neuroanatomy may shed light on this question. We have already seen how specific areas of brain tissue are associated with different aspects of language: Broca's area with expressive language and Wernicke's area with receptive language. Memory, on the other hand, can be attributed to subcortical limbic system structures (for example, the hippocampus) and unspecified areas of the entire cerebral cortex. The difference between language and memory (with respect to their correlation with neuroanatomy) might help to answer the traditional question of localization. That is, there may not be any universal principle determining the extent to which sophisticated functions (such as language, learning, and memory) can be localized in brain tissue. Rather, the extent of neuroanatomical localization may depend upon the specific function considered.

Similarities between the development of long-term semantic memory and language may underscore an important point. Some of these similarities are their common normal progression from simple to complex, the positive correlation between their emergence and maturation as assessed by myelinization and dendritic differentiation, and their mediation by the cerebral cortex, in particular the association areas. These similarities are probably not accidental; rather, they reflect the tremendous interplay of human language and long-term semantic memory. Indeed, efficient long-term memory is necessary for a complex language. Conversely, much of human long-term memory is encoded, labeled, and rehearsed through linguistic processes. As you may recall, the use of verbal mnemonic strategies is thought to represent an important stage in the development of long-term memory. The interrelatedness of language and memory exposes a difficulty in exploring complex behaviors or functions in humans. Not only does the brain operate as an integrated unit whose constituent parts interact tremendously, but human functions also interact, are interdependent, and are difficult to separate.

In conclusion, we hope that the student not only has acquired some useful and interesting information on the development of language and memory, but also has gained an understanding of the complexities encountered when studying human behavior. An appreciation of such complexities provides an appropriate perspective from which to view information on other brain-behavior relationships.

REFERENCES

ACHENBACH, T. M. *Developmental psychopathology.* New York: Ronald, 1974.

AGHAJANIAN, G. K., & BLOOM, F. E. The formation of synaptic junctions in developing rat brain: A quantitative electron microscopic study. *Brain Research*, 1967, *6*, 716–727.

ALAJOUANINE, T. Verbal realization in aphasia. *Brain*, 1956, *79*, 1–28.

ALAJOUANINE, T., & LHERMITTE, F. Acquired aphasia in children. *Brain*, 1965, *88*, 653–662.

ALTMAN, J., & BAYER, S. Postnatal development of the hippocampal dentate gyrus under normal and experimental conditions. In R. L. Isaacson & K. H. Pribram (Eds.), *The hippocampus* (Vol. 1). New York: Plenum Press, 1975.

ARENBERG, D., & ROBERTSON, E. A. Learning. In J. E. Birren & W. K. Schaie (Eds.), *Handbook of the psychology of aging.* New York: Van Nostrand Reinhold, 1977.

BAKER, L. J., BAKER, T. B., & KESNER, R. P. Taste aversion learning: A comparison between young and adult rats. *Journal of Comparative and Physiological Psychology*, 1977, *91*, 1168–1178.

BARBIZET, J. *Human memory and its pathology.* San Francisco: W. H. Freeman, 1970.

BASSER, L. Hemiplegia of early onset and the faculty of speech with special reference to the effects of hemispherectomy. *Brain*, 1962, *85*, 427–460.

BENSON, D. F., & GESCHWIND, N. The aphasias and related disturbances. In A. B. Baker & L. H. Baker (Eds.), *Clinical neurology*. New York: Harper & Row, 1976.

BERMAN, R. F., & KESNER, R. P. Posttrial hippocampal, amygdaloid and lateral hypothalamic electrical stimulation: Effects upon memory of an appetitive experience. *Journal of Comparative and Physiological Psychology*, 1976, *90*, 260–267.

BICKFORD, R., MULDER, D. W., DODGE, H. W., SUIEN, H. J., & ROME, H. P. Change in memory function produced by electrical stimulation of the temporal lobe. *Research Publications of the Association for Research in Nervous and Mental Diseases*, 1958, *36*, 227–243.

BOGEN, J., & GORDON, H. Musical tests for functional lateralization with intracarotid amobarbital. *Nature*, 1971, *230*, 524–525.

BOROWY, T., & GOEBEL, R. Cerebral lateralization of speech: The effects of age, sex, race, and socioeconomic class. *Neuropsychologia*, 1976, *14*, 363–370.

BOTEZ, M. I., & CRIGHEL, E. Partial disconnection syndrome in an ambidextrous patient. *Brain*, 1971, *94*, 487–494.

BROWN, A. L. The development of memory: Knowing, knowing about knowing, and knowing how to know. In H. W. Reese (Ed.), *Advances in child development and behavior* (Vol. 10). New York: Academic Press, 1975.

BUCHWALD, N. A., & HULL, C. D. Some problems associated with interpretation of physiological and behavioral responses to stimulation of caudate and thalamic nuclei. *Brain Research*, 1967, *6*, 1–11.

BURKLUND, C. W. Cerebral hemisphere function in the human: fact versus tradition. In L. W. Smith (Ed.), *Drugs, development and cerebral function*. Springfield: Charles C. Thomas, 1972.

BUTTERS, N., & CERMAK, L. Some analyses of amnesic syndromes in brain-damaged patients. In R. L. Isaacson & K. H. Pribram (Eds.), *The hippocampus* (Vol. 2). New York: Plenum Press, 1975.

CAMPBELL, B. A., & CAMPBELL, E. H. Retention and extinction of learned fear in infant and adult rats. *Journal of Comparative and Physiological Psychology*, 1962, *55*, 1–8.

CAMPBELL, B. A., JAYNES, J. R., & MISANIN, J. Retention of a light-dark discrimination in rats of different ages. *Journal of Comparative and Physiological Psychology*, 1968, *66*, 467–472.

CAMPBELL, B. A., & SPEAR, N. E. Ontogeny of memory. *Psychological Review*, 1972, *79*, 215–236.

CAMPBELL, B. A., MISANIN, J. R., WHITE, B. C., & LYTLE, L. D. Species differences in ontogeny of memory: Support for neural maturation as a determinant of forgetting. *Journal of Comparative and Physiological Psychology*, 1974, *87*, 193–202.

CHOMSKY, N. *Aspects of the theory of syntax*. Cambridge, Mass.: MIT Press, 1965.

CHOMSKY, N. *Language and mind*. New York: Harcourt, Brace, and World, 1972.

COLEMAN, P. D., & RIESEN, A. H. Environmental effects on cortical dendritic fields, Part I. Rearing in the dark. *Journal of Anatomy*, 1968, *102*, 363–374.

CONEL, J. L. *The postnatal development of the human cerebral cortex*. Cambridge, Mass.: Harvard University Press, 1939–1967.

COTMAN, C., TAYLOR, D., & LYNCH, G. Ultrastructural changes in synapses in the dentate gyrus of the rat during development. *Brain Research,* 1973, *63,* 205–213.

CRAGG, B. G. The development of cortical synapses during starvation in the rat. *Brain,* 1972, *95,* 143–150.

CRAGG, B. G. The development of synapses in the visual system of the cat. *Journal of Comparative Neurology,* 1975, *160,* 147–166.

CRAIN, B., COTMAN, C., TAYLOR, D., & LYNCH, G. A quantitative electron microscopic study of synaptogenesis in the dentate gyrus of the rat. *Brain Research,* 1973, *63,* 195–204.

CUNNINGHAM, D. F. *Contribution to the surface anatomy of the cerebral hemispheres.* Dublin, Ireland: Royal Irish Academy, 1892.

DELAY, J. *Les dissolutions de la memoire.* Paris: Presses Universitaires de France, 1942.

DESCARTES, R. *Discourse on method and meditations* (Translated by L. Lafleur). Indianapolis: Bobbs-Merrill, 1960. (Originally published 1637.)

DRACHMAN, G. Adaptation in the speech tract. In R. J. Binnick, A. Davison, G. Green, & J. L. Morgan (Eds.), *Papers from the Fifth Regional Meeting of the Chicago Linguistic Society.* Chicago: Department of Linguistics, University of Chicago, 1969.

EAYRS, J. T., & GOODHEAD, B. Postnatal development of the cerebral cortex of the rat. *Journal of Anatomy,* 1959, *93,* 385–402.

ERVIN–TRIPP, S. M. Language development. In L. W. Hoffman & M. L. Hoffman (Eds.), *Review of child development research* (Vol. 2). New York: Russell Sage Foundation, 1966.

ESCOBAR, A. Cytoarchitechtonic derangement in the cerebral cortex of the undernourished rat. In J. Cravioto, L. Hambraeus, & L. Vahlquist (Eds.), *Early malnutrition and mental development.* Swedish Nutrition Foundation, Uppsala: Almquist and Wiksell, 1974.

FEIGLEY, D. A., & SPEAR, N. E. Effect of age and punishment condition on long-term retention by the rat of active- and passive-avoidance learning. *Journal of Comparative and Physiological Psychology,* 1970, *73,* 515–526.

FIFKOVA, E. The effect of monocular deprivation on the synaptic contacts of the visual cortex. *Journal of Neurobiology,* 1970, *1,* 285–294. (a)

FIFKOVA, E. Changes of axosomatic synapses in the visual cortex of monocularly deprived rats. *Journal of Neurobiology,* 1970, *2,* 61–71. (b)

FLAVELL, J. H. *Cognitive development.* Englewood Cliffs, N.J.: Prentice-Hall, 1977.

FOLCH-PI, J. Chemical constituents of the brain during development and in maturity. In *The biology of mental health and disease, the 27th annual convention of the Milbank Memorial Fund.* New York: Hoeber, 1952.

FOLCH-PI, J. Composition of the brain in relation to maturation. In H. Waelsch (Ed.), *Biochemistry of the developing nervous system: Proceedings of the First International Neurochemical Symposium.* New York: Academic Press, 1955.

FOUTS, R. S. Acquisition and testing of gestural signs in four young chimpanzees. *Science*, 1975, *180*, 978–980.

FOX. M. *Integrative development of brain and behavior in the dog.* Chicago: University of Chicago Press, 1971.

FROMKIN, V., KRASHEN, S., CURTISS, S., RIGLER, D., & RIGLER, M. The development of language: A case of language acquisition beyond the "critical period." *Brain and Language*, 1974, *1*, 81–107.

GAZZANIGA, M. S. *The bisected brain.* New York: Appleton-Century-Crofts, 1970.

GEFFNER, D., & HOCHBER, I. Ear laterality performance of children from low and middle class socioeconomic levels on a verbal dichotic listening task. *Cortex*, 1971, *7*, 193–203.

GESCHWIND, N. Disconnection syndromes in animals and man. Part I. *Brain*, 1965, *88*, 237–294. (*a*)

GESCHWIND, N. Disconnection syndromes in animals and man. Part II. *Brain*, 1965, *88*, 585–644. (*b*)

GESCHWIND, N., & LEVITSKY, W. Human brain: Left-right asymmetries in temporal speech region. *Science*, 1968, *161*, 186–187.

GLOBUS, A., ROSENZWEIG, M. R., BENNETT, E. L., & DIAMOND, M. C. Effects of differential experience on dendritic spine counts in rat cerebral cortex. *Journal of Comparative and Physiological Psychology*, 1973, *82*, 175–181.

GOTT, P. S. Language after dominant hemispherectomy. *Journal of Neurology, Neurosurgery and Psychiatry*, 1973, *36*, 1082–1088.

GREENOUGH, W. T., WOOD, W. E., & MADDEN, T. C. Possible memory storage differences among mice reared in environments varying in complexity. *Behavioral Biology*, 1972, *7*, 717–722.

GREENOUGH, W. T., VOLKMAR, F. R., & JURASKA, J. M. Effects of rearing complexity on dendritic branching in frontolateral and temporal cortex of the rat. *Experimental Neurology*, 1973, *41*, 371–378.

GREENOUGH, W. T., & VOLKMAR, F. R. Pattern of dendritic branching in occipital cortex of rats reared in complex environments. *Experimental Neurology*, 1973, *40*, 491–504.

HARDYCK, C., & PETRINOVICH, L. F. Left-handedness. *Psychological Bulletin*, 1977, *84*, 385–404.

HARNAD, S., & DOTY, R. W. Introductory overview. In S. Harnad, R. W. Doty, L. Goldstein, J. Jaynes, & G. Krauthamer (Eds.), *Lateralization in the nervous system.* New York: Academic Press, 1977.

HEBB, D. O. The effects of early experience on problem solving at maturity. *American Psychologist*, 1947, *2*, 306–307.

HEBB, D. O. *A textbook of psychology.* Philadelphia: Saunders, 1958.

HIMWICH, W. A. Biochemical processes of nervous system development. In E. Tobach, L. R. Aronson, & E. Shaw (Eds.), *The biopsychology of development.* New York: Academic Press, 1971.

HIMWICH, W. A. Problems in interpreting neurochemical changes occurring in developing and ageing animals. *Progress in Brain Research,* 1973. *40,* 13-24.

HOLLOWAY, R. L. JR. Dendritic branching: Some preliminary results of training and complexity in rat visual cortex. *Brain Research,* 1966, *2,* 393-396.

HUTTENLOCHER, P. R. Dendritic development in neocortex of children with mental defect and infantile spasms. *Neurology,* 1974, *24,* 203-210.

IVERSEN, S. Do hippocampal lesions produce amnesia in animals? *International Review of Neurobiology,* 1976, *19,* 1-49.

JACKSON, J. H. *Selected writings.* London: Hodder and Stoughton, 1932.

JOHNS, D. F., & LA POINTE, L. L. Neurogenic disorders of output processing: Apraxia of speech. In H. Whitaker & H. A. Whitaker (Eds.), *Studies in neurolinguistics* (Vol. 1). New York: Academic Press, 1976.

JOUVET, M. The states of sleep. *Scientific American,* 1967, *216,* 62-72.

KESNER, R. P. Brain stimulation: Effects on memory. In R. F. Thompson & J. L. McGaugh (Eds.), *Neurobiology of learning and memory.* New York: Plenum Press, 1980 (in press).

KESNER, R. P., & CONNER, H. S. Effects of electrical stimulation of limbic system and midbrain reticular formation upon short and long-term memory. *Physiology and Behavior,* 1974, *12,* 5-12.

KESNER, R. P. DIXON, D. A., PICKETT, D., & BERMAN, R. F. Experimental animal model of transient global amnesia: Role of the hippocampus. *Neuropsychologia,* 1975, *13,* 465-480.

KIMURA, D. Speech lateralization in young children as determined by an auditory test. *Journal of Comparative and Physiological Psychology,* 1963, *56,* 899-902.

KIMURA, D. Left-right differences in the perception of melodies. *Quarterly Journal of Experimental Psychology,* 1964, *16,* 355-358.

KIMURA, D. Functional asymmetry of the brain in dichotic listening. *Cortex,* 1967, *3,* 163-178.

KINSBOURNE, M. Mechanisms of hemispheric interaction in man. In M. Kinsbourne & W. L. Smith (Eds.), *Hemispheric disconnection and cerebral function.* Springfield, Ill.: Charles C. Thomas, 1974.

KIRBY, R. H. Acquisition, extinction, and retention of an avoidance response in rats as a function of age. *Journal of Comparative and Physiological Psychology,* 1963, *56,* 158-162.

KNOX, C., & KIMURA, D. Cerebral processing of non-verbal sound in boys and girls. *Neuropsychologia,* 1970, *8,* 227-237.

KOHN, B., & DENNIS, M. Patterns of hemispheric specialization after hemidecortication for infantile hemiplegia. In M. Kinsbourne & W. L. Smith (Eds.), *Hemispheric disconnection and cerebral function.* Springfield, Ill.: Charles C. Thomas, 1974.

KRASHEN, S. Language and the left hemisphere. *Working Papers in Phonetics,* 1972, No. 24.

KRASHEN, S. Lateralization, language learning, and the critical period. Some new evidence. *Language Learning,* 1973, *23,* 63-74.

KREUTZER, M. A., LEONARD, C., & FLAVELL, J. H. An interview study of children's knowledge about memory. *Monographs of the Society for Research in Child Development*, 1975, *40* (whole no. 159).

LASHLEY, K. S. In Search of the engram. In F. A. Beach, D. O. Hebb, C. T. Morgan, & H. W. Nissen (Eds.), *Neuropsychology of Lashley*. New York: McGraw-Hill, 1950.

LENNEBERG, E. H. Understanding language without ability to speak: A case report. *Journal of Abnormal Psychology*, 1962, *65*, 419–425.

LENNEBERG, E. H. *Biological foundations of language*. New York: John Wiley and Sons, 1967.

LEVY, J. Psychobiological implications of bilateral asymmetry. In S. J. Dimond & J. G. Beaumont (Eds.), *Hemisphere function in the human brain*. London: Paul Elek, 1974.

LIEBERMAN, P. D., KLATT, H., & WILSON, W. Vocal tract limitations of the vocal repertoires of rhesus monkeys and other nonhuman primates. *Science*, 1969, *164*, 1185–1187.

LIMBER, J. Language in child and chimp? *American Psychologist*, 1977, *32*, 280–295.

LINDSLEY, D. B. The reticular system and perceptual discrimination. In H. H. Jasper (Ed.), *Reticular formation of the brain*. Boston: Little, Brown, 1958.

LURIA, A. R. *Higher cortical functions in man*. New York: Basic Books, 1966.

LURIA, A. R. *Traumatic aphasia*. The Hague, The Netherlands: Mouton, 1970.

MARLER, P. A comparative approach to vocal learning: Song development in white-crowned sparrows. In M. E. P. Seligman & J. L. Hager (Eds.), *Biological boundaries of learning*. New York: Appleton-Century-Crofts, 1972.

MEDIN, D. L. Form perception and pattern reproduction by monkeys. *Journal of Comparative and Physiological Psychology*, 1969, *68*, 412–419.

MILNER, B. Laterality effects in audition. In V. Mountcastle (Ed.), *Interhemispheric relations and cerebral dominance*. Baltimore, Md.: Johns Hopkins University Press, 1962.

MILNER, B. Memory and the medial temporal regions of the brain. In K. H. Pribram and D. E. Broadbent (Eds.), *Biology of memory*. New York: Academic Press, 1970.

MILNER, B. CNS maturation and language acquisition. In H. Whitaker & H. A. Whitaker (Eds.), *Studies in neurolinguistics* (Vol. 1). New York: Academic Press, 1976.

MOHR, J. P. Broca's area and Broca's aphasia. In H. Whitaker & H. A. Whitaker (Eds.), *Studies in neurolinguistics* (Vol. 1). New York: Academic Press, 1976.

NASH, J. *Developmental psychology: A psychobiological approach*. Englewood Cliffs, N.J.: Prentice-Hall, 1970.

NIELSON, J. M. *Agnosia, apraxia, aphasia: Their value in cerebral localization*. New York: Hoeber, 1946.

NOTTEBOHM, F. Ontogeny of bird song. *Science*, 1970, *167*, 950–956.

NOTTEBOHM, F. Neural lateralization of vocal control in a passerine bird I. Song. *Journal of Experimental Zoology*, 1971, *177*, 229–262.

NOTTEBOHM, F. Asymmetries in neural control of vocalization in the canary. In S. Harnad, R. W. Doty, L. Goldstein, J. Jaynes, & G. Krauthamer (Eds.), *Lateralization in the nervous system*. New York: Academic Press, 1977.

OLSON, G. M. An information-processing analysis of visual memory and habituation in infants. In T. J. Tighe & R. N. Leaton (Eds.), *Habituation: Perspectives from child development, animal behavior and neurophysiology*. New York: John Wiley, 1976.

PARNAVELAS, J. G., GLOBUS, A., & KAUPS, P. Continuous illumination from birth affects spine density of neurons in the visual cortex of the rat. *Experimental Neurology*, 1973, *40*, 742–747.

PENFIELD, W. Memory and perception. *Research Publications of the Association for Research in Nervous and Mental Diseases*, 1970, 48, 108–122.

PENFIELD, W., & ROBERTS, L. *Speech and brain mechanisms*. Princeton, N.J.: Princeton University Press, 1959.

PREMACK. D. On the assessment of language competence in the chimpanzee. In A. M. Schrier & F. Stollnitz (Eds.), *Behavior of non-human primates* (Vol. 4). New York: Academic Press, 1971.

PURPURA, R. P. Dendritic spine "dysgenesis" and mental retardation. *Science*, 1974, *186*, 1126–1128.

REESE, H. W. The development of memory: Life-span perspectives. In H. W. Reese (Ed.), *Advances in child development and behavior* (Vol. 11). New York: Academic Press, 1976.

RIOPELLE, A. J., & ROGERS, C. M. Age changes in chimpanzees. In A. M. Schrier, H. F. Harlow, & F. Stollnitz (Eds.), *Behavior of nonhuman primates* (Vol. 2). New York: Academic Press, 1965.

ROBERTS, L. Aphasia, apraxia, and agnosia in abnormal states of cerebral dominance. In P. J. Vinken & G. W. Bruyn (Eds.), *Handbook of clinical neurology*. New York: Wiley & Sons, 1969.

ROSENZWEIG, M. R. Effects of environment on development of brain and of behavior. In E. Tobach, L. R. Aronson, & E. Shaw (Eds.), *The biopsychology of development*. New York: Academic Press, 1971.

ROSENZWEIG, M. R., BENNETT, E. L., & DIAMOND, M. C. Chemical and anatomical plasticity of brain: Replications and extensions. In J. Gaito (Ed.), *Macromolecules and behavior* (2nd ed.). New York: Appleton-Century-Crofts, 1972.

ROZIN, P. The psychobiological approach to human memory. In M. R. Rosenzweig & E. L. Bennett (Eds.), *Neural mechanisms of learning and memory*. Cambridge, Mass.: MIT Press, 1976.

RUBENS, A. B. Anatomical asymmetries of human cerebral cortex. In S. Harnad, R. W. Doty, L. Goldstein, J. Jaynes, & G. Krauthamer (Eds.), *Lateralization in the nervous system*. New York: Academic Press, 1977.

RUMBAUGH, D. M., VON GLASERFELD, E. C., WARNER, H., PISANI, P., & GILL, T. V. Lana (chimpanzee) learning language: A progress report. *Brain and Language*, 1974, *1*, 205–212.

SALAS, M., DIAZ, S., & NIETO, A. Effects of neonatal food deprivation on cortical spines and dendritic development of the rat. *Brain Research*, 1974, *73*, 139–144.

SATZ, P., BAKKER, D. J., TEUNISSEN, J., GOEBEL, R., & VAN DER VLUGT, H. Developmental parameters of the ear asymmetry: A multi-variate approach. *Brain and Language*, 1975, 2, 171–185.

SCHADE, J. P., & VAN GROENIGEN, W. B. Structural organization of the human cerebral cortex. *Acta Anatomica*, 1961, 47, 74–111.

SEARLEMAN, A. A review of right hemisphere linguistic capabilities. *Psychological Bulletin*, 1977, 84, 503–528.

SHAPIRO, S., & VUKOVICH, K. R. Early experience effects upon cortical dendrites: A proposed model for development. *Science*, 1970, 167, 292–294.

SLOBIN, D. I. The acquisition of Russian as a native language. In F. Smith & G. A. Miller (Eds.), *The genesis of language: A psycholinguistic approach.* Cambridge, Mass.: MIT Press, 1966.

SMITH, A. Speech and other functions after left (dominant) hemispherectomy. *Journal of Neurology, Neurosurgery, and Psychiatry*, 1966, 29, 461–471.

SMITH, A., & BURKLUND, C. W. Dominant hemispherectomy. *Science*, 1966, 153, 1280–1282.

SMITH, N. Effects of interpolated learning on the retention of an escape response in rats as a function of age. *Journal of Comparative and Physiological Psychology*, 1968, 65, 422–426.

SPERRY, R. W., Mental unity following surgical disconnection of the cerebral hemispheres. *The Harvey Lectures*, 1968, 62, 293–323.

THOMPSON, R. F. *Introduction to physiological psychology.* New York: Harper & Row, 1975.

TULVING, E. Episodic and semantic memory. In E. Tulving (Ed.), *Organization of memory.* New York: Academic Press, 1972.

TURKEWITZ, G. The development of lateral differences in the human infant. In S. Harnad, R. W. Doty, L. Goldstein, J. Jaynes, & G. Krauthamer (Eds.), *Lateralization in the nervous system.* New York: Academic Press, 1977.

TURNER, O. A. Growth and development of cerebral cortical pattern in man. *Archives of Neurology and Psychiatry*, 1948, 59, 1–12.

TURNER, O. A. Postnatal growth changes in the cortical surface area. *Archives of Neurology and Psychiatry*, 1950, 64, 378–384.

VALVERDE, F. Apical dendritic spines of the visual cortex and light deprivation in the mouse. *Experimental Brain Research*, 1967, 3, 337–352.

VALVERDE, F. Rate and extent of recovery from dark rearing in the visual cortex of the mouse. *Brain Research*, 1971, 33, 1–11.

VICTOR, M., ADAMS, R. D., & COLLINS, G. H. *The Wernicke-Korsakoff syndrome.* Philadelphia: F. A. Davis, 1971.

WADA, J. A., CLARKE, R., & HAMM, A. Cerebral hemispheric asymmetry in humans: Cortical speech zones in 100 adult and 100 infant brains. *Archives of Neurology*, 1975, 32, 239–246.

WILBURN, M. W., & KESNER, R. P. Effects of caudate nucleus stimulation upon initiation and performance of a complex motor task. *Experimental Neurology,* 1974, *45*, 61–71.

WITELSON, S. F., & PAILLE, W. Left hemisphere specialization for language in the newborn: Neuroanatomical evidence of asymmetry. *Brain,* 1973, *96*, 641–646.

YAKOVLEV, P. I., & LECOURS, A. R. The myelogenetic cycles of regional maturation of the brain. In A. Minkowski (Ed.), *Regional development of the brain in early life.* Philadelphia: F. A. Davis, 1967.

ZAIDEL, E. Auditory vocabulary of the right hemisphere following brain bisection or hemidecortication. *Cortex,* 1976, *12*, 191–211.

ZAIDEL, E. Unilateral auditory language comprehension on the token test following cerebral commissurotomy and hemispherectomy. *Neuropsychologia,* 1977, *15*, 1–18.

ZANGWILL, O. L. *Cerebral dominance and its relation to psychological function.* Edinburgh, Scotland: Oliver & Boyd, 1960.

ZANGWILL, O. L. Speech and the minor hemisphere. *Acta Neuropsychiatrica,* 1967, *67*, 1013–1020.

FIVE

The Development
of Prosocial Behavior and
Moral Judgment

Donna M. Gelfand and Donald P. Hartmann

A thirteen-year-old boy comes upon a burning house, hears a baby crying inside, and rushes into the house to rescue the baby. Later the boy's feat is reported in the newspapers and on local television news broadcasts. He is interviewed, given a good citizen award, and becomes something of a local celebrity. Most observers of his behavior would term his act *altruistic*, *moral*, or *prosocial*. But let us examine more closely the conditions under which such labels would apply. First, let us consider the action itself. Clearly, there was an element of risk to the actor and potential great benefit to the recipient (the endangered baby). Almost all theorists maintain that an act must benefit another person in order to qualify as prosocial or altruistic. At this point, the consensus among authors breaks down. For some, any behavior that benefits some other person is regarded as prosocial, regardless of the degree of benefit, the nature of the actor's motives, or the amount of sacrifice involved (Staub, 1975a, p. 2). The crucial feature is that the actor benefits rather than harms others. Readers may detect a potential problem with such a definition, however. What if, in attempting to rescue the baby, the boy actually inflicted harm or injury? In the confusing and dangerous situation, the teenager could have panicked and tossed the infant out of a second-story window to someone who failed to catch it. In this case, the actor was indeed imperiled, but he certainly did not benefit the victim. Would such an action qualify as prosocial? Observers might reasonably conclude that the boy's intent was commendable although the results were fatal for the baby.

Other writers have viewed the actor's intent and expectations as the crucial determinants of the behavior's status. For example, Macaulay and Berkowitz (1970) define altruism as, ''behavior carried out to benefit another without anticipation of rewards from external sources'' (p. 3). Mussen and Eisenberg-Berg (1977) concur in the opinion that prosocial behavior must not involve the actor's anticipation of external rewards. The difficulty with definitions based upon intentions and expectations, however, is that such private events are extremely difficult, perhaps impossible, to verify. Regarding the rescue in our opening example, who can tell whether the boy fleetingly considered whether he would become a celebrated hero? Would only one such thought disqualify his act as altruistic? If our perception of our own motivation is frequently erroneous (Nisbett & Wilson, 1977), how much more difficult it must be to infer the motives of another, whose circumstances we know even less well than our own. All of these considerations suggest that although it is intuitively appealing to define prosocial behavior by reference to the actor's motives, the motivational criterion may prove impossible to apply in practice. We simply cannot rule out the possibility that the helper may expect or may experience some reward for heroic behavior.

Hoffman (1976) has offered a working definition of altruism that includes the possibility that there may be some benefit for the actor. In Hoffman's opinion, altruism has been implicitly defined in research as, "any purposive action on behalf of someone else which involves a net cost to the actor" (p. 124). But how can one calculate net cost, and at what point does the calculation cease—at the time of the act or later? To return to our example, perhaps the teenaged boy experienced only momentary stress, and very little physical danger, but later received a cash reward, public recognition, and a scholarship. By calculating all of the psychological and material rewards, one could conclude that there was a net gain rather than a net cost to the actor.

This brings us to one of the central issues regarding the nature of helpful actions: Are such behaviors produced by rewards to the helper, or are they personally costly actions motivated by generous impulses to help others in distress? How can an activity be maintained if it requires self-sacrifice rather than self-benefit? Rosenhan (1972) has referred to this issue as the "altruistic paradox," a phenomenon we will discuss later in this chapter.

It may now be clear why researchers of prosocial behavior have employed *operational definitions* in which concepts are defined in terms of the procedures used to measure or observe them. Charitable behavior has been defined as monetary donations to a charity, rescue as entering a room from which calls for help emanate, helping as assisting the experimenter pick up spilled materials, and so forth. Such operational definitions allow research to proceed without general agreement on the ultimate nature of moral behavior. Operational definitions are not without problems of their own. They may be overly restrictive, may differ considerably from everyday usage of terms, and may vary widely from one study to another, thus leading to inconsistent usage of terms. Despite their limitations, operational definitions have been useful in research on prosocial behavior and moral judgment.

Moral judgment involves the consideration of the ethics of various courses of action and the weighing of costs and benefits to the actor, the beneficiary, and the social order. For example, deciding whether one should endanger oneself in order to rescue an accident victim involves moral judgment. Such a question can be posed in the abstract, or it can have an influence on actual conduct. Presumably, moral judgment enters into moral behavior as the first step in the prosocial behavior sequence. In order to rescue the baby, the boy in our example first had to realize that the fire posed a danger and then had to decide whether or not to intervene. The latter decision lies within the realm of moral judgment. As will become apparent, however, many investigators of moral reasoning confine their interest to the judgmental process and are less directly concerned with exploring the relationship between reasoning and action.

In the following pages, we will describe and evaluate three major contemporary views regarding the development of prosocial behavior: the cognitive-developmental or structural position; the operant-learning approach; and the cognitive social-learning theory approach. Additional sections will discuss what is known about children's prosocial behavior and the criteria for an adequate theory of prosocial development.

WHAT IS KNOWN ABOUT CHILDREN'S PROSOCIAL BEHAVIOR

Even infants offer to share things with others. At the age of about ten months the share gesture appears and children offer toys, eating utensils, and other objects to other people, particularly to their mothers (Escalona, 1973). The meaning of the share gesture is ambiguous, however. Rheingold, Hay, and West (1976) believe that the infant's share gesture is not necessarily indicative of altruism, in part because the infant frequently demands the immediate return of the object given the recipient. On the other hand, toddlers' sharing does closely match the dictionary definition of granting to another the "partial use, enjoyment, or possession of a thing though it may merely imply a mutual use or possession" (*Webster's Seventh New Collegiate Dictionary*, 1969).

Bronson (1974) interprets the share gesture as a bid for the mother's attention. Bronson studied a group of twelve- to twenty-four-month-old toddlers, and found that nearly 30 percent of the twelve- and eighteen-month-olds' bids to their mothers consisted of showing, offering, or giving an object. Although the toddlers' intent was not clear, all of these behaviors brought the child into greater proximity with the mother and thus commanded her attention. Moreover, the mothers were more likely to respond to share offers than to other potential social initiators such as toddlers' frequent visual checks of their mothers. The share gesture decreased in frequency as the children approached their second birthdays; it was partially replaced by even more powerful methods for obtaining the parents' attention such as comments, requests for help, and signals of distress or frustration.

The sharing of play materials is relatively infrequent among groups of preschool children between the ages of two and five years. Angry and aggressive behavior is nearly five times as common as are generous acts (Murphy, 1937), and children are much more likely to quarrel over the possession of toys than to share them. Tonick, Gelfand, Hartmann, Cromer, and Millsap (1977) studied sharing within three-child groups during three fifteen-minute play sessions held once a week in a nursery school. Every five minutes the children were given a single attractive toy, and their interactions were observed and recorded. The children made frequent verbal and physical bids for the toy, but they showed a low rate (just over two instances) of sharing per fifteen-minute session. Also, demands were more likely to win the child possession of the toy than were polite requests, a phenomenon we shall discuss later.

The demandingness and relative lack of generosity of preschoolers changes gradually to increased sharing and donating as the child becomes older. The rate of prosocial behavior increases significantly with age during the first decade of life, but not thereafter (Bryan & London, 1970; Mussen & Eisenberg-Berg, 1977). During this same period, children become more empathic and better able to take the role of the other and to appreciate the feelings of others (Shantz, 1975). The evidence on the effect of role-taking ability is mixed, with some studies finding that role-taking skill is positively associated with helping (Iannotti, 1978; Rubin & Schneider, 1973), and others finding no relationship between the two (Emler & Rushton, 1974). It seems intuitively persuasive that the child who can apprehend another person's distress would be more helpful than a child who cannot.

With increasing age, there is a regular and predictable sequence of modes of reasoning about moral dilemmas. When faced with a hypothetical quandary about how one should behave in ambiguous circumstances, younger children are more concerned about the physical consequences of an act or with potential reward or punishment than they are about more lofty moral considerations (Kohlberg, 1976a). Older children become increasingly aware of and responsive to other people's opinions and of social rules and the maintenance of social order. Finally, in young adulthood, some individuals achieve a postconventional or principled level of reasoning in which right conduct is determined by appeal to self-chosen abstract ethical principles such as the Golden Rule. There is a modest but reliable positive relationship between moral judgment and helpful behavior during childhood (Rushton, 1976).

The child who is helpful in one situation may or may not behave helpfully in other circumstances. Rushton (1976) reviewed a number of studies and concluded that the interrelationships among children's altruistic behaviors average about .30 in magnitude. This may be a statistically significant level of relationship, but it is hardly an impressive one. Poor reliability may artifically depress the correlations among measures of helping, and there may be individual differences in cross-situation consistency. Some individuals may show great consistency in helping while others may not. Also, the degree to which the child perceives the tasks as similar (as all representing opportunities for helping) may well determine the level of consistency in the child's behavior. The degree to which the child views himself or herself as characteristically generous or not generous may be an influential factor as well (Bem & Allen, 1974; Gergen, Gergen, & Meter, 1972). In any case, there is a great deal of variability in children's altruism under differing circumstances.

There are relatively few sex differences in prosocial behavior, although those differences that do emerge tend to show girls as more helpful (Krebs, 1970). In fact, girls are likely to be perceived as more helpful than they actually are (Hartshorne, May, & Maller, 1929), perhaps because they surpass boys in expressions of empathy (sympathetic emotional arousal) in response to another person's distress (Hoffman, 1977b). Because girls are more likely to appear distressed by someone else's suffering, they may seem to be more helpful than is actually the case. In contrast, boys' failure to express empathy may lead to their helpfulness being underestimated by peers and adult observers.

Certain situational and child-rearing variables enhance children's helpfulness. Exposure to concerned and helpful adult models often increases similar responses in children (Harris, 1970). Children's generosity and helpfulness are particularly affected by adults who are nurturant, and who both practice and preach concern for others (Yarrow & Waxler, 1976). Those adults who verbally advocate nurturance and helpfulness but do not practice what they preach do not heighten children's helpfulness. Moreover, their attempts to praise the children's generous acts prove ineffective (Midlarsky, Bryan, & Brickman, 1973).

Although hypocritical adults are not effective praise agents, others are. Adult praise can powerfully reinforce children's donations, particularly in conjunction with instructions to be generous or with modeled demonstrations of donating (Gelfand, Hartmann, Cromer, Smith, & Page, 1975). With children who are initially consistently unhelpful, it is necessary first to model helping and to verbally instruct the children to help so that they can begin to earn reinforcement for their prosocial behavior. When modeling alone fails to produce prosocial responding, the addition of praise and material rewards may prove effective (Warren, Rogers-Warren, & Baer, 1976).

Other situational factors that have been found to promote children's helping include the provision of specific permission for the child to intervene (Staub, 1974), uncoerced practice or rehearsal of helpful acts that have been demonstrated by live or televised models (Friedrich & Stein, 1975; Rosenhan & White, 1967), and taking the role of a tutor or supervisor of other children (Staub, 1975b). In order to act helpfully, the child must realize that it is permissible to intervene or must have a role that necessitates helping, as well as knowing how to intervene effectively.

The foregoing section presented a brief overview of the established facts regarding the development of moral judgment and prosocial conduct. Next, we shall summarize and evaluate the major theories that have been formulated to account for these facts. In discussing these theories, we shall examine the research findings in greater detail.

COGNITIVE-DEVELOPMENTAL APPROACHES

Cognitive-developmental theories of moral development are concerned with the *structures of thought* or the reasoning processes underlying the *moral concepts* which are characteristic of different *stages of development*. This focus on developmental changes in ways of thinking about the social world, about right and wrong, and about these in relation to the self differentiates cognitive-developmental theories from the learning-based approaches discussed later in this chapter. Learning theories, whether cognitive or operant, are less concerned with underlying thought structure and developmental changes, and are more directly concerned with overt prosocial behavior and with the motives and affect (emotions such as guilt) that regulate moral actions.

The core of cognitive-developmental positions—the doctrine of cognitive structures—was reviewed in the chapter on Piaget. According to the structural doctrine, moral reasoning progresses in a series of stages whose end product is a universal sense of justice or concern for equity among individuals (Hoffman, 1970). These stages have the following characteristics:[1]

1. The pattern or structure of moral reasoning typical of each stage forms a coherent whole; thus, a child's reasoning about moral issues should be *consistent* whatever the content of the issues—responsibility, justice, or punishment.

2. Each stage develops out of its predecessor, so that it is a synthesis of the old and the new. However, change is not simply an addition of elements to one stage to form another stage; rather, it is the result of a major reorganization so that each stage is *qualitatively different* from the previous stage.

3. Each successive stage is more comprehensive and provides new perspectives and criteria for making moral judgments. The stages are, therefore, *hierarchically arranged.*

4. Because each stage is a necessary part of the successive stages, each individual must go through the same sequence of stages *(invariant sequence).* Individual capability, cultural and other environmental events determine only how quickly and how far each person moves through the stage sequence.

---

[1]See Flavell (1971) for a more detailed description of the properties of stages in cognitive-developmental theory and Kessen (1970) for a general discussion of the role of stages in developmental theory.

Movement from one stage to the next is due both to the child's social experiences and to existing thought structures. The existing structures influence how the social environment is experienced; the interaction of the existing structures and social experiences leads to a reorganization of the structures. Structural change is not a matter of passive incorporation; the child comes to develop new moral structures through active coping with the social environment and through attempts to order and organize social experiences.

The stage is not solely a descriptive concept as used in this framework. It both describes the nature of the child's moral reasoning at a given time and serves as an explanatory concept. According to Turiel (1969), "a given stage helps explain how the environment affects the individual, and also provides understanding of how the subsequent stage develops" (p. 99).

To summarize, cognitive-developmental theories of moral development posit a series of qualitatively distinct, coherent, hierarchically arranged, and invariant stages which develop through the individual's active coping with the social environment. There are many theories that meet this general description; Kohlberg (1976a, p. 48) lists some ten different theories including his own, and there are some more recent additions (Turiel, 1975; Damon, 1977). Our discussion will be limited to the work of two representatives of this approach, notably Piaget (1932/1965) and Kohlberg (1969).

Piaget's Position

Piaget's inquiries were focused on the beliefs expressed by four- to thirteen-year-old boys toward the origins, legitimacy, and availability of rules in the game of marbles (marbles was then exclusively a boys' game in Switzerland); on children's attitude toward lies; and finally on children's responses to stories concerning motives and justice.

Piaget describes two major stages in the development of moral reasoning. The first stage is called the stage of *"moral realism,"* morality of constraint, or heteronomous morality. During this stage, children feel an obligation to comply with rules because they are sacred and unalterable. Behavior is viewed as being totally right or completely wrong, and everyone is believed to think similarly. Whether an action is judged to be right or wrong depends upon the magnitude of its consequences, the extent to which it conforms to established rules, and whether it is punished. Finally, children at the stage of moral realism believe in expiatory punishment and immanent justice (automatic punishment emanates directly from objects).

The second and more cognitively mature stage is labeled *"autonomous morality"* or the morality of reciprocity or cooperation. Children in this stage, which typically commences during middle to late childhood, conceive of rules as established and maintained through reciprocal agreement and thus subject to modification. Actions are judged to be right or wrong based on the intentions of the actor, rather than merely in terms of the consequences of the actions. Punishment, instead of being harsh, arbitrary, and immediate, is reciprocally related to the misdeed, for example, through restitution. Finally, children at the stage of autonomous morality define duty and obligation in terms of peer expectations rather than in terms of obedience to authority.[2]

The initial stage of moral realism is produced by children's generalized feelings of respect for adults and by two cognitive limitations: egocentrism (the confusion of one's own perspective with that of others) and realism (the confusion of subjective with objective experiences). The shift from moral realism to a morality of reciprocity occurs primarily as a result of changes in cognitive ability as well as the child's broadened social experiences. According to Hoffman's (1977a) interpretation of Piaget, these social experiences operate in two ways:

1. By growing older the child attains relative equality with adults and other children, which lessens his unilateral respect for them and gives him confidence to participate with peers in decisions about applying and changing rules on the basis of reciprocity. This new mode of interaction makes the child's initial conception of rules no longer tenable (p. 110).

2. Interacting with peers often requires taking alternate and reciprocal roles with them; thus the child becomes sensitized to the motives that underlie the acts of others and is more likely to consider intention in judging the actions of others.

Social encounters, then, serve to challenge and sometimes contradict the child's expectations, and in so doing produce a state of cognitive disequilibrium. This state of disequilibrium or uncertainty in turn motivates the child to employ his or her newly attained cognitive skills to resolve the inconsistencies between experiences and expectations. It is through this effort that preexisting patterns of moral reasoning are reorganized.

In summary, Piaget views mature moral reasoning as the outcome of an active process involving the development of cognitive capacities in conjunction with exposure to new social experiences which provide the basis for a changed—and broadened—perspective on authority, intentions, and duty, and for enhanced role-taking skills.

A Challenge to Piaget's Position

In a test of Piaget's theory of moral development, Bandura and his associates (Bandura & McDonald, 1963; Bandura & Walters, 1963) questioned three presumed aspects of his cognitive-developmental position:

[2]See Kohlberg (1963) for a more extensive description of the heteronomously and autonomously moral child.

(1) stage invariance, (2) performance consistency within a stage (coherence), and (3) the role of cognitive disequilibrium in producing a change in stage. Box A describes the classic study by Bandura and McDonald (1963) which provoked these questions.

Box A
Modifying Children's Intentional and Consequence-Based Judgments

Bandura and McDonald studied five- to eleven-year-old children's use of either intentions or consequences in judging the seriousness of acts. The choice of this age span is important, because it should include children at the stage of moral realism, in which judgments of responsibility are based predominately on consequences (objective responsibility), children at the stage of autonomous morality, in which judgments of responsibility are based primarily on intentions (subjective responsibility), as well as children who are in transition.

The subjects were initially asked to indicate who was "naughtier" from each of twelve pairs of stories in which one character performed a well-intentioned act that resulted in considerable material damage, and a second character engaged in a selfishly or maliciously motivated act producing minor consequences; for example, breaking fifteen cups accidentally while complying with a parental request versus breaking one cup while pilfering a cookie. This baseline phase of the study provided a basis for classifying children as either predominately *objective* or predominately *subjective* in their conception of responsibility. The data obtained during the baseline phase also served as a check on Piaget's normative findings (such as that younger children's choices should be based predominantly on consequences) and allowed for an assessment of the degree to which children were consistent in their performance across tasks.

Children were then exposed to one of three experimental conditions. One group of subjects observed adult models who expressed moral judgments counter to the children's predominant orientation, and the children were reinforced with verbal approval for adopting the model's evaluative response. A second group observed the model but received no reinforcement for matching the model's behavior. A third group had no exposure to the model, but the children were reinforced whenever they expressed moral judgments that ran counter to their dominant evaluation tendencies.[3] The measures of learning were the percentage of objective judgmental responses produced by the initially "subjectively" oriented children and the percentage of subjective responses performed by the initially "objectively" oriented children in response to twelve new pairs of stimulus items that were similar to those used in the baseline assessment phase. Following the treatment procedure, the stability and generality of the children's judgmental

---

[3]While the results of Bandura and McDonald's study have been used to attack Piaget's position, the study was originally designed to compare predictions based on cognitive-learning theory with predictions derived from operant theory.

responses were tested in a different experimental room in the absence of both the model and the social reinforcement. Again twelve story pairs were used in the posttest assessment.

The results indicated that children exposed to the modeling cues that ran contrary to their own initial judgments not only modified their moral orientations but also maintained these changes in their postexperiment judgmental behavior. Bandura and his associates (Bandura & McDonald, 1963; Bandura & Walters, 1963, p. 206) interpreted the relative ease with which the children's evaluative judgments could be altered as a challenge to the notion of stage invariance as well as to Piaget's position that change from one stage to the next requires cognitive disequilibrium and a long period of consolidation. Furthermore, the finding that a majority of the children (86 percent) responded with a mixture of objective and subjective choices on the baseline measure called into question the alleged property of consistent responding within a stage. Other baseline performance data clearly supported Piaget's position; younger children's choices indicated that they tended to discount intentions in assigning moral blame.

Not surprisingly, this study and its interpretations sparked a heated controversy in which Bandura and McDonald were accused of misinterpreting Piaget and were criticized on both methodological and conceptual grounds (Cowan, Langer, Heavenrich, & Nathanson, 1969; Lickona, 1969; also see Bandura's [1969b] reply). Although Bandura and McDonald's basic findings have been subsequently replicated (Cowan et al., 1969), most psychologists would agree that their results were overinterpreted. For example, the expectation that children would show a high degree of consistency runs counter to Piaget's (1932/1965) own observation that children displayed substantial variability when faced with conflicts over intentions and consequences.[4] And, although training studies can provide information about the modifiability of children's behavior under highly controlled circumstances, they may be much less informative regarding developmental changes and the factors producing these changes under ordinary life circumstances.

The most frequent criticism of Bandura and McDonald is that the judgments modified by exposure to models were surface responses and did not reflect changes in the children's cognitive structure (Turiel, 1966). If Turiel was correct, then we might expect that the effects of training would be transitory, specific to the training stimuli, and unrelated to changes in the understanding of the principles that presumably underlie the judgments of typical subjects. But subsequent studies have found that training effects (1) generalize to some (Le Furgy & Woloshin, 1969) but not all aspects (Prentice, 1972) of moral responding; (2) produce

[4]In his work on moral development, Piaget (1932/1965) held less rigorous stage assumptions than those outlined at the beginning of this section (see, for example, Ginsburg & Opper, 1969, p. 108).

changes not only in evaluative responses but also in the understanding of the principles presumably underlying these judgments (Dorr & Fey, 1974); and (3) persist for at least six months (Glassco, Milgram, & Youniss, 1970). Persistence of the effects of training is, however, greater for children trained to make more mature rather than less mature judgments (Le Furgy & Woloshin, 1969). As suggested by Lickona (1976b, p. 236), this finding can be taken as evidence of a natural developmental direction—from objective to subjective.

Although the contributions of training studies do not end here, we can perhaps see from this brief discussion the progress achieved through the use of this methodology.

(1) The developmental nature of the bases of children's assignment of blame has been upheld, based on both the baseline performance differences between younger and older children and on the greater persistence of changes produced in children trained to make more mature judgments. (2) Piaget's often misunderstood position concerning stage consistency has been clarified as well as supported. (3) On the other hand, Piaget's notion that performance changes require a long period of consolidation has proven incorrect; brief exposure to models (and other powerful intervention techniques) can produce immediate changes in children's choice behavior. (4) Turiel's position has not been supported. The changes produced do not appear to be superficial; instead, they generalize, persist, and are associated with increased understanding of principles. (5) We now better understand what implications the training study methodology has, or doesn't have, for testing the invariance property of stage theories. (6) Finally, we have a better understanding of the basic processes governing the modification of moral judgments.

Kohlberg's Position

Kohlberg's influential theory (Kohlberg, 1958, 1969) represents an extension and refinement of Piaget's stage theory of moral development.[5] Like Piaget's, Kohlberg's original position was based on the response of seven- to seventeen-year-old boys to brief stories depicting moral dilemmas. An example is the story of Heinz, who is faced with the conflict of allowing his wife to die or of stealing a drug so that she might live. Kohlberg was not interested in the specific content of the subjects' responses to these stories in which laws, rules, or commands of authority conflict with the needs or welfare of other persons. His interest focused on the quality of individuals' judgments as indicated by the justifications they gave for their replies. Kohlberg's method of assigning individuals to a stage of moral reasoning was based on the scoring of some twenty-five different aspects grouped under seven moral issues such as value, choice,

---

[5]For a discussion of the correspondence between the stages of moral development described by Piaget and Kohlberg, see Hoffman (1970, pp. 227–278).

and rules (Kohlberg, 1958). Later and more refined and objective scoring systems are described by Kohlberg (1976*a*).

The six stages of moral reasoning described by Kohlberg are divided into three levels. The levels are hierarchically arranged, as are the two stages within each level (see Table 5-1). In the first level, variously termed "premoral" or *"preconventional,"* control of conduct is viewed as external to the self—the standards to be conformed to consist of external commands, rules, or pressures; the motives are to avoid external punishment, obtain rewards, and have favors returned. A stage 1 child might respond to the Heinz dilemma by stating that Heinz should steal the drug because "if you let your wife die, you will get in trouble."[6] Actions at this stage are motivated by the fear of punishment administered by higher authorities, and in the second stage, by anticipated benefits and reciprocity. A stage 2 child might justify Heinz's theft of the drug by saying "you wouldn't get much time even if you got caught; a little time is OK if you have your wife."

Table 5-1

Levels and Stages of Moral Development

Level	Stage
I. Premoral or preconventional level	1. Punishment and obedience orientation ("Do what you're told.")
	2. Naive instrumental hedonism ("Let's make a deal.")
II. Morality of conventional role conformity	3. Good-person morality of maintaining social approval and good relations
	4. Authority and social-order maintaining orientation
III. Morality of self-accepted moral principles	5. Morality of contract and of democratically accepted law
	6. Morality of individual principles of conscience

Note: Adapted from Kohlberg (1969), and Kurtines and Greif (1974), and Rest (1977).

In level two, called *"conventional morality,"* judgments are based on the maintenance of conventional social order or upon the expectations of other individuals. Individuals at stage 3 are oriented to approval and to pleasing and helping others. Heinz's theft of the drug might be justified by the fact that "people won't think you're bad if you steal it to save your wife, but they'd think you're a dog if you didn't." The more advanced reasoning of a stage 4 advocate of theft of the drug is based on duty rather than approval and on guilt rather than shame: "It's your responsibility if

[6]The examples of reasoning at each of the six stages are based on Rest (1968).

she dies. You can pay the druggist later." According to Kohlberg (1976*a*) stage 4 responding is typical of the majority of adults in our society.

The final level, postconventional or *principled morality*, is reached by a minority of American adults, and then only after the age of twenty. At this level, justification for moral actions indicates that the person has differentiated him or herself from the rules and expectations of others and defined his or her values in terms of self-chosen principles. At stage 5, concern is directed toward maintaining the respect of equals and of the community (assuming this respect is based on reason and not emotions). An individual classified at this stage might justify theft of the drug by stating that "the law wasn't meant for this kind of situation; you'd lose other people's respect if you stuck to the letter of the law and allowed your wife to die." The stage 6 individual is more concerned about violating his or her own principles rather than about losing the respect of rational others: "You wouldn't be able to live with your conscience if you allowed your wife to die."

The examples we have used all justify Heinz's theft of the drug. The reader may find it interesting to provide reasons at each stage to justify the opposite action—Heinz's not stealing the drug.

Although Kohlberg's stage conception is a substantial improvement over Piaget's in comprehensiveness, neither position details how children progress to higher levels of moral thought. Like Piaget, Kohlberg (1969, 1976*a*) assigns important roles to logical reasoning, to role-taking skills, and to social experiences that promote the development of these abilities. Kohlberg also stresses the importance of social experiences which encourage dialogue on moral issues. In order for such dialogues to be effective in promoting moral development, they should include moral reasoning slightly in advance of the child's current level of functioning (Kohlberg, 1976*a*; Turiel, 1966).

A Challenge to Kohlberg

Kohlberg's position has been most forcefully questioned by Kurtines and Greif (1974). Although their criticisms included both methodological and substantive aspects of Kohlberg's work, their most extensive commentary was directed at the procedure used to assess moral reasoning, Kohlberg's dilemmas. The question of the adequacy of the measure is particularly important because Kohlberg's theory was originally based on subjects' responses to the dilemmas and because much of the subsequent empirical work on the theory has used some variant on Kohlberg's method.

Any measuring instrument, whether it attempts to assess interests, competencies, or typical behavior must meet certain technical requirements including standardization of administration and scoring, reliability, and validity. These technical aspects of Kohlberg's method have been thoroughly evaluated by Kurtines and Greif (1974) and by Rest (1976); our discussion will rely heavily upon their reviews.

Administration and Scoring. The first problem one experiences in attempting to compare the results of moral-reasoning studies is the substantial range (from two to nine) in the number of dilemmas employed. While this would not pose a problem if the test stimuli could be considered equivalent, evidence indicates that subjects' responses differ as a function of their familiarity with the dilemmas and of the explicitness of the dilemmas (Rest, 1977).

Even within a study, responses are not strictly comparable from subject to subject. Because scoring focuses on the subject's reasoning, the test administrator is frequently required to engage in extensive probing to clarify the nature of the subject's response. Since the probe questions vary in accordance with the subject's initial response, each subject receives a different set of questions and, in a sense, a different test.

Scoring a subject's responses and arriving at a stage score also present problems. Scoring the responses from Kohlberg's projective test involves complex interpretations and inferential leaps from the data, factors that can promote scorer bias. In addition, the scoring procedure varies across experiments, and Kohlberg (1976a) himself has experimented with four different scoring schemes, with stage scores assigned variously to each sentence, to each story, or to each issue within a story.

After scoring has been completed, the subject must be classified into one of the six stages. This also is not a simple task inasmuch as most subjects display considerable variability or scatter. In fact, Kohlberg (1969) indicates that less than 50 percent of subjects' responses are at their assigned stage level. One classification technique is based on the subject's most frequently achieved score on the individual sentences, issues, or dilemmas. Thus, if an adolescent had 15 percent stage 1 responses, 20 percent stage 2 responses, 25 percent stage 3 responses, and 40 percent stage 4 responses, the adolescent would be classified as a stage 4 responder according to the predominant stage method. Another technique uses a weighted average of the individual's responses. According to this method, the preceding example would be scored as follows: $(1 \times 15) + (2 \times 20) + (3 \times 25) + (4 \times 40) = 290$ (a score of 300 corresponds to stage 3). As you can see from this example, these two methods may lead to nonequivalent stage assignments. Still other discrepancies can be produced by variations in other aspects of scoring and administration. Therefore, one must exercise considerable caution when comparing moral reasoning scores between studies.

Reliability. Three reliability questions should be raised when evaluating Kohlberg's scale. First, do raters agree in the stage scores they assign to subjects (scorer reliability)? This is the only kind of reliability for which sufficient data are available to make a confident judgment. In general, raters do agree in assigning stage designations; the agreement or correlational statistics typically range in the high .80s.

Second, do subjects perform consistently on different dilemmas (internal-consistency reliability)? The data available on internal consistency suggest that the test is much less adequate in this regard. For example, Fishkin, Keniston, and MacKinnon (1973) report that not one of seventy-five college students employed moral reasoning that was exclusively rated at any single level of development on five of Kohlberg's dilemmas. And, as we have already seen, Kohlberg (1969) reports that less than 50 percent of subjects' responses are at their assigned level. These findings do not provide grounds for optimism when Kohlberg's theory would lead us to suspect a substantial degree of consistency across stories.

Third, do subjects obtain the same stage score across testing sessions separated by a brief time interval (test-retest reliability or temporal stability)? Temporal stability appears as low as does internal consistency, at least for young children (see Rest, 1977, for a summary of studies reporting test-retest reliability). For example, we calculated test-retest reliabilities for two of Kohlberg's dilemmas from data reported by Kuhn (1976, p. 165). Kuhn tested fifty children from kindergarten through second grade three times at six-month intervals with the two dilemmas. Our estimate of the correlation between first and second testing was +.40, and between second and third testing was only +.24. In fairness to Kohlberg, it should be noted that the test-retest correlations almost certainly would have been larger if the children had responded to more than two stories. Nevertheless, inasmuch as the time periods between testing were brief, and Kuhn's subjects were not experiencing significant stage advances, the substantial performance fluctuations associated with these modest stability values raise doubts about the validity of the invariance property of Kohlberg's stage theory.

Validity. The type of validity most relevant to evaluating Kohlberg's method of assessing moral reasoning is construct validity—the degree to which the test data are consistent with Kohlberg's theory. Many forms of evidence can be used to evaluate the construct validity of Kohlberg's method. We have already discussed results in the reliability section that serve that function: the very modest test-retest reliabilities and the substantial inconsistency of performance across dilemmas. Unfortunately, neither of these findings is entirely consistent with Kohlberg's theory. As in any properly conducted construct validity study that provides findings that are inconsistent with theory, one is uncertain whether the fault lies with the theory or with the measuring instrument. In either case, Kohlberg cannot escape criticism as both the theory and the instrument are his creation.

Next, we will examine one more construct validity issue—the degree to which Kohlberg's method provides results that are consistent with the notion of stage invariance. Support for the hypothesis of stage invariance was originally obtained from studies that used cross-sectional designs in which subjects of different ages were each tested on a single occasion. These studies indicated that older subjects were more likely to be classified at the more advanced stages, younger subjects at earlier stages, and children of intermediate ages at the intermediate stages. While findings such as these are suggestive, they do not provide direct evidence for stage invariance (Kuhn, 1976). They do not guarantee, for example, that college students currently in stage 6 went through all the lower stages in the required order, with no skipping or backsliding. In order to demonstrate stage invariance, one must use a longitudinal design in which subjects are tested through part or all of their progression through the stages (Wohlwill, 1973).

The results from longitudinal studies of individuals' moral reasoning are not entirely consistent with Kohlberg's theory. For example, Holstein's (1972) data, collected over a three-year period for fifty-three families, showed substantial skipping of stages as well as some regression (retreat to a lower level). Similarly, Kuhn (1976) found backsliding in approximately one-quarter of her five- through eight-year-old subjects over six-month time intervals, and in 10 percent of these same subjects over a twelve-month period. The data shown in Table 5–2 are adopted from Kuhn (1976) and show the number of children whose stage designations increased, decreased, and remained the same from the first test to a retest on the same two stories six months later.

Table 5–2

Stages of Moral Reasoning Based on Two Test Administrations Separated by Six Months

Stage Assignment		Second Test				
		1	1(2)	2(1)	2	2(3)
	2(3)		1		1	1
First Test	2			1	1	
	2(1)		4	4	1	4
	1(2)	3	7	6	3	1

Note:
Stage number in parenthesis indicates substages, for example, 1(2) and 2(1) are substages between Kohlberg's stage 1 and stage 2. Consistent performers are shown in the shaded diagonal. Children whose scores decreased are shown above the shaded diagonal; those whose scores increased are shown below the shaded diagonal. Children incapable of change in either direction, that is, those performing at substage 1 or 3(2) on the first test, were excluded.

(From Kuhn, 1976).

Based on these and other research reports, we must agree with Kurtines and Greif (1974) that the adequacy of Kohlberg's method has yet to be demonstrated. Moreover, because of the interdependence between theory and measurement technique, the status of Kohlberg's theory must also remain suspect, despite its intuitive appeal.

Fortunately, both Kohlberg (1976a) and Rest (1976) have developed new and more objective techniques for assessing moral development. As Rest (1976) suggests, methods may differ in their utility at different stages of the scientific development of an area of inquiry. At the onset, methods which include open-ended questions and which allow subjects to generate their own alternatives may be necessary to insure that the method of measurement does not predetermine response options. Later, more objective, response-constraining techniques (such as multiple-choice) formats may be advantageous. While it is too early to judge the adequacy of these latter measurement devices, recent work with Rest's Defining Issues Test seems promising. The test is objectively scored, and a growing body of reliability and validity data provide support for its utility (Martin, Shafto, & Vandeinse, 1977; Rest, 1977).

Cognition, Role Taking, and Moral Development

Piaget and Kohlberg both view moral development as an outgrowth of the interaction of cognitive and social experiences. Because of the relevance of cognitive and social (role-taking) development to these theoretical positions, we will next examine the relationship of these two variables to moral development.

Moral Development and Cognitive Development.

In speculating about the relationship between cognitive and moral development, both Piaget and Kohlberg suggest that the development of logical operations parallels the development of moral reasoning. According to Kohlberg (1976a, p. 32), "A person whose logical stage is only concrete operational is limited to the preconventional moral stages, stages 1 and 2. A person whose logical stage is only 'low' formal operational is limited to the conventional moral stages (Stages 3 and 4)."

In an attempt to test the hypothesized positive relationship between moral and cognitive development, some investigators have correlated performance on IQ tests with moral stage scores. A substantial number of these studies have found performance on standardized IQ tests to be positively related to aspects of moral development as described by Piaget (see review by Hoffman, 1970) and by Kohlberg (see review by Keasey, 1975). Keasey (1971), for example, reports a modest correlation of +.31 between IQ scores on the Lorge-Thorndike Intelligence Test and stages of moral development as assessed from five of Kohlberg's moral dilemmas with fifth and sixth graders. Studies in this genre have been criticized because the conception of intelligence held by the developers of traditional IQ tests differs considerably from that held by cognitive-developmentalists

(Elkind, 1970). At best, traditional IQ tests only indirectly assess *stages* of cognitive development.

When stage measures of cognitive development are employed, the speculations by Piaget and Kohlberg have generally been supported (see review by Keasey, 1975). Damon (1975), for example, has reported a close correspondence between the development of concrete-operational reasoning and the development of positive justice conceptions in four-through eight-year-old children. The children's reasoning about positive justice (sharing, fairness, and property rights) was assessed by means of a structured interview and responses to four specially constructed dilemmas. Cognitive reasoning was assessed on the basis of performance on five of Piaget's mathematical and physical tasks (such as seriation and spatial perspective taking). Both positive justice and cognitive reasoning correlated substantially with age (from .59 to .85) and with one another (from .76 to .88). While results such as these indicate a sizable relationship between cognitive and moral reasoning performance, they do not indicate the nature of the relationship. The relationship may be parallel but independent (Lee, 1971), both domains may be structurally identical (Damon, 1975), or cognitive development may be a necessary antecedent of moral development (Kohlberg, 1969). The choice among these alternatives must await further research.

Moral Development and Role Taking.   Role taking, or "ability to understand what another person thinks, feels, sees, and intends" (Shantz, 1975, p. 311), is almost uniformly viewed as having a necessary, though not sufficient, relationship to moral reasoning. Piaget (1932/1965), for example, held that children could not manifest autonomous (second stage) morality until they had begun to include the perspective of others. In a similar vein, Kohlberg (1971) asserted that all moral rules are interpreted through the process of role taking.

In general, the research literature provides results consistent with these expectations (see reviews by Olejnik, 1975; Selman, 1976; and Selman & Damon, 1975. Moir (1974), for example, investigated the relationship between moral reasoning and role-taking ability in eleven-year-old New Zealand girls. Moral reasoning was assessed using nine of Kohlberg's dilemmas. Role-taking ability was assessed by a number of tasks, each of which made somewhat different demands on the subjects. One task required the children to see physical objects from different perspectives; another required the subjects to perceive the strategy of another player and to cooperate in order to "win"; and a third task required the children to listen to brief audiotaped conversations and then to describe the feelings and motivations of the characters. The correlation between the moral reasoning and role-taking scores was a robust +.64.

A correlation of this size is particularly impressive when one considers (1) that the subjects were homogeneous with respect to age and SES, (2) that variability due to IQ differences was statistically partialled-out, and

(3) that quite different methods were used to assess moral reasoning and role-taking ability. In some studies (Selman and Damon, 1975), moral dilemmas are used to assess both moral reasoning and role-taking ability. In such instances, the overlap in the methods of assessment could itself produce positive correlations, even if the variables were themselves conceptually independent (Campbell & Fiske, 1959).

In summary, the research literature is consistent with the predictions from cognitive-developmental theory in finding substantial and positive relationships between moral development and both role playing and cognitive development. The specific nature of the causal connections between these variables is not entirely clear, however.

Critique of Cognitive-Developmental Approaches

We have already touched on some of the difficulties encountered by the cognitive-developmental position: variability in the performance of individual subjects, the lack of detail as to how stage changes normally occur, the ease with which stage reasoning can be modified, and the measurement problems associated with the most commonly used measure of moral reasoning, Kohlberg's dilemmas. The criticisms do not end here, however.[7] For example, Turiel (1975) has argued that both Piaget's and Kohlberg's theories are too global and include issues such as law, conventions, honesty, responsibility, and justice which may have quite different patterns of development. Other writers have commented on the modest relationships between moral reasoning and moral behavior (DePalma & Foley, 1975; Mischel & Mischel, 1976; Mussen & Eisenberg-Berg, 1977; Wright, 1971).[8] Baier (1974) has pointed out apparent inconsistencies in Kohlberg's theory; Alston (1971) has argued that a given moral stage— even one logically dependent on an earlier stage—is not necessarily morally superior to its predecessor, as Kohlberg has contended (1969); and Simpson (1974) has criticized Kohlberg for claiming universality for his stages when they are actually based on Western cultural traditions.

On the basis of these criticisms one might be tempted to minimize the value of cognitive-developmental theories. Such a conclusion would be in error for, despite flaws, these theories have made substantial contributions.

First, as good theories should, cognitive-developmental theories have clarified the nature of the domain to which they apply. Aronfreed (1976), for example, states that cognitive-developmental theories "provide a

---

[7]Detailed criticisms of Piaget can be found in Kohlberg (1963), in Hoffman (1970), and in Lickona (1976*b*); criticisms of Kohlberg are Kurtines and Greif (1974), in Lickona (1976*a*) and in Rest (1977).

[8]While Piaget (1932/1965) is tentative in his discussion of the relationship between moral reasoning and behavior, Kohlberg (1976*b*, p. 818) states that "moral judgment, while only one factor in moral behavior, is the *single* most important or influential factor yet discovered in moral behavior" (italics added). See Rest (1977) for an excellent discussion of this issue.

welcome antidote to a behavioristic paradigm in which an act is regarded as 'moral' by virtue of its conformity to an external norm" (p. 56). These theories have also served an important systemizing function. According to Jessor (1975), "beyond the Kohlbergian stage notions, there is little in the moral development field that provides a logical basis for coordinating concepts and linking them to actual behavior" (p. 170).

Moreover, cognitive-developmental theories have stimulated renewed interest in methodologies previously out of vogue in the area of prosocial behavior. When an area of inquiry is dominated by theories that emphasize *change-producing processes,* as do the learning-based theories, developmental normative investigations wane, and even classic studies of the past are forgotten (Murphy, 1937). Descriptive studies of the typical behavior of different-aged children are now regaining some of their deserved status. Cross-cultural investigations, which decreased in popularity since the heyday of psychoanalytic theory (Whiting & Child, 1953), also have reestablished their importance as a method of assessing the validity of Kohlberg's claim of stage universality. In addition, longitudinal studies are experiencing a similar resurgence due in part to their ability to provide critical tests of invariant stage propositions.

Perhaps most importantly, cognitive-developmental theories have stimulated and redirected the focus of considerable research in the moral area. A more balanced and integrated perspective including attention to behavior and cognitions has been forced upon researchers who previously disregarded cognitions. Cognitive-development theorists have also been largely responsible for the growing interest in social cognition, an area that includes not only moral development but also developmental changes in role playing and person perception (see reviews by Shantz, 1975; and Youniss, 1975). And last, the cognitive-developmental perspective, and Kohlberg's theory in particular (Kohlberg, 1971), has provided guidelines for major—though perhaps premature (DePalma & Foley, 1975; Fraenkel, 1976; Rest, 1974)—new efforts in moral education.

OPERANT-LEARNING APPROACH

The cognitive-developmental approach focuses on changes in the developing child's interpretations of events and transformations in the child's reasoning processes. In contrast, learning formulations concentrate on environmental events and general processes which affect the child's behavior regardless of age or developmental status. The same principles of operant or classical conditioning are thought to apply equally to the infant and to the mature adult. And, unlike cognitive-developmental theories, the operant-learning approach emphasizes the environmental control of social behavior. In the operant view, as first described by Skinner (1953), prosocial behavior is simply one type of voluntary, learned behavior. It is responsive to the same situational variables that control other forms of operant behavior. This behavior is termed *"operant"* because it has certain effects on or operates on the environment. These environmental effects control the occurrence of the behavior and determine its rate. To illustrate, children share their building blocks with playmates, are praised by their nursery school teacher for sharing, and then continue to share in future play. The sharing, a voluntary rather than a reflex reaction, would be considered an operant behavior because its rate is controlled by an environmental consequence —the teacher's praise. The praise is observed to follow the sharing and to cause high rates of sharing, so praise acts as a positive reinforcer of sharing for these children at this time. Environmental consequences that increase the rate of responding and maintain the behavior at a high rate are termed *"positive reinforcers."*

Any specific event such as praise cannot be presumed to act equivalently for all children, however. For example, seriously disturbed autistic children may not find praise reinforcing or may actually respond to the praise as if it were punishing. Or normal children may reject and avoid praise from a disliked teacher. In fact, the same child who responds positively to a particular person's expressions of approval at one time may not find them reinforcing at another, for example, when the child has just been praised copiously. A stimulus that signals the availability of reinforcement for a certain type of action or sets the occasion for that action is called a *"discriminative stimulus."* If preschool children receive reinforcement for sharing when their teacher is in the room, the teacher's presence can come to serve as a discriminative stimulus, and the children would be more likely to share when the teacher was nearby.

A general principle of the operant approach is that one must analyze the behavior of the individual child to determine the functional relationships between environmental events and the child's behavior. When the environmental stimulus increases the rate of a preceding behavior and maintains that behavior at a rate higher than its original level, then and only then is the stimulus a positive reinforcer. Consequences that decrease the rate of responding are punishing or *aversive stimuli* and those that increase the rate of escape or avoidance maneuvers are *negative reinforcers.*

Operant behaviors are influenced by antecedent events as well as by their consequences. *Setting events* such as the child's state of health, the general social atmosphere, and the child's mood can all affect the probability that the child will behave helpfully. For example, various forms of positive mood induction can increase generosity. Research studies have shown that in some situations positive mood states produced by success or receipt of gifts appear to promote behaviors such as donating and offering help (Isen & Levin, 1972). Also, instructions to think about happy events have increased children's donations of pennies (Moore, Underwood, & Rosenhan, 1973). Such antecedents may not be very potent or consistent in their influence over behavior, however, as suggested by reports of failure to find increased prosocial behavior as a result of success experiences (Atkinson, 1974), or of reflecting on happy events

(Harris & Siebel, 1975). Moreover, by itself the positive mood effect is fairly transient, lasting about twenty minutes (Isen, Clark, & Schwartz, 1976), but the behavior may be more durable if the resulting helping has positive consequences.

Experimental Analysis of Behavior

A standard of comparison is needed to determine whether a given stimulus acts as a reinforcer; for example, does praise truly affect the rate of prosocial activity? To do this, we must know how frequently the behavior occurs in the absence of the presumed reinforcing stimulus. For this reason, operant experimental analyses most frequently begin with the observation of a behavior prior to the introduction of a suspected reinforcer. This is termed the "*baseline* period of observation," and the behavior is said to be at its "*operant rate*" or level. Observation continues until a stable operant rate is determined. Then the presumed reinforcing stimulus is introduced, and its effect on the rate of responding is observed. Sidman (1960) has argued that the essence of the demonstration of causal relationships in experimentation is *replication*. If we apply the same manipulation to the behavior of many individuals, or to the behavior of the same individual many times, and we observe the same behavioral result (such as increased sharing), then we have replicated the effect. These replications allow us to make the inference that the manipulation (such as praising the sharing) causes the observed increase in the sharing.

Box B describes an experiment by Gelfand, Hartmann, Cromer, Smith, and Page (1975) that illustrates the operant experimental analysis of sharing and also demonstrates the reinforcing action of adult praise on children's donating.

Box B
Increasing Donating Through Verbal Prompts and Praise

In a research trailer, kindergarten and first-grade children individually played a marble-drop game to earn pennies toward purchase of a prize. The size and attractiveness of the prize was determined by the number of pennies the child amassed. A second (fictitious) child was supposedly playing a similar game in a nearby room and, on an automatically programmed schedule, this other child's game would occasionally become inoperative, thus reducing the number of pennies the second child could earn. The child under study (first child) could see a flashing light indicating that the second child's game had stopped, and would be restarted only if the subject child would deposit a penny.

Under the first, or baseline 1, condition, the child's donations were simply observed. As can be seen in Figure 5–1, some children helped initially (panel A child), while others did not (panel B child). Children who consistently gave under the baseline conditions were excused, because it was impossible to increase their donation rates further through reinforcement. Panel A shows data for a child who donated at first and then ceased to donate. A verbal prompt proved necessary to produce some donating which could then be reinforced. In this study, a within-subject replication procedure was used to test the effectiveness of the praise in producing donations. The praise was introduced in the praise 1 condition, and then withdrawn in the baseline 2 condition, whereupon the children's donation rates declined. Then, praise was reintroduced in the praise 2 condition, and the rates of donating increased once more. These results indicate that adult praise can act as a positive reinforcer for helping for some children.

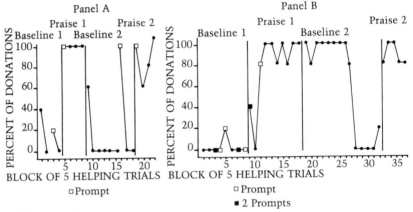

Figure 5-1

Representative data for children who participated in all phases of the experiment. Subject 32, a first-grade boy whose data are shown in panel *A*, was prompted to donate during both baseline 2 and praise 2 phases. Subject 3, a kindergarten girl whose data are shown in panel *B*, was not prompted to donate during either baseline 2 or praise 2 phases. Open squares (□) indicate trials that included a single prompt; closed squares (■) indicate trials that included two prompts.

From Gelfand et al., 1975, with permission of the authors and the Society for Research in Child Development.

Other studies have also demonstrated that young children's sharing can be reinforced by praise (Midlarsky, Bryan, & Brickman, 1973), by candy (Fischer, 1963), and by a combination of the two (Warren, Rogers-Warren, & Baer, 1976). Although such demonstrations do not preclude the possibility that prosocial behavior can be acquired and maintained through other means, they do indicate that some prosocial behavior is operant in nature and can be increased through positive reinforcement.

Practical Applications
Although laboratory experiments do reveal that selected prosocial behaviors can be increased through positive reinforcement, naturalistic

studies are required to demonstrate the utility of reinforcement procedures in educational settings. Teachers and parents are not always able to provide the continuous monitoring of the children's interactions that is necessary if helpful acts are to receive immediate reinforcement. For this reason, investigators have sought effective, but indirect, methods for increasing children's desirable behavior, such as reinforcing children's verbal reports of their sharing. Rogers-Warren, Warren, and Baer (1977) have found that it is possible to train preschool children to make accurate reports of their sharing of play materials, and then to increase their sharing by giving the children treats and trinkets for their reports of their sharing. These investigators found that only when accurate reports were reinforced did the children's sharing increase. However, reinforcement of inaccurate reports of sharing failed to produce reliable increments in the children's sharing. Once accurate reporting is established, it will not be time consuming for teachers or parents to maintain helpful behavior by providing praise or material reinforcers for the child's verbal reports.

Sometimes it is not necessary to train children in accurate reporting because positive consequences for prosocial speech are sufficient to promote helpful nonverbal behavior as well. Slaby and Crowley (1977) found that teachers could increase preschool children's nonverbal cooperation and helping through attending to the children's cooperative statements. It was noteworthy that the teachers' attention to cooperative acts increased the children's prosocial *behavior* despite the fact that the comments had a low base rate, the teachers applied the contingency to only 11–16 percent of the cooperative comments, and the procedure was applied for only two weeks. It appears that the reinforcement of prosocial comments and of accurate reports of helping and sharing constitutes a practical and effective method for increasing rates of helpful behavior among preschool youngsters.

Control by Aversive Stimuli

Other types of learning can affect prosocial behavior as well. Many times the natural behavioral consequences of accidents or of failure to help or share are aversive ones. The injured child may thrash about and scream in pain; the rejected playmate may weep or whine unpleasantly. Such reactions may provide aversive social stimuli to the potential helper. To the extent that children can escape the victim's cries by simply leaving the situation, they may follow that course of action, particularly in the case of younger, less socially adept children. But often children remain in the situation and, insofar as the situation is aversive, the children's attempts to help may be *negatively reinforced*. The word "negative" indicates that a negative state of affairs exists, and that the performer's behavior negates or eliminates the aversive stimulus. The result in this case is the reinforcement of the rescue or consolation attempt. For instance, providing aversive consequences or *punishment* for selfish acts can suppress these types of behavior, but children frequently need an explanation of the reason for the punishment if it is to be effective (Hartmann, Gelfand, Smith, Paul, Cromer, Page, & LeBenta, 1976; Parke, 1970). It is often necessary to provide explanations of the punishment contingency, to provide models of desirable alternative actions, and to reinforce the children for any prosocial responses. Otherwise, the children could become generally inhibited. If their selfish behavior is punished, and no other alternatives are immediately available, children may withdraw from social interaction.

Aronfreed and Paskal (reported in Aronfreed, 1968) demonstrated how avoidance conditioning can be used to train helpful or sympathetic behavior. Unlike the operant interpretation, however, Aronfreed's explanation of the training effect presumes the presence of an empathic emotional reaction of the helper to the victim's distress. In the Aronfreed and Paskal study, some children witnessed an adult's display of pain reactions (holding her head, grimacing, lowering her head to the table) paired with their own exposure to a loud, unpleasant noise. Later, the children saw the adult wearing earphones and supposedly hearing occasional blasts of noise. The children were tested for their willingness to operate a switch to turn off the supposed noise whenever the adult emitted the pain reaction. Some children just viewed the adult's discomfort, some just heard the noise, some experienced both together, and some experienced both, but not in conjunction. The children who experienced the noise and the adult's display of pain in conjunction were more likely to press the switch to turn off the noise in order to relieve the adult's discomfort than were the other three groups. In the operant view, pairing the noise with the adult's pained expression would confer conditioned aversive properties on the adult's pain cues. Thereafter, the child would work to reduce exposure to these conditioned aversive stimuli and, in order to do so, the child would help the adult. In Aronfreed's analysis, the pairing of the loud noise (which the child heard) with the adult's pained expression produced an empathic reaction in the child. The child would vicariously experience the other person's distress and would act to relieve the suffering of the other as well as the child's own psychological distress. This is another example of the process of negative reinforcement. In contrast to Aronfreed's interpretation, the operant-learning explanation would omit the consideration of the presumed unobservable mediator (the child's empathic reaction).

Everyday Contingencies for Sharing

In the operant view, there must be some desirable consequence for sharing if sharing is to continue in naturalistic settings. If the natural results of prosocial actions are aversive or neutral ones, the child will become less likely to share or to help. In a clever study conducted by Warren, Rogers-Warren, and Baer (1976), nursery-school children were taught to share their play materials by informing them that they might receive something if they shared. After each five-minute segment of daily ten-minute play sessions, the children who had offered to share their toys received praise and small candies. Needless to say, their rates of offering to share increased greatly. But the more frequent their offers, the less likely their playmates were to accept each offer, with classmates ignoring or rejecting nearly 70 percent of the offers made. Perhaps this wholesale rejection occurred because the other children, too, had to make share offers in order to receive candy and praise. Since they could not accept and make offers at the same time, they probably preferred to spend their time in the reinforced activity (making offers).

Next, the children were reinforced for making share offers only one or two times per five-minute segment. When they received reinforcement for low offer rates, they complied and their playmates tended to accept about 75 percent of their offers. This study suggests that high rates of prosocial behavior can be produced through reinforcement, but that high rates may not prove socially adaptive, and that children must be helped to perform at optimal rather than maximal levels.

Observation of children's play interactions has revealed some possible reasons why preschool children's natural rates of sharing may be so low. Tonick et al. (1977) studied sharing patterns within nursery-school play groups during weekly sessions over a period of three weeks. The children's sharing decreased over time, which was perhaps not surprising because there appeared to be no positive (reinforcing) consequences for sharing. In only three instances did the recipient thank the sharer during 405 minutes of interaction, nor were there any other expressions of gratitude such as smiles or comments. Most often the sharing was reluctant and occurred when the possessor of the toy could no longer keep the others entertained or fend off their verbal demands and attempts to grab the toy.

In the operant-learning analysis of such observations, the rather low rate of sharing (an average of 2.2 shares per fifteen-minute session) would be attributed to the apparent absence of positive consequences for sharing. The relatively high rates of verbally and physically demanding the toy were attributed to the positive reinforcement. That is, demands were more likely to win the child possession of the toy than were polite requests. This analysis suggests that in order to increase prosocial exchanges among young children, we must introduce positive consequences for sharing and for polite requests rather than for demands for desirable play materials.

Summary of Operant Approach

According to the operant-learning formulation, prosocial acts are operant behaviors which are affected by antecedent setting events and are controlled by their consequences. Prosocial behaviors are increased in rate through positive reinforcement (the provision of positive consequences) or through negative reinforcement (the elimination of negative or aversive consequences). In order to have an immediate effect both positive and negative reinforcement contingencies must be explained to the children. Helpful behaviors that are not reinforced will decrease in frequency, as seems to be the case in play groups of preschool children.

Critique of Operant Approach

Reinforcement procedures have been demonstrated to have a powerful impact on children's rates of donating and sharing. Even when modeling influences have proved ineffective, reinforcement has been shown to promote helpful and cooperative behavior (Rogers-Warren & Baer, 1976; Rogers-Warren, Warren, & Baer, 1975). The operant-learning interpretation has an elegant parsimony. It is conservative in that it assumes the minimum of speculation regarding private thoughts and feelings and other events incapable of direct public observation. Principles that account for other forms of voluntary behavior are also used to explain prosocial behavior.

Even when no reinforcing events can be observed, operant principles can be invoked to explain self-sacrificing behavior. As Goldiamond (1968) has pointed out, an observer would not be able to witness the reinforcement or prosocial behavior if the behavior is being maintained on a very sparse intermittent schedule of reinforcement, perhaps on an average of one reinforcement for each 100 helpful acts. Alternatively, there may be a very large, but very delayed, reinforcer for helping, for example, a good-citizen award or a promotion; or the reinforcers involved may be very subtle social ones such as an easing of tension in the facial expression of the person helped. The reinforcement effect would be no less powerful if the reinforcing event were effective only with that particular performer or if the reinforcer were social rather than material in nature. Also, the helping could be imitative. The imitative helping could be one member of a *response class* of imitative or matching behaviors that are all maintained through intermittent reinforcement of some members of the response class (Gewirtz & Stingle, 1968). Finally, if the victim's cries for help constituted an aversive stimulus for the rescuer, seemingly altruistic actions could actually be negatively reinforced and so reduce the rescuer's own distress. It appears, then, that operant-behavior principles can account for various, seemingly unreinforced acts of helping. Note, however, that the various operant explanations offered presume the existence of various subtle interpersonal reinforcers which are postulated on a post hoc basis. Not everyone will find such explanations convincing.

Even when interpersonal reinforcers are operative, their true impact may not be perceived. The social psychology of attribution processes provides an explanation for the common belief that altruistic behavior is unrewarded. Some stimulus events are more likely than others to be perceived as causing certain behavioral outcomes. For example, whereas material rewards (especially material or physical punishment) are highly likely to be considered causes of human behavior, other types of rewards are not (Kelley, 1971; Rothbart, 1968). Reinforcing consequences such as praise and social influences such as modeling (Grusec, Kuczynski, Rushton, & Simutis, 1978) are not often seen as causing or as powerfully affecting behavior. An experiment conducted by Smith, Gelfand, Hartmann, and Partlow (1979) revealed that children did perceive material consequences as promoting their help giving, but that social consequences such as praise or reproof were not considered to be conducive to helping. In fact, many children did not even remember the experimenter's positive or negative comments regarding the children's helping or, if the statements were remembered, they were dismissed as motivationally unimportant. As we have seen, however, praise can substantially increase children's donating, though both the praise agent and the child may fail to recognize the power of such seemingly innocuous comments.

We do not yet know just how much independence from external reinforcement contingencies is possible or desirable. Some writers have asserted that giving children material rewards for engaging in activities that the children at first found attractive undermines the children's intrinsic interest in the activity (Condry, 1977; Lepper & Green, 1975). In these studies, when the material rewards were no longer available, the children who had been promised and had received the material rewards earlier showed less interest in the activity than did children who had received an unexpected reward or those who had received no reward for engaging in the play activity. Other writers (Feingold & Mahoney, 1975; Reiss & Sushinsky, 1975) have reported that there is no reduction in children's willingness to perform an act that has been previously materially reinforced. In fact, Ross (1976) has found that when children were rewarded for meeting certain performance standards their interest in the activity increased. It seems that, depending upon the fashion in which rewards are administered, they can increase, decrease, or leave unchanged the child's willingness to continue a previously reinforced activity (Bandura, 1977).

It has not been demonstrated that the subtle social reinforcers or the thin, intermittent reinforcement schedules posited to explain heroic or altruistic acts actually do exist. Although there are a small number of laboratory demonstrations we can draw upon, we must make a leap of faith in interpreting everyday behavior in terms of the principles formulated in the laboratory. There are, however, abundant examples of the utility of reinforcement procedures in applications in education, rehabilitation, and child rearing (see any issue of the *Journal of Applied Behavior Analysis*). So it can confidently be asserted that many forms of prosocial behavior are responsive to the laws of operant learning. And critics of the operant approach find that it is not at all easy to prove the negative; that is, to prove that there is *no* reinforcement for a particular act of helping or sharing.

The learning approach has also been criticized for failing to deal explicitly with developmental differences in moral reasoning and behavior. For example, there are age-related changes in the effects of exposure to selfish playmates. Peterson, Hartmann, and Gelfand (1977) found that third graders were significantly less affected by a peer's refusal to share pennies than were first graders. The younger children abided more closely to a practice of strict reciprocity in peer relationships than did the third graders. Both groups, however, were significantly less likely to share with children who had failed to reciprocate their earlier generosity than to share with reciprocating peers. The question of why one finds age-related differences in ideas and practices relating to reciprocity in practice and in moral judgment has received very little attention in the operant literature. To be sure, cognitive developmental theory also takes a more descriptive than explanatory approach to developmental changes, so it might be argued that no contemporary viewpoint deals adequately with the mechanisms of development.

In summary, operant interpretations of prosocial behavior are characterized by their parsimony and directness. Mediational constructs are little used, and persistence of helpful behavior is explained in terms of intermittent reinforcement, negative reinforcement, and subtle or delayed reinforcers. Typically, neither these mechanisms nor their absence are demonstrable in everyday examples of prosocial behavior, although a large body of literature suggests that operant principles are useful in generating effective practices in teaching, therapy, and child rearing. However, like cognitive social-learning explanations, operant analyses deemphasize systematic developmental differences in moral reasoning and prosocial behavior.

COGNITIVE SOCIAL-LEARNING THEORY

As its name implies, cognitive social-learning theory combines elements of cognitive psychology and of learning theory in the explanation of social behavior. One common set of cognitive and learning processes is held to account for various forms of social behavior including both prosocial acts and aggressive, socially deviant, and neutral ones. Cognitive processes enter into the person's interpretations of environmental events, plans, selection of goals, and self-evaluations. In this view it is not so much the actual events and physical stimuli as the individual's interpretation of them which influence the person's actions. Yet many of these interpretations are learned directly or through observation, so both cognitive and learning processses are determinants of behavior.

Although cognitive social-learning theory draws upon both cognitive and learning formulations, the approach is not merely derivative. New information regarding processes such as imitation and internalization of performance standards has emerged during the development of the social-learning approach. Although many writers have made theoretical as well as research contributions to the development of this approach, this chapter will give major consideration to the two theorists whose work has stimulated the most research and attention—Albert Bandura and Walter Mischel.

In contrast to the structural focus of the cognitive developmental formulation, the cognitive social-learning model emphasizes the *processes* through which information is acquired and behavior is motivated and performed. In this sense, cognitive social-learning theory is not developmental. Cognitive social-learning theorists do not search for stages or sequences in moral judgment and altruistic behavior; instead they examine the situational variables and the personal characteristics which would lead a person of any age to act in an altruistic or an egocentric manner. Of course, any account must consider the limitations imposed upon acquisition and performance by both physical maturation and past experience. Even should they desire to do so, toddlers could not act prosocially in many situations calling for strength, dexterity, acquaintance with the norms of social conduct, control over resources which could be shared, and skills in self-expression. It is the means by which children acquire these various skills that primarily interest social-learning proponents.

The social-learning emphasis on the impact of *situational variables* contrasts with the cognitive developmental focus on mental structures and stage considerations. Because social situations vary in complex ways and may activate diverse motives, one should not expect to find a high degree of consistency in a person's altruistic or aggressive behavior in various contexts. The same boy who helps his grandfather find his glasses may also throw rocks at a stray dog, share candy with a friend, tease a newcomer to his school, and help a smaller child ward off an attack by a gang of older boys. In some situations the boy's primary motivation may be loyalty to family and friends, in others an attempt to appear fearless and grown-up or to assert his status, and in still others to help those in need. And physical barriers or social conventions may inhibit helping in certain situations but be absent from others. Consequently, *situational specificity* in behavior is often found, particularly in children, although there appears to be a modest relationship of about .30 among altruistic behaviors across situations (Rushton, 1976).

The cognitive social-learning position of Bandura (1977; Bandura & Walters, 1963) and of Mischel (1968; Mischel & Mischel, 1976) stresses the impact of the individual's behavior in creating social climates as well as recognizing the effect of environmental factors on the individual. In contrast, the operant approach emphasizes environmental controls over individual behavior, a one-way rather than a bidirectional causal pattern. Both Bandura and Mischel see the person as influential in constructing his or her own environment. By behaving aggressively, the individual produces hostile reactions from others who, in turn, provide antagonistic models and aversive stimuli which provoke further negative encounters. Similarly, by helping others and by expressing interest in and sympathy for them, the person builds an environment conducive to additional prosocial behavior. Thus, there is a continuing *interaction* between the individual's personal characteristics and environmental outcomes.

Learning Processes

In the cognitive social-learning view, altruistic behavior is acquired in a fashion similar to that of other social behavior, namely through direct or through vicarious experience. The child may receive praise or some other form of reinforcement for spontaneously helping a younger child who has fallen. This process was described in detail in the preceding section on the operant-learning formulation. The child may also learn helpful acts as a result of witnessing family members or television characters engaging in such prosocial behavior. In practice, it is nearly impossible to trace the roots of any child's observed behavior. There have been thousands of occasions for observing prosocial models (persons who demonstrate positive social behavior) in real life, films, television, and books, and probably thousands of occasions in which the child has acted helpfully and has been reinforced for doing so.

Bandura's View of Observational Learning

One of the major contributions of the cognitive social-learning approach has been to illuminate the central role of observational learning in human socialization. Although previous writers had directed their attention toward imitative responding (Miller & Dollard, 1941), none has so thoroughly analyzed and investigated modeling processes as has Bandura (1971; 1977; Bandura & Walters, 1963). In Bandura's formulation, observational learning involves four subprocesses: attention, retention, motor reproduction, and reinforcement. The first process to occur is *attention* to the model. Variables such as the novelty of the act and the status and prior behavior of the model affect the likelihood that the observer will attend to the model. If the observer fails to notice the model's actions, it is impossible for observational learning to take place.

Then, because an observer might not have an opportunity to emulate the model's actions until a later time, *retention* processes are required. The observer must somehow symbolically encode the model's actions so that they can be remembered and later recalled for imitation. Verbal descriptions of the model's acts are particularly effective in aiding retention (Bandura & Jeffrey, 1973), although visual mental images can also prove helpful. In addition, the statement of a rule or principle that governs the model's behavior is beneficial in producing imitative responding. Rule statements aid memory and may also aid the observer in generating beneficial acts in novel situations. Rule statement is a particularly effective technique to use with preschool children who, unlike older ones, are often unable to deduce the rule underlying the behavioral model (Zimmerman & Rosenthal, 1974). Such rules, however, are often insufficient by themselves to produce helpful behavior in children, especially when the models' behavior belies their moralistic admonitions. Bryan and Walbek (1970) have found that when adults preach generosity but practice greed, children's actions will be influenced by the adults' selfishness, although they, too, may verbally advocate generosity.

Motoric reproduction skills are also required for imitation to occur. The child must not only remember what the model did but must also have the physical and social skills to match the model's performance. In Mischel and Mischel's (1976) formulation, the individual must have certain competencies in order to act in a prosocial manner. The person must know how to act appropriately, must be able to generate an acceptable plan of action to help the other person, and must possess the behavioral skills necessary to carry out that plan. A very young child may lack the strength or coordination to give physical assistance to an accident victim or may not possess the vocabulary to express sympathy in any way other than breaking into tears, an action hardly likely to reassure the victim.

Finally *reinforcement* processes will also help to determine the occurrence of imitative responses. Children may acquire information on how to help through observing helpful models. Whether or not the child puts this information into operation may well depend upon the incentives available for doing so. If, through direct past experience or through the observation of models who received rewards, children have come to expect reinforcement for imitating the model, then they will imitate. But if past imitation has resulted in no benefits or in punishment, then little imitation can be expected. Similarly, children are reluctant to imitate infrequently reinforced or punished models, because the negative consequences experienced by the model indicate that the behavior demonstrated is likely to produce similar ill effects for the observing child. Altruistic models are often less effective than aggressive ones because imitating their behavior may entail some cost in time, effort, and resources, and may have little, if any, benefit for the imitator.

Bryan and his associates (see Bryan, 1975) have found that helpful models who express positive emotional reactions after helping (for example, smiling and commenting that they like to help) are particularly likely to produce imitation. Simply providing the model with some type of reinforcement, such as praise, does not typically increase imitation in brief laboratory interactions. It seems necessary for the model to express happiness, either with or without additional reward from others. Whether the model receives praise, material benefits, or engages in obvious self-congratulation, the effect seems to be one of *vicarious rein-*

forcement for the observer. As Bandura (1977) has pointed out, vicarious reinforcement can have a variety of effects. It provides information regarding the likelihood of a rewarding consequence for engaging in the modeled behavior. Also, the observer may become motivated to act prosocially in order to obtain reward and may learn prosocial values that are exemplified in the model's behavior.

How does vicarious reinforcement increase the observer's helpfulness? Aronfreed (1968) has suggested that the emotional cues emitted by others may come to have reinforcing effects for observers through a process of conditioning. If children receive rewarding hugs and expressions of affection at the same time as they witness another's expressions of pleasure, the other person's behavior may come to have reinforcing value for the children. Consequently, the children may even sacrifice attractive rewards for themselves in order to produce positive consequences for others, as indicated by the other person's expressions of pleasure (Aronfreed & Paskal, 1965, cited in Aronfreed, 1968; Midlarsky & Bryan, 1967). It is presumed that the pairing of rewarding hugs and the other person's expressions of pleasure confer conditioned reinforcing properties on the signs of the other's pleasure, which come to induce empathy and to exert control over the observer's behavior. This is another way in which vicarious reinforcement could be effective.

The Development of Imitation

The social learning position is that observational learning facility depends not so much on the child's achieving any particular stage of development as on his or her skill in the use of the various component processes of imitation (Bandura, 1977). The child who has skills in selective attention, memory encoding, and motoric reproduction and who has learned to anticipate consequences will be able to learn from observation. Younger children typically are unskilled in symbolic encoding of observed behaviors for later cognitive retrieval and matching, so they are greatly handicapped in delayed imitation. Infants can, however, imitate simple motor acts immediately after they are modeled (Bower, 1976; Meltzoff & Moore, 1977). In fact, Bower (1976) has demonstrated that six-day-old infants may be able to imitate actions such as protruding one's tongue, but that early imitative ability may disappear with increasing age, to reappear only when the infant is about one year old. This successive appearance and disappearance of skills is not readily explained by cognitive-developmental theories which postulate incremental, irreversible phases of development.

However, it is also true that, as Piaget (1946/1951) postulated, the earliest imitative acts are simple motor responses (such as tongue protrusion) that are already within the infant's repertoire. Piaget maintains that at seven to eight months infants begin to distinguish between environmental stimuli and events and their perception of or action upon them, a developmental achievement which should produce imitation of novel acts. The research literature confirms this position. At seven to eight months the infant begins to imitate novel behaviors never before displayed (McCall, Parke, & Kavanaugh, 1977). Piaget's view that the development of symbolic functioning at eighteen to twenty-one months should permit deferred rather than only immediate imitation is also supported by research findings that deferred imitation begins at this age (McCall et al., 1977).

In Bandura's social-learning view, an infant or young child's failure to imitate a model could be due to many factors unrelated to cognitive development. For example, many repetitions (rather than a single modeling display) may be required before imitation occurs. Powerful incentives may be necessary for young children to be motivated to display their imitative abilities. Perhaps certain model characteristics are essential. For example, the toddler may imitate a parent or sibling much more readily than a stranger. Bandura does believe, however, that verbal encoding of modeled sequences greatly facilitates later reproduction of those sequences by an observer. Older children and adults, who have greater verbal facility, are greatly advantaged in observational learning of complex behavioral sequences. Bandura maintains that in order to enhance imitative performance one would do better to teach children component skills, such as verbal encoding, than to wait until they have achieved a particular cognitive developmental level. Although recognizing that level of maturation places some limits on imitative ability, Bandura emphasizes the modifiability of behavior, even in very young children.

Functions of Altruistic Models

Modeling stimuli can have three types of effects (Bandura, 1969a; 1977). First, models can teach observers novel behaviors. A very young child may never before have witnessed anyone deposit coins in a canister to make a contribution to help handicapped persons. When the youngster first sees a parent doing so, the child learns how and where to deposit the money; if the parent explains why one should do so, the child learns prosocial values as well. Learning a modeled behavior that is new to the observer is termed a *"modeling effect."*

A second effect of exposure to a model, *disinhibition*, is somewhat more general. Young children may be inhibited about helping others because they are unsure about the appropriateness of doing so. In fact, children may require explicit permission to put their helping skills into practice (Staub, 1971). Exposure to nonpunished or rewarded helping models can also reduce children's inhibitions regarding prosocial behavior. Disinhibition occurs with antisocial as well as with prosocial behavior. Say that a little boy sees a gunfight and a wrestling match on television, and then goes outside to play, whereupon he quarrels with and hits another boy. The exposure to the aggressive television models could be said to have a disinhibiting effect on the boy's aggressive behavior. Even when no new responses are learned, exposure to the antisocial model promotes many types of antagonistic activities in the observing child. Models can powerfully encourage customarily prohibited behavior, especially when the model is not punished for hostility. These disinhibition effects are very strong, and there is considerable imitation of aggressive models because children's aggression is quite likely to earn them the toys of their victims as well as the respect and approval of other children (Patterson & Cobb, 1971).

A third effect of exposure to models is the simple *facilitation* of previously learned behaviors such as looking in a particular direction, yawning, toying idly with a piece of string, using a certain phrase in conversation, humming a tune, and so forth. Liebert and Fernandez (1970) have found that exposure to a single generous model was sufficient to instigate some donating among nursery-school boys. That is, the modeling display probably *facilitated* the occurrence of a previously learned donation response. In contrast, exposure to two models who consistently donated equal amounts of tokens produced exact matching of the amount donated by the observing children. This development of specific standards for the amount shared could be considered true learning of a new performance. Liebert and Fernandez concluded that the presentation of a single exemplar of prosocial behavior is more likely to produce a facilitation effect, while consistent multiple exemplars are more like to produce exact matching of the models' behavior, indicating learning rather than facilitation.

Summary of Cognitive Social-Learning Approach

Both cognitive and learning functions affect altruistic performance. The child learns helpful behavior either through direct experience and reinforcement or, more likely, through modeling. Four components jointly determine the behavioral effects of exposure of modeling stimuli—attention, retention, motoric reproduction, and reinforcement. If any one subprocess fails, then modeling stimuli may not produce imitative behavior. Ability to imitate depends more upon skill with the component processes (which can be acquired through instruction) than upon cognitive maturity. Models can act to teach observers new responses, can disinhibit socially proscribed activities, and can facilitate performance of previously learned behaviors, regardless of the child's age, so long as the component skills have been mastered.

Model Characteristics

Certain types of models have been shown to be particularly effective transmitters of prosocial behavior. Factors such as the model's status, prestige, similarity to the observer, and general attractiveness may determine the model's influence over the observer. *Powerful* adults, those who have control over play materials or other resources valued by the child, are more potent prosocial models than are strangers or those with less power (Grusec, 1971). The adult's actual *nurturance* toward the child may promote prosocial imitation in some situations but inhibit it in others. Warm and permissive models may encourage children to over-reward themselves for minimal accomplishments. When self-denial of treats for substandard game performance is examined, nurturant models appear to promote undeserved self-gratification in children (Bandura, Grusec, & Menlove, 1967). On the other hand, when the behaviors studied are attempts to rescue accident victims, prior interaction with a nurturant adult promotes helping (Staub, 1971). Perhaps the warm and approving adult signals to the child that the child's behavior will surely be acceptable and that caution and guardedness are not required. The child then feels free to take gratuitous rewards as well as to defy an implicit prohibition against leaving an assigned task in order to assist an accident victim.

In an important and ambitious study of nursery-school children's learning of helping behavior, Yarrow, Scott, and Waxler (1973) found that an adult caretaker who (1) was consistently nurturant in doll-play enactments of helping, (2) was helpful to persons who had hurt themselves or required other help, and (3) was helpful toward the children themselves was influential in teaching the children to be helpful in a wide variety of contexts. Children exposed to the consistently nurturant model were highly likely to express concern for and to aid those in need. Other children who interacted with an adult who was less responsive to the children themselves (low nurturance model) were less helpful. Thus, the nurturant model transmits prosocial values such as concern for others, as well as offering training in how to help. These findings suggest that it is crucial that parents and teachers who desire altruistic children should exemplify prosocial values in their own behavior.

Rehearsal and Role Playing

Once a child has witnessed a helpful model, rehearsal of the model's behavior may promote the child's later helpfulness. Rosenhan and White (1967) have proposed that rehearsing modeled contributions to an orphan's fund in the model's presence can promote future generosity. Those who did not imitate the model initially failed to give when they had another opportunity to do so (but see White & Burnham, 1975, for a failure to replicate). Rosenhan and White believed that the rehearsal of the donating behavior in the model's presence promoted future generosity. But an alternative explanation could be that some other factor, such as the child's initial inclination to be generous, promoted donating both in public and in private at a later time.

It is not yet clear what prompts children to imitate or not imitate immediately. In an effort to promote immediate rehearsal, some researchers have explicitly instructed the children to imitate. It is important that such rehearsal not appear coercive, because in another study, White (1972) found that children who had been coerced into donating through demanding instructions tended not to give in a later private test, and that some actually stole gift certificates. More permissive instructions produced donations on both the immediate, public and the later, private occasions.

Boys appear to be particularly likely to resist instructions that exert social pressure to behave helpfully, and coercive tactics sometimes even suppress boys' helpfulness (Feinberg & Staub, 1975; Staub, 1976). Thus, it is not engaging in helpful acts itself, but the circumstances under which one does so, which promote future helpfulness. In some recent research, Staub has found that when children engage in positive behaviors such as role-playing helpful acts and tutoring other children, an increase is found in their prosocial behavior (Staub, 1975b). Staub suggests that acting as a teacher or helper places the children in an important role which enhances self-esteem, produces feelings of satisfaction, and promotes the internalization of prosocial values. All of these factors encourage positive social activities.

Internalization and Self-regulation

The cognitive social-learning approach holds that individuals can transcend immediate social influences through the use of self-evaluation and self-reward for their own conduct. The individuals' own values may motivate prosocial action even though short-term, external consequences might favor greed or failure to help. In addition, behaving selfishly may produce feelings of guilt and self-contempt, whereas helping is rewarded by pride and satisfaction. The original sources of self-standards and self-regulation are external, however. Parents and other socialization agents exemplify social standards and enforce them in evaluating children's conduct. The children, in turn, accept these standards as their own and come to apply the standards to their own behavior. Bandura and Kupers (1964) have demonstrated that children imitate adults' standards in rewarding themselves with candies for performance in a bowling game. After the model's departure, the children played the bowling game by themselves and denied themselves freely available candies for performance that failed to meet the modeled standards. Bandura argues that this type of learning governs our behavior in many situations in which we provide ourselves with intangible, psychological rewards contingent upon actions that meet self-prescribed social standards.

Our values and our goals, our standards of self-reinforcement, and our self-regulation practices are all acquired during socialization. For the most part, socialization influences reflect broadly based cultural values. These values are internalized by children and are used to guide their own conduct. For a minority of individuals, however, very small and highly unusual reference groups might exist and might promote atypical behavior. Thus, the child may exhibit unusual dress, or strange eating habits, or particularly selfless behavior because of the influence of a particular religious sect or cultural subgroup to which the child's family belongs. For example, some religions prohibit use of weapons even in self-defense; other prescribe vegetarian diets. There are idiosyncratic as well as subcultural sources for atypical behavior, however. Some people's behavior may actually be governed by hallucinations or by delusional reference groups, as happens with certain psychotic individuals.

Mostly, however, the larger society's values are adopted by its members. To the extent that the culture's values are altruistic ones, the individual will act in a prosocial manner and will receive both external and self-reinforcement for doing so. But when individual achievement and monetary gain are the society's preeminent goals, people may be reluctant to sacrifice time, money, or effort or to risk status in order to help others in need.

Critique of Cognitive Social-Learning Approach

The cognitive social-learning approach has yielded considerable information regarding the determinants of positively valued social behavior and has produced powerful methods for increasing desired behavior. Modeling has proven particularly useful in this regard. Although it might be possible to train a child to act prosocially without exposure to prosocial models, modeling has emerged as an extremely important influence in actual socialization. Recent studies by Friedrich and Stein (1975) have demonstrated that prosocial television content ("Mr. Rogers' Neighborhood," a program presented on the Public Broadcasting System) produced significant gains in children's knowledge about and involvement in helping and sharing. The combination of watching the helpful and sympathetic television character and of using hand puppets to reenact scenes from the program was particularly effective in enhancing the kindergarten children's helpfulness. These results suggest that televised models could be used more extensively to increase the low rates of helpfulness (Murphy, 1937) typically found among children of preschool and kindergarten ages.

It is possible that the behavioral effects of modeling displays are due largely to demand characteristics in the experimental situations studied (see Bryan, 1975). Perhaps the children simply are behaving as they believe the experimenter wishes them to. The findings of generalizability and durability of modeling effects suggest that something other than demand characteristics is operating, however. Strong demands may create reactance, as the work of White (1972) and Staub (1976) has shown. Moreover, the charge that demand characteristics produce modeling effects is contested by studies that have demonstrated potent effects of prosocial and of aggressive television models on children's free play in naturalistic contexts (see, for example, Stein, Friedrich, & Vondracek, 1972; Steuer, Applefield, & Smith, 1971). It seems highly unlikely that the young participants in such research perceived the televised entertainment programs employed as demands to act in a helpful or a quarrelsome manner.

Like the operant approach, the cognitive social-learning formulation largely neglects the study of systematic changes in moral reasoning and in prosocial behavior which accompany age increases in children. Rather, both approaches emphasize the learning processes which are presumed to produce change at all developmental levels. Some critics view this emphasis on process as disregarding important structural changes which occur during development (for example, Kohlberg, 1976a). From the operant-learning position, cognitive social-learning theory is seen as including excess theoretical baggage. Although the transmission of modeled standards of material self-reward has been demonstrated (Bandura & Kupers, 1964), it is extremely difficult, perhaps impossible, to provide a public demonstration of cognitive or mental self-reward, or of plans, or of standard setting. Descriptions of one's own thoughts, reasoning, and motivation are notoriously unreliable. Nevertheless, one could ask subjects to make public their thoughts by stating them aloud, but this operation may simply result in the manipulation of public statements, which possibly differ from private cognitions (Rachlin, 1977). Thus, one is forced to argue by analogy that covert actions follow the same behavioral laws as do overt ones. Whether or not this parallelism holds may be untestable, however reasonable it appears to be.

CRITERIA FOR A THEORY OF MORAL DEVELOPMENT

Thus far, this chapter has discussed some of the vast array of research findings on moral judgment and behavior. A comprehensive theory of the development of prosocial behavior must define a domain of relevant behavior and must consider, organize, and account for these many and diverse empirical results. The theory must also generate new studies which, ideally, should yield predictions that are confirmed in behavioral tests. To be most useful, the account should deal both with moral judgment and with prosocial behavior (Mischel & Mischel, 1976); but, as we have seen, no contemporary theory actually covers both topics. The cognitive developmental theorists focus upon differences in moral judgment among individuals at various stages of development; the behavior analysts and the cognitive social-learning theorists study the effects of situational variables on children's sharing, helping, and cooperation. None of the current theories considers both the judgmental and the behavioral realm in any detailed fashion. The future should see the development of more comprehensive theories which will describe the causal relationships between cognitive and behavioral variables and which will specify the conditions under which judgments and actions will correspond or fail to correspond.

Motivation is a central issue in any theory of moral development. When and why will children act to promote the welfare of others? To what degree are we hedonistically or altruistically motivated? Philosophers such as Bentham and John Stuart Mill long ago asserted that humans are primarily motivated to seek pleasure and to avoid pain, and this view has never gone either unchampioned or uncontested. Today's psychologists debate whether altruistic behavior defies known laws of operant behavior and is motivated solely out of concern for others, or whether this belief is a flattering illusion and conduct is influenced primarily by environmental reinforcement contingencies. Theories of prosocial behavior must take a position on this issue, and the position taken must explain the outcomes of experiments that have demonstrated that rewards affect helping, as well as those in which no personally advantageous results of helping can be identified. One cannot simply assert the negative and state that since no extrinsic rewards were observed the helping was purely altruistically motivated. Rather, the conceptual model must first specify the sources of the altruistic motivation posited and then demonstrate the existence of that motive *independent from* observation of the behavior which the motive is supposed to explain. One cannot at the same time appeal to the motive to explain the behavior and to the behavior to demonstrate the existence of the motive. For example, we might observe that a child anonymously donates some gift certificates to charity without receiving either recognition or material rewards for the donation; we might then, perhaps mistakenly, conclude that the child's motivation for donating was a purely altruistic one. The donating is the behavior to be explained. It is neither logically nor scientifically acceptable to explain the donating by reference to altruistic motivation and simultaneously to demonstrate the existence of the altruistic motivation through the observation of that same charitable behavior. Somehow, we must provide a measure of the inferred motivational state independent of its presumed effect on the dependent variable. Our theory should suggest just how we can do so and what additional effects the altruistic motive should have.

Each theory must weigh the impact of experience on the one hand and of genetic and hereditary endowment on the other, and nearly all accounts posit some interaction between heredity and environment in determining behavior. Present theories range widely between the biological extreme represented by E. O. Wilson's theory of sociobiology (Wilson, 1975), and the environmental extreme of the operant-learning approach. Wilson believes that we act instinctively to rescue our immediate relatives from danger in order to maximize the chances of passing on our genes to future generations. Sociobiology contrasts with the operant view that we repeat actions of the type that previously have been reinforced, whether the behavior is selfish or prosocial in nature. The accumulation of research evidence ultimately will decide the utility of these competing explanations. Experimentation to verify predictions drawn from the sociobiology formulation is virtually impossible to conduct because of the vast evolutionary history that is assumed to produce social behavior. Therefore, the decisive evidence on the adequacy of the contrasting viewpoints must come from experiments that investigate the role of cognitive and environmental variables.

An adequate theory should be truly developmental. That is, the account should not only describe age-related changes in behavior but also identify the mechanisms producing developmental changes. Current accounts are much better at description than at explanation. Thus, we have detailed descriptions of a sequence of developmental levels of moral judgment (Piaget, 1932/1965; Kohlberg, 1976a) or social cognition (Selman & Jaquette, 1978), but there is much less specificity in the discussion of the factors—such as ego structures and cognitive/moral conflict—that are supposed to produce the developmental changes. Granted that both maturation and experience are necessary, the theory should detail just what types of experiences are crucial, and how these experiences affect judgment. The theory should relate levels of moral reasoning to the child's general cognitive development. It should state, as Kohlberg (1976a) does, whether moral development is a separate realm or an integral part of intellectual functioning. The theory should allow us to predict the magnitude of the correlations between tests of moral reasoning and of cognitive development and general intelligence. Developmental issues pose problems for operant and cognitive social-learning positions as well. There do seem to be age-related changes in the effectiveness of certain types of modeling demonstrations, such as those provided by nonreciprocating models (Peterson, Hartmann, & Gelfand, 1977). The learning theories are largely silent on the issue of why one would expect such developmental changes and how they might be predicted.

Then there is the issue of consistency in behavior, whether within the same individual in different situations or across individuals in the same situation. Each theory must address the available evidence which suggests a rather modest, but often reliable, association of prosocial behaviors for individuals across situations and types of prosocial behavior (Rushton, 1976). There is also a body of research suggesting that modeling and other situational influences produce often reliable, but sometimes rather weak, effects on prosocial behavior across individuals. The task for a theory is to explain and to predict the levels of consistency observed. Different theorists offer various explanations regarding consistency. The accounts range from the learning position—that the individual's past history may interact with present situational influences—to the cognitive-developmental position of Kohlberg (1976a; see also Lickona, 1976a)—which predicts behavioral inconsistencies for individuals at less advanced levels of moral reasoning and greater consistency for those operating at postconventional levels. There is disagreement, too, regarding the very definition of consistency, with the learning theorists referring to behavioral consistency (for example, Mischel & Mischel, 1976), and the cognitive-developmentalists maintaining that consistency resides in the individual's perception of the situation and of the meaning of his or her actions (Lickona, 1976a, p. 17). With such differences existing in the definitions of basic terminology, it becomes especially important that theorists take care to define their terms and concepts explicitly.

The theorists we have reviewed in the preceding pages do take definite positions on the role of biological factors, on the importance of reward and punishment, on consistency in prosocial behavior, and on the existence of unselfish, altruistic motivation. There is, as yet, little serious attempt to reach beyond the confines of a single judgmental or behavioral domain and to explain the findings from diverse research traditions within a single conceptual framework. Theorists have limited themselves to attempting to deal either with moral judgments or with prosocial behavior; none has considered both. Consequently, current accounts would be rated low both on the scope of the explanations attempted and on the variety of empirical demonstrations accounted for. Although it seems generally true that theoretical perspectives are, of necessity, based on a limited domain of observation and experimentation (Aronfreed, 1976), theories of prosocial development have, perhaps, been overly restrictive in their purview. On the other hand, present theories of moral development are generating vigorous research activity and so must be judged to be successful on this latter criterion. Upon considering the rise and fall in popularity of past theories of learning, of cognitive development, and of personality, one is tempted to conclude that the search for the perfect theory is much like the search for the unicorn. The goal may prove unattainable, but the process of exploration can, itself, yield rich rewards in our understanding and prediction of human behavior.

To summarize, criteria for judging the adequacy of a theory of moral development include the ability of the theory to organize and to explain empirical evidence of the greatest possible diversity, to address basic motivational and developmental issues, and to predict new research findings. Current theories do best at generating new research and at dealing with a single judgmental or behavioral domain. They are considerably weaker in specifying mechanisms supposed to produce developmental change and in the scope of their coverage. It would, perhaps, be wise to recognize that although a perfect theory may never be devised, the attempt to develop one may prove rewarding nevertheless.

REFERENCES

ALSTON, W. P. Comments on Kohlberg's "From is to ought." In T. Mischel (Ed.), *Cognitive development and epistemology*. New York: Academic Press, 1971.

ARONFREED, J. *Conduct and conscience*. New York: Academic Press, 1968.

ARONFREED, J. Moral development from the standpoint of a general psychological theory. In T. Lickona (Ed.), *Moral development and behavior: Theory, research, and social issues.* New York: Holt, Rinehart and Winston, 1976.

ARONFREED, J., & PASKAL, V. Altruism, empathy, and the conditioning of positive affect. Unpublished manuscript, University of Pennsylvania, 1965. Cited in Aronfreed, J. *Conduct and conscience: The socialization of internalized control over behavior.* New York: Academic Press, 1968.

ATKINSON, C. A. *The effects of success, failure, and age on children's sharing.* Unpublished master's thesis, University of Utah, 1974.

BAIER, K. Moral development. *Monist*, 1974, *58*, 601–615.

BANDURA, A. *Principles of behavior modification.* New York: Holt, Rinehart and Winston, 1969. (a)

BANDURA, A. Social learning of moral judgments. *Journal of Personality and Social Psychology*, 1969, *11*, 275–279. (b)

BANDURA, A. *Psychological modeling: Conflicting theories.* New York: Aldine-Atherton, 1971.

BANDURA, A. *Social learning theory.* Englewood Cliffs, N.J.: Prentice-Hall, 1977.

BANDURA, A., GRUSEC, J. E., & MENLOVE, F. L. Some social determinants of self-monitoring reinforcement systems. *Journal of Personality and Social Psychology*, 1967, *5*, 449–455.

BANDURA, A., & JEFFERY, R. W. Role of symbolic and rehearsal processes in observational learning. *Journal of Personality and Social Psychology*, 1973, *26*, 122–130.

BANDURA, A., & KUPERS, C. J. Transmission of self-reinforcement through modeling. *Journal of Abnormal and Social Psychology*, 1964, *69*, 1–9.

BANDURA, A., & McDONALD, F. J. Influence of social reinforcement and the behavior of models in shaping children's moral judgments. *Journal of Abnormal and Social Psychology*, 1963, *67*, 274–281.

BANDURA, A., & WALTERS, R. H. *Social learning and personality development.* New York: Holt, Rinehart and Winston, 1963.

BEM, D. J., & ALLEN, A. On predicting some of the people some of the time: The search for cross-situational consistencies in behavior. *Psychological Review*, 1974, *81*, 506–520.

BOWER, T. G. R. Repetition processes in child development. *Scientific American*, 1976, *235*, 38–47.

BRONSON, W. C. Mother-toddler interaction: A perspective on studying the development of competence. *Merrill-Palmer Quarterly*, 1974, *20*, 275–301.

BRYAN, J. H. Children's cooperation and helping behaviors. In E. M. Hetherington (Ed.), *Review of child development research* (Vol. 5). Chicago: University of Chicago Press, 1975.

BRYAN, J. H., & LONDON, P. Altruistic behavior by children. *Psychological Bulletin*, 1970, *73*, 200–211.

BRYAN, J. H., & WALBEK, N. H. The impact of words and deeds concerning altruism upon children. *Child Development*, 1970, *41*, 747–757.

CAMPBELL, D. T., & FISKE, D. Convergent and discriminant validation by the multi-trait, multi-method matrix. *Psychological Bulletin*, 1959, *56*, 81–105.

CONDRY, J. Enemies of exploration: Self-initiated versus other-initiated learning. *Journal of Personality and Social Psychology*, 1977, *35*, 459–477.

COWAN, P. A., LANGER, J., HEAVENRICH, J., & NATHANSON, M. Social learning and Piaget's cognition theory of moral development. *Journal of Personality and Social Psychology*, 1969, *11*, 261–274.

DAMON, W. Early conceptions of positive justice as related to the development of logical operations. *Child Development*, 1975, *46*, 301–312.

DAMON, W. *The social world of the child*. San Francisco: Jossey-Bass, 1977.

DePALMA, D. J., & FOLEY, J. M. Toward the future. In D. J. DePalma & J. M. Foley (Eds.), *Moral development: Current theory and research*, Hillsdale, N.J.: Erlbaum, 1975.

DORR, D., & FEY, S. Relative power of symbolic adult and peer models in the modification of children's moral choice behavior. *Journal of Personality and Social Psychology*, 1974, *29*, 335–341.

ELKIND, D. *Children and adolescents: Interpretation essays on Jean Piaget.* London: Oxford University Press, 1970.

EMLER, N. P., & RUSHTON, J. P. Cognitive-developmental factors in children's generosity. *British Journal of Social and Clinical Psychology*, 1974, *13*, 277–281.

ESCALONA, S. K. Basic modes of social interaction: Their emergence and patterning during the first two years of life. *Merrill-Palmer Quarterly*, 1973, *19*, 205–232.

FEINBERG, H., & STAUB, E. *Learning to be prosocial: The effects of reasoning and participation in prosocial action on children's prosocial behavior.* Paper presented at the meetings of the Eastern Psychological Association, New York, April, 1975.

FEINGOLD, B. B., & MAHONEY, M. J. Reinforcing effects on intrinsic interest: Undermining the overjustification hypothesis. *Behavior Therapy*, 1975, *6*, 723–729.

FISCHER, W. F. Sharing in preschool children as a function of amount and type of reinforcement. *Genetic Psychology Monographs*, 1963, *68*, 215–245.

FISHKIN, J., KENISTON, D., & MacKINNON, C. Moral reasoning and political ideology. *Journal of Personality and Social Psychology*, 1973, *27*, 109–119.

FLAVELL, J. H. Stage-related properties of cognitive development. *Cognitive Psychology*, 1971, *2*, 421–453.

FRAENKEL, J. R. The Kohlberg bandwagon: Some reservations. In D. Purpel & K. Ryan (Eds.), *Moral education...it comes with the territory.* Berkeley, Calif.: McCutchan, 1976.

FRIEDRICH, L. K., & STEIN, A. H. Prosocial television and young children: The effects of verbal labeling and role playing on learning and behavior. *Child Development*, 1975, *46*, 27–38.

GELFAND, D. M., HARTMANN, D. P., CROMER, C. C., SMITH, C. L., & PAGE, B. C. The effects of instructional prompts and praise on children's donation rates. *Child Development*, 1975, *46*, 980–983.

GERGEN, K. J., GERGEN, M. M., & METER, K. Individual orientations to prosocial behavior. *Journal of Social Issues*, 1972, *28*, 105–130.

GEWIRTZ, J. L., & STINGLE, K. G. Learning of generalized imitation as the basis for identification. *Psychological Review*, 1968, *75*, 374–397.

GINSBURG, H., & OPPER, S. *Piaget's theory of intellectual development: An introduction.* Englewood Cliffs, N. J.: Prentice-Hall, 1969.

GLASSCO, J. A., MILGRAM, N. A., & YOUNISS, J. Stability of training effects on intentionality in moral judgment in children. *Journal of Personality and Social Psychology*, 1970, *14*, 360–365.

GOLDIAMOND, I. Moral behavior: A functional analysis. *Psychology Today*, 1968, *2*, 31–34.

GRUSEC, J. E. Power and the internalization of self-denial. *Child Development*, 1971, *42*, 93–105.

GRUSEC, J. E., KUCZYNSKI, L., RUSHTON, J. P., & SIMUTIS, Z. Modeling, direct instruction, and attributions: Effects on altruism. *Developmental Psychology*, 1978, *14*, 51–57.

HARRIS, M. B. Reciprocity and generosity: Some determinants of sharing in children. *Child Development*, 1970, *41*, 313–328.

HARRIS, M. B., & SIEBEL, C. E. Affect, aggression, and altruism. *Developmental Psychology*, 1975, *11*, 623–627.

HARTMANN, D. P., GELFAND, D. M., SMITH, C. L., PAUL, S. C., CROMER, C. C., PAGE, B. C., & LeBENTA, D. V. Factors affecting the acquisiton and elimination of children's donating behavior. *Journal of Experimental Child Psychology*, 1976, *21*, 328–338.

HARTSHORNE, J., MAY, M. A., & MALLER, J. B. *Studies in the nature of character* (Vol. 2). *Studies in service and self-control.* New York: MacMillan, 1929.

HOFFMAN, M. L. Moral development. In P. H. Mussen (Ed.), *Carmichael's manual of child psychology* (Vol. II, 3rd Ed). New York: Wiley, 1970.

HOFFMAN, M. L. Empathy, role taking, guilt, and development of altruistic motives. In T. Lickona (Ed.), *Moral development and behavior: Theory, research, and social issues.* New York: Holt, Rinehart and Winston, 1976.

HOFFMAN, M. L. Moral internalization: Current theory and research. In L. Berkowitz (Ed.), *Advances in experimental social psychology* (Vol. 10). New York: Academic Press, 1977. *(a)*

HOFFMAN, M. L. Sex differences in empathy and related behavior. *Psychological Bulletin*, 1977, *84*, 712–722. *(b)*

HOLSTEIN, C. B. The relation of children's moral judgment level to that of their parents and to communication patterns in the family. In R. C. Smart & M. S. Smart (Eds.), *Readings in child development and relationships.* New York: MacMillan, 1972.

IANNOTTI, R. J. Effect of role-taking experiences on role-taking, empathy, altruism, and aggression. *Developmental Psychology*, 1978, *14*, 119–124.

ISEN, A. M., CLARK, M., & SCHWARTZ, M. F. Duration of the effect of good mood on helping: "Footprints on the sands of time." *Journal of Personality and Social Psychology*, 1976, *34*, 385–393.

ISEN, A. M., & LEVIN, P. F. The effect of feeling good on helping: Cookies and kindness. *Journal of Personality and Social Psychology*, 1972, *21*, 384–388.

JESSOR, S. L. Recent research on moral development: A commentary. In D. J. DePalma & J. M. Foley (Eds.), *Moral development: Current theory and research.* Hillsdale, N. J.: Erlbaum, 1975.

KEASEY, C. B. Social participation as a factor in the moral development of preadolescents. *Developmental Psychology*, 1971, *5*, 216–220.

KEASEY, C. B. Implicators of cognitive development for moral reasoning. In D. J. DePalma & J. M. Foley (Eds.), *Moral development: Current theory and research.* Hillsdale, N. J.: Erlbaum, 1975.

KELLEY, H. H. Causal schemata and the attribution process. In E. E. Jones et al. (Eds.), *Attribution: Perceiving the causes of behavior.* Morristown, N. J.: General Learning Press, 1971.

KESSEN, W. "Stage" and "structure" in the study of children. In R. Brown (Ed.), *Cognitive development in children.* Chicago: University of Chicago Press, 1970.

KOHLBERG, L. *The development of modes of moral thinking and choice in the years ten to sixteen.* Unpublished doctoral dissertation, University of Chicago, 1958.

KOHLBERG, L. Moral development and identification. In H. Stevenson (Ed.), *Child Psychology, 62nd Yearbook of the National Society for the Study of Education.* Chicago: University of Chicago Press, 1963.

KOHLBERG, L. Stage and sequence: The cognitive-developmental approach to socialization. In D. A. Goslin (Ed.), *Handbook of socialization theory and research.* Chicago: Rand McNally, 1969.

KOHLBERG, L. Stages of moral development as a basis for moral education. In C. M. Beck, B. S. Crittenden, & E. V. Sullivan (Eds.), *Moral education: Interdisciplinary approaches.* Toronto: University of Toronto Press, 1971.

KOHLBERG, L. Moral stages and moralization: The cognitive-developmental approach. In T. Lickona (Ed.), *Moral development and behavior: Theory, research, and social issues.* New York: Holt, Rinehart and Winston, 1976. *(a)*

KOHLBERG, L. The cognitive-developmental approach to moral education. In D. Purpel & K. Ryan (Eds.), *Moral education...it comes with the territory.* Berkeley, Calif.: McCutchan, 1976. *(b)*

KREBS, D. L. Altruism—an examination of the concept and a review of the literature. *Psychological Bulletin*, 1970, *73*, 258–302.

KUHN, D. Short-term longitudinal evidence for the sequentiality of Kohlberg's early stages of moral development. *Developmental Psychology*, 1976, *12*, 162–166.

KURTINES, W., & GREIF, E. B. The development of moral thought: Review and evaluation of Kohlberg's approach. *Psychological Bulletin*, 1974, *81*, 453–470.

LEE, L. C. The concomitant development of cognitive and moral modes of thought: A test of selected deductions from Piaget's theory. *Genetic Psychology Monographs*, 1971, *83*, 93–146.

LE FURGY, W. G., & WOLOSHIN, G. W. Immediate and long-term effects of experimentally induced social influence in the modification of adolescents' moral judgments. *Journal of Personality and Social Psychology*, 1969, *12*, 104–110.

LEPPER, M. R., & GREENE, D. Turning play into work: Effects of adult surveillance and extrinsic rewards on children's intrinsic motivation. *Journal of Personality and Social Psychology*, 1975, *31*, 479–486.

LICKONA, T. Piaget misunderstood: A critique of the criticisms of his theory of moral development. *Merrill-Palmer Quarterly*, 1969, *16*, 337–350.

LICKONA, T. Critical issues in the study of moral development and behavior. In T. Lickona (Ed.), *Moral development and behavior: Theory, research, and social issues.* New York: Holt, Rinehart and Winston, 1976. *(a)*

LICKONA, T. Research on Piaget's theory of moral development. In T. Lickona (Ed.), *Moral development and behavior: Theory, research and social issues.* New York: Holt, Rinehart and Winston, 1976. *(b)*

LIEBERT, R. M., & FERNANDEZ, L. E. Effects of single and multiple modeling cues on establishing norms for sharing. *Proceedings of the 78th Convention, American Psychological Association*, 1970, *5*, 437–438. (Summary)

MACAULAY, J. & BERKOWITZ, L. (Eds.), *Altruism and helping behavior.* New York: Academic Press, 1970.

MARTIN, R. M., SHAFTO, M., & VANDEINSE, W. The reliability, validity, and design of the Defining Issues Test. *Developmental Psychology*, 1977, *13*, 460–468.

MCCALL, R. B., PARKE, R. D., & KAVANAUGH, R. D. Imitation of live and televised models by children one to three years of age. *Monographs of the Society for Research in Child Development*, 1977, *42*, (5, Serial No. 173).

MELTZOFF, A. N., & MOORE, M. K. Imitation of facial and manual gestures by human neonates. *Science*, 1977, *198*, 75–78.

MIDLARSKY, E., & BRYAN, J. H. Training charity in children. *Journal of Personality and Social Psychology*, 1967, *5*, 408–415.

MIDLARSKY, E., BRYAN, J. H., & BRICKMAN, P. Aversive approval: Interactive effects of modeling and reinforcement on altruistic behavior. *Child Development*, 1973, *44*, 321–328.

MILLER, N. E., & DOLLARD, J. *Social learning and imitation.* New Haven, Conn.: Yale University Press, 1941.

MISCHEL, W. *Personality and assessment.* New York: Wiley, 1968.

MISCHEL, W., & MISCHEL, H. N. A cognitive social-learning approach to morality and self-regulation. In T. Lickona (Ed.), *Moral development and behavior: Theory, research, and social issues.* New York: Holt, Rinehart and Winston, 1976.

MOIR, D. J. Egocentrism and the emergence of conventional morality in preadolescent girls. *Child Development*, 1974, *45*, 299–304.

MOORE, B. S., UNDERWOOD, B., & ROSENHAN, D. L. Affect and altruism. *Developmental Psychology*, 1973, *8*, 99–104.

MURPHY, L. B. *Social behavior and child personality.* New York: Columbia University Press, 1937.

MUSSEN, P. H., & EISENBERG-BERG, N. *Roots of caring, sharing, and helping.* San Francisco, Calif.: Freeman, 1977.

NISBETT, R. E., & WILSON, T. D. Telling more than we can know: Verbal reports on mental processes. *Psychological Review*, 1977, *84*, 231–259.

OLEJNIK, A. B. *Developmental changes and interrelationships among role-taking, moral judgments, and children's sharing.* Paper presented at the Biennial meeting of the Society for Research in Child Development, Denver, 1975.

PARKE, R. D. The role of punishment in the socialization process. In R. Hoppe, G. Milton, & E. Simmel (Eds.), *Early experiences and the process of socialization.* New York: Academic Press, 1970.

PATTERSON, G. R., & COBB, J. A. A dyadic analysis of "aggressive" behaviors. In J. P. Hill (Ed.), *Minnesota symposia on child psychology* (Vol. 5). Minneapolis: University of Minnesota Press, 1971.

PETERSON, L., HARTMANN, D. P., & GELFAND, D. M. Developmental changes in the effects of dependency and reciprocity cues on children's moral judgments and donation rates. *Child Development*, 1977, *48*, 1066–1070.

PIAGET, J. *Play, dreams, and imitation in childhood.* (C. Gattengo & F. M. Hodgson, trans.). New York: Norton, 1951. (First published in Paris: Delachaux & Nieslè, 1946.)

PIAGET, J. *The moral judgment of the child*, trans. Marjorie Gabain. New York: Free Press, 1965. (First published in London: Kegan Paul, 1932.)

PRENTICE, N. M. The influence of live and symbolic modeling on promoting moral judgments of adolescent delinquents. *Journal of Abnormal Psychology*, 1972, *80*, 157–161.

RACHLIN, H. Review of *Cognition and behavior modification* by M. J. Mahoney. *Journal of Applied Behavior Analysis*, 1977, *10*, 369–374.

REISS, S., & SUSHINSKY, L. W. Overjustification, competing responses, and the acquisition of intrinsic interest. *Journal of Personality and Social Psychology*, 1975, *31*, 1116–1125.

REST, J. R. *Development hierarchy in preference and comprehension of moral judgment.* Unpublished doctoral dissertation, University of Chicago, 1968.

REST, J. R. Developmental psychology as a guide to value education: A review of "Kohlbergian" programs. *Review of Educational Research*, 1974, *44*, 241–259.

REST, J. R. New approaches in the assessment of moral judgment. In T. Lickona (Ed.), *Moral development and behavior: Theory, research, and social issues.* New York: Holt, Rinehart and Winston, 1976.

REST, J. R. *Development in judging moral issues.* Unpublished manuscript, University of Minnesota, 1977.

RHEINGOLD, H. L., HAY, D. F., & WEST, M. J. Sharing in the second year of life, *Child Development*, 1976, *47*, 1148–1158.

ROGERS-WARREN, A., & BAER, D. M. Correspondence between saying and doing: Teaching children to share and praise. *Journal of Applied Behavior Analysis*, 1976, *9*, 335–354.

ROGERS-WARREN, A., WARREN, S. F., & BAER, D. M. *Modeling, self-reporting, and reinforcement: A component analysis.* Paper read at the meeting of the American Psychological Association, Chicago, September 1975.

ROGERS-WARREN, A., WARREN, S. F., & BAER, D. M. A component analysis: Modeling, self-reporting, and reinforcement of self-reporting in the development of sharing. *Behavior Modification*, 1977, *1*, 307–322.

ROSENHAN, D. L. Learning theory and prosocial behavior. *Journal of Social Issues*, 1972, *28*, 151–163.

ROSENHAN, D. L., & WHITE, G. M. Observation and rehearsal as determinants of prosocial behavior. *Journal of Personality and Social Psychology*, 1967, *5*, 424–431.

ROSS, M. The self perception of intrinsic motivation. In J. H. Harvey, W. J. Ickes, & R. Kidd (Eds.), *New directions in attribution research*. Hillsdale, N.J.: Erlbaum, 1976.

ROTHBART, M. Effects of motivation, equity, and compliance on the use of reward and punishment. *Journal of Personality and Social Psychology*, 1968, *9*, 353–362.

RUBIN, K. H., & SCHNEIDER, F. W. The relationship between moral judgment, egocentrism, and altruistic behavior. *Child Development*, 1973, *44*, 661–665.

RUSHTON, J. P. Socialization and the altruistic behavior of children. *Psychological Bulletin*, 1976, *83*, 898–913.

SELMAN, R. L. Social-cognitive understanding: A guide to educational and clinical practice. In T. Lickona (Ed.), *Moral development and behavior: Theory, research, and social issues*. New York: Holt, Rinehart and Winston, 1976.

SELMAN, R. L., & DAMON, W. The necessity (but insufficiency) of social perspective taking for conceptions of justice at three early levels. In D. J. DePalma & J. M. Foley (Eds.), *Moral development: Current theory and research*. Hillsdale, N.J.: Erlbaum, 1975.

SELMAN, R. L., & JAQUETTE, D. Stability and oscillation in interpersonal awareness: A clinical-developmental analysis. In C. B. Keasey (Ed.), *Nebraska Symposium on motivation* (Vol. 25). Lincoln, Nebraska: University of Nebraska Press, 1978.

SHANTZ, C. U. The development of social cognition. In E. M. Hetherington (Ed.), *Review of child development research* (Vol. 5). Chicago: University of Chicago Press, 1975.

SIDMAN, M. *Tactics of scientific research*. New York: Basic Books, 1960.

SIMPSON, E. L. Moral development research: A case study of scientific cultural bias. *Human Development*, 1974, *17*, 81–106.

SKINNER, B. F. *Science and human behavior*. New York: MacMillan, 1953.

SLABY, R. G., & CROWLEY, C. G. Modification of cooperation and aggression through teacher attention to children's speech. *Journal of Experimental Child Psychology*, 1977, *23*, 442–458.

SMITH, C. L., GELFAND, D. M., HARTMANN, D. P., & PARTLOW, M. P. Children's causal attributions regarding help-giving. *Child Development*, 1979, *50*, 203–210.

STAUB, E. A child in distress: The influence of modeling and nurturance on children's attempts to help. *Developmental Psychology*, 1971, *5*, 124–133.

STAUB, E. Helping a distressed person: Social, personality, and stimulus determinants. In L. Berkowitz (Ed.), *Advances in experimental social psychology* (Vol. 7). New York: Academic Press, 1974.

STAUB, E. *The development of prosocial behavior in children.* Morristown, N.J.: General Learning Press, 1975. *(a)*

STAUB, E. To rear a prosocial child: Reasoning, learning by doing, and learning by teaching others. In D. DePalma & J. Foley (Eds.), *Moral development: Current theory and research.* Hillsdale, N.J.: Erlbaum, 1975. *(b)*

STAUB, E. *The development of prosocial behavior: Directions for future research and applications to education.* Paper presented at the Moral Citizenship/ Education Conference. Philadelphia, June 1976.

STEIN, A. H., FRIEDRICH, L. K., & VONDRACEK, F. Television content and young children's behavior. In J. P. Murray, E. A. Rubinstein, & G. A. Comstock (Eds.), *Television and social behavior* (Vol. 2), *Television and social learning.* Washington, D. C.: Government Printing Office, 1972.

STEUER, F. B., APPLEFIELD, J. M., & SMITH, R. Televised aggression and the interpersonal aggression of preschool children. *Journal of Experimental Child Psychology,* 1971, *11,* 442–447.

TONICK, I. J., GELFAND, D. M., HARTMANN, D. P., CROMER, C. C., & MILLSAP, R. *A naturalistic study of children's prosocial behavior.* Paper presented at the meeting of the American Psychological Association, San Francisco, August 1977.

TURIEL, E. An experimental test of the sequentiality of developmental stages in the child's moral judgments. *Journal of Personality and Social Psychology,* 1966, *3,* 611–618.

TURIEL, E. Developmental processes in the child's moral thinking. In P. H. Mussen, J. Langer, & M. Covington (Eds.), *Trends and issues in developmental psychology.* New York: Holt, Rinehart and Winston, 1969.

TURIEL, E. The development of social concepts: Mores, customs, and conventions. In D. J. DePalma & J. M. Foley (Eds.), *Moral development: Current theory and research.* Hillsdale, N.J.: Erlbaum, 1975.

WARREN, S. F., ROGERS-WARREN, A., & BAER, D. M. The role of offer rate in controlling sharing by young children. *Journal of Applied Behavior Analysis,* 1976, *9,* 491–497.

Webster's Seventh New Collegiate Dictionary (17th ed). Springfield, Mass.: Merriam, 1969.

WHITE, G. M. Immediate and deferred effects of model observation and guided and unguided rehearsal on donating and stealing. *Journal of Personality and Social Psychology,* 1972, *21,* 139–148.

WHITE, G. M., & BURNHAM, M. A. Socially cued altruism: Effects of modeling, instructions, and age on public and private donations. *Child Development,* 1975, *46,* 559–563.

WHITING, J. W., & CHILD, I. L. *Child training and personality: A cross-cultural study.* New Haven, Conn.: Yale University Press, 1953.

WILSON, E. O. *Sociobiology: The new synthesis.* Cambridge, Mass.: Belknap Press, 1975.

WOHLWILL, J. F. *The study of behavioral development.* New York: Academic Press, 1973.

WRIGHT, D. *The psychology of moral behavior.* Middlesex, England: Penguin, 1971.

YARROW, M. R., SCOTT, P. M., & WAXLER, C. Z. Learning concern for others. *Developmental Psychology*, 1973, *8*, 240-260.

YARROW, M. R. & WAXLER, C. Z. Dimensions and correlates of prosocial behavior in young children. *Child Development*, 1976, *47*, 118-125.

YOUNISS, J. Another perspective on social cognition. In A. D. Pick (Ed.), *Minnesota symposium on child psychology* (Vol. 9). Minneapolis: University of Minnesota Press, 1975.

ZIMMERMAN, B. J., & ROSENTHAL, T. L. Observational learning of rule-governed behavior by children. *Psychological Bulletin*, 1974, *81*, 29-42.

SIX

The Development of Antisocial Behavior

Charles W. Turner and David K. Dodd

INTRODUCTION

The material in this chapter reviews several major theoretical positions which are designed to explain the learning of antisocial behaviors. By antisocial behavior we mean acts that are generally considered to be inappropriate within the particular cultural group. Many behaviors that are judged to be inappropriate in one culture can be appropriate or even desirable in another culture. For example, Wolfgang (1968) proposed that a subculture of violence exists in the United States in which fighting or violence is seen as being both necessary and appropriate. The relative acceptability of sexually explicit language, film portrayals, and printed material varies greatly across groups within the United States. Material considered to be profane and obscene by one group is seen as art by another group. The acceptability of a behavior, then, often depends directly upon the particular cultural norms within a group. There does seem to be fairly general agreement that aggressive, coercive, and obnoxious behaviors are inappropriate. Hence, our discussion of the development of antisocial behavior will focus on this class of behaviors.

First, we review the social-learning perspective and apply its principles to the learning of coercive behaviors in the age range from infancy to three years. This perspective seems particularly appropriate for that age range since these children do not have elaborate conceptual or verbal skills to modify or be modified by their parents' reactions. The perspective emphasizes the role of reinforcement as a determinant of learning. Hence, it implies that the learning of obnoxious behaviors in young children usually results from the pattern of reinforcements the child receives for being obnoxious, especially in the exchange of consequences among family members. The orientation also helps us to understand how many parents reinforce obnoxious behavior even though they are irritated by the behavior.

A second section of the chapter offers one possible limitation to the learning perspective of the development of antisocial behavior. In that section, we discuss the possible role of physiological dysfunctions in modifying the probability of risk for antisocial behavior. These physiological processes may influence the development of antisocial behavior at all ages, but the effects of these dysfunctions seem most pronounced at the time children enter school. It is possible that as many as 15 million American children and adolescents suffer some degree of physiological dysfunction which can increase the risk that these youths will display antisocial or inappropriate behavior. Physiological dysfunctions frequently influence the development of antisocial behavior by increasing the child-rearing difficulties that the parents experience. Generally, the physiological problems are likely to be an indirect rather than a direct cause of antisocial behavior in young children.

We need a more elaborate model to explain adequately the learning process of children as they develop greater conceptual and verbal facility. The third general theoretical perspective—cognitive social-learning theory—explores the role of memory and information-processing mechanisms which influence the development of antisocial behavior through observational learning. This theoretical position helps us to understand how children can learn antisocial behavior by watching the actions and consequences of other people. For example, many young children are exposed to a wide variety of appropriate and inappropriate behaviors through television. An avid television watcher may view thousands of killings on television by the age of twenty. It seems reasonable to think that all of these modeled behaviors in the media may eventually have some impact on the viewer. However, the modeled behavior on the television might be counteracted by the modeled behavior of the immediate family or of peers. Hence, television is only one possible source of antisocial behavior for young people.

The final section of the chapter is designed to explain the development of serious delinquent behavior in adolescents and young adults as mediated by long-term changes in family structure. We have employed a theoretical model based on demographic and social psychological principles to account for the acquisition of antisocial behavior in these age groups. Some researchers have proposed that a disintegrating family structure (reflected in higher divorce rates) may be at the root of the increased rate of social problems such as crime and delinquency. We will propose a contrasting view that the increased rate of a number of social problems can be traced to population waves which result from changing family size and birth rates. Although the principles describe changes at a societal rather than an individual level, the analysis can alert us to the changing problems which young people will face as they mature. Rather than predicting an increased rate of delinquency, divorce, and unemployment, current research leads to the prediction of a substantial (40 percent) decline in youthful social problems between 1975 and 1985. However, alcohol-related problems, such as "driving under the influence," probably will increase.

Any antisocial act is likely to have many sources. Each of the theoretical positions which we have discussed can help us to understand part of the complex nature of the development of appropriate and inappropriate social behaviors. Some of the social forces may become more salient at one time of a child's life than at another, but each of these processes may add to an accumulative risk of displaying serious antisocial acts.

THE SOCIAL-LEARNING ORIENTATION

Parents often inadvertently teach their children to be obnoxious, to develop tantrum behavior, or to be habitual liars, even though these antisocial behaviors are irritating and contradictory to the parents' child-rearing goals. By demonstrating to parents how they reinforce these unwanted behaviors, Patterson and his colleagues have been able to terminate these undesirable outcomes. Most of the material in this section is based on Patterson's work (such as Patterson & Cobb, 1973).

To appreciate how parents achieve these undesirable outcomes, it is useful to review some of the basic principles of the reinforcement orientation. A central proposition in reinforcement theory is that the consequences for one's actions are a major determinant of what one does. A researcher, practitioner, or parent attempts to modify the rate or strength of a response by applying an appropriate consequence immediately after the behavior occurs. For example, children may receive a piece of candy after they perform an act that parents like. Inappropriate responses can be reinforced inadvertently; a child may gain a desired toy by hitting the owner of the toy. The aggressive child is reinforced by peers if they yield an attractive toy to the attacking child.

Reinforcing stimuli are defined as events that increase the strength or frequency of a response preceding the reinforcer. There are two distinct types of reinforcing events: positive and negative. Positive reinforcement increases the rate of the behavior it follows. For example, receiving candy or a toy increases the likelihood of the response preceding the receipt of the candy or toy. Negative reinforcement increases a behavior which leads to the removal or avoidance of aversive or painful stimuli. If some response enables a child to escape from a distressing situation (such as being hit, spanked, or scolded), then the particular activity (such as crying or striking out at an attacker) which removed the aversive stimuli is "reinforced." In future experiences with this distressing event, children are likely to use the same avenue of escape from the aversive events which previously proved successful. A study by Patterson, Littman, and Bricker (1967) demonstrated how victimized children on the playground learn to use either counterattacks or passive behavior in order to terminate or avoid the aggressive attacks of other children.

Initially passive children who were successful in their first aggressive encounter rapidly began to use aggressive acts to terminate attacks from others. However, those passive children who were unsuccessful in their early aggressive encounters eventually became even more passive and withdrawn. Apparently, the children used that response (aggression or avoidance) which enabled them to stop the attacks of the other children. As we will see in the following sections, the concept of negative reinforcement is particularly useful in explaining how children can be trained in antisocial behavior by their parents, even though the parents may be trying to prevent inappropriate behaviors.[1]

Punishment can also modify behavior; it is defined as a stimulus (usually aversive) which *decreases* the probability of behavior. For example, a child who touches a hot pan (aversive stimulus) is less likely to touch the pan at a later time. The concept of negative reinforcement is easily confused with the idea of punishment. Since we often think of positive reinforcement as a positive outcome for the organism, it only seems natural to think of negative reinforcement as a negative event. However, it is important to remember that reinforcers are events which *increase* the probability of behavior (and in a sense can be conceptualized as favorable outcomes), while punishment *decreases* the probability of a response. In other words, we can think of punishment as the exposure to an aversive event after a particular response (which will decrease its likelihood). If the individual can engage in another response to avoid the aversive event, then this second response will become more frequent (it is negatively reinforced). One of the major problems in using punishment as a technique for controlling a behavior is that the individual will frequently find a secondary response for escaping from the punishment. As we will discover, this alternative response can be as undesirable as the original response which was being punished (Patterson & Cobb, 1973).

The reinforcement orientation assumes that behavioral change is controlled by the different types of consequences which follow different responses. However, when many social acts are examined superficially, there do not appear to be any reinforcements following the act. For example, students often study for many hours without receiving explicit reinforcement. The relative absence of positive and negative consequences for most social behavior seems to be contradictory to reinforcement principles. Actually, one of the most interesting features of the reinforcement perspective is the prediction that the *infrequent* reinforcers which we experience are particularly effective in maintaining social behaviors.

[1]The explanation of aggressive behavior by the concept of negative reinforcement is quite similar to the idea of frustration-induced aggression. Current formulations of the frustration/aggression theory (Berkowitz, 1974) specify that frustrating events (such as aversive stimuli) increase the probability of aggressive behavior. Since aggression can be a highly effective means of terminating frustrating events, it is easy to see how aggressive reactions to frustrations are easily learned responses.

Advocates of the reinforcement orientation have extensively examined the effects of different types of reinforcement schedules (Skinner, 1957). While the entire topic of reinforcement schedules is too complicated to cover in much detail here, a few of the basic principles can be outlined. First, we can consider the differential effects of continuous reinforcement (reinforcement following every response) versus partial reinforcement (reinforcement following only some responses). While you might not be surprised to learn that continuous reinforcement typically produces faster learning than partial (irregular) reinforcement, the opposite pattern seems to occur for "forgetting" (extinction) of the learned response. That is, when we stop reinforcing someone for a response acquired under a particular schedule of reinforcement, that person will maintain the unreinforced response for longer periods of time if the response was learned under partial rather than continuous reinforcement. Some attacks on the reinforcement orientation fail to appreciate the power of partial reinforcement notions in accounting for apparently unreinforced behavior.

Discriminative Stimuli

Children eventually learn that reinforcements are more likely to occur on some occasions than on others. Discriminative stimuli are defined as events which set the occasion for reinforcement. In other words, if a particular stimulus signals that a reinforcer can be earned by engaging in a specific response, then the individual will be more likely to produce the required response. Similarly, if a stimulus signals that a particular response will lead to punishment, the individual will avoid the potentially punished response. For example, a misbehaving child may quickly learn that the approaching footsteps of the parent (discriminative stimulus) are likely to lead to some form of punishment. Hence, the child may engage in a response to avoid the anticipated consequences (for example, he or she may hide behind a curtain to avoid being spanked). As we will see later, discriminative stimuli can sometimes play a very important function in modifying behavior, even though there do not appear to be reinforcers in the individual's environment. Cognitively oriented theorists use the term "retrieval cue" (Tulving, 1968) instead of discriminative stimulus, but both terms refer to similar processes. After we have introduced cognitive and information-processing notions, we will use interchangeably the idea of retrieval cues and discriminative stimuli.

Learning of Obnoxious Behaviors

Typically, we think of parents as the active training or socializing agent and the child as the somewhat passive recipient of socialization. Bell (1977) reasons that we should consider the process more as a system or reciprocal-influence process. In the early stages of growth, the child often has more control over the parents' reactions than the other way around. Citing DeVries (1954), Bell suggests that rather than thinking of marriage as an institution where adults produce children, it may make more sense to argue that the institution permits children to socialize their parents! The following material is based partly on Bell's observations, and it will help us to see how the young child socializes and controls the parents.

During the earliest stages of infancy, both the parents' and the child's behavior are controlled by negative reinforcement of each other. Numerous writers have observed that the newborn infant comes into the world kicking and yelling. While some writers see these responses as reflections of a biologically predisposed aggressive reaction (Storr, 1968), another interpretation may be more appropriate. First, it is important to note that the infant's crying does not require learning since the response is genetically predisposed; in most mammalian species, the newborn displays some type of yelp or cry as a "distress sign" (Freedman, 1974). Second, most adults seem to find the crying response of children to be highly aversive. While some parents are attracted to the crying infant with the anticipation of being able to soothe the child, other parents respond to the crying in an effort to terminate their own unpleasant reactions to the crying (Bell, 1977). Third, although the cry of a newborn infant is uncontrolled and unmodulated, the two-month-old infant has the ability to control crying (the response can be varied in intensity and duration).

The unlearned crying in the newborn is usually stimulated by one of several possible sources of distress. The child may experience pain, hunger, colic, cold, or sudden noises in the environment. By relieving the child's distress, the parents negatively reinforce the child's crying (Gewirtz & Boyd, 1976). Similarly, since the child stops crying when the distress is relieved, the parents are also negatively reinforced for attending to the child's problem. In short, both the parents and the child exert negative reinforcement control over each other.

By terminating the crying response at the appropriate time, the child may produce superstitious behavior in the parents. To relieve their own distress (which results from the child's crying), parents check for possible sources of the child's distress. First, they are likely to determine if the child is hungry; next, they may check for obvious sources of distress such as sticking pins, cold, or a rash. If none of these tactics quiets the child, then parents may pick up the child. In the process, they will jostle or vibrate the child, and these vibrations frequently relieve distress produced by gastric pains (Bell, 1977). Occasionally, the parents also may talk or sing to the child while rocking and jostling. Although the child shortly may become quiet due to the rocking motions, the parents may think that the words or singing soothed the child. Since the termination of the child's distress and crying also relieves the parents' distress, the singing response has been negatively reinforced for the parents. The parents may then superstitiously repeat the singing when the child is again in distress.

After the first two months, the child is able to modulate the level of crying and cries less frequently. For example, the child has developed two different types of crying (Etzel & Gewirtz, 1967). One of the two cries is similar to the unlearned, unmodulated response which occurs at full intensity. This response seems to result from intense stimulation or distress (sometimes termed "respondent crying"). A second, modulated, crying and fussiness does not have a clear antecedent (sometimes termed "operant crying"). Hence, it is difficult for the parents to terminate this secondary crying response since the parents cannot easily identify and remove the source of the child's distress (and consequently their own distress). A difficult dilemma faces the parents. One strategy that parents attempt to follow is to ignore children's crying. Children may continue to cry because a serious source of distress needs careful attention; as the distress increases, the intensity of the crying is also likely to increase. Hence, the parents eventually will try to relieve their own distress (due to the crying) by determining the cause of the crying. If the parents isolate a possible reason for the distress (for example, it is time for the child to be fed), then they will attend to the child. If they attend to the loudly crying child, then loud rather than soft crying will be reinforced and loud crying will occur more frequently in the future. By *unsuccessfully* trying to ignore the child's crying, they have unwittingly reinforced (negatively) the child's *intense* crying response.

On some occasions, the parents may decide that there is no real source of the child's distress, so that they do not attend to the child. Hence, they sometimes successfully ignore the child and the child eventually will stop crying. If we consider the consequences of partial reinforcement processes, we can see that the parents have unwittingly increased the likelihood of the child's crying behavior in future situations. That is, since behavior learned under a partial reinforcement (irregular payoff) schedule is slower to extinguish than behavior learned under continuous reinforcement, the inconsistent response of the parent (sometimes attending, sometimes not attending) increases the chances that the child will cry at a later time even though the parents (sometimes) successfully ignore the crying.

Eventually most parents learn to discriminate between the different types of crying that the child displays, and they can tell whether or not the child is experiencing serious distress. If the parents manage to ignore the crying for several evenings at bedtime, they are able to extinguish the crying response. However, any mistakes in judgment on the parents' part may lead to negative reinforcement on a very irregular schedule that greatly exaggerates the problem of extinguishing the child's crying.

One of the important principles which is being described is that the child's earliest and most adaptive method for controlling parents is by being aversive to them. This mutual, negative-reinforcement system of parent and child behavior is not a very satisfactory basis for establishing a healthy relationship among them. Fortunately, the child has other behaviors which can be employed to win the parent's affection. By the third month most children begin to develop a variety of social behaviors such as visual gaze, social smile, and babbling (Bell, 1977; Kagan, 1974; Moss, 1967). By observing parents, it is easy to see that these responses are much more pleasurable for them than crying (Moss, 1967). One can guess, however, that the aversive control through negative reinforcement is sufficiently powerful and effective that the child is not likely to terminate this response very quickly (Patterson & Cobb, 1973).

Tantrum Behavior

As the child grows older, a wider assortment of obnoxious behavior can be employed to gain control over one's parents (Patterson & Cobb, 1973). Consider the example of a child who does not want to go to bed. First of all, the child may be too tired to use more subtle means of distracting the parents' attention away from their goal of getting the child to go to bed. Children quickly learn a number of prosocial responses such as requests for "one more story" or "a few more minutes" of play with a particular toy. Or the child might ask for a glass of water or juice. These tactics are likely to work often enough (partial reinforcement) to sustain the effort. If these tactics fail, the child may opt for the (by now) well-learned aversive-control strategy. While the tactic contains some risks of parental retaliation (as we will see later), it also can be quite effective. A marginally prosocial response is to ask to be taken to the bathroom (with the implicit threat of wetting the bed if the parent does not comply). If these tactics have failed, the child can then begin to whine and cry (getting progressively louder). The parents will probably be somewhat skilled in handling this problem and they will try to ignore the child. As we saw for younger children, the parents are still in somewhat of a dilemma. Under some conditions, the crying might really represent major distress such as a stomachache. Hence, the parents really cannot be sure that the child's cry is primarily a response to being put to bed. If the parents are a little uncertain about the reason for the crying, they may occasionally check on the child to make sure that there are no major problems. During these times, the child can reinstitute the strategies of asking to be read to, and so forth. Since parents occasionally surrender to the requests, they effectively reinforce the child on an intermittent schedule (Patterson & Cobb, 1973). Thus, the parents are likely to train (or be trained by) their children under conditions which maximize the chance that the obnoxious behaviors will be retained for long periods of time, even though the parents may be firmly opposed to the outcome. As parents become more and more irregular in surrendering to the child's crying strategy, they are more likely to ensure that the crying will be difficult to extinguish completely (due to partial reinforcement effects). One solution for the parent, then, is to avoid placing the child on the irregular reinforcement schedule. Of course, the child does run the risk that the crying will be so aversive to the parents that they are more willing to punish or abuse the child than to comply with the aversive control (Patterson & Cobb, 1973).

In the supermarket an analogous problem emerges. Parents may be quite involved in the problems of shopping, remembering what needs to be purchased, and trying to find reasonably priced foods (especially if a sharply restricted budget must be managed). Hence, initial signs of distress from children are likely to be ignored. Again, children are likely to begin escalating their aversive behavior to attract parents' attention. The supermarket setting is further complicated because parents do not have immediately available all of the toys or games with which children can be distracted at home. A common solution for many parents is to attempt to "bribe" their children with gum or candy which is readily available. If parents ignore the early warning signs too long, children are likely to have escalated their behavior to a high level before the parents respond. It is not uncommon to see children whose aversive behavior elicits a spanking or shaking in retaliation for their aversive behavior. Because of the subsequent guilt reactions of the parents, especially if they realize others are watching, they may overcompensate for striking the child by attending to the child and offering candy or other bribes. If the child is eventually going to be reinforced in these environments, it certainly seems to make more sense to reinforce them for good behavior rather than bad behavior by being prepared for the earliest signs of distress. The pressures of supermarket shopping, however, seem to make the "inappropriate" response of the parent the most likely. The time that the parents need to pay most attention to the child is exactly the time when they are most involved in some alternate task. Hence, the child has to use unusually aversive behavior to get parental attention.

Crying and the Battered Child Syndrome

If the parents are not able to consistently ignore the child or are unaware of the effects of partial reinforcement, they are likely to become quite irritated at the child for crying with no "apparent" reason (especially if the child is infrequently reinforced). Robson and Moss' (1970) findings suggest that excessive crying after the first month leads to reduced levels of maternal attachment. Some parents, in their aggravation or frustration, may attempt to suppress the child's crying by punishment. As most parents can readily observe, the application of punishment to a distressed child is likely to lead to even higher levels of distress and/or crying. This intensification often makes the parents feel guilty so that they bend over backward to be nice to the child, who has been reinforced for more intense crying. Again the parents have executed a counterproductive strategy which will lead to an outcome opposite to the one they were trying to achieve. Obviously, this entire state of affairs can be highly frustrating to some parents. If they are awakened at three o'clock in the morning, they may have very little tolerance for the child's crying. Bell (1977) reasons that the battered child syndrome should be thought of as a bidirectional influence process. For every battered child, there may also be a parent "abused" by a child. Correlational evidence obtained in interviews of abusing parents suggests that the most salient immediate antecedent of child abuse is a constant fussing and/or a highly irritating cry (Gil, 1970). Abusing parents frequently claim that they had attempted to soothe or calm the distressed child; but, after repeated failures, the parents seem to strike the child impulsively (Weston, 1974).

There is some evidence that the battered child is more likely to have a history of medical or learning problems (Klaus & Kennell, 1970; Klein & Stern, 1971; see also the following section on physiological factors related to antisocial behavior). The parents report that the battered child seems to be an unusually difficult child (Parke, 1977). Perhaps these children are more likely to display higher levels of unexplained fussiness. Hence, parents may not be reliably able to relieve the child's distress and consequently cannot relieve their own distress. In a sense, children's problems make it difficult for them to effectively train their parents in good caretaking skills. If we add to this problem the fact that the family may be distressed by additional problems such as unemployment, constant job changes, and marital tensions, the parents' tolerance of the child's problems may be very low. Perhaps we should not be surprised that so many young children are struck by their parents under these very trying circumstances (Gil, 1970).

Learning to Tell Lies

Another form of antisocial behavior which can be very frustrating to parents is habitual lying by a child. The model which we have previously described can help us to understand how the parent/child interaction sequence, using positive- and negative-reinforcement processes, can contribute to the learning of deceptive behavior, even though the parents do not want to teach their child to use this type of behavior.

What Is a Lie?   First we have to distinguish between someone telling a lie versus someone who simply is in error about the facts. Another complication is that the concept of lie telling usually implies that a known fact is being distorted. We also need to distinguish opinion statements from other types of statements. Since it may be difficult to determine whether opinion statements are true or false, it may not be easy to determine objectively whether or not people are telling the truth. Actually, all that we need to assume is that lie tellers believe that the truth is being distorted. Finally, we need to distinguish lying behavior from "make believe" or play behavior in which children are permitted or even encouraged to pretend that something is other than what it is.

Antecedents of Lie Telling.   Consider the following example. Johnny, who is watching his favorite television program, is asked by his parents whether or not he has completed his homework. Johnny is told that he will not be able to watch any more of the program if the homework is not completed. Johnny replies that his homework is finished. Later, Johnny's parents learn that he has not completed his homework. In the past, Johnny has frequently told lies and his parents are afraid that he is becoming a habitual liar. Since they think lying is bad, they cannot understand why he tells lies so much and wonder if there might be something "wrong" with him. However, the parents have permitted Johnny to avoid an unpleasant consequence by telling a lie; hence, they have negatively reinforced Johnny's lying behavior.

Children learn from a very early age that they must sometimes tell lies, if for no other reason than to avoid hurting someone's feelings. Consider a recurring theme in the "Dennis the Menace" comic strips. A neighbor, Mary, is visiting Dennis' home, and she has been described in a derogatory fashion by Dennis' parents when they are alone. When Dennis sees Mary, we can expect him to say something like, "Hello, Mrs. Blabbermouth." After Mary leaves in a huff, Dennis is firmly punished for his honesty.

Many of the rules of politeness which each person is expected to learn require individuals to hide their true feelings in public. Similarly, social norms often require us to distort our true feelings. When we encounter a cashier in a supermarket who says, "How are you today?" we rapidly learn that the cashier really does not want to know how we feel. Instead social norms require us to answer, "Fine, thank you, and how are you?" Truth telling can lead to embarrassment or inconvenience.

In short, a number of social situations require us to distort the expression of our true feelings. Presumably, the rules of politeness or social norms have a primarily beneficial goal of protecting privacy or preventing someone else from being hurt. These polite lies, or social lies, are sometimes referred to as "white" lies, while inappropriate lies are referred to as "black" lies. Apparently, it is not always bad to tell lies; rather, only some lies are considered bad. The young child who sees his parents telling appropriate and inappropriate lies may not easily distinguish between them.

A colleague described an interesting example of how his five-year-old daughter began to distinguish appropriate and inappropriate lies. When asked, the daughter said that she had "been to the bathroom." However, her agitated behavior clearly indicated that she had not gone to the bathroom. Her father then said, "You know if you tell lies, your nose will grow to be this long" (measuring about one foot with his hands). He was referring to the story of Pinocchio, which he had recently read to his daughter. Whereupon the daughter replied, "Daddy, if you won't tell lies, then I won't either."

When children observe products being advertised on television, they may ask their parents to buy one of the products. Since the attractiveness of the toy is frequently exaggerated, the child is likely to be disappointed when the toy is purchased. Hence, the child may quickly learn that other people tell lies when they are trying to sell you something. The advertiser was positively reinforced by distorting the truth. Apparently, under such circumstances, a little lying is not considered too inappropriate. Research cited by Liebert, Neale, and Davidson (1973) indicates that most children learn to discriminate many of the distortions in television advertisements by the time they are seven years old.

Lying or deception, then, is a well-learned response which can have great utility for people who distort the truth (provided they are not discovered in the deception). By avoiding unpleasant consequences or achieving pleasant consequences, deception is both negatively and positively reinforced.

Potential Long-term Effects of Negative Reinforcement

It would be misleading to imply that children typically have cognitive control over their lying or tantrum behavior. Unlike responses to positive reinforcements, the negative reinforcement or escape reaction often seems to involve highly emotional, impulsive reactions. These impulsive reactions sometimes persist long after the initial exposure to aversive stimulation. The long-term effects of negatively reinforced behavior can be demonstrated with work by Solomon and his associates (such as Solomon & Brush, 1956). First, they placed dogs in a cage from which escape was possible. Then, they rang a bell just before the dog was exposed to a very intense and painful foot shock. The dogs displayed various signs of distress such as pilo-erection (hair raising), defecation, and yelping. After repeating the bell and shock episode for a few trials, the dogs rapidly learned to escape from the cage when the bell rang. Hence, the dogs were able to escape any further shock. One of the important findings of the research was the fact that the animals continued to escape for hundreds of trials without ever receiving another shock. The bell, serving as a discriminative stimulus or retrieval cue for punishment, continued to control the dogs' reactions long after the initial shocks.

After a few trials, the dogs began to escape from the cage without strong displays of distress; the pilo-erection, defecation, and yelping disappeared. Other than the fact that the dogs always escaped when the bell rang, the dogs did not appear distressed by the situation. However, other conditions demonstrated how potentially distressing this event really was for the dogs. After some dogs had learned to escape very reliably without distress signs when the bell was rung, Solomon and his associates blocked the escape route. For these dogs, the ringing of the bell reinstated the strong distress reactions which occurred when they were originally shocked. Although we always have to be cautious in comparing the results from one species to another, if we extend the findings from dogs to humans a potentially important conclusion is suggested. Humans may be able to escape from distressing situations without apparent displays of emotion (in other words, they are negatively reinforced for their escape). Yet the potential for highly emotional behavior may exist and be revealed if the person's normal means of escape from distress are blocked by situational pressures. Cues associated with an earlier punishing situation (similar to the bell with Solomon's research) may serve as discriminative stimuli or retrieval cues to remind the child of the earlier episode. As with Solomon's dogs, the previously punished child may not display signs of distress other than avoidance or escape behavior. However, strong emotional responses might occur if a retrieval cue occurs when the individual's previous avoidance response is blocked.

When we see apparently irrational behavior from adults who strongly avoid some event that does not appear to be threatening to other people, we describe the person as having a phobic reaction. Suppose a young girl was attacked and seriously injured by a dog when she was younger; her avoidance behavior as an adult in the presence of apparently safe dogs may seem inappropriate. Yet she may be displaying a reaction very similar to the experimentally induced avoidance reaction seen in Solomon's animals. If the negatively reinforced escape behavior is not possible, then a highly emotional behavioral display may appear unless the victim has learned to control her emotional reactions under the presence of retrieval cues reminding her of the earlier assault. As with attacks by dogs, sexual assaults, severe physical abuse, or severe snake or insect bites may be remembered for many years after the initial episode.

PHYSIOLOGICAL FACTORS IN THE DEVELOPMENT AND MAINTENANCE OF ANTISOCIAL BEHAVIOR

Up to this point, antisocial childhood behavior has been discussed primarily in terms of environmental models, such as the social-learning approach. On the other hand, certain well recognized, if poorly understood, physiological conditions may directly or indirectly influence antisocial behavior. The following section investigates the possible role of physiological syndromes in the development of antisocial behavior at the individual level and also explores possible implications on a societal scale. The hyperactive child syndrome, allergic tension-fatigue syndrome, and the hypoglycemic aggressive reaction are each described briefly in terms of their physical and behavioral correlates. While it is generally agreed that the physical symptoms result directly from underlying physiological dysfunctioning, there is much less agreement regarding the development of the behavioral correlates. We propose that antisocial behavior can be developed and maintained as a consequence of the interaction of physical symptoms with the environment, rather than directly from physiological processes. Finally, a research study relating untreated physiological disorders with antisocial behavior at the societal level is presented and discussed.

Physiological Syndromes Related to Antisocial Behavior

While the hyperactive child syndrome has been widely recognized in recent years with respect to its impact on academic performance and social development, other physiologically based problems such as allergies and hypoglycemia (low blood sugar) are still considered to be primarily medical problems. A distinction between severe and mild to moderate levels of these two syndromes seems in order. Severe hypoglycemic or allergic reactions result in very obvious and serious medical complications which can even necessitate hospitalization. In such cases, diagnosis is relatively easy, although isolating the exact cause of the reaction may be difficult. On the other hand, at mild to moderate levels, the disorders are likely to be unrecognized by the victims and their doctors alike, even though behavior might be substantially affected (Moyer, 1976). At intermediate levels of severity, these two syndromes are very poorly understood and more research is needed to determine incidence rates and specific effects on behavior. However, the literature to date suggests that the hypoglycemic and allergic reaction syndromes may indeed contribute to the development and maintenance of antisocial behavior in many individuals. Thus, we are including these syndromes in our current analysis of physiologically based dysfunctions in social behavior.

Hyperactive Child Syndrome. While there is much disagreement among researchers and clinicians regarding terminology and etiology, there is very little controversy about the major symptoms which identify the hyperactive child syndrome.[2] In describing the syndrome, it is important to distinguish between primary (physical) and secondary (behavioral) symptoms (Patternite, Loney, & Langhorne, 1976). Physical symptoms frequently cited include hyperactivity, perceptual-motor impairment, coordination defects, attentional deficits (short span, distractibility, perseveration), memory deficits, and impulsivity (Cantwell, 1975a; Clements, 1966; Conners, 1967). Behavioral symp-

---

[2]Terms such as "minimal brain dysfunction, minimal brain damage, minimal cerebral palsy, learning disability, and hyperkinesis" are all used to describe a set of behavioral symptoms; each assumes the existence of some underlying central nervous system abnormality. However, actual neurological evidence of such impairment is only rarely and inconsistently found (Dubey, 1976; Hartocollis, 1968; Schmitt, 1975), and even indirect indication of impairment such as prenatal and perinatal stresses have not been demonstrated (Haller & Axelrod, 1975; Schmitt, 1975). Therefore, the term "hyperactive childhood syndrome" (Cantwell, 1975a), which refers only to the existence of behavioral symptoms without regard to assumed etiology, will be used. While we, too, are assuming that some physiological abnormality underlies the syndrome, we are not willing to suggest specifically that it is a central nervous system deficit.

toms include emotional lability, specific learning disabilities, aggressiveness, and deficient interpersonal relationships (Bernstein, Page, & Janicki, 1974; Cantwell, 1975a; Huessy, Marshall, & Gendron, 1974).

While this symptomatology has been derived largely from clinical reports, there has been some empirical validation of the primary symptoms. For example, hyperactive children, compared to normals, show smaller heart rate and galvanic skin responses to stimuli, slower simple reaction times, and more impulsive errors in judgment (Dykman, Ackerman, Peters & McGrew, 1974), as well as attentional deficits and poor impulse control on experimental tasks (Douglas, 1974). On the other hand, research on behavioral symptoms has not identified consistent differences between hyperactive and normal children. For example, Klein and Gittelman-Klein (1974) found that only 63 of 120 children referred to therapists for "hyperactivity" met even the minimal behavioral criteria for hyperactivity. Also, studies utilizing actometers to measure body movement have failed to reveal heightened activity among the "hyperactive" (Cantwell, 1975a), except during the REM stage of sleep (Klein & Gittelman-Klein, 1974). In sum, while the physical symptoms of the hyperactivity syndrome are more consistently reported and more clearly documented, behavioral symptoms (such as academic underachievement, hyperactivity, and antisocial behavior) are more highly visible and disruptive and are thus more likely to result in certain children being labeled "hyperactive."

Allergic Tension-Fatigue Syndrome. Although this term was first coined by Speer (1954), the syndrome has been clinically recognized for sixty years. Substances which produce allergic reactions are called "allergens;" common ones are various foods (such as milk, eggs, grains, chocolate, and cola), pollens, molds, and drugs. Physical symptoms such as skin reactions and nasal congestion are more common, but some allergic children develop behavioral symptoms which fall under the general categories of tension and fatigue (Speer, 1954). The child may be restless, hyperactive, apprehensive, inattentive, and very irritable. Thus, much of the behavioral symptomatology of this syndrome is quite similar to that of the hyperactive syndrome (Kittler, 1970; Speer, 1970). In addition, the child with the allergic tension-fatigue syndrome is plagued by general sluggishness and constant fatigue; unlike physiologic fatigue, however, additional rest commonly exacerbates the child's condition. Occasionally, extremely violent and irrational outbursts are linked to particular allergens such as bananas or wheat (Moyer, 1976).

Hypoglycemic Aggressive Reaction. Hypoglycemia (low blood sugar) can result from a variety of abnormalities related to glucose-regulating mechanisms of the body (Moyer, 1976). Common physical symptoms include faintness, weakness, palpitations, hunger, and nervousness (Glittler, 1962). In addition, emotional symptoms such as anxiety, depression, and impulsivity frequently occur (Moyer, 1976). Our concern here, however, is with the antisocial behaviors which are sometimes associated with hypoglycemic reactions. Moyer (1976) provides examples of extreme behavior which apparently results from severe hypoglycemia. Individuals may become quite confused and disoriented, and their behavior may become extremely irrational and violent. Total amnesia for such behavior during these episodes is often reported. While such extreme cases are probably rare, Moyer (1976) argues that mild to moderate levels of hypoglycemia are more common and may be associated with general irritability and restlessness which can be quickly converted into overt aggressiveness given provocative environmental conditions.

Implications for Development

Estimates of rates of incidence among the three syndromes are similar and relatively high, especially when projected upon the entire population. Commonly reported incidence rates are 4–20 percent for hyperactivity (Bernstein, et al., 1974; Cantwell, 1975a; Clements, 1966); 25 percent for allergies (Feingold, 1973); and 2–30 percent for hypoglycemia (Bolton, 1973). The projection of even modest rates of 5 percent onto a population of 100 million children and adolescents reveals that 5–15 million young persons might be affected by at least one of the syndromes.

Drug therapy has been moderately successful in alleviating physical symptoms of hyperactivity (Cantwell, 1975b, 1975c; Whalen & Henker, 1976). That is, perceptual-motor, attentional, and coordination deficits are sometimes dramatically reduced by the use of medication, primarily psychostimulants. Similarly, medication (Kittler, 1970) or dietary control (Feingold, 1968, 1973; Moyer, 1976) quite frequently relieve physical symptoms of allergic reactions; hypoglycemia can also be controlled through drug or diet therapy (Shafer, Sawyer, McClusky, Beck, & Phipps, 1971). However, positive therapeutic effects of dietary and medical treatments on behavioral symptoms have not been consistently demonstrated (Whalen & Henker, 1976). Well-rehearsed antisocial behaviors commonly either persist after dietary and drug treatments are introduced or return after their removal.

Cantwell (1975c) reviewed seven studies which suggest that childhood behavior problems associated with the hyperactive syndrome persist through adolescence and into adulthood. Hyperactive adolescents commonly show antisocial behavior, poor academic performance, poor self-image, and depression; adulthood can bring with it alcoholism, sociopathy, hysteria, and even psychosis.[3] Although symptoms such as hyperactivity, distractibility, excitability, and aggression decrease with

---

[3]The reader is warned that these studies are based on clinical reports or correlational data, and hence must be considered suggestive only.

age and even reach or approach normal levels, rates of juvenile delinquency and psychological disturbance remain high during adolescence
(Weiss & Minde, 1974).

For each of the syndromes described above, there seems to be a great
deal of disagreement over whether behavioral symptoms result directly
from underlying physiological mechanisms or indirectly through an
interaction with the environment. Those who would support a primary
(direct) hypothesis (such as Moyer, 1976) claim that physiological processes affect certain parts of the central nervous system which control
aggression and impulse control. Supporters of the secondary (indirect)
hypothesis (such as Cantwell, 1975*a*) concur that general irritability and
restlessness may result directly from underlying physiological processes,
but the behavioral symptoms probably are mediated by reinforcement
contingencies in the environment. Although much research is needed to
identify particular causal relationships, it is quite possible that children
with physiologically related deficits in attention, coordination, and
impulse control simply do not respond to the same teaching or child-
rearing methods used to train normal children. Failure at learning tasks
may produce a substantial amount of frustration for both the children and
their parents or teachers, and each may resort to punishment in an
attempt to "manage" the other. By resisting the punishment efforts of
the other, negatively reinforced antisocial tendencies may develop and
become quite resistant to change. Such a hypothesis is partly supported
by the research cited in previous sections of this chapter. While primary
physical symptoms can be treated medically and tend to decrease with
age, behavioral problems tend to persist, suggesting that environmental
contingencies may be crucial in maintaining the antisocial behavior.

Physiological disorders may be particularly influential during certain
developmental periods in which new behavior patterns are emerging. For
example, during infancy the presence of undetected physiological disturbances might significantly affect parent/child interactions, as
discussed earlier in the chapter, so that negative reinforcement and coercive control patterns predominate. Likewise, during the preschool years
when the child first begins to interact more regularly with peers,
physiological problems may greatly interfere with developing patterns of
social interaction. Physiological dysfunctions occurring during the first
year or two of school may contribute to learning disabilities and behavioral problems which persist throughout the child's academic career. In
short, physiological factors may play an especially crucial role during any
developmental period characterized by increased exposure to novel learning situations, peers, or authority figures. Learned behavior patterns may
persist for many years, even after the physiological condition itself has
subsided or been successfully diagnosed and treated.

Although the preceding discussion has focused primarily on factors
related to the development and control of antisocial behavior on the

individual level, it is also important to study the impact of these physiological syndromes on antisocial behavior at the societal level, especially
given the relatively high incidence rates and the low to moderate rates of
treatment success. Bolton's (1973) study of the role of hypoglycemia on
societal conflict illustrates a number of important points which are
highly relevant to the discussion of antisocial behavior. His study
(described below) suggests that antisocial behavior rarely if ever has a
single, simple cause. Instead, there are a variety of environmental, cultural, and psychological factors which may play a major role in antisocial
behavior, and physiological processes may be important in mediating this
complex interaction of factors.

The Qolla: The Effect of Hypoglycemia on Aggression. The Qolla
Indians of Peru are well known to anthropologists for their high level of
societal conflict. The Qolla personality has been characterized by
extreme aggressiveness, hostility, and distrust (Bolton, 1973). Because
the Qolla use litigation extensively to resolve interpersonal conflicts and
because careful records are kept, Bolton was able to establish that antisocial behavior is indeed quite high and that the Qolla's reputation is
probably deserved. Fights, insults, stealing, destruction of crops and live-
stock, and threats against person and property occur quite frequently.
The homicide rate among the Qolla is perhaps the highest of any reported
culture (possibly as high as 55 per 100,000 population) and is twice as
high as it is in most cultures. Despite their vicious behavior and
infamous character, the Qolla actively maintain a moral code which
stresses charity, compassion, and cooperation and, in fact, they have
established exceedingly high moral standards for themselves. They seem
somewhat unaware of the discrepancy between their moral code and
their behavior and are unable to explain typical aggressive episodes other
than to describe them as irrational or insane. After examining social and
cultural factors, Bolton was still unable to explain the high rate and
degree of hostility and aggression and thus turned his attention to physiological factors.

Bolton reviewed the medical literature on hypoglycemia and found a
curvilinear relationship between blood glucose level and aggression. That
is, at normal or very high levels of hypoglycemia, aggressive behavior is
rare, while at mild to moderate levels it is more common. He then hypothesized that there would be a very high incidence of hypoglycemia
among the Qolla and that those persons with mild to moderate
hypoglycemia would show more aggression than those with severe hypoglycemia or normal glucose levels. Sixty-six males, from an original
random sample of 124, were rated for aggressiveness and then given a
standard glucose tolerance test. The incidence of hypoglycemia among
the sample was 55.5 percent, compared to an estimated U.S. incidence
rate of 2–30 percent. Also, as Bolton had hypothesized, those males with
mild to moderate levels of hypoglycemia were rated as more aggressive

than either the normals or the severely hypoglycemic individuals. However, within the mild to moderate range, hypoglycemia failed to predict aggressiveness, suggesting that other factors such as environmental or social influences interact with physiological state.

Bolton hypothesized two possible ways in which hypoglycemia might produce aggression. First, by increasing irritability hypoglycemia may lower thresholds for frustration tolerance, thus making social conflict more likely. Secondly, Bolton proposed that aggression itself might be a coping strategy for removing the irritability and tenseness associated with hypoglycemia. That is, anger tends to raise blood glucose, thus perhaps alleviating some of the unpleasant physical sensations associated with hypoglycemia, and hypoglycemic individuals may actually learn to act aggressively in order to alleviate these sensations. If this is true, the individuals are negatively reinforced for their antisocial behavior. They might be expected to increase their level of aggression in the future, particularly in response to reduced blood glucose.

Bolton's data is obviously correlational and thus no direct causal links between hypoglycemia and aggression can be verified. While aggression, or any physical exertion, can *lower* blood glucose (that is, produce mild hypoglycemia), anger and anxiety produce adrenal secretions (Klopper 1964) which actually *increase* glucose levels. In addition, extensive clinical evidence cited by Bolton suggests that insulin-induced hypoglycemia can produce irritability and radical personality changes and sometimes immediately precedes extremely violent and irrational behavior. Thus, while there has been no solid experimental evidence demonstrating that hypoglycemia directly causes aggression, the bulk of clinical experience suggests that hypoglycemia probably precedes, rather than follows, irritability and aggressive behavior.

There are a number of unusual features of the Qolla culture and environment that are highly relevant. The weather is highly unpredictable with extreme fluctuations in temperature. The high elevation (12,000 feet) is associated with hypoxia (decreased oxygen supply). The land is overpopulated, agriculture is primitive, and food production is low, so diets tend to be deficient and competition for resources is high. Medical care is also poor, and premature births, infant mortality, and childhood disease are quite high. Thus, there are a number of environmental and economic factors which contribute to harsh, stressful living conditions; these factors could be related to either aggression or hypoglycemia, or both.

The high level of aggression and hostility, possibly a consequence of the environment, may also contribute to the environmental stress. For example, the high level of competition, suspiciousness, and hostility prevents the Qolla from farming cooperatively and thus improving their food production and ultimately their diets. Abuse of alcohol and coca (a tropical shrub which is the source of cocaine) is widespread and may represent a coping strategy for dealing with environmental and interpersonal stress; however, such drug abuse may also complicate glucose homeostasis and/or increase the likelihood of aggression through disinhibiting effects. In short, antisocial behavior among Qolla is not a simple phenomenon with a single cause but rather a complex system of factors which may affect and in turn be affected by aggression. If Bolton's hypothesis is correct, hypoglycemia, in the Qolla culture at least, best accounts for the influence of the various environmental and social stresses. While he was unable to examine all of the potential factors mentioned above, Bolton cited clinical evidence which linked most of the factors directly to hypoglycemia. Furthermore, he examined stressor variables such as high density and protein deficiency among his sample and found them to be more highly correlated with hypoglycemia than with aggressiveness, again suggesting that hypoglycemia may be the important mediating factor.

While Bolton's hypothesis lacks direct experimental evidence, it is deserving of further attention, since the possible implications for a society such as ours are fascinating. The many parallels between hypoglycemia, hyperactivity, and the allergic reaction syndrome, plus the relatively high incidence of each, suggest that such physiological disorders may have a profound impact on antisocial behavior at the societal level, particularly in economically deprived environments. Our society is relatively sophisticated in detecting and treating individuals who experience severe physiological disturbances. However, Bolton's findings suggest that those individuals with mild to moderate physiological disorders (which are difficult to diagnose) may represent the group with the greatest risk for developing antisocial behavioral syndromes.

Summary and Conclusions

Hyperactivity, allergic reactions, and hypoglycemia are three syndromes which occur relatively frequently in our culture and which have very similar symptomatology. While medical treatment is somewhat successful in alleviating the primary physiological symptoms, social learning apparently plays a major role in the development and maintenance of secondary symptoms including antisocial behavior such as aggression, delinquency, and sociopathy. Bolton's (1973) study of the relationship between physiological factors and societal factors suggests that the physiological syndromes may have a major impact on antisocial behavior at the societal level, particularly when one assumes that while mild levels of physiological abnormality may go undetected and untreated they still predispose an individual toward antisocial behavior. In conclusion, students of childhood antisocial behavior must be well aware of the possible contributions of physiological factors, especially as they interact with social learning. Physiological dysfunctions may be especially important during certain developmental periods that are characterized by exposure to demanding interpersonal and academic situations.

COGNITIVE SOCIAL LEARNING

As children grow older, they develop greater cognitive abilities, especially with the acquisition of language. These rapidly expanding conceptual processes enable children and parents to use a much wider range of behaviors to influence each other. Subsequently, the socialization process is not restricted to events and consequences in the child's immediate environment. As a consequence, reinforcement mechanisms become less central in the acquisition of new behavior, and we need a more elaborate theory to explain the learning of new social behaviors.

One of the most influential theories to account for the expanding role of cognitive processes in the acquisition of social behavior in children is the social-learning theory of Albert Bandura (1971, 1973; see Chapter Five of this text for further detail). Bandura's position is in general agreement with many reinforcement theorists; namely, that the anticipated consequences of behavior are one of the most important determinants of what people will do. That is, we can expect people to seek pleasant outcomes and to avoid unpleasant outcomes. However, there are two central features of Bandura's model which distinguish it from other social-learning theories. First, Bandura emphasized the role of retention or memory processes in the learning of social behavior. Second, Bandura explained reinforcement effects both in terms of their incentive value and of their informational value. Suppose one child observed another being reinforced for some activity. Both children are likely to repeat the reinforced activity; the reinforced child may repeat the activity because of the contingent reinforcements for past behavior (incentive value) and the observing child may engage in the same activity because the observed reinforcements indicate what consequences might be expected if the response is imitated (information value).

By employing memory and information-processing principles in his theory, Bandura was able to distinguish between processes which influence the acquisition or the performance of social behavior. One important source of information stored in a child's memory is the pairing of acts and their consequences for salient people (models) in the child's environment. For example, a child can remember the pleasant and unpleasant consequences that other people experience when they attempt to do something. These lessons can be particularly valuable when the outcomes to others are very painful and produce permanent injury or disfigurement.

Theoretically, the child need not receive any reinforcement in order to learn that a particular sequence of behaviors is likely to lead to either a positive or a negative outcome. If the behavioral sequence is simple, the child may be able to imitate the required acts in order to achieve the reinforcements that others receive. If the behavioral sequence is too difficult, the child may require extensive rehearsal in order to perform the potentially reinforcing sequence. For example, children may learn that an Olympic Gold Medal winner receives considerable respect and admiration from others, but they probably will not be able to imitate the athlete until they have practiced for many hours. Still, children can learn to predict favorable outcomes for future behavior if they see others reinforced for their actions. Similarly, young children who see someone punished for playing in the street can anticipate similar consequences if they also play in the street. In the following sections we consider the role of attention and retention processes in the development of social processes.[4]

Attention

The typical child is exposed to a very complex set of events during any given day. Only a small amount of the information we encounter is attended to and processed carefully (Neisser, 1967). One characteristic of the attention process is that it is highly selective. We are able to divide our attention among tasks depending on the relative effort or complexity of the tasks. Selective attention permits an individual to monitor several events simultaneously if each task is not too complex. More complicated tasks may require our undivided attention to process and understand the event (Fitts & Posner, 1967; Griffiths & Johnston, 1973). Experienced drivers can monitor the gas pedal, the brake, the clutch and gears, the steering wheel, and traffic on the roadway while listening to the radio or talking with a passenger. Drivers can perform all these tasks simultaneously because each task is quite familiar and overlearned. However, while learning to drive (especially without automatic transmissions), most people experience great difficulty in coordinating the clutch, gas pedal, brake, and gear shift. Initially each task is so difficult that it requires almost all of our attention with little capacity remaining to coordinate the additional activities.

We pay special attention to novel information whenever it appears. As a consequence, we frequently stop paying attention to familiar features of our environment even though they influence our reactions. For example, if you have been sitting down to read this chapter, the particular posture you have adopted was probably influenced by the type of chair in which you are sitting. Many features of our environment can influence our behavior without our really attending to these features (Altman, 1975). We can learn to direct our attention to these environmental features if we can break our perceptual habits.

We can also apply the same reasoning to "nonconscious" social determinants of behavior. For example, most Americans seem to carefully regulate the distance that they stand from other people when they engage in casual conversation. The typical American standing distance is about thirty inches (Hall, 1966). If we stand too close, others may feel uncom-

---

[4]The two important processes of motoric reproduction and reinforcement (especially self-reinforcement) are not discussed here. An excellent discussion of these processes can be found in Bandura (1973).

fortable; if we stand too far away, others will think that we are cold and distant (Altman & Vinsel, 1977). In short, a great number of social cues and social processes may operate at a nonconscious level, although we can focus our attention on these processes. Since most of us are very familiar with these social cues, we no longer attend to their effects on our inferences and behavior. One interesting example of this process is revealed in our use of eye contact. We learn to use eye contact to signal interest in other people, to regulate verbal interaction, and to indicate friendship and intimacy. And yet, too much eye contact can be embarrassing or threatening (Argyle & Kendon, 1967; Ellsworth & Carlsmith, 1973). Although we can learn to attend to these nonconscious determinants of our social interaction, we can also underestimate their effects because they are so familiar. One of the interesting questions which deserves future research attention is what determines the direction of our focus and gaze, especially as these factors influence which types of models children will observe.

Retention

A second major element of Bandura's approach is the description of processes which facilitate the retention of the material we perceive. First of all, an enormous amount of our past experience is encoded in memory and is potentially accessible at some later time. Information stored in memory is frequently "organized" into a network of associations. By remembering part of the network, we can sometimes reconstruct and retrieve events which seemed to be forgotten. We seem to have the capacity to recall remote events after many years, even though we have not had much opportunity to rehearse these events or scenes in the intervening period. Research cited in Chapter Three by Linton provides further examples of the complex memory processes which can facilitate the recall of remote events.

It is easy to underestimate the complexity and detail of information that are potentially available from our memories as a result of socialization processes. One potentially important source of information for children about antisocial behavior is the mass media. Anecdotal observations about the amount of information remembered from television is revealed by the annual springtime complaints about summer reruns. It is instructive to watch these reruns to see how long it takes to recognize the program as one that was or was not watched previously. This exercise is most informative if only about one-half of the programs were watched at the first showing. Students in our classes indicate that they can determine within a few minutes whether or not they previously watched the television program. In fact, if they can make such accurate judgments, an interesting question is raised. How much of the television material which they viewed over the past year is still potentially accessible from memory?

Squire (1974) has conducted a series of studies on the long-term accuracy of recall for television programming. His main purpose in pursuing these remote memory experiences was to identify possible memory loss from electroconvulsive shock therapy (ECS). Although we have all heard about possible abuses of ECS from novels such as Kesey's *One Flew over the Cuckoo's Nest*, ECS seems to be one of the few successful treatments for patients suffering from severe depression. While some researchers originally thought the painful experiences associated with ECS might be responsible for the beneficial effects, more recent evidence casts doubt on this possibility. First, Squire noticed that patients receiving several ECS treatments often complained of amnesia for events of the past few months. In addition, the beneficial effects of ECS have been shown to occur even though the client is sedated and receives muscle relaxants before shock so that they feel nothing. Squire postulated that the beneficial effects of ECS might not result from pain but rather that treatment might erase one's memory for some past events.

To test these memory losses, Squire needed to identify some type of information that would be closely time tagged (that is, events occurring within a restricted time period). As his stimulus material, Squire selected television programs which were cancelled after one year. Hence, he knew the programs would not be rerun in following years and would be limited to exposures within a single year. By asking questions about the main characters of these programs, Squire could estimate how rapidly the information about programs was lost for nontreated clients and he could compare this decay rate to that of the clients receiving ECS. Squire found that the loss of memory from ECS was primarily concentrated over the previous few months. Events stored for longer periods of time seemed to be relatively invulnerable to the ECS.

If we consider Squire's finding with respect to social behavior, it suggests that many important social events are retrievable over long periods of time. For some reason events seem to be held in a relatively active memory for a period of weeks and months after these events occurred. This relatively active memory seems to be most susceptible to ECS. Moreover, the absolute amount of memory for these earlier television programs is somewhat surprising. If we can remember so much about these programs after several years, imagine how much information might be remembered by children for a period of a few hours or days. The sections which follow describe how memory and retention processes might be involved in the expression of aggressive behavior.

Memory Induced Mediators of Aggressive Behavior

Numerous studies have investigated the short-term effects of exposure to aggressive material (such as live models, films, words, toys, and weapons associated with aggression). Numerous findings demonstrated that aggressive material can facilitate the expression of aggressive behavior, especially from provoked and uninhibited individuals (Bandura, 1973; Berkowitz, 1974). However, the short-term effects of aggressive material may be blocked by strong inhibitions against aggression. Children watching television violence might not become more aggressive immediately after exposure since they either might not be aroused or they may expect negative consequences for displaying the witnessed antisocial behavior. Even if there are no immediate effects of observing media violence, delayed effects might occur when the parents are no longer present or when the children are playing outside the home.

Since inhibitions might mask short-term effects of exposure to aggressive material, it is important to investigate variables which can influence delayed reactions in order to fully understand the effects of media portrayals of violence. Both Bandura (1973) and Berkowitz (1974) have proposed that memory or mediational mechanisms can influence the delayed effects of aggressive material on aggressive behavior. Presumably, variables such as imagery, rehearsal, coding strategies, and retrieval cues—which increase the probability of delayed recall for material—are important determinants of the material's delayed effects on aggressive behavior.

Berkowitz (1970) has proposed an interactive model to explain the effects of exposure to mass-media portrayals of violence on aggressive behavior. Aggressive behavior is assumed to be an interactive function of arousal (such as frustration), inhibitions, and aggressive stimulation. Theoretically, subjects are most aggressive following exposure to aggressive stimuli (such as films, aggressive words, weapons, or pictures) and also when they experience low inhibitions and high arousal. Several studies have demonstrated that subjects delivered significantly more intense or numerous electric shocks to a former frustrator after being exposed to a brutal boxing film (aggressive stimulation) and being aroused by electric shocks than subjects who were not aroused or were not exposed to the aggressive film (Berkowitz, 1970).

Strong inhibitions or low arousal might mask the short-term effects of mass-media violence. Nevertheless, there may be important delayed or long-term effects of exposure to aggressive stimulation. Presumably, Berkowitz's (1970) model concerning the effects of exposure to aggressive stimuli can be extended to include situations where stimulation occurs from *either* external or internal (memory) sources. If conditions facilitate recall of aggressive stimuli from earlier exposures, then an individual might respond in the same manner as someone recently exposed to external aggressive stimuli. That is, if aggressive material is easily recalled in situations where arousal is high and inhibitions are low, then the material may produce delayed effects. Thus, an understanding of such delayed and long-term effects of exposure to aggressive material requires an assessment of conditions under which aggressive material is likely to be *remembered* and to evoke aggression some time after exposure.

Memory and Aggressive Stimulation. Quite often in research on social behavior, the behavioral effects of stimulus materials are measured when relatively long time intervals have elapsed following exposure to some experimental treatment (Bandura, 1973; Bandura & Jeffery, 1973). More research is needed to evaluate the memory and information-processing limitations of the subject in order to be able to assess the delayed effects of exposure to some critical stimulus. Both the social-learning approaches of Bandura (1969; 1971), Walters (1964), and Aronfreed (1968) and the S-R mediational approach of Berkowitz (1970) emphasize the importance of memory processes. However, there has not been sufficient research on memory and information-processing limitations in the context of emotional and antisocial *behavior* (cf. Bandura, 1973; Gerst, 1971; Hicks, 1965, 1968; Liebert & Baron, 1972; Turner & Layton, 1976).

It may be especially important to differentiate the immediate from the delayed effects of aggressive material (Liebert & Baron, 1972). Human memory research indicates that learned material is often inaccessible or unretrievable after five minutes if the material was imbedded in a complex array of unrelated information (Neisser, 1967). In many investigations of aggressive material the subject's aggressive behavior was observed shortly after the last exposure to aggressive stimulation. However, it might be expected that aggressive stimulation in the context of complex environmental cues often does not have much influence on behavior after five or more minutes unless the subject can be reminded of the earlier material or earlier frustrations. If information-processing and memory limitations do not prevent recall of the aggressive material, then it might produce delayed reactions when the material is remembered.

In some naturally occurring settings, exposure to aggressive stimulation may occur when inhibitions are high or when arousal is low. For example, many individuals saw violent films such as *In Cold Blood*, *The Godfather*, *Straw Dogs*, and *Clockwork Orange*. Apparently, there was no widespread increase in social violence immediately following these films as might be expected from the previously described research. Perhaps most of these viewers experienced strong inhibitions or were not strongly aroused immediately after the film. Suppose, however, one of these film viewers went to a bar or attended an informal party shortly afterward, had a few drinks, and became involved in an argument. Perhaps the drinks and party atmosphere might lower the film viewer's inhibitions (Bandura, 1973; Clark, 1952; Shupe, 1954; Shuntich & Taylor, 1972), while the noise of the party and the argument might increase the person's arousal level (Geen & O'Neal, 1969). If the individual recalled or was reminded of the previous film, then Berkowitz's (1970) interaction model of aggressive behavior suggests that the person would be highly predisposed to engage in aggressive behavior even when the film had been seen much earlier.

There may also be important immediate and delayed effects of aggressive stimulation in the home environment. Aggressive behavior may frequently occur in some homes since inhibitions may be particularly low in such familiar surroundings, strong arousal or frustration may be frequent, and effective exposure to aggressive stimuli is high. Apparently, a high proportion (82 percent) of murders and aggravated assaults occur in or around the home following *frustration-related altercations* among acquaintances (Newton & Zimring, 1969). Moreover, the average American is exposed to aggressive stimulation through television quite frequently, viewing forty to one hundred aggressive episodes every week (Gerbner, 1972). Thus, the simultaneous occurrence of low inhibitions, high arousal, and aggressive stimulation through television or other mass media is frequently experienced in some homes.

To summarize, it is proposed that the effects of exposure to aggressive stimulation through films and television could endure beyond the immediate situation in which the individual was exposed. For example, viewers who are exposed to high levels of aggressive stimulation might be easily reminded of the television violence in their daily activities away from the television set. Apparently, the aggression-inducing effects of mass-media violence could occur in situations quite removed from the initial exposure, situations where inhibitions are low, arousal is high, and the aggressive material is easily recalled.

Memory, Retrieval Cues, and Modeling.   Retrieval cues might also mediate the delayed effects of aggressive modeling on subsequent behavior if the cues remind a person of earlier models. For example, suppose a man is in a bar and observes a fight. When this observer leaves the bar, he will probably forget the fight as he moves into other situations which occupy his attention. If our hypothetical individual subsequently becomes involved in a heated argument and hears his opponent use a term or phrase that occurred during the earlier fight, the expression (even if neutral in connotation) may remind the individual of the earlier bar fight. When our observer is reminded of the earlier fight, he might respond as if he were recently exposed to aggressive modeling.

Similarly, retrieval cues might stimulate recall of modeling sequences from mass-media portrayals of violence. Considerable evidence indicates that aggressive models can influence the probability of subsequent aggressive behavior (Bandura, 1973). Presumably, a critical variable in determining whether aggressive models influence behavior is whether the individual happens to remember the modeled behavior (including the consequences). Ostensibly insignficant stimuli encoded at the same time as the modeled sequence might serve as a retrieval cue.

A speculative analysis of a brutal murder that occurred in the Roxbury district of Boston ("Crime: Murder in Roxbury," 1973) provides an example of how the present argument might be applied to an analysis of mass-media effects on violent behavior. A Boston television station broadcast a violent film *(Fuzz)* which portrayed a juvenile gang throwing gasoline over "bums" and burning them to death. A few days later, a gang of youths stopped a young woman who was carrying a can of gasoline. The youths forced the woman to enter an alley and to pour the gasoline over herself. One youth then tossed a lighted match on the woman engulfing her in flames; she died several hours later from the burns. It is possible that the earlier television program had influenced the occurrence of this killing. Two major ambiguities exist about the murder. First, it is not clear whether the youths had seen the program. Second, there were many details that differed between the two episodes (such as age, race, and sex of the victim, setting of the crime, and, possibly, motives of the actors). If too many differences existed between the modeling stimuli and the subsequent situation, one might question whether the modeling stimuli are an important determinant of the observers' behavior.

However, the proposed paradigm, which predicts interactive effects of arousal, inhibitions, and recall, might be used to explain delayed effects in novel situations. The youths had threatened the woman on the previous day (suggesting that they were angry with her). Moreover, the youths had forced her into an alley, perhaps indicating that they felt they would not be seen there. Thus, the youths might have experienced strong arousal (Geen & O'Neal, 1969) and low inhibitions since they were not watched (Turner & Simons, 1974). Finally, if the youths had seen *Fuzz* or heard about the film, then the presence of the gasoline can carried by the woman might have served as a retrieval cue to remind the youths of the filmed murders. Perhaps without the presence of a salient retrieval cue the youths would not have remembered the bizarre means for harming the woman. Moreover, if they had not seen the film, the presence of the gasoline can might not have caused the youths to think of killing the woman with gasoline. Thus, the presence of a salient cue in the film and the murder situation might have been necessary for the previous modeling to have delayed effects on the youths. Although admittedly speculative, the present analysis of the Boston killing suggests that stimuli encoded at the same time as some modeled sequence might serve as retrieval cues to remind the observer of the entire modeled sequence. If the observer also experiences low inhibitions and strong arousal simultaneously with recall of the previous modeled behavior, then the modeling stimuli could produce delayed effects on the observer.

Memory, Retrieval Cues, and Aggressive Stimulation. Tulving (1968) proposed that the main question to be investigated about memory processes is that of retrievability. Presumably, recall could be stimulated for any material in memory if the correct retrieval cues are used. His findings indicated that the appropriate retrieval cues associated with a to-be-remembered response facilitated response retrieval even though the subjects seemed to have forgotten the response when tested by conventional recall procedures. Apparently, stimuli encoded at the same time as a critical (to-be-remembered) stimulus are likely to be the most effective retrieval cues (Thomson & Tulving, 1970; Tulving & Osler, 1968; Tulving & Pearlstone, 1966). One additional issue derived from these memory considerations for an explanation of aggressive behavior is that neutrally connotated stimuli associated with aggressive stimulation or frustration might serve as retrieval cues to remind the subject of the aggressive material at a later time and in another situation. For example, Berkowitz (1971, 1974) proposed that neutral stimuli such as an individual's name could increase aggressive responding when it was associated with previous aggressive material (Berkowitz & Geen, 1966) or a frustrating episode (Berkowitz & Knurek, 1969). Perhaps the names used to stimulate aggression served as retrieval cues to produce recall of previous aggressive stimulation or of frustration. Presumably, the analysis of memory processes associated with retrieval cues could serve to clarify delayed effects of aggressive stimulation.

One possible retrieval cue for media violence is a drawn weapon. Our research indicates that toy weapons can increase the rate of antisocial behavior in a free play setting for young children (Turner & Goldsmith, 1976). Moreover, systematic observation of forty hours of evening television programs indicated that drawn weapons had both a high rate of appearance and a strong contingent association with physical aggression (Turner, Simons, Berkowitz, & Frodi, 1977). Approximately 80 percent of the portrayals of a weapon carried in someone's hand were followed shortly by some form of physical aggression. These portrayals occurred approximately three times per hour in crime drama programs. Other cues which potentially could be associated with aggression, such as police cars, alcohol consumption, pistols in holsters, police uniforms, or knives either had much lower frequencies of occurrence or weaker association with aggression since they also were associated with many nonaggressive scenes. These findings were replicated by Wilson and Higgins (1977). Children using toy weapons, then, might be reminded of earlier portrayals of violence while other kinds of toys previously viewed on television (such as Sesame Street puppets or cowboy hats and spurs) might remind children of many nonaggressive behaviors. In other words, the joint portrayal of weapons and violence could be important in determining whether children can spontaneously recall material which they had witnessed previously.

Television Research and Policy Implication

Although previous research has demonstrated that television portrayals of violence can stimulate antisocial behavior in some observers, these findings suggest also that there are strong individual differences in reactions to the media. For example, several studies suggest that the stimulating effects of violence are strongest for viewers who are especially likely to be aggressive even in the absence of media portrayals of violence (Parke, Berkowitz, Leyens, West, & Sebastian, 1977).

In order to understand fully the effects of media violence in a way that permits reasonable, policy-oriented action, it is necessary to have a better idea about the actual risks involved in media portrayals of violence. There is some reason to believe that only a small proportion of television watchers may be strongly influenced by television violence (Kaplan & Singer, 1976). Suppose that only one person in 1,000 is influenced by television enough to intensify harmful attacks against others. The remaining 999 out of 1,000 individuals who were not influenced by television violence may not forego their favorite television programs to reduce the risk of violence unless they were clearly convinced that a causal relationship could be established linking television and aggression. Hence, a fairly sizable risk might have to be demonstrated before program changes could be implemented. However, a single assault each year to 1/1,000 of the United States' population could result in 200,000 serious assaults per year. Even for this large number of assaults, it might be quite difficult to identify a causal relationship of television portrayals and actual assaults unless a much clearer model is available to predict when individuals are a risk to be influenced by television programming. At the present level of research, it is still not clear what features of television programming might be most likely to stimulate aggression in viewers. It is possible that some individuals might be provoked by the assaultive behavior of the "bad" characters on television while other individuals are more likely to be influenced by the retaliatory responses of the main characters who punish the behavior of the antagonists (Liebert et al., 1973).

Need for Estimates of Actual Rates of Instigation. While numerous studies indicate that media violence can have stimulating effects on the majority of viewers under very special circumstances (Berkowitz, 1974), it remains to be demonstrated that television viewing does stimulate overt acts of aggression in the viewing public under everyday viewing situations. Even the most casual observation of television viewers in their homes indicates that the vast majority of individuals do not become assaultive toward those around them following portrayals of violence. Although television violence can influence viewers, several other factors are also important determinants of whether aggression will occur.

First, researchers have repeatedly found that observers are more likely to respond aggressively when they are also physiologically aroused at the same time that they are exposed to the aggressive material (Tannenbaum & Zillmann, 1975). Moreover, highly aggressive or sexually explicit material seems to contribute to physiological arousal. Even background white noise in the viewing setting can contribute to arousal which may intensify the physiological reactions of the observer (Geen & O'Neal, 1969). Probably two of the most consistent sources of arousal are frustrations and provocations caused by other individuals (Berkowitz, 1974).

In addition to physiological arousal, other conditions may be required for aggression to be stimulated in viewers. Several studies suggest that there is a higher risk of impulsive aggressive behavior if the observers of aggressive stimuli are relatively uninhibited (Ellis, Weinir, & Miller, 1971; Turner, Layton, & Simons, 1975). Alternatively, if the individual feels that others are likely to negatively evaluate or punish aggressive behavior or if the target might strongly retaliate, then the viewers might inhibit aggressive impulses (Turner & Simons, 1974). Apparently most individuals are moderately successful in monitoring their own reactions; when they think they might be inappropriately aggressive, they are likely to bend over backward to avoid displaying aggressive reactions (Berkowitz & Turner, 1974). However, individuals who are unconcerned about how others would react to their behavior (such as people who have consumed a considerable amount of alcohol) may respond with strong aggressive reactions (Shuntich & Taylor, 1972). The combination of conditions which promote aggression may be quite infrequent in most homes. Hence, the actual effect on the viewing public might be quite minimal if the joint occurrence of high arousal, low inhibitions, a safe target, and aggressive acts on television is infrequent. One important consideration for future research is that a better prediction must be made of the actual occurrence of aggressive behavior in the viewing public if clearer policy implications can be drawn for modifying television programming. While most researchers seem to agree that television violence *can* stimulate aggression in viewers (Comstock & Rubinstein, 1972), there still remains considerable controversy about whether the actual occurrence of instigation of attacks is very common. Informal observations of families in naturalistic settings strongly suggest that the instigation rate is actually very low.

The Viewing Audience at Home. Parke et al. (1977) have suggested that the reactions of the audience watching with an individual also may be an important determinant of an individual's reactions to violence. People watching television violence with an audience that strongly endorses aggression with cheers, applause, and similar behavior may have very different reactions than people watching at home with a family that disapproves of violence. For example, if a child imitated aggressive behavior viewed on television, and the child's parents discouraged that imitation, the child may be much less likely to imitate the behavior at a later time, especially if the parents are present and serve as a discriminative stimulus for negative consequences resulting from earlier imitation situations. Failure to consider the effects of the viewing audience may be one important limitation in generalizing earlier findings to the typical viewing environment, which is with other family members in the home.

Our informal observations suggest that reactions to media violence portrayed at home could sharply differ from reactions in other settings.

Most parents seem to be especially likely to punish strongly the immediate imitation of behavior performed on television. Moreover, most teenagers watch television violence with their parents. When watching alone, they are likely to chose nonviolent programming (Chaffee & Tims, 1976). Many children have learned that imitation of aggression around the home television set can lead to quick and certain consequences. If this parental response is as common as our informal data suggests, children may learn to be nonaggressive most of the time that they watch television programs in their own homes. However, the inhibiting effects of negative consequences at home may not generalize very well beyond the home. If children see television programs at school or in other novel research settings, the inhibitions learned at home might not influence their behavior. Yet if they can remember programs shown at home while they are playing on the school yard, the earlier presentations might produce delayed reactions on the children. In summary, the present reasoning suggests that reactions to television out of the home might be quite different than reactions within the home environment. Since most of the earlier research on effects of television violence was not conducted in the home—where parental control could moderate reactions to media violence—earlier research may not correctly predict how children typically respond to media violence viewed in the home.

There is another reason that previous findings may not correctly predict how children respond to television violence in the home, as opposed to the typical research settings used in the past. Children playing in the home may have a well-established pattern or hierarchy of play behavior. If they have developed fairly strong habitual patterns of play in one setting, then a single television portrayal may not have much effect in modifying the children's typical play behavior in that setting. However, if the children were moved to a highly novel setting where no habits of play had been established, then a single television program might have relatively strong effects on the children. In other words, we need to know whether children can be stimulated to imitate media portrayals both in highly familiar environments and in strange or novel environments.

In the typical research study conducted previously, children were introduced in their classroom to a stranger who led them to a novel setting, showed them a television program, and then observed their reactions. In this novel setting, stimulating effects of films were frequently observed. When these children were brought back to this room weeks and months later, they frequently could correctly recall what they had previously seen and what they had done the last time they were in this room (Hicks, 1965, 1968; Kniveton, 1973). However, we can wonder what effects the program would have if it had been shown in a room where children had already established very familiar patterns of play. On the one hand, we might expect the children to attend to the television program because of its novelty in a familiar room. However, the children's imitation of the modeled behaviors might be much weaker if they had already strongly established patterns of play in the same room.

DEMOGRAPHIC DETERMINANTS OF ANTISOCIAL BEHAVIOR

Up to this point we have examined environmental and physiological factors related to the development of antisocial behavior, primarily at the individual or family level. In the following section we shall explore some of the relatively major changes our society is undergoing. Rapidly changing population characteristics, particularly those resulting from the relative number of individuals in certain age groups, seem to be at the root of many current societal changes. While there is no direct evidence about these relationships, it is quite likely that the learning environments of children and adolescents and the economic and social environments of young adults have been substantially influenced by the effects of population fluctuation over the past fifty years. However, the precise relationship between demographic factors and antisocial behavior appears to be highly complex and poorly understood.

In this section, some societal trends are outlined, recent research projects which attempted to relate demographic factors to specific crime rates are described, and finally two hypotheses regarding possible explanations for the relationship between societal changes and antisocial behavior are discussed.

A Changing American Society

There can be little doubt that major changes are occurring in our society which have produced changes in family structure. In the last decade, for example, annual crime, divorce, and unemployment rates have climbed dramatically, while the birth rate has dropped to an all-time low (*Vital Statistics*, 1960–1976). Accompanying these changes are major modifications in norms and values. Sex roles appear to be rapidly changing and women are entering the labor market at an increasing rate. Divorce laws have been greatly liberalized (Goode, 1976; Kenkel, 1977), and factors such as smaller family size, availability of day-care centers, and the increased ability of women to compete successfully in the labor market have had a major effect not only on the divorce rate but also on society in general (Kenkel, 1977).

It is often claimed that the modern family as an institution is disintegrating (Kenkel, 1977; Yorburg, 1973), perhaps due to its inability to adapt to technological advancements (Schulz, 1976). Thus, the changing family is often blamed for the high divorce rate and other social ills. An alternative view is that, instead of acting as a cause of social change, the American family is itself responding to societal change. In fact, some view the rising divorce rate as evidence of healthy changes in values and expectations among young people (Kenkel, 1977; Kirkpatrick, 1963;

Schulz, 1976; Yorburg, 1973). In any event, it is clear that our society is changing in rather significant ways, and that the family institution is involved in much of the change.

It is interesting to note that many of the changes which are occurring in the United States are occurring in other societies as well. For example, since 1910, divorce has risen in practically every western European nation, often at a rate higher than that of the U.S. (Goode, 1976; Kenkel, 1977; Kerckhoff, 1976; Thamm, 1975); the divorce and birth rates of the Soviet Union closely paralleled those of the U.S. from 1964–1974 (Coser, 1974). Such cross-national similarity in societal change suggests the role of a universal factor such as population change.

The widespread effects of population changes on society are well known (Hauser, 1971; Heer, 1975; Merton & Nisbet, 1976). For decades demographers have been aware that the birth rate has a major impact on the entire economic and social structure, including industry, commerce, education, and politics (Whelpton, 1932). More specifically, the increasing U.S. birth rate from 1940–1960 has been related to increases in crime and delinquency, alcoholism and drug addiction, and political alienation (Hauser, 1971). Yet the relationship of population to social change is not a simple one. For example, while the birth rate affects economic conditions, the reverse might also be true. That is, economic conditions may also affect marriage, divorce, and birth rates (Thamm, 1975; van de Walle, 1972).

In addition to absolute size, the age structure of the population may also be related to societal change. Hauser (1969), for instance, outlined and predicted the influence of birth rate on the population age structure. He then discussed the global effects of a changing age structure on the educational system, the institution of marriage, family formation, and economic systems and the more specific effects on juvenile delinquency, marriage, and automobile accident rates.

Heer (1975) similarly discussed the societal impact of the age structure on the labor force, patterns of consumption, political attitudes, welfare, and the women's rights movement. While these rather global influences of the changing population have been recognized by demographers for some time, attempts to relate specific demographic factors, such as birth rate, to specific social behavior have been infrequent. Using national data, we have completed two research projects (Cole & Turner, 1977; Dodd, Cole, & Turner, 1977) relating fluctuations in birth rates to shifts in the crime rate.

Crime Rates as a Function of the Post-World War II Baby Boom

Not all individuals in the population are equally at risk for committing criminal offenses. While most serious crimes are committed by males aged fifteen to twenty-four, each class of crime can be characterized by different age-specific risk values. For example, the modal age of arrest for robbery and aggravated assault is eighteen years, while the modal age for burglary is sixteen, and twenty-one for homicide (*Uniform Crime Reports*, 1960–1976). In order to understand the increased frequency of crime over the past twenty years, it is important first to account for the increased numbers of individuals in the specific age groups for which the risk of crime is highest. While previous research has related the increase in crime rates to the effects of a changing age structure of the U.S. population (Ferdinand, 1969) and to changing birth rates (Wellford, 1973), Cole and Turner (1977) analyzed both of these factors simultaneously as they relate to specific crimes.

Cole and Turner noted that there have been major fluctuations in the U.S. birth rate from 1920–1975 (see Figure 6–1). During the Depression of the 1930s, the birth rate dropped substantially, probably due to the effect of the Depression on marriage rates as well as upon the willingness of married couples to increase the size of their families. Following the Depression, the birth rate began to climb slowly and then skyrocketed in 1946, immediately following World War II. The birth rate continued to climb markedly until 1957, when it leveled off; since 1960 it has dropped steadily. A major contributor to the birth-rate fluctuation has been the expanding and contracting family size with larger families occurring between 1920–1930 and 1950–1960. Assuming that the effects of mortality and migration are minor compared to the birth-rate fluctuations, it is possible to estimate the number of individuals in our population for any given year and age group from previous birth data. That is, since the birth rate was quite low during the 1930s, one can assume that the relative number of twenty-year-olds during the 1950s was also low (1930 + 20 years). Likewise, the high birth rate following WWII produced a "population wave" which has greatly inflated the numbers of young adults in our society currently.

Various crimes in the U.S. are characteristically age specific. That is, serious crimes against the individual (such as robbery, rape, and homicide) are most frequently committed by individuals in the eighteen to twenty-four year age group. Other crimes are characterized by younger and older age structures (vandalism and public intoxication, respectively). Thus, Cole and Turner's model, based on changing birth rates and the "at risk" age structure related to various crimes, was an attempt to explain the increasing crime rate and make predictions about future trends.

Multiple regression[5] analysis revealed that both previous birth rates and the "at risk" age factor were highly correlated with changes in crime rates,[6]

[5]Multiple regression is a correlational method for analyzing the collective and separate contributions of two or more predictor variables to the variation of a single dependent variable (Kerlinger & Pedhazur, 1973).

[6]While it can be debated whether "crime" is the commission, detection, or conviction of an illegal act, arrest rate was selected as the indicator of crime since such a measure would seem to be the most reliable, it is readily available from the FBI *Uniform Crime Reports*, and it is also possible to obtain the age at arrest.

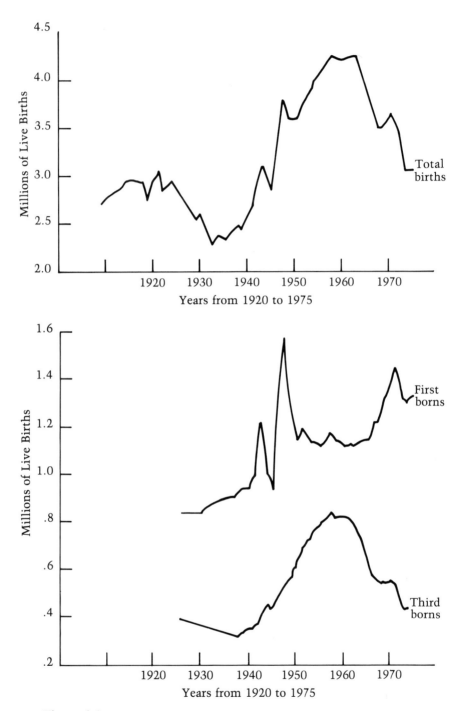

Figure 6-1

Numbers of live births by birth order from 1920–1975.

within twelve different age groups and across different crimes (homicide, robbery, burglary, and aggravated assault). That is, the changing number of individuals in a particular age group (based on birth data) from 1960–1975 was highly correlated with the actual number of arrests of suspects in that age group, regardless of which of several crimes and age groups were examined. Figure 6-2 depicts the actual, statistically estimated and forecast rates of homicide from 1960–1985. As the baby-boom group passes through young adulthood into middle age during the next decade, the age

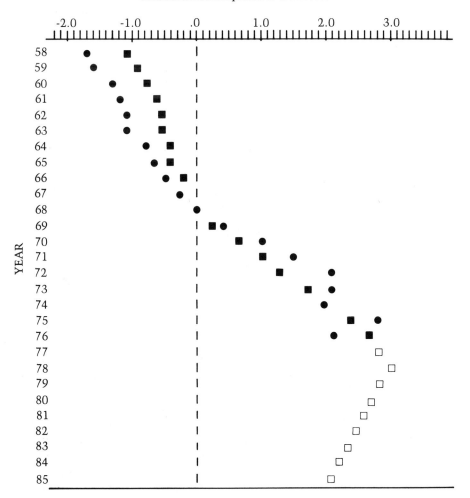

Figure 6-2

Actual (●) and estimated (■) standardized frequencies of arrests for homicide in high risk age groups during 1958–1976, and forecast frequencies (□) for 1977–1985.

structure of the population will begin to shift and, as the figure indicates, the research model predicts a 40 percent decline in the number of youth-oriented crimes such as homicide between 1975 and 1985. Concomitantly, there will be increased rates of those crimes committed by older adults, such as various nonviolent, alcohol-related crimes.

The Age Structure of Arrests for Crime

Adolescents (fourteen to eighteen), young adults (eighteen to twenty-four), and older adults (twenty-five to thirty or thirty to forty-five) are typically arrested for different types of crimes. If we compute the median age for arrests reported in the FBI's *Uniform Crime Reports* in each criminal category (robbery, assault, and so on), some interesting patterns begin to emerge. Adolescents seem to be involved in status-related crimes (acts which would not be illegal for older persons) such as alcohol consumption and running away, or crimes which have a strong thrill-seeking element such as vandalism, shoplifting, and auto-theft. As teenagers grow older and begin to enter the labor market at the age of sixteen to eighteen, the nature of crimes committed begins to change. For example, robbery and serious drug problems begin to emerge. These crimes seem to be especially likely for those individuals who do not have easy access to legitimate occupational opportunities. At this age, we also see the appearance of serious violent crimes such as aggravated assault and rape. Each of these violent acts is frequently committed under the influence of alcohol. Perhaps young people beginning to drink alcohol have serious difficulty in monitoring their social behavior while drinking. Research by Shuntich and Taylor (1972) indicates that alcohol does increase the risk of aggressive behavior. (Interestingly, the same research indicates that the consumption of marijuana decreases the likelihood of aggressive acts, at least for college students.) Since the maximum birth rate occurred in 1957, we can expect the annual rate of these adolescent crimes to decrease after 1975 as the post-WWII population wave passes beyond the adolescent age range.

Among young adults over the age of twenty, the most serious of all crimes—homicide—becomes substantially more likely. The most likely killer is a young, unemployed, nonwhite, male from a large urban neighborhood. His victim is likely to be a friend or acquaintance with whom he has been arguing. Young adulthood also increases the risk of crimes even for those individuals who are successful in seeking employment. The median age of arrest for embezzlement is twenty-three. Apparently as young people gain several years of employment experience, they have increased access to large amounts of money. Some of these individuals apparently become too tempted by the money they handle. However, the opportunity to commit the crime is limited by their social experiences. Similarly, slightly older individuals become more likely to commit assaults against their children and their spouses. These later crimes usually require the individuals to be married for several years before they have children against whom they can commit assaults. Thus, individuals seem to become maximally at risk for these offenses for a fairly limited period of their lives. Since the median age of arrest for this crime is twenty-eight, and since the maximum birth rate occurred in 1957, then we can expect a continuing increase in child-abuse and wife-beating cases to come to the attention of the courts until 1985–1988 (1957 + 28). After that period of time, the rate of occurrence for this crime should begin to decline.

For individuals over thirty, a different type of alcohol-related problem begins to occur. Public intoxication, driving under the influence, and public vagrancy are all alcohol-related offenses. The median age of arrest for these offenses is in the thirty to thirty-five age range. Unlike younger people whose alcohol-related problems lead to assaults, these older individuals seem more at risk for "passive" emotional reactions when they consume alcohol. These crimes should also continue to increase for the next ten to fifteen years, reaching a peak in 1990.

Finally, as people become even older members of society, their risk of being arrested for gambling increases. In addition, the risk of self-inflicted injuries such as suicide increases substantially (median age is sixty-five). Collectively, the arrest and suicide data suggest that people of different ages respond quite differently with antisocial and inappropriate behaviors. Further research may help us to understand why people seek these different means of expressing antisocial behaviors.

In summary, two major points emerge from a discussion of age-related crime rates. First, the data clearly demonstrate that the antisocial behavior expressed by various age groups takes quite different forms. A possible explanation for such findings is that the social and economic demands which living environments place on individuals may vary with age and lead to quite different forms of antisocial behavior. More research is obviously needed to clarify the relationship between environment and behavior. Second, since people seem to be at risk for different crimes at different ages, the post-World War II population wave is likely to cause the rates of specific crimes to rise and then fall as the baby boom reaches and then passes the age of risk for each crime.

It is important to observe that the increase in birth rate was not associated simply with a one-to-one increase in arrest rates. That is, within a given age group, the frequency of arrests increased at a rate approximately three times faster than the expanding number of individuals within that age group. Hence, the expanding crime rate cannot be explained solely by increased numbers of individuals available to commit crimes. Possible explanations for this phenomenon are discussed in the following section.

The Role of Demographic Factors on Antisocial Behavior

While the results outlined above are quite impressive, the interpretation of such findings is quite complex. Assuming that the changing population wave has been a major cause of the increases in antisocial behavior such as crime, the mechanism for such an effect remains unclear. Two possible hypotheses stand out.

First, population waves may directly affect access to labor markets, and there is reason to believe that young people suffer most from depressed economic conditions. As previously mentioned, the unemployment rate among teenagers and young adults has skyrocketed in the past ten years, compared to only slight increases among other age groups. Cloward and Ohlin's (1960) well-known theory of crime and delinquency is based on the premise that illegitimate methods are pursued when legitimate opportunities for reaching one's aspirations are restricted.

Severe unemployment undoubtedly reduces or eliminates legitimate opportunities, and those who cannot compete successfully for rewarding jobs may turn instead to burglary, drug dealing, and embezzlement. Individuals may seek out groups who share similar predicaments, and criminal subcultures which model and reinforce antisocial behavior may develop. Rather than turning directly to criminal activities, other individuals who are economically and socially stressed may begin to abuse alcohol or drugs. Hard-drug usage, especially heroin addiction, has long been associated with crime (Wilson, 1975), and alcohol overconsumption is frequently stated as a precipitating factor in a variety of crimes (Newton & Zimring, 1969; Shuntich & Taylor, 1972).

To a degree, crime may also be self-generating. That is, as crime rates begin to rise, law enforcement and judicial systems may be unable to maintain arrest and conviction rates (relative to total crimes committed), so the subjective (and objective) probability of being apprehended and punished may decline sharply. Similarly, there may be a dramatic increase in the numbers of individuals who model successful criminal behavior, that is, those who have achieved material success through illegal channels and yet eluded the law. In sum, then, demographic factors such as a changing age structure of the population may influence antisocial behavior by creating stressful events in the economic and social environments of "at risk" age groups; once initiated, the increases in antisocial behavior may prove to be self-generating.

A second hypothesis focuses upon the possible influence of demographic factors on family structure and family interaction patterns. Changes in the birth rate almost inevitably produce changes in the average family size. The post-WWII baby boom expanded the average family size in the United States from approximately three to five children. The decline in the birth rate since 1960 has now contracted the average family size to less than three children. Aside from family size, there is also reason to believe that the changing age structure of the population has affected divorce rates in the same fashion that it has affected crime rates. Like crime rates, divorce rates have increased dramatically (over 200 percent) during the past fifteen years; married individuals in their 20s and early 30s are particularly vulnerable. Using a model similar to that developed by Cole and Turner (1977), Dodd, Cole, and Turner (1977) found that the increasing number of young people can account for 68 percent of the variance in divorce rates from 1960–1973. Furthermore, there were twice as many children involved in divorces and annulments in 1975 than in 1963 (1,123,000 compared to 562,000 [*Vital Statistics*, 1976]). If the current trend persists, it has been estimated that one-sixth of all children will have been involved in divorce by the age of eighteen (Bronfenbrenner, 1973). A contrasting perspective is offered in the findings from Dodd, Cole, and Turner (1977), which relates the increased divorce rate to population waves. This data lead to the prediction that divorce will decline by 25–40 percent between 1980 and 1990 as the population wave moves beyond the age of maximum risk for divorce (twenty-two to thirty).

While there is no evidence that large families or single-parent families *directly* produce antisocial behavior in their children, there is some evidence to suggest that the interaction and child-rearing patterns of such families may be more conducive to the development of antisocial behavioral tendencies, relative to families with two parents and/or fewer children. Heer (1975) cited three studies which suggest that family size is inversely related to social adjustment, especially among working-class children; he suggested that children of large families may receive less individual adult attention and thus have less opportunity for the development of a wide range of social skills. Heer further examined research which demonstrated that the number of siblings is negatively related both to educational and vocational achievement in adulthood, even when the father's educational or occupational level was held constant.

Zajonc and Markus (1975) proposed an intriguing but controversial hypothesis about the effects of family size and birth order on the development of intelligence. While their research focused primarily on intellectual development, the findings might be relevant to the development of social behavior as well. Based on data from a sample of 400,000 nineteen-year-olds, they found that intelligence is related to both family size and birth order; that is, children from large families have slightly lower intelligence than those from small families, and later borns have lower IQs than early borns. While children from small families, as well as early borns in larger families, are exposed to learning environments dominated by adults (the parents), later borns, and especially those from large families, receive proportionally more of their intellectual training from siblings, who presumably are poorer teachers than adults. In addition, Zajonc and Markus (1975) briefly reviewed theories about birth-order effects which have intrigued psychologists in the past, including speculations regarding birth-order effects on affiliation, frustration tolerance, marital adjustment, conformity, alcoholism, and juvenile delinquency.

Mischel has extensively studied preference for delayed versus immediate reinforcement in children from several different cultures; many of his findings are quite relevant to the current discussion. A preference for delayed reinforcement is consistently related to social responsibility, as well as personal and social adjustment and maturity; furthermore, juvenile delinquents clearly showed a preference for immediate, small rewards as opposed to larger, delayed rewards (Mischel, 1961*b*). Mischel (1961*a*) also reported that the absence of a father was strongly related to preference for immediate reinforcement and, in addition, he suggested that the presence of a father in the family may be crucial for the transmission of many cultural values. Similarly, it has been noted that families experiencing marital stress, as well as single-parent families, tend to rely more heavily upon negative reinforcement in child management and that marital stress or divorce severely impedes therapeutic efforts to modify parenting skills (Patterson, Reid, Jones, & Conger, 1975).

While the preceding research is intriguing and highly relevant to the argument that demographic factors such as birth rate and divorce rate may affect the developmental environments of children, a word of caution is in order. Such correlational research as has been presented here can only be considered to be suggestive, and statements about causation are merely speculative. Additional research is definitely needed to investigate further the effects of family structure and interaction on the development of antisocial behavior.

Who Is at Risk to Become a Criminal?

According to estimates derived from Feldman (1977), most of us are at some risk for being arrested and convicted of criminal behavior. Feldman's estimates are based, in part, on self report data which might be distorted to some degree; however, efforts at cross validation within samples and replications across samples suggest that his estimates are quite reasonable. Feldman reasoned that we could learn a great deal about the actual rates of criminal acts by interviewing samples of individuals to determine whether they had committed illegal acts. As Feldman indicates, many reports by offenders may be biased because of suppression of reports, because of fear of detection, or because of a desire to appear brave or glamorous—leading to distorted claims. Feldman reviewed a number of studies with various procedures to detect deceptive individuals; (one such procedure was to get validating reports from peers). These studies suggest that 70–80 percent of adolescent males and 30 percent of adolescent females have committed at least one serious criminal offense (such as theft from a store). One major reason for the high offense rate is the low probability of being apprehended. Feldman (1977) cited an informal report of shoplifting in New York City which indicated that only one shoplifter in 1,000 is likely to be apprehended, even when a security guard is available to control shoplifting. In short, a very high percentage of the population commits serious illegal acts which are not detected.

Approximately 10 percent of the male population will be arrested at some time in their lives. However, about 98 percent of all individuals over the age of fourteen commit what is considered a minor offense at some time in their lives, and, *if* they were detected in the act, they could receive a citation requiring the payment of a fine. For example, people cross streets at inappropriate places, make errors while driving, or fail to follow laws concerning the proper riding of a bicycle. Nearly 90 percent of all adolescents and adults commit more major offenses for which they could be arrested if they were detected in the act. If convicted, they would be required to pay a fine. For example, these individuals have taken something of minor value which they knew did not belong to them. About 80 percent of people over fourteen commit offenses serious enough that judges are empowered to send them to jail as punishment. These acts include stealing inexpensive items from stores, serious mischief and vandalism, or violations of alcohol and tobacco ordinances. Nearly 50 percent of all individuals commit offenses serious enough to result in imprisonment if the person were convicted. These acts include illegal sale or consumption of alcohol and drugs, illegal sex acts, theft of items valued at more than $50, and similar offenses.

Wolfgang (1968) studied the criminal histories of a cohort of 5,000 youths in Philadelphia. A "cohort" is a carefully identified group of individuals of the same age who are studied in a longitudinal design. For example, all of the members of a cohort born in the same year start school together. A careful inspection of the city court records permitted the researchers to examine what types of individuals were arrested and what happened to these offenders. The results indicated that 10 percent of the males were likely to be arrested once. Of this group, approximately one-half were rearrested (within the ten years of the study). About thirty percent of this rearrested group was arrested a third time. Hence, about 1.5 percent of the cohort was arrested more than twice, and only 15 percent of the first offenders became serious repeat offenders. Based on these findings, Wolfgang recommended that most of the treatment efforts within the criminal-justice system should be reserved for those people who become repeat offenders. Even a casual inspection of policy in most courts indicates that Wolfgang's recommendation is followed; most first and second offenders are given suspended sentences and placed on probation.

In one sense, the question to be raised about first offenders is not whether they are criminals but why they were apprehended among all of the actual offenders in the population. Are these individuals less skilled in committing offenses, are they likely to commit more serious offenses so that they come to the attention of the police, do they commit multiple offenses that increase the risk that they will be detected in one of the offenses, or is their arrest a matter of luck? A disturbing question raised by Feldman (1977) is that the risk of arrest and conviction for low income and/or ethnic minority individuals is substantially higher than it is for middle- to high-income nonminority groups even though the rate of criminal behavior might not differ. When we examine the frequency of arrest in court cases, the rate from low-income neighborhoods is four and a half times the middle- and high-income neighborhoods while the self-reported offense rates in low-income neighborhoods is only one and a half times that of middle- and high-income neighborhoods. Findings from Stark and McEvoy (1970) indicate that high-income individuals actually report more physical assaults against other people than are reported by low-income males.

If these findings are correct, they suggest that low-income adolescents are unfairly overrepresented in court. Feldman speculates that the discretionary power of victims in reporting crime, of police in deciding whether a law was broken, of criminal prosecutors in filing charges, and in legal representations for poor defendants may each contribute to a higher likelihood that low-income persons will be arrested for and convicted of criminal offenses. Perhaps the overrepresentation of low-income people in the courts is the result of subtle biases which affect what types of behaviors are judged to be criminal, who is likely to be under surveillance by the police, who is released by the courts on bail and who is able to be released on their own recognizance, who is able to hire an effective lawyer to defend them, or who is able to plea bargain an alternative restitution which will permit the charges to be dropped. As with other resources in the community, financial prosperity seems to offer greater protection for middle- and upper-income than for low-income individuals when they are confronted by the criminal-justice system.

Misleading Meanings of Official Criminal Statistics. One of the important implications of these findings is that official statistics about crime and offenders can be quite misleading in representing the seriousness of crime in a community. It can be argued somewhat humorously that the higher the level of (official statistics for) crime in one's neighborhood, the better one's police force and the lower the risk of becoming a victim of crime. To see how this could be the case, let us suppose that a newly elected police chief embarks on a comprehensive law and order campaign to eliminate corruption and crack down on crime. (The following example is based largely upon actual events and evidence presented by Campbell, 1969; Kamisar, 1964.) Three major reforms are instituted. First, as many corrupt police officers as possible are identified and removed from the police force. Second, the record-keeping system is revamped so that all crime reports are officially filed and forwarded to the central administrative office. Finally, a public-relations campaign is undertaken to increase the confidence of the public in the law-enforcement system and to encourage citizens to report all crimes promptly. Let us examine how each of these reforms might lead to a sharp increase in the number of reported crimes, *independently* of the actual number of criminal offenses.

If the police chief were successful in eliminating corrupt officers from the police force, criminal acts—such as prostitution, drug violations, gambling, and possibly even assaults and robberies—which were previously overlooked or unreported (due to bribery) would be reported and pursued by the new police officers. The increased efficiency of the new record-keeping system would also increase the number of offenses which were officially reported and recorded. Finally, the public-relations campaign, if successful, would sensitize the public to crime and to the efforts of the police to combat it, increase the public's confidence in the law-enforcement system, and thus increase the likelihood that witnesses and victims would report criminal offenses or suspicious activities.

In short, a higher official crime rate in one's city could reflect an improved police force. One primary reason that this strange relationship can exist is that a high proportion of crime, especially minor crimes, is unreported in official police statistics. Hence, the "increased" crime may simply reflect the fact that the gap between the official crime rate and the actual crime rate has been narrowed. Of course, changes in the opposite direction might occur also. That is, a police force might produce a false impression of increased efficiency by lowering the quality of service. The poorer service would increase the gap between the true and the official crime rate which would give the appearance of a declining crime rate. In this case, the true crime rate might be increasing while the official rate was declining.

Summary and Conclusions

Our society is clearly undergoing rapid and significant changes in several areas. Specifically, rates of crime, divorce, and unemployment are on the rise, and many social norms and values, such as women's rights, are also changing. While it is tempting to blame such changes on disorganization of the family or disintegration of traditional societal values, such "explanations" have little empirical basis. Changes in population, both in total size and more specifically in terms of age structure, have been associated with increasing crime and divorce rates. While statistical models account for much of the fluctuation in crime and divorce rates and further predict a decline in these rates, the reasons for such associations need further explication.

It is possible that population waves place immediate stress on economic and social systems and thus produce negative effects, such as rising unemployment and crime rates. On the other hand, it is possible that the effects of population on antisocial behavior are more subtle and result instead from child-development environments associated with large family size or single-parent families. Such possibilities are intriguing and deserve the attention of the scientific community.

In sum, demographic variables may play a major role in antisocial behavior through their influence on the social and economic environments of adults and through the developmental environments of children and adolescents. While understanding of antisocial behavior might be achieved by analyzing environmental and physiological components at the individual level, understanding at the societal level necessitates serious consideration of the role of demographic factors, such as population size and structure, on society in general and on the family in particular.

REFERENCES

ALTMAN, I. *The environment and social behavior.* Belmont, Calif.: Brooks Cole, 1975.

ALTMAN, I., & VINSEL, A. M. Personal space: An analysis of E. T. Hall's proxemics framework. In I. Altman & J. F. Wohlwill (Eds.), *Human behavior and environment: Advances in theory and research,* (Vol. 2). New York: Plenum Press, 1977.

ARGYLE, M., & KENDON, A. The experimental analysis of behavior. In L. Berkowitz (Ed.), *Advances in experimental social psychology,* (Vol. 3). New York: Academic Press, 1967.

ARONFREED, J. A. *Conduct and conscience.* New York: Academic Press, 1968.

BANDURA, A. *Principles of behavior modification.* New York: Holt, Rinehart and Winston, 1969.

BANDURA, A. *Social learning theory.* New York: General Learning Press, 1971.

BANDURA, A. *Aggression: A social learning analysis.* Englewood Cliffs, N. J.: Prentice-Hall, 1973.

BANDURA, A., & JEFFERY, R. W. Role of symbolic coding and rehearsal processes in observational learning. *Journal of Personality and Social Psychology,* 1973, *26,* 122–130.

BELL, R. Q. Human infant-effects in the first year. In R. Q. Bell & L. V. Harper (Eds.), *Child effects on adults.* Hillsdale, N. J.: Erlbaum, 1977.

BERKOWITZ, L. The contagion of violence: An S—R mediational analysis of some effects of observed aggression. *Nebraska Symposium on Motivation,* 1970, *19,* 95–135.

BERKOWITZ, L. The "weapons effect," demand characteristics, and the myth of the compliant subject. *Journal of Personality and Social Psychology,* 1971, *20,* 332–338.

BERKOWITZ, L. Some determinants of impulsive aggression: Role of mediated associations with reinforcements for aggression. *Psychological Review,* 1974, *81,* 165–176.

BERKOWITZ, L., & GEEN, R. Film violence and the cue properties of available targets. *Journal of Personality and Social Psychology,* 1966, *3,* 525–530.

BERKOWITZ, L., & KNUREK, D. A. Label-mediated hostility generalization. *Journal of Personality and Social Psychology,* 1969, *13,* 200–206.

BERKOWITZ, L., & TURNER, C. Perceived anger level, instigating agent, and aggression. In H. London & R. Nisbett (Eds.), *Cognitive alteration of feeling states*. Chicago: Aldine, 1974.

BERNSTEIN, J. E., PAGE, J. G., & JANICKI, R. S. Some characteristics of children with minimal brain dysfunction. In C. K. Conners (Ed.), *Clinical use of stimulant drugs in children*. New York: American Elsevier, 1974.

BOLTON, R. Aggression and hypoglycemia among the Qolla: A study in psychobiological anthropology. *Ethnology*, 1973, *12*, 227–257.

BRONFENBRENNER, U. The origins of alienation. *Scientific American*, (August) 1973, *231*, 53–61.

CAMPBELL, D. T. Reforms as experiments. *American Psychologist*, 1969, *24*, 409–429.

CANTWELL, D. P. Clinical picture, epidemiology and classification of the hyperactive child syndrome. In D. P. Cantwell (Ed.), *The hyperactive child: Diagnosis, management, current research*. New York: Spectrum Publications, 1975. (*a*)

CANTWELL, D. P. A critical review of therapeutic modalities with hyperactive children. In D. P. Cantwell (Ed.) see above, 1975. (*b*)

CANTWELL, D. P. Natural history and prognosis in the hyperactive child syndrome. In D. P. Cantwell (Ed.), see above, 1975. (*c*)

CHAFFEE, S. H., & TIMS, A. R. Interpersonal factors in adolescent television use. *Journal of Social Issues*, 1976, *32*, 98–115.

CLARK, R. A. The projective measurement of experimentally induced levels of sexual motivation. *Journal of Experimental Psychology*, 1952, *44*, 391–400.

CLEMENTS, S. D. Minimal brain dysfunction in children (U. S. Dept. of Health, Education and Welfare). Washington, D. C.: U. S. Government Printing Office, 1966.

CLOWARD, R. A., & OHLIN, L. E. *Delinquency and opportunity*. New York: Free Press, 1960.

COLE, A. M., & TURNER, C. W. Effects on crime rates of changing birth orders during the post World War II baby boom. Paper presented at the Western Psychological Association meeting, Seattle, Wash., April 1977.

COMSTOCK, G. A., & RUBINSTEIN, E. A. (Eds.), *Television and social behavior*. Vol. 1, *Media content and control*. Washington, D. C.: U. S. Government Printing Office, 1972.

CONNERS, C. K. Syndrome of minimal brain dysfunction: Psychological aspects. *Pediatric Clinics of North America*, 1967, *14*, 749–766.

COSER, L. A. Some aspects of Soviet family policy. In R. L. Coser (Ed.), *The family: Its structures and functions* (2nd ed.), New York: St. Martin's Press, 1974.

"Crime: Murder in Roxbury." *Newsweek*, October 15, 1973, Pp. 30, 35.

DEVRIES, P. *The tunnel of love*. Boston: Little, Brown & Co., 1954.

DODD, D. K., COLE, A. M., & TURNER, C. W. Effects of post World War II baby boom on U. S. divorce rate. Paper presented at the American Psychological Association meeting, San Francisco, Calif., August 1977.

DOUGLAS, V. Differences between normal and hyperkinetic children. In C. K. Conners (Ed.), *Clinical use of stimulant drugs in children.* New York: American Elsevier, 1974.

DUBEY, D. Organic factors in hyperkinesis: A critical evaluation. *American Journal of Orthopsychiatry,* 1976, *46,* 353–366.

DYKMAN, R. A., ACKERMAN, P. T., PETERS, J. E., & McGREW, J. Psychological tests. In C. K. Conners (Ed.), *Clinical use of stimulant drugs in children.* New York: American Elsevier, 1974.

ELLIS, D. P., WEINIR, P., & MILLER, L. Does the trigger pull the finger? An experimental test of weapons as aggression eliciting simtuli. *Sociometry,* 1971, *34,* 453–465.

ELLSWORTH, P. C., & CARLSMITH, J. M. Eye contact and gaze aversion in an aggressive encounter. *Journal of Personality and Social Psychology,* 1973, *28,* 280–292.

ETZEL, B. C., & GEWIRTZ, J. L. Experimental modification of caretaker maintained high-rate operant crying in a 6- and a 20-week-old infant *(Infans tyrannotearus)*: Extinction of crying with reinforcement of eye contact and smiling. *Journal of Experimental Child Psychology,* 1967, *5,* 303–317.

FEINGOLD, B. F. Recognition of food additive as a cause of symptoms of allergy. *Annals of Allergy,* 1968, *26,* 309–313.

FEINGOLD, B. F. Food additive and child development. *Hospital Practice,* 1973, *8,* 11–21.

FELDMAN, M. P. *Criminal behavior: A psychological analysis.* New York: Wiley, 1977.

FERDINAND, T. Reported index crime increases between 1950 and 1965 due to urbanization and changes in the age structure of the population alone. In D. J. Mulvihill & M. M. Tumin (Eds.), *Crimes of violence.* Washington, D. C.: U.S. Government Printing Office, 1969.

FITTS, P. M., & POSNER, M. I. *Human performance.* Belmont, Calif.: Brooks Cole, 1967.

FREEDMAN, D. G. *Human infancy: An evolutionary perspective.* Hillsdale, N. J.: Erlbaum, 1974.

GEEN, R. C., & O'NEAL, E. C. Activation of cue-elicited aggression by general arousal. *Journal of Personality and Social Psychology,* 1969, *11,* 289–292.

GERBNER, B. Violence in television drama: Trends and symbolic functions. In G. A. Comstock & E. A. Rubinstein (Eds.), *Television and social behavior. Vol. 1, Media content and control.* Washington, D.C.: U.S. Government Printing Office, 1972.

GERST, M. A. Symbolic coding processes in observational learning. *Journal of Personality and Social Psychology,* 1971, *19,* 7–17.

GEWIRTZ, J. L., & BOYD, E. F. Experiments in mother-infant interaction, mutual attachment, acquisition: The infant conditions his mother. In T. Alloway, L. Krames, & P. Pliner (Eds.), *Advances in the study of communication and affect* (Vol. 3). New York: Plenum Press, 1976.

GIL, D. G. *Violence against children*. Cambridge, Mass.: Harvard University Press, 1970.

GLITTLER, R. E. Spontaneous hypoglycemia. In M. Ellenberg & H. Rifkin (Eds.), *Clinical diabetes mellitus*. New York: McGraw-Hill, 1962.

GOODE, W. J. Family disorganization. In R. K. Merton and R. Nisbet (Eds.), *Contemporary social problems* (4th ed.). New York: Harcourt Brace Jovanovich, 1976.

GRIFFITHS, D., & JOHNSTON, W. A. An information processing analysis of visual imagery. *Journal of Experimental Psychology*, 1973, *100*, 141–146.

HALL, E. T. *The hidden dimension*. New York: Doubleday, 1966.

HALLER, J. S., & AXELROD, P. Minimal brain dysfunction: Another point of view. *American Journal of Diseases in Children*, 1975, *129*, 1319–1324.

HARTOCOLLIS, P. Syndrome of minimal brain dysfunction in young adult patients. *Bulletin of the Menninger Clinic*, 1968, *32*, 102–114.

HAUSER, P. M. The population of the United States, retrospect and prospect. In American Assembly, Columbia University (Ed.), *The population dilemma* (2nd ed.). Englewood Cliffs, N. J.: Prentice-Hall, 1969.

HAUSER, P. M. On population and environmental policy and problems. In N. Hinricks (Ed.), *Population, environment and people*. New York: McGraw-Hill, 1971.

HEER, D. M. *Society and population* (2nd ed.). Englewood Cliffs, N. J.: Prentice-Hall, 1975.

HICKS, D. J. Imitation and retention of film-mediated aggressive peer and adult models. *Journal of Personality and Social Psychology*, 1965, *2*, 97–100.

HICKS, D. J. Short and long-term retention of affectively varied modeled behavior. *Psychonomic Science*, 1968, *11*, 369–370.

HUESSY, H. R., MARSHALL, C. D., & GENDRON, R. A. Five hundred children followed from grade 2 through grade 5 for the prevalence of behavior disorder. In C. K. Conners (Ed.), *Clinical use of stimulant drugs in children*. New York: American Elsevier, 1974.

KAGAN, J. Discrepancy, temperament, and infant distress. In M. Lewis & L. A. Rosenbaum (Eds.), *Origins of fear*. New York: Wiley, 1974.

KAMISAR, Y. On the tactics of police-persecution oriented critics of the courts. *Cornell Law Quarterly*, 1964, *49*, 436–477.

KAPLAN, R. M., & SINGER, R. D. Television violence and viewer aggression: A re-examination of the evidence. *Journal of Social Issues*, 1976, *32*, 35–70.

KENKEL, W. F. *The family in perspective* (4th ed.). Santa Monica, Calif.: Goodyear, 1977.

KERCKHOFF, A. C. Patterns of marriage and family formation and dissolution. *Journal of Consumer Research*, 1976, *2*, 261–275.

KERLINGER, F. N., & PEDHAZUR, E. J. *Multiple regression in behavioral research*. New York: Holt, Rinehart and Winston, 1973.

KIRKPATRICK, C. *The family: Process and institution* (2nd ed.). New York: Ronald Press, 1963.

KITTLER, F. J. The effect of allergy on children with minimal brain damage. In F. Speer (Ed.), *Allergy of the nervous system.* Springfield, Ill.: Charles C. Thomas, 1970.

KLAUS, M. H., & KENNELL, J. H. Mothers separated from their newborn infants. *Pediatric Clinics of North America,* 1970, *17,* 1015–1037.

KLEIN, D. F., & GITTLEMAN-KLEIN, R. Diagnosis of minimal brain dysfunction and hyperkinetic syndrome. In C. K. Conners (Ed.) *Clinical use of stimulant drugs in children.* New York: American Elsevier, 1974.

KLEIN, M., & STERN, C. Low birth weight and the battered child syndrome. *American Journal of Diseases of Childhood,* 1971, *122,* 15–18.

KLOPPER, A. Physiological background to aggression. In J. D. Carthy & F. J. Ebling (Eds.) *The Natural History of Aggression.* New York: Academic Press, 1964.

KNIVETON, B. H. The effect of rehearsal delay on long-term imitation of filmed aggression. *British Journal of Psychology,* 1973, *64,* 259–265.

LIEBERT, R. M., & BARON, R. A. Short-term effects of televised aggression on children's aggressive behavior. In J. P. Murray, E. A. Rubenstein, & G. A. Comstock (Eds.), *Television and social behavior.* Vol. 2. *Television and social learning.* Washington, D. C.: U.S. Government Printing Office, 1972.

LIEBERT, R. M., NEALE, J. M., & DAVIDSON, E. S. *The early window: Effects of television on children and youth.* Elmsford, N. Y.: Pergamon Press, 1973.

MERTON, R. K., & NISBET, R. (Eds.). *Contemporary social problems* (4th ed.). New York: Harcourt Brace Jovanovich, 1976.

MISCHEL, W. Father-absence and delay of gratification. *Journal of Abnormal and Social Psychology,* 1961, *63,* 116–124. (*a*)

MISCHEL, W. Preference for delayed reinforcement and social responsibility. *Journal of Abnormal and Social Psychology,* 1961, *62,* 1–7. (*b*)

MOSS, H. A. Sex, age, and state as determinants of mother-infant interaction. *Merrill-Palmer Quarterly,* 1967, *13,* 19–36.

MOYER, K. E. *The psychobiology of aggression.* New York: Harper & Row, 1976.

NEISSER, U. *Cognitive psychology.* New York: Meredith, 1967.

NEWTON, G. C., & ZIMRING, F. E. *Firearms and violence in American life.* Washington, D. C.: U.S. Government Printing Office, 1969.

PARKE, R. D. Socialization into child abuse: A social interactional perspective. In J. L. Tapp & F. J. Levine (Eds.), *Law, justice, and the individual in society: Psychological and legal issues.* New York: Holt, Rinehart, and Winston, 1977.

PARKE, R. D., BERKOWITZ, L., LEYENS, J. P., WEST, W., & SEBASTIAN, R. M. Some effects of violent and nonviolent movies on the behavior of juvenile delinquents. In L. Berkowitz (Ed.), *Advances in experimental social psychology,* (Vol. 10). New York: Academic Press, 1977.

PATTERNITE, C. E., LONEY, J., & LANGHORNE, J. E. Relationships between symptomatology and SES-related factors in HK/MBD boys. *American Journal of Orthopsychiatry,* 1976, *46,* 291–301.

PATTERSON, G. R., & COBB, J. A. Stimulus control for classes of noxious behaviors. In J. F. Knutson (Ed.), *The control of aggression*. Chicago: Aldine, 1973.

PATTERSON, G. R., LITTMAN, R. A., & BRICKER, W. Assertive behavior in children: A step toward a theory of aggression. *Monographs of the Society for Research in Child Development, 1967, 32* (5, Serial No. 113).

PATTERSON, G. R., REID, J. B., JONES, R. R., & CONGER, R. C. *Families with aggressive children*. Eugene, Ore.: Castalia Publishing Co., 1975.

ROBSON, K. S., & MOSS, H. A. Patterns and determinants of maternal attachment. *Journal of Pediatrics*, 1970, 77, 976–985.

SCHULZ, D. A. *The changing family: Its function and future*. Englewood Cliffs, N.J.: Prentice-Hall, 1976.

SCHMITT, B. D. The minimal brain dysfunction myth. *American Journal of Diseases in Children*, 1975, 129, 1113–1118.

SHAFER, K. N., SAWYER, J. R., McCLUSKY, A. M., BECK, E. L., & PHIPPS, W. J. *Medical-surgical nursing*. St. Louis: C. V. Mosby, 1971.

SHUNTICH, R. J., & TAYLOR, S. P. The effects of alcohol on human physical aggression. *Journal of Experimental Research in Personality*, 1972, 6, 34–38.

SHUPE, L. M. Alcohol and crime: A study of the urine alcohol concentration found in 882 persons arrested during or immediately after the commission of a felony. *Journal of Criminal Law, Criminology, and Police Science*, 1954, 44, 661–664.

SKINNER, B. F. *Verbal behavior*. New York: Appleton-Century-Crofts, 1957.

SOLOMON, R. L. & BRUSH, E. S. Experimentally derived conceptions of anxiety and aversion. In M. R. Jones (Ed.), *Nebraska symposium on motivation*. Lincoln, Neb.: University of Nebraska Press, 1956.

SPEER, F. The allergic tension-fatigue syndrome. *Pediatric Clinics of North America*, 1954, 1, 1029–1037.

SPEER, F. The allergic tension-fatigue syndrome. In F. Speer (Eds.), *Allergy of the nervous system*. Springfield, Ill.: Charles C. Thomas, 1970.

SQUIRE, L. R. Amnesia for remote events following electroconvulsive therapy. *Behavioral Biology*, 1974, 12, 119–125.

STARK, R., & McEVOY III, J. Middle class violence. *Psychology Today*, 1970, 4, 52–54, 110–112.

STORR, A. *Human aggression*. New York: Atheneum, 1968.

TANNENBAUM, P. M., & ZILLMANN, D. Emotional arousal in the facilitation of aggression through communication. In L. Berkowitz (Ed.), *Advances in experimental social psychology*, (Vol. 8). New York: Academic Press, 1975.

THAMM, R. *Beyond marriage and the nuclear family*. San Francisco: Canfield Press, 1975.

THOMSON, C. M., & TULVING, E. Associative encoding and retrieval: Weak and strong cues. *Journal of Experimental Psychology*, 1970, 86, 255–262.

TULVING, E. Theoretical issues in free recall. In R. U. Dixon & D. L. Horton (Eds.), *Verbal behavior and general behavior theory*. Englewood Cliffs, N. J.: Prentice-Hall, 1968.

TULVING, E., & OSLER, S. Effectiveness of retrieval cues in memory for words. *Journal of Experimental Psychology*, 1968, 77, 593–601.

TULVING, E., & PEARLSTONE, Z. Availability versus accessibility of information in memory for words. *Journal of Verbal Learning and Verbal Behavior*, 1966, 5, 381–391.

TURNER, C. W., & GOLDSMITH, D. Effects of toy guns and airplanes on children's anti-social free play behavior. *Journal of Experimental Child Psychology*, 1976, 21, 303–315.

TURNER, C. W., & LAYTON, J. F. Verbal imagery and connotation as memory induced mediators of aggressive behavior. *Journal of Personality and Social Psychology*, 1976, 33, 755–763.

TURNER, C. W., LAYTON, J. F., & SIMONS, L. S. Naturalistic studies of aggression: Aggressive stimuli, victim visibility, and horn honking. *Journal of Personality and Social Psychology*, 1975, 31, 1098–1107.

TURNER, C. W., & SIMONS, L. S. Effects of subject sophistication and evaluation apprehension on aggressive responses to weapons. *Journal of Personality and Social Psychology*, 1974, 30, 341–348.

TURNER, C. W., SIMONS, L. S., BERKOWITZ, L., & FRODI, A. The stimulating and inhibiting effects of weapons on aggressive behavior. *Aggressive Behavior*, 1977, 3, 355–378.

Uniform Crime Reports, 1960–1976. Washington, D. C.: U. S. Government Printing Office.

VAN DE WALLE, E. Marriage and marital fertility. In D. V. Glass & R. Revelle (Eds.), *Population and social change*. London: Edward Arnold, 1972.

Vital Statistics of the United States, 1960–1976. Washington, D. C.: U.S. Government Printing Office.

WALTERS, R. H. Delay of reinforcement gradients in children's learning. *Psychonomic Science*, 1964, 1, 307–308.

WEISS, G., & MINDE, K. K. Follow-up studies of children who present with symptoms of hyperactivity. In C. K. Conners (Ed.), *Clinical use of stimulant drugs in children*. New York: American Elsevier, 1974.

WELLFORD, C. F. Age composition and the increase in recorded crime. *Criminology*, 1973, 11, 61–70.

WESTON, J. T. The pathology of child abuse. In R. E. Helfer & C. H. Kempe, *The battered child*. Chicago: The University of Chicago Press, 1974.

WHALEN, C. K., & HENKER, B. Psychostimulants and children: A review and analysis. *Psychological Bulletin*, 1976, 83, 1113–1130.

WHELPTON, P. K. The future growth of the population of the United States. In G. H. L. J. Pitt-Rivers (Ed.), *Problems of population*. Port Washington, N. Y.: Kennikat Press, 1932.

WILSON, J. *Thinking about crime*. New York: Random House, 1975.

WILSON, M., & HIGGINS, P. B. Television's action arsenal: Weapon use in prime time. Paper read at the United States Conference of Mayors, 1977.

WOLFGANG, M. Crime: Homicide. In D. L. Sells (Ed.), *International encyclopedia of the social sciences* (Vol. 3). New York: Macmillan, 1968.

YORBURG, B. *The changing family.* New York: Columbia University Press, 1973.

ZAJONC, R. B., & MARKUS, G. B. Birth order and intellectual development. *Psychological Review*, 1975, *82*, 74–88.

Author Index

A

Achenbach, T.M., 164
Ackerman, P.T., 281
Adams, R.D., 176
Aghajanian, G.F., 190, 191
Alajouanine, T., 170, 194
Allen, A., 220
Allen, T.W., 38, 39, 43
Altman, I., 288, 289
Altman, J., 188
Alston, W.P., 234
Anglin, J.M., 72, 73, 90
Applefield, J.M., 254
Arenberg, D., 186
Argyle, M., 289
Arlin, P.K., 34
Armah, K., 29
Arnold, M., 29
Aronfreed, J., 234, 240, 248, 292
Atkinson, C.A., 236
Atkinson, K., 57
Atkinson, R.C., 110, 141, 143
Ault, R.L., 8
Axelrod, P., 280n

B

Baddeley, A.D., 113
Baer, D.M., 220, 238-241
    passim
Baier, K., 234
Baker, L.J., 186
Baker, T.B., 186
Bakker, D.J., 196n
Bandura, A., 223-225, 243,
    245-246, 248, 249, 251,
    252, 254, 287, 289,
    291-293; theory of moral
    development, 223-236
Banuazizi, A., 32
Barbizet, J., 176
Barclay, J.R., 118
Baron, R.A., 292
Bartels, B., 121
Bartlett, F.C., 118
Basser, L., 194, 195, 196n
Bates, E., 58
Baumeister, A.A., 136
Bayer, S., 188
Beach, D.R., 132
Beck, E.L., 282
Beilin, H., 38

Bell, R.Q., 271, 272, 274, 276
Bellugi, U., 52, 75, 78-81
    passim
Belmont, J.M., 133n
Bem, D.J., 220
Bennett, E.L., 202
Benson, D.F., 172, 193n
Berman, R.F., 177
Berkowitz, L., 216, 270n, 291,
    292, 295-297 passim
Bernbach, J.A., 141
Bernstein, J.E., 281, 282
Bever, T.G., 55, 87
Bickford, R., 177
Blake, J., 130
Bloom, F.E., 190, 191
Bloom, L., 54
Bogen, J., 195
Bolton, R., 284-286
Bonvillian, J.D., 55
Borowy, T., 196, 197
Botez, M.I., 193
Botvin, G.J., 38
Bouchard, M., 32
Bovet, M., 38
Bower, T.G.R., 127, 248
Bowerman, M., 52, 71, 72
Boyd, E.F., 272
Boyes-Braem, P., 73
Brackbill, Y., 123
Brainerd, C.J., 7, 8, 13, 15n,
    17, 19, 20, 21, 23, 27, 28,
    34, 38, 39, 42, 43
Brainerd, S.H., 26
Bransford, J.D., 118
Brekke, B., 31
Bricker, W., 269
Brickman, P., 220, 238
Broen, P.A., 62
Bronfenbrenner, U., 307
Bronson, W.C., 218
Brown, A.L., 137, 138, 184, 186
Brown, J., 131
Brown, R., 51-52, 54, 64, 73,
    75-76, 88, 115, 124
Brownell, C.A., 38
Bruner, J., 58, 59
Brush, E.S., 278
Bryan, J.H., 219, 220, 238,
    247-248, 253
Buchwald, N.A., 162

Budiansky, J., 108
Burklund, C.W., 195
Burnham, M.A., 251
Butterfield, E.C., 133n
Butters, N., 176

C

Caldwell, R.C., 126-127
Campbell, B.A., 186, 187
Campbell, D.T., 234, 310
Campbell, E.H., 186
Campbell, H., 121
Cannizzo, S.R., 132
Cantwell, D.P., 280-283 passim
Carlsmith, J.M., 289
Caron, A.J., 126-127
Caron, R.F., 126-127
Carpenter, G., 126
Carskaddon, G., 126
Carter, A.L., 58
Carter D.J., 128
Cavanagh, J.P., 136
Cazden, C.B., 52
Cermak, L., 176
Chaffee, S.H., 298
Charles, D.C., 31
Chase, H.H., 124
Child, I. L., 135
Chinsky, J.M., 132
Chomsky, C., 82, 87
Chomsky, N., 52, 180
Clark, E.V., 51, 55, 67, 69-71,
    87, 88
Clark, H.H., 55, 67, 70n, 87, 88
Clark, M., 237
Clark, R.A., 292
Clarke, R., 174
Clements, S.D., 280, 282
Cloward, R.A., 306
Cobb, J.A., 250, 269, 270, 274,
    275
Cohen, L.B., 120, 121, 122
Cole, A.M., 300, 301, 307
Cole, M., 29, 30
Coleman, P.D., 201
Collins, A.M., 92, 116-117
Collins, G.H., 176
Comalli, P.E., 31
Comstock, G.A., 297
Conrad, R., 132
Condry, J., 243

321

Subject Index